# The Dow Jones-Irwin Guide to Using
# The Wall Street Journal

The **Dow Jones-Irwin**
**Guide to Using**
The **Wall Street Journal**

Michael B. Lehmann

DOW JONES-IRWIN, INC.
Homewood, Illinois 60430

© Michael B. Lehmann, 1984

ISBN 0-87094-309-X
Library of Congress Catalog Card No. 83–70874

*Printed in the United States of America*

3 4 5 6 7 8 9 0   K   1 0 9 8 7 6 5 4

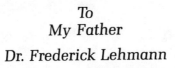

*To*
*My* Father

Dr. Frederick Lehmann

# Preface

When I first proposed this book to Dow Jones-Irwin, they asked me if its purpose was to show the reader "how to be your own economist." Not exactly, I said. The objective was to show the reader "how to use *The Wall Street Journal* to be your own economist."

After all, the *Journal* is the authoritative source for business news in America; it is published coast to coast; and it has the largest daily circulation of any newspaper in the country. By focusing on a handful of key statistical reports in the *Journal*, you can acquire a surprisingly quick and firm comprehension of the ups and downs of the American business economy. This book will facilitate that comprehension, clearly and accurately—but, I hope, in a pleasing and nontechnical manner.

A word of caution. This is not a get-rich-quick manual; it is not designed to offer investment advice. You should always seek competent professional counsel before placing business or personal capital at risk.

It is the purpose of this book to develop a sound overview of our economy so that your grasp of economic events as well as your business and investment decisions will be more informed and more confident.

**Michael B. Lehmann**

# ACKNOWLEDGMENTS

I would like to express my gratitude to the people who assisted me in developing, writing, and producing this work. First, I wish to thank my good friend and colleague Alan Heineman, associate professor of English at the University of San Francisco, and my principal editor. To the extent that the book reads well, it is in large measure due to his efforts; any stylistic defects remain only because there was not time to refine it further. I also want to express gratitude to my wife, Millianne, for her patient assistance in sorting through draft after draft, weeding out the unimportant material, identifying topics that demanded inclusion, and revising the text with grace and wisdom.

Jonathan Miller, a free-lance writer in Los Angeles and an old friend, helped me focus on the central facets of the Federal Reserve System; Chapters Three and Four are much better because of his contribution. Peter Lindert, whom I've known since student days, now professor of economics at the University of California at Davis, made valuable comments on the international transactions chapter. Tom Soden, vice president of Davis, Skaggs and Company in San Francisco and a former student of mine, provided significant commentary on the financial markets.

Betty Blecha, Yuan-Li Wu, Martin Brown, and Fr. Richard Mulcahy, S.J., my colleagues in the Economics Department at USF, also read the text and provided helpful comments. Further appreciation goes to the University of San Francisco for providing the opportunity to develop the course that launched this entire project. I am grateful to all my students who sat through it from beginning to end while it was being developed, and whose responses have reinforced my sense of what most needed to be said on these topics.

Associate Dean John Dwyer was very cooperative in providing secretarial support; Lou Martin, Emily White, and Monica Roskos heroically typed rough drafts of the text, and Terry Harned had the monumental job of putting the final drafts on the university's computer and doing the word processing necessary to produce the text. Kathy Woo, USF's periodicals librarian, helped me find several elusive *Wall Street Journal* articles. I wish also to express my appreciation to the entire university computer center staff, especially Chuck Wilcher, who gave up his nights and weekends to help me meet the deadline.

Let me record, finally, my acknowledgments to the staffs of *The Wall Street Journal* and Dow Jones-Irwin who assisted me along the way. Without their help, there would be no book, let alone a book that came out on time.

**M. B. L.**

# Contents

xii    Contents

# CHAPTER ONE

## Introduction

GNP, consumer price index, Treasury bills, housing starts, labor productivity, the money supply . . .

Can you effectively analyze these statistical series and reports? Can you use them to gain an understanding of developing economic and business trends? Or are your judgments and opinions based on popular analyses and secondary sources?

Perhaps you would like to deal with the data on your own but don't know how. It's worth some time and effort to learn, because until you come to grips with the data you can't honestly say that you have formed your own opinion of current economic and business events, let alone of what the future holds in store. The news media now serve as intermediaries between you and the data. Furthermore, no matter how many experts are quoted, you still aren't dealing with the facts, only with someone else's interpretation of them. And these interpretations are often contradictory—and therefore confusing. At some point you have to wonder, do the experts know what they're talking about?

Your desire to master the data may stem from your own business needs. Will demand for your product be weak or strong two quarters from now or two years from now? Is this the time to lay in additional inventory, hire key personnel, and build more plant? Or, despite the current level of orders, would it be more prudent to cancel those plans? Can you beat the competition to the punch, one way or another? Are interest rates likely to rise or to fall? Is disinflation (as deflation is sometimes called) merely a buzzword, or has

1

inflation really been licked? That's just a hint of the issues you can begin to analyze on your own: all it takes is learning to come to grips with no more than a few dozen regularly released statistical reports.

You may wish to conduct your own analysis of current economic events because they are the foundation for so many other social and political developments. Was President Reagan's tax cut responsible for the decline in inflation *and* the increase in unemployment? Or should the Federal Reserve System take the credit—and the blame? Do your answers to these questions reflect your analysis of the data, your political point of view, or the opinions of your favorite commentator? Maybe they should reflect all three, but they can reflect only the last two until you learn to deal with the numbers on your own. Once you do that, your views will be of greater importance to yourself and others.

Don't misunderstand. Dispensing with expert advice is not the objective. Even the world's leading authority on a subject must consult other experts as a continual check on his or her understanding. This challenges the authority and helps prevent sloppy thinking. The point is: become the expert by handling the data on your own, and you will know whether or not the other experts make sense. Otherwise, you'll never be certain whether you're being given sound or flimsy advice.

If you want to be your own economist, if you wish to master the data, you need two things: (1) a readily available, reliable, and comprehensive statistical source; and (2) a guide to organize and interpret the information you receive.

As to the first requirement, *The Wall Street Journal* is your best source of business and economic information; you really don't need anything else. It contains all of the reports necessary to conduct your own analysis.

With respect to the second requirement, this book can be your guide. In it, the nature of the statistics will be explained so that what they measure and how they are computed will be clear. GNP, the money supply, the Consumer Price Index, and the Dow Jones Industrial Average cannot remain vague and indefinite terms.

For example, when the *Journal* reports that the money supply has increased, it is important to know that this fact has virtually nothing to do with the availability of paper money. The money supply is composed largely of checking accounts. Currency is the petty cash of the economy.

An understanding of the nature of the various statistical series is, of course, not enough. You must be able to place them in both historical and contemporary context. These essential skills will develop and gain strength with each chapter. Your historical perspective will deepen, providing the context or benchmark for evaluating contemporary events. When a *Journal* article states that the prime interest rate is the highest ever, or that the unemployment rate is the highest since the Great Depression, or that the factory operating rate is the lowest since World War II, the comparison can provide perspective only if you grasp the frame of reference, for knowledge of the past aids evaluation of the present by providing a standard against which to measure contemporary events. Auto sales or housing starts may be lower than they were a year earlier, but if they hit bottom six months ago, after several years' decline, and the *Journal* has reported improvement in each successive month, your perspective gives evidence of recovery, not decline.

As you read on you will become aware that none of the statistical reports stands alone. Understanding the relationships among them provides insight into the economy's operation. Each is a piece of the puzzle, and together they compose the picture. Mortgage interest rates and home construction are examples that have been featured in the *Journal* lately, and there is a simple, vital link between them: as mortgage interest rates fall, home construction increases.

Consider another example. The dollar became stronger during the latest recession because Americans demanded far fewer imported goods, which in turn reduced our purchases of foreign currency. Meanwhile, the attraction of high interest rates here caused foreign investors to buy dollars.

All of the statistics analyzed in this book can be grouped in this fashion, so that they need not be a series of unrelated events, released piecemeal on a day-to-day basis. Instead, they will form an unfolding pattern that clearly reveals the direction of economic and business activity.

Finally, you need a framework, a device to structure these historical insights and contemporary interrelationships. The business cycle, that wavelike rise and fall of economic activity, provides the necessary framework. You are already familiar with the cycle in your own business or personal situation, and the news media have provided increased coverage of the ups and downs of the economy in recent years. Economic expansion and contraction, easy or tight credit conditions, inflation and unemployment are recurring facts of life. Who escapes them?

The business cycle is the best vehicle for illuminating the *Journal's* regularly appearing statistical series. Its phases bring life and meaning to the statistical reports. They establish the perspective through which the illustrations and examples in the book are interwoven into a unified exposition.

Each chapter will introduce one or more statistical series, and will be devoted to a theme (such as the money and credit markets) that is used to describe and explain the statistical series introduced in the chapter, beginning with the simplest and most basic elements of the business cycle and proceeding to additional topics that will complete your understanding. This step-by-step progression of topics will not, however, prevent you from breaking into any chapter, out of order, if you wish to examine a particular statistical series or group of series. Indeed, you may already have a firm grasp of some of these topics, and need only fill in the missing elements to round out your comprehension of the essential workings of American business. A complete listing of all the statistical series discussed in this guide can be found in the Appendixes following Chapter Sixteen.

Each chapter will describe the statistical series under discussion in the context of the business cycle and explain the relationship of the new series to the ones discussed up until then. Analysis will be based on charts drawn from official publications so that you can visualize the data and put the current information in perspective. Recent *Wall Street Journal* articles containing the statistical series will be reproduced and discussed so that you can interpret the data in light of the visual presentation made by the charts. Finally, you will be alerted to what future developments can be expected.

You will enjoy putting the puzzle together yourself. Anyone can do it, with a little help. The ebb and flow of the business cycle will channel the stream of data which now flood you in seemingly random fashion, and you will experience a genuine sense of accomplishment in creating order out of something which has appeared chaotic.

A word of caution before you begin. This will be neither an economics or business cycle course or text nor a precise forecasting device. There will be no formula or model. The business cycle is used strictly as a vehicle to make the statistical information usable in as easy a manner as possible. The objective is not to make a professional economist out of you but to enable you to conduct your own analysis of the data just as soon as you are able. You will dive into the data and "get your hands dirty" by taking apart the cycle, analyzing it, and reassembling it. When you have finished this book, you will feel confident that you can deal with the data on your own.

Finally, please realize that this work is designed to help you understand *The Wall Street Journal* in the context of the business cycle. It is not an investment guide. To understand, for example, how the stock market fits into our economy, which this book tries to help you do, is a very different matter than knowing which stock to invest in at any particular moment. Seek competent professional counsel before you invest your money.

Now before exploring the business cycle in detail, take time for a leisurely overview.

# CHAPTER TWO

## The Business Cycle

The business cycle is nothing new. It's been a characteristic of every capitalist economy in the modern era. Nations have endured boom followed by bust, prosperity and then depression, a period of growth and confidence trailing off into a decade of despair.

It is all so familiar to us that images of its human effects are scattered among our popular stereotypes. Men in top hats peer at ticker tape emerging from a little glass dome. They wheel and deal, corner wheat markets, play with railroads, and organize steel companies. Fortunes are quickly won and just as quickly lost. Former tycoons are seen selling apples on street corners. Factory gates shut and signs go up saying, "No help wanted." Soup kitchens appear, and desperate families flee the dust bowl in Model A pickup trucks.

These caricatures—based on real history, actual power, blows of ill fortune, human suffering—persist in our collective consciousness, permanently etched by the Great Depression. Although the stock market collapse of 1929 is the most notorious such event in our history, it is by no means unique. Cycles in the American economy can be traced and analyzed going back to the beginning of the 19th century.

The settlement of the West is an example. The frontier assumes such importance in our history and folklore that we tend to think of the westward migration as a smooth, inevitable flow, driven by the doctrine of manifest destiny. It didn't happen that way. The settlement of the West proceeded in a cyclical pattern.

Farmers and ranchers were (and are) businesspeople. The sod house and subsistence farming of the 1800s were a temporary inconvenience, converted as quickly as possible to growing cash crops and raising livestock for the market. The settlers wanted to know the bottom line, the difference between revenue and expense. They wanted the best price for their cotton, corn, cattle, wheat, and hogs. They wanted to maximize production and minimize cost by using modern cultivation techniques and the latest equipment. Railroads and banks concerned them because transportation and interest rates affected the cost of doing business and thus their profit margin. Finally, and most important, the typical farmer wanted his capital to grow. He expected his net worth to increase as his farm appreciated in value and his mortgage was paid.

This experience was not confined to the United States; European settlers in Canada, Australia, and Argentina produced the same commodities under similar conditions. All were part of the growing world economy. Every farmer and rancher counted on industrialization and urbanization at home and in Europe to build demand for his commodities.

And worldwide demand for food and fiber did increase rapidly. Farmers responded by boosting production as best they could on existing holdings. Eventually, however, their output reached its limit even though demand continued to grow. As a result, prices began to creep, and then race, upward. The venturesome dreamed of moving west and doubling or tripling their acreage. Record crop and livestock prices made the costs of moving and financing a new spread seem manageable, and existing farms could always be sold to the less intrepid. Thousands upon thousands of families streamed across the frontier, claiming millions of acres offered by generous government policies or buying from speculators who held raw land.

Nobody planned the westward migration; nobody coordinated it; nobody governed it. Everyone made his or her own calculation of the market. Farmers borrowed in order to purchase land and building materials and to buy livestock, seed, and equipment. Newly opened banks faced an insatiable demand for credit. Towns sprang up at railroad sidings where grain elevators and livestock yards were constructed. Merchants and Main Street followed. High prices brought a land boom, and the land boom brought settlement and opened the West.

It took a while for the newly converted prairie to produce a cash crop. But when it did, thousands of new farms began dumping their output on the market. The supply of agricultural commodities increased dramatically. Shortage changed to surplus, and prices dropped. Time after time during the 19th century, commodity prices fell to record lows after a period of inflation and the subsequent land rush.

Many farmers were wiped out. They could not pay their debts while commodity prices scraped bottom and banks foreclosed on farm property. If a bank made too many loans that went bad, then it was dragged down too. Merchants saw their customers disappear and had to close up shop. Settlers abandoned their land, and boomtowns became ghost towns.

Prices remained low for years, and most farmers barely made it, living on returns far below expectations. In every instance, it took a while before the steady growth in world demand absorbed the excess agricultural commodities.

But as time passed, the cycle would repeat itself. After the inflation which accompanied the Civil War, western settlement continued to occur in waves until the end of the century, despite 30 years of deflation. The process happened at least half a dozen times until the frontier closed in the last years of the 19th century.

By the turn of this century, progress had been spectacular. Untold thousands of acres of prairies had been transformed into productive field and pasture. Commodities worth billions of dollars were produced annually for the domestic and world markets. Billions of dollars of wealth had been created in the form of improved farmland. But the discipline of the business cycle governed the advance. For every two steps forward, there had been one step backward, as those who borrowed or lent the least wisely, settled the poorest land, or had the worst luck went broke.

What was true for farming was equally true for the nation's railroads: they developed in the same cyclical pattern. On the eve of World War I, America's railway system was complete, representing a total capital investment second only to that of agriculture. It was a remarkable feat of creative engineering and equally creative financing.

History refers to the builders of the railways as robber barons, and we marvel at the exploits of the Goulds, Fisks, Drews, Vanderbilts, Stanfords, Hills, et al. Some of these characters seemed to skim off one dollar for every two invested, and it's a wonder that the railway system was ever completed or operated safely. Yet there it was, the largest in the world, a quarter of a million miles of track moving the nation's freight and passenger traffic with unparalleled efficiency.

Promoters speculatively pushed the railroads westward in anticipation of the freight and passenger traffic that settlement would bring. Federal, state, and local governments vying for the routes that would bring progress and development gave the railroad companies 10 percent of the nation's land. Improving rights-of-way, laying track, building trestles, stations, and marshaling yards, and purchasing locomotives and rolling stock required the railway company to raise more capital than had been mobilized for any other single business venture. The companies floated billions of dollars in stocks and bonds, and investors eagerly ventured their capital to take advantage of prospective success. Flush with funds, the railroads raced toward the Pacific Coast, hoping that revenue would grow quickly enough to justify their huge investment. Periodically, however, the generous rate of expansion exceeded the growth in traffic. Prospects for profits, which had seemed so bright, grew dim. Investors stopped providing funds, and railroad track construction came to a halt. Since operating revenues could not recover costs, many railroads were forced into receivership and were reorganized. Stock and bond prices plunged, wiping out investors long after the promoters had made off with their killings.

Eventually, traffic grew sufficiently to justify existing lines and raise hopes that construction could profitably resume. Investors were once again lured into advancing their funds, and a new cycle of railway expansion began. It too was followed by a bust, and then by another wave of construction, until the nation's railway system was complete.

The tracks spanned a continent, from New York, Philadelphia, and Baltimore to Chicago, and from there to New Orleans, Los Angeles, San Francisco, Portland, and Seattle. Profit had motivated the enterprise, and enormous tangible wealth had been created. Losses had periodically and temporarily halted the undertaking and impoverished those who had speculated unwisely or had been duped. Construction had been in waves, an unplanned and often disorganized adventure. Given the institutions of the time, no other method could have built the system as rapidly.

In this century, we have seen the business cycle not only in the heroic proportions of the Roaring Twenties and the Great Depression but also during every succeeding business expansion or recession. We're in the cycle now, and will be tomorrow and next year.

Most people realize that there are cyclical fluctuations as business activity expands and then contracts; that there are periods when production, employment, and profits surge ahead, each followed by a period when profits and output fall and unemployment increases; and that the entire cycle then repeats itself once again. During the expansion, demand and production, income and wealth grow. Homes and factories are constructed, and machinery and equipment are put in place. The value of these assets grows too, as home prices and common stock prices increase. But then comes the inevitable contraction, and all the forces that mark the expansion shift into reverse. Demand, production, and income fall. The level of construction and the production of machinery and equipment are drastically curtailed. Assets lose their value as home prices and common stock prices fall.

Why do business cycles occur in this fashion, repeating themselves over and over again? No completely satisfactory theory of the cycle has been created. No one can accurately predict the length and course of each cycle. Economics, unlike physics, cannot be reduced to experiments, repeated over and over again under ideal conditions. There is no economic equivalent to Galileo on the tower of Pisa, proving that objects of unequal weight fall with equal speed, because the economic "tower" is never quite the same height; the "objects" keep changing in number, size, and even nature; and the "laws of gravity" apply unequally to each object. Yet this is certain: the business cycle is generated by forces within the economic system, not by outside forces. These internal forces create the alternating periods of economic expansion and contraction. And certain crucial features of the cycle endure and should be recognized.

*First, the forces of supply and demand condition every cycle.* Our ability to enjoy increasing income depends on our ability to supply or create increased production or output; we must produce more to earn more. But the level of demand, and the expenditures made in purchasing this output, must justify the level of production. That is, we must sell what we produce in order to earn. With sufficient demand, the level of production will be sustained and will grow, and income will increase; if demand is insufficient, the reverse will occur. During the expansionary phase of the cycle, demand and supply forces are in a relationship which permits the growth of production and income; during the contractionary phase, their relationship compels a decrease in production and income.

*Second, neither consumers nor businesses are constrained to rely solely upon the income they have generated in the process of production.* They have recourse to the credit market; they can borrow money and spend more than they earn. Spending borrowed funds permits demand to take on a life of its own and bid up a constantly and rapidly growing level of production. This gives rise to the expansionary phase of the cycle. Eventually, the growth in production becomes dependent upon the continued availability of credit, which sustains the growth in demand. But once buyers can no longer rely on borrowed funds because of market saturation, the exhaustion of profitable investment opportunities, or tight credit, demand falls, and with it, the bloated level of production and income. The contractionary phase has begun.

*Third, every expansion carries with it the inevitability of "overexpansion" and the subsequent contraction.* Overexpansion may be impelled by businesses which invest too heavily in new plant and equipment in order to take advantage of a seemingly profitable opportunity, or by consumers who borrow too heavily in order to buy homes, autos, or other goods. Businesses realize that the expected level of sales will not support additional plant and equipment, and consumers realize that they will have difficulty paying for that new home or car. Thus, businesses and consumers curtail their borrowing and expenditure. Since production and income spurted ahead to meet the growth in demand, when the inevitable contraction in demand takes place, production and income fall.

*Fourth, during contractions, production and income recede to a sustainable level, that is, to a level not reliant upon a continuous growth in credit.* The contraction returns the economy to a more efficient level of operation.

*Fifth, every contraction sows the seeds of the subsequent recovery.* Income earned in the productive process, rather than bloated levels of borrowing, maintains the level of demand. Consumers and businesses repay their debts. Eventually, lower debt burdens and interest rates encourage consumer and business borrowing and demand. The economy begins expanding once more.

Yet there is progress over the course of the cycle. Overall growth takes place because some, or even most, of the increase in output remains intact. Nor is all the wealth which was created subsequently destroyed.

The plant and equipment used to make Mustangs will remain on-stream; the tools and dies needed to make the Edsel will be scrapped. Subdivisions developed in 1976, when interest rates were low, will turn a profit for their developers, while those completed in 1980, when interest rates rose, may be liquidated at a loss after standing empty for a year. And so on. The tree grows, but the rings in its trunk mark the cycles of seasons which were often lush but on occasion were beset by drought.

The following chapters will trace recent cyclical developments in the course of showing you how to use the economic data published in *The Wall Street Journal*. But the money and credit markets are so important in the progress of the business cycle over its phases, and the Federal Reserve System has had such a heavy impact on these markets, that you should first acquaint yourself with their operation and with the role of the Federal Reserve System.

# CHAPTER THREE

## The Federal Reserve System

The United States was the last major industrial nation to establish a central bank. The modern German state commissioned a central bank in 1875; the Bank of France was founded in 1800; and the Bank of England had entered its third century of operation when the Federal Reserve System was created in 1913.

America's tardiness was due to our traditional suspicion of centralized financial power and authority. Historically, we have felt more comfortable with small banks serving a single community. For instance, some states limit or even forbid branch banking to this day, requiring that all of a bank's business be conducted under one roof. Ironically, the Continental Illinois National Bank in Chicago is one of the nation's biggest, even though Illinois law requires that it operate without benefit of branches. California's liberal branch banking laws helped Bank of America build its position as the nation's largest bank, while the big New York City banks (until recently) were hampered by legislation which confined them to the city and its suburbs and kept their branches out of upstate New York.

Alexander Hamilton proposed a central bank shortly after the country's founding, and there were two early attempts to create one. Both failed when confronted with the nation's suspicion of the Eastern financial community. Consequently, our economy grew until the eve of World War I without benefit of coordination or control of its banking activity. Banking, like the sale of alcohol following repeal of Prohibition, was largely a matter of local option.

Under these circumstances, the banks had to fend for themselves, and the business cycle created perils for them as well as opportunities for profit. During periods of recession, when business income was down (usually following periods of speculative excess), banks found it difficult to collect on loans.

At the same time, nervous businesspersons and investors made large withdrawals, sometimes demanding payment in gold or silver specie. These precious metal coins composed the ultimate reserve for deposits; however, no bank possessed enough of them to secure every depositor, and the banking system functioned on the assumption that only a minority of depositors would demand their funds on any one day. If panic set in and a queue formed out the door and around the block, a bank could be wiped out in a matter of hours. As rumor spread, one bank after another would fail, until only the most substantial institutions, with the greatest specie reserve, were left standing. The chain reaction damaged many people, not the least of whom were innocent depositors who could not reach their funds in time.

Congress took up the issue after the panic of 1907. In that crisis—as the story goes—J. P. Morgan kept New York's most important bankers locked up in his home overnight until they agreed to contribute a pool of specie to be lent to the weakest banks until the run subsided. It was clear that the time had come to establish an American central bank with the capability of lending to all banks in time of panic. The nation's financial system could no longer rely on the private arrangements of J. P. Morgan. Thus, the Federal Reserve System was established by Congress in 1913. All member banks were required to make deposits to the system, creating a pool of reserves from which financially strapped banks could borrow during a financial crisis.

The system was originally conceived as a lender of last resort. In times of financial crisis, it would use the pooled reserves of the banking system to make loans to banks under stress. When conditions improved, the loans were to be repaid. As time went by, however, *the Fed* (as the Federal Reserve System came to be known) discovered two things: first, that the reserve requirement could be used to control banking activity; and second, that control over the banking system provided a means of influencing the business cycle.

The reasoning was straightforward; it will be outlined here and developed more fully later. Bank lending is a key ingredient in the business cycle, driving the cyclic expansion of demand. It cannot, however, grow beyond the limits set by bank reserves, so when the Fed wants to give the economy a boost by encouraging banks to lend more, it increases reserves. On the other hand, by decreasing reserves and thereby shrinking available credit, the Fed exerts a restraining effect on the economy.

The mechanism used by the Fed to manipulate the banking system's reserves is astonishingly simple: it buys or sells securities on the open market. Briefly put, when the Fed buys securities, the sellers deposit the proceeds of the sale in their banks and the banking system's reserves grow. On the other hand, when the Fed sells securities, buyers withdraw funds from their banks in order to make the purchases and bank reserves fall.

The Fed exercised increasing power over the economy as the years passed, and the exercise of this power led to conflict with the president and Congress. On occasion, politicians took the Fed to task for being too restrictive, for not permitting the economy to grow rapidly enough. At other times, the Fed was criticized for being too lenient and permitting demand to grow so rapidly that inflation threatened.

Why the conflict? Shouldn't the Fed's policy reflect the wishes of Congress and the president? Maybe, but it need not, for—as many do not realize—the Fed is not an agency of the U.S. government. It is a corporation owned by banks which have purchased shares of stock. Federally chartered banks are required to purchase this stock and be members of the Federal Reserve System; state-chartered banks may be members if they wish. All banks, however, are subject to the Fed's control.

True, the Fed does have a quasi-public character because its affairs are managed by a Board of Governors appointed by the president of the United States with the approval of Congress. Nonetheless, once appointed, the Board of Governors is independent of the federal government and is free to pursue policies of its own choosing. New laws could, of course, change its status. That's why Paul Volcker, chairman of the board, is so frequently called upon to defend the policies of the Fed before Congress, and why Congressmen often remind the Fed that it is a creature of Congress, which can enact legislation to reduce, alter, or eliminate the Fed's powers. Indeed, Congressmen and others suggest from time to time that the Fed be made an agency of the U.S. government in order to remove its autonomy. Be that as it may, the fed is now independent and seems likely to remain so, exercising its best judgment in guiding the nation's banking activity.

In some ways, the Fed's control over the banking system's reserves is the most important relationship between any two institutions in the American economy. It can increase or reduce bank reserves at will, making it easier or more difficult for the banks to lend, thus stimulating or restricting business and economic activity. This chapter will show you how to use the weekly report of the

Fed's operations to understand the impact of the Fed's actions on the banks. The report appears each Monday in *The Wall Street Journal* under the caption "Federal Reserve Data," and is usually printed in the *Journal's* second section.


## FEDERAL RESERVE DATA

*"Federal Reserve Data"* is published every Monday in *The Wall Street Journal.* These are Wednesday figures released on Friday for publication the following Monday. Thus, the statistics for Wednesday, May 11, 1983, appeared five days later, on Monday, May 16, 1983.

Look at **Free Reserves**, the last line under the heading **Member Bank Reserve Changes**. It reveals the impact of the Fed's actions upon the banking system. This section will explain its derivation and how to use it.

In examining free reserves, keep in mind that the discussion refers to all banks collectively, not to individual banks. This distinction is important. Banks can competitively drain one another of reserves to augment their ability to lend, but this activity does not increase the entire system's reserves. That explains the fierce rivalry among banks for deposits. When deposits are moved from one bank to another, the reserves of the first bank fall and those of the second bank increase. The first bank must restrain its lending, while the second bank is able to lend more. This competitive reshuffling of reserves, however, has not altered the overall level of reserves, and so the lending ability of the banking system remains the same.

Thus, the reserves of the entire banking system depend on the Fed's open-market operations. The banks cannot augment their reserves independently through their own actions. The Fed supplies the banking system with reserves by buying securities, and it deprives the system of reserves by selling securities. When the Fed buys securities, the seller deposits the proceeds of the sale in his bank, increasing bank reserves. When it sells them, the buyer pays with funds withdrawn from his bank, thus decreasing bank reserves. More reserves make it easier for the banks to lend, stimulating economic activity; less reserves make it difficult for the banks to lend, restraining economic activity.

That sounds very hard on the banks. Suppose the Fed's policy becomes restrictive in the midst of an economic expansion, and it sells securities, thus depriving the banks of reserves? If the banks are making loans while the Fed is reducing the level of bank reserves, the banking system will be short of reserves. Do the banks have a cushion which protects them in such an event?

## Federal Reserve Data

**KEY ASSETS AND LIABILITIES OF 10 WEEKLY REPORTING MEMBER BANKS IN NEW YORK CITY**
(in millions of dollars)

| ASSETS: | May 4, 1983 | Change from Apr. 27, 1983 |
|---|---|---|
| Total assets | 233,988 | + 6,979 |
| Total loans and investments | 142,756 | + 757 |
| Includes: | | |
| Commercial and industrial loans | 57,119 | + 194 |
| Domestic | 55,616 | + 185 |
| Foreign | 1,503 | + 9 |
| Acceptances, comm'l paper | 1,165 | + 214 |
| Finance company loans | 3,864 | − 79 |
| Personal loans | 11,620 | + 79 |
| Loan loss reserve | 2,531 | + 38 |
| U.S. Treasury securities | 9,718 | + 318 |
| Federal agency securities | 1,458 | + 11 |
| Municipal issues | 11,631 | − 145 |
| Due in one year or less | 1,466 | − 52 |
| Longer term | 10,165 | − 93 |
| LIABILITIES: | | |
| Demand deposits | 121,299 | + 2,426 |
| Demand deposits adjusted (a) | 25,619 | + 384 |
| Time and savings deposits | 72,127 | − 601 |
| Negotiable CDs ($100,000 and up) | 23,774 | − 1,284 |
| Borrowings | 61,242 | + 4,417 |

a-Excludes government and bank deposits and cash items being collected.

**Member Bank Reserve Changes** ⟶

**MEMBER BANK RESERVE CHANGES**

Changes in weekly averages of reserves and related items during the week and year ended May 11, 1983 were as follows (in millions of dollars)-b

| | May 11, 1983 | Chg fm May 4, 1983 | wk end May 12, 1982 |
|---|---|---|---|
| Reserve bank credit: | | | |
| U.S. Gov't securities: | | | |
| Bought outright | 138,058 | − 120 | + 9,395 |
| Held under repurch agreemt | .... | − 1,812 | .... |
| Federal agency issues: | | | |
| Bought outright | 8,908 | .... | − 100 |
| Held under repurch agreemt | .... | − 114 | .... |
| Acceptances−bought outright | | | |
| Held under repurch agreemt | .... | − 366 | .... |
| Borrowings from Fed | 709 | − 219 | − 408 |
| Seasonal borrowings | 91 | − 10 | − 127 |
| Extended credit | 506 | + 13 | + 314 |
| Float | 2,095 | − 181 | − 39 |
| Other Federal Reserve Assets | 9,667 | + 14 | − 113 |
| Total Reserve Bank Credit | 159,436 | − 2,799 | + 8,733 |
| Gold Stock | 11,134 | − 1 | − 15 |
| SDR certificates | 4,618 | .... | + 800 |
| Treasury currency outstanding | 13,786 | .... | + 30 |
| Total | 188,974 | − 2,800 | + 9,548 |
| Currency in circulation | 156,993 | + 1,235 | +12,337 |
| Treasury cash holdings | 530 | + 6 | + 38 |
| Treasury dpts with F.R. Bnks | 3,812 | − 2,041 | − 882 |
| Foreign dpts with F.R. Bnks | 223 | − 35 | − 94 |
| Other deposits with F.R. Bnks | 554 | − 146 | + 78 |
| Other F.R. liabilities & capital | 4,894 | − 279 | − 363 |
| Total | 167,695 | − 1,217 | +11,621 |
| Reserves | | | |
| With F.R. Banks | 21,278 | − 1,583 | − 2,073 |
| Total inc. cash | 37,904 | − 1,646 | − 1,254 |
| Required reserves | 37,568 | − 1,376 | − 1,326 |
| Excess reserves | 336 | − 270 | + 72 |
| Free reserves | 224 | − 48 | .... |

**Free Reserves** ⟶

b-The figures reflect adjustment for new Federal Reserve rules that impose reserve requirements on most deposit-taking institutions, including non-member commercial banks, mutual savings banks and savings and loan associations.

**MONETARY AND RESERVE AGGREGATES**
(daily average in billions)

| | One week ended: May 4, | Apr. 27, |
|---|---|---|
| Money supply (M1) sa | 499.5 | 495.3 |
| Money supply (M1) nsa | 497.9 | 493.7 |
| | May 11, | May 4, |
| Monetary base | 181.8 | 182.5 |
| Total Reserves | 40.73 | 41.61 |
| Nonborrowed Reserves | 40.02 | 40.69 |
| Required Reserves | 40.39 | 41.01 |
| | Four weeks ended: May 4, | Apr. 6, |
| Money supply (M1) sa | 496.2 | 497.6 |

sa-Seasonally adjusted. nsa-Not seasonally adjusted.

**KEY INTEREST RATES**
(weekly average)

| | May 11, | May 4, |
|---|---|---|
| Federal funds | 8.48 | 8.80 |
| Treasury bill (90 day) | 8.03 | 8.06 |
| Commercial paper (dealer, 90 day) | 8.17 | 8.26 |
| Certfs of Deposit (resale, 90 day) | 8.31 | 8.35 |
| Eurodollars (90 days) | 8.71 | 8.88 |

The Wall Street Journal, *May 16, 1983.*

Yes, the banks may borrow reserves from the Fed at a rate of interest called "the discount rate." And to avoid a penalty for falling short, banks initiate such borrowing before their reserves are completely exhausted, thus maintaining a margin of "excess reserves."

Now you can calculate the "free reserve" figure for the entire banking system, which appears in the "Member Bank Reserve Changes" section of "Federal Reserve Data."

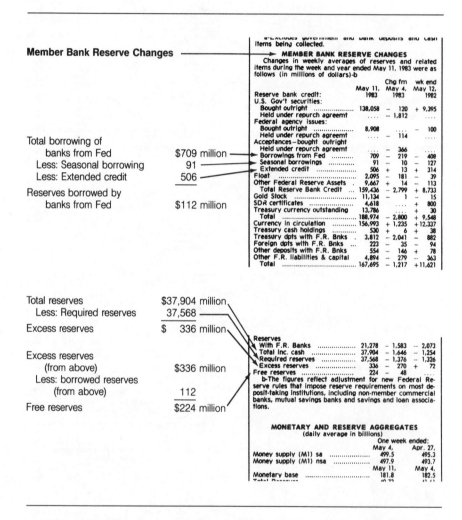

**Member Bank Reserve Changes**

Total borrowing of
    banks from Fed — $709 million
    Less: Seasonal borrowing — 91
    Less: Extended credit — 506

Reserves borrowed by
    banks from Fed — $112 million

Total reserves — $37,904 million
    Less: Required reserves — 37,568

Excess reserves — $   336 million

Excess reserves
    (from above) — $336 million
Less: borrowed reserves
    (from above) — 112

Free reserves — $224 million

a-Excludes government and bank deposits and cash items being collected.

**MEMBER BANK RESERVE CHANGES**
Changes in weekly averages of reserves and related items during the week and year ended May 11, 1983 were as follows (in millions of dollars)-b

| | May 11, 1983 | Chg fm wk end May 4, 1983 | May 12, 1982 |
|---|---|---|---|
| Reserve bank credit: | | | |
| U.S. Gov't securities: | | | |
| Bought outright | 138,058 | − 120 | + 9,395 |
| Held under repurch agreemt | .... | − 1,812 | .... |
| Federal agency issues: | | | |
| Bought outright | 8,908 | .... | − 100 |
| Held under repurch agreemt | .... | − 114 | .... |
| Acceptances – bought outright | | | |
| Held under repurch agreemt | ... | − 366 | .... |
| Borrowings from Fed | 709 | − 219 | − 408 |
| Seasonal borrowings | 91 | − 10 | − 127 |
| Extended credit | 506 | + 13 | + 314 |
| Float | 2,095 | − 181 | − 39 |
| Other Federal Reserve Assets | 9,667 | + 14 | − 113 |
| Total Reserve Bank Credit | 159,436 | − 2,799 | + 8,733 |
| Gold Stock | 11,134 | − 1 | − 15 |
| SDR certificates | 4,618 | ... | + 800 |
| Treasury currency outstanding | 13,786 | ... | + 30 |
| Total | 188,974 | − 2,800 | + 9,548 |
| Currency in circulation | 156,993 | + 1,235 | +12,337 |
| Treasury cash holdings | 530 | + 6 | + 38 |
| Treasury dpts with F.R. Bnks | 3,812 | − 2,041 | − 882 |
| Foreign dpts with F.R. Bnks | 223 | − 35 | − 94 |
| Other deposits with F.R. Bnks | 554 | − 146 | + 78 |
| Other F.R. liabilities & capital | 4,894 | − 279 | − 363 |
| Total | 167,695 | − 1,217 | +11,621 |

**Reserves**
| | | | |
|---|---|---|---|
| With F.R. Banks | 21,278 | − 1,583 | − 2,073 |
| Total inc. cash | 37,904 | − 1,646 | − 1,254 |
| Required reserves | 37,568 | − 1,376 | − 1,326 |
| Excess reserves | 336 | − 270 | + 72 |
| Free reserves | 224 | − 48 | .... |

b-The figures reflect adjustment for new Federal Reserve rules that impose reserve requirements on most deposit-taking institutions, including non-member commercial banks, mutual savings banks and savings and loan associations.

**MONETARY AND RESERVE AGGREGATES**
(daily average in billions)

| | One week ended: | |
|---|---|---|
| | May 4, | Apr. 27, |
| Money supply (M1) sa | 499.5 | 495.3 |
| Money supply (M1) nsa | 497.9 | 493.7 |
| | May 11, | May 4, |
| Monetary base | 181.8 | 182.5 |
| Total Reserves | 40.73 | 41.61 |

When bank lending grows rapidly and the Fed is not supplying the banks with sufficient reserves, the banks will be obliged to borrow heavily from the Fed. If borrowing exceeds excess reserves, free reserves is a negative ( − ) figure. This is a signal that bank lending is expanding at a rapid pace and that the Fed is trying to restrain the banks and the expansion of economic activity.

On the other hand, during a period of slack economic activity, bank lending, and hence required reserves, will decline. Banks will not have to borrow reserves from the Fed. When excess reserves are large and bank borrowing is negligible, free reserves will be positive ( + ). A high level of free reserves shows that the Fed is not restraining the banks.

Return to the May 11, 1983, "Federal Reserve Data."

You can see that free reserves were $224 million in the week ending May 11, 1983. The Fed had provided banks with sufficient reserves. Excess reserves exceeded the banks' borrowing from the Fed, so free reserves were positive ( + ). (See page 18.)

A week later, on May 18, 1983, free reserves were negative ( − ) $96 million. The Fed was exercising a degree of restraint, obliging the banks to borrow $96 million from the Fed over and above their excess reserves. (See page 19.)

In summary, free reserves will be positive ( + ) when the Fed is supplying the banks with ample reserves and negative ( − ) when the Fed is restricting bank reserves. When, in the course of the business cycle, the former is true, the Fed's actions are referred to as an *easy money policy* or an *expansionary monetary policy*. When the latter is true, and free reserves are negative by a large amount, the Fed's actions are referred to as a *tight money policy* or a *contractionary monetary policy*.

What are the Fed's objectives in implementing these policies?

*Expansionary policy*: If the Fed buys securities, thus increasing member bank reserves, the banks will be able to lend more, stimulating demand. Such an expansionary policy has traditionally been pursued during a period of recession when the economy is at the bottom of the business cycle.

*Contractionary policy*: If the Fed sells securities, and bank reserves are reduced, the banks will not be able to lend as much, which will curtail the share of demand that depends on borrowing, and hence will reduce the total level of demand. This policy has been followed at the peak of the cycle to restrain the growth of demand and inflationary increases in prices.

These relationships can be easily summarized in the following manner. Read ↑ as "up," ↓ as "down," and → as "leads to."

**Expansionary policy:** *Fed buys securities* → *Bank reserves* ↑ → *Bank lending* ↑ → *Demand* ↑.

**Contractionary policy:** *Fed sells securities* → *Bank reserves* ↓ → *Bank lending* ↓ → *Demand* ↓.

Thus, free reserves are positive ( + ) when the Fed pursues an expansionary policy, because open-market operations (Fed buys securities) have provided banks with such a large volume of reserves that excess reserves exceed bank borrowing from the Fed. Free re-

# Federal Reserve Data

## KEY ASSETS AND LIABILITIES OF 10 WEEKLY REPORTING MEMBER BANKS IN NEW YORK CITY
(in millions of dollars)

| ASSETS: | May 4, 1983 | Change from Apr. 27, 1983 |
|---|---|---|
| Total assets | 233,988 | + 6,979 |
| Total loans and investments | 142,756 | + 757 |
| Includes: | | |
| Commercial and industrial loans | 57,119 | + 194 |
| Domestic | 55,616 | + 185 |
| Foreign | 1,503 | + 9 |
| Acceptances, comm'l paper | 1,165 | + 214 |
| Finance company loans | 3,864 | − 79 |
| Personal loans | 11,620 | + 79 |
| Loan loss reserve | 2,531 | + 38 |
| U.S. Treasury securities | 9,718 | + 318 |
| Federal agency securities | 1,458 | + 11 |
| Municipal issues | 11,631 | − 145 |
| Due in one year or less | 1,466 | − 52 |
| Longer term | 10,165 | − 93 |
| LIABILITIES: | | |
| Demand deposits | 121,299 | + 2,426 |
| Demand deposits adjusted (a) | 25,619 | + 384 |
| Time and savings deposits | 72,127 | − 601 |
| Negotiable CDs ($100,000 and up) | 23,774 | − 1,284 |
| Borrowings | 61,242 | + 4,417 |

a-Excludes government and bank deposits and cash items being collected.

## MEMBER BANK RESERVE CHANGES

Changes in weekly averages of reserves and related items during the week and year ended May 11, 1983 were as follows (in millions of dollars)-b

| | May 11, 1983 | Chg fm May 4, 1983 | wk end May 12, 1982 |
|---|---|---|---|
| Reserve bank credit: | | | |
| U.S. Gov't securities: | | | |
| Bought outright | 138,058 | − 120 | + 9,395 |
| Held under repurch agreemt | .... | − 1,812 | .... |
| Federal agency issues: | | | |
| Bought outright | 8,908 | .... | − 100 |
| Held under repurch agreemt | .... | − 114 | .... |
| Acceptances−bought outright | | | |
| Held under repurch agreemt | .... | − 366 | .... |
| Borrowings from Fed | 709 | − 219 | − 408 |
| Seasonal borrowings | 91 | − 10 | − 127 |
| Extended credit | 506 | + 13 | + 314 |
| Float | 2,095 | − 181 | − 39 |
| Other Federal Reserve Assets | 9,667 | + 14 | − 113 |
| Total Reserve Bank Credit | 159,436 | − 2,799 | + 8,733 |
| Gold Stock | 11,134 | − 1 | − 15 |
| SDR certificates | 4,618 | .... | + 800 |
| Treasury currency outstanding | 13,786 | .... | + 30 |
| Total | 188,974 | − 2,800 | + 9,548 |
| Currency in circulation | 156,993 | + 1,235 | +12,337 |
| Treasury cash holdings | 530 | + 6 | + 38 |
| Treasury dpts with F.R. Bnks | 3,812 | − 2,041 | − 882 |
| Foreign dpts with F.R. Bnks | 223 | − 35 | − 94 |
| Other deposits with F.R. Bnks | 554 | − 146 | + 78 |
| Other F.R. liabilities & capital | 4,894 | − 279 | − 363 |
| Total | 167,695 | − 1,217 | +11,621 |
| Reserves | | | |
| With F.R. Banks | 21,278 | − 1,583 | − 2,073 |
| Total inc. cash | 37,904 | − 1,646 | − 1,254 |
| Required reserves | 37,568 | − 1,376 | − 1,326 |
| Excess reserves | 336 | − 270 | + 72 |
| Free reserves | 224 | − 48 | .... |

**Free Reserves** — Positive (+) $224 million for week ending May 11, 1983

b-The figures reflect adjustment for new Federal Reserve rules that impose reserve requirements on most deposit-taking institutions, including non-member commercial banks, mutual savings banks and savings and loan associations.

## MONETARY AND RESERVE AGGREGATES
(daily average in billions)

| | One week ended: May 4, | Apr. 27, |
|---|---|---|
| Money supply (M1) sa | 499.5 | 495.3 |
| Money supply (M1) nsa | 497.9 | 493.7 |
| | May 11, | May 4, |
| Monetary base | 181.8 | 182.5 |
| Total Reserves | 40.73 | 41.61 |
| Nonborrowed Reserves | 40.02 | 40.69 |
| Required Reserves | 40.39 | 41.01 |
| | Four weeks ended: May 4, | Apr. 6, |
| Money supply (M1) sa | 496.2 | 497.6 |

sa-Seasonally adjusted. nsa-Not seasonally adjusted.

## KEY INTEREST RATES
(weekly average)

| | May 11, | May 4, |
|---|---|---|
| Federal funds | 8.48 | 8.80 |
| Treasury bill (90 day) | 8.03 | 8.06 |
| Commercial paper (dealer, 90 day) | 8.17 | 8.26 |
| Certfs of Deposit (resale, 90 day) | 8.31 | 8.35 |
| Eurodollars (90 days) | 8.71 | 8.88 |

The Wall Street Journal, *May 16, 1983.*

**KEY ASSETS AND LIABILITIES OF 10 WEEKLY
REPORTING MEMBER BANKS IN NEW YORK CITY**
(in millions of dollars)

| ASSETS: | May 11, 1983 | Change from May 4, 1983 |
|---|---|---|
| Total assets | 230,295 | − 3,693 |
| Total loans and investments | 142,079 | − 677 |
| Includes: | | |
| Commercial and industrial loans | 56,364 | − 755 |
| Domestic | 54,856 | − 760 |
| Foreign | 1,508 | + 5 |
| Acceptances, comm'l paper | 1,171 | + 6 |
| Finance company loans | 3,800 | − 64 |
| Personal loans | 11,612 | − 8 |
| Loan loss reserve | 2,537 | + 6 |
| U.S. Treasury securities | 10,485 | + 767 |
| Federal agency securities | 1,450 | − 8 |
| Municipal issues | 11,785 | + 154 |
| Due in one year or less | 1,602 | + 136 |
| Longer term | 10,183 | + 18 |
| LIABILITIES: | | |
| Demand deposits | 118,873 | − 2,426 |
| Demand deposits adjusted (a) | 25,630 | + 11 |
| Time and savings deposits | 72,055 | − 72 |
| Negotiable CDs ($100,000 and up) | 23,639 | − 135 |
| Borrowings | 60,775 | − 467 |

a-Excludes government and bank deposits and cash
items being collected.

**MEMBER BANK RESERVE CHANGES**

Changes in weekly averages of reserves and related
items during the week and year ended May 18, 1983 were as
follows (in millions of dollars)-b

| | May 18 1983 | Chg fm May 11 1983 | wk end May 19 1982 |
|---|---|---|---|
| Reserve bank credit: | | | |
| U.S. Gov't securities: | | | |
| Bought outright | 139,806 | + 1,748 | +10,872 |
| Held under repurch agreemt | .... | .... | − 793 |
| Federal agency issues: | | | |
| Bought outright | 8,908 | .... | − 100 |
| Held under repurch agreemt | .... | .... | − 89 |
| Acceptances−bought outright | | | |
| Held under repurch agreemt | .... | .... | − 233 |
| Borrowings from Fed | 1,074 | + 365 | + 108 |
| Seasonal borrowings | 91 | .... | − 141 |
| Extended credit | 519 | + 13 | + 340 |
| Float | 1,521 | − 673 | − 230 |
| Other Federal Reserve Assets | 8,684 | − 983 | − 322 |
| Total Reserve Bank Credit | 159,993 | + 458 | + 9,213 |
| Gold Stock | 11,132 | − 2 | − 17 |
| SDR certificates | 4,618 | .... | + 800 |
| Treasury currency outstanding | 13,786 | .... | + 30 |
| Total | 189,529 | + 456 | +10,026 |
| Currency in circulation | 157,363 | + 372 | +12,467 |
| Treasury cash holdings | 535 | + 3 | + 47 |
| Treasury dpts with F.R. Bnks | 3,131 | − 681 | + 9 |
| Foreign dpts with F.R. Bnks | 272 | + 49 | + 13 |
| Other deposits with F.R. Bnks | 560 | + 6 | + 60 |
| Other F.R. liabilities & capital | 4,867 | − 27 | − 336 |
| Total | 167,423 | − 272 | +12,769 |
| Reserves | | | |
| With F.R. Banks | 22,105 | + 728 | − 2,744 |
| Total inc. cash | 38,132 | + 129 | − 1,583 |
| Required reserves | 37,764 | + 196 | − 1,511 |
| Excess reserves | 368 | − 67 | − 72 |
| Free reserves | −96 | − 419 | .... |

b-The figures reflect adjustment for new Federal Reserve rules that impose reserve requirements on most deposit-taking institutions, including non-member commercial
banks, mutual savings banks and savings and loan associations.

**Free Reserves**
Negative (−) $96 million for week
ending May 18, 1983

**MONETARY AND RESERVE AGGREGATES**
(daily average in billions)

| | One week ended: May 11 | May 4 |
|---|---|---|
| Money supply (M1) sa | 506.9 | 499.9 |
| Money supply (M1) nsa | 493.6 | 492.2 |
| | May 18 | May 11 |
| Monetary base | 182.86 | 181.87 |
| Total Reserves | 41.12 | 40.82 |
| Nonborrowed Reserves | 40.04 | 40.11 |
| Required Reserves | 40.75 | 40.39 |
| | Four weeks ended: May 11 | Apr. 13 |
| Money supply (M1) sa | 499.1 | 496.4 |

sa-Seasonally adjusted. nsa-Not seasonally adjusted.

**KEY INTEREST RATES**
(weekly average)

| | May 18 | May 11 |
|---|---|---|
| Federal funds | 8.59 | 8.48 |
| Treasury bill (90 day) | 8.09 | 8.03 |
| Commercial paper (dealer, 90 day) | 8.26 | 8.17 |
| Certfs of Deposit (resale, 90 day) | 8.41 | 8.31 |
| Eurodollars (90 days) | 8.89 | 8.71 |

The Wall Street Journal, *May 23, 1983.*

serves are negative ( − ) when Fed policy turns contractionary and open-market sales of securities deprive banks of reserves, obliging them to borrow more than their excess reserves from the Fed.

Now examine the Fed's record of expansionary (free reserves positive) and contractionary (free reserves negative) monetary policies since World War II. Negative free reserves are called *net borrowed reserves*.

Remember that the Fed's objective has always been to counteract the natural swing of the cycle, stimulating demand at the trough by making it easy for the banks to lend and curbing inflation at the peak by making it difficult for the banks to lend. The peaks and valleys of the cycle are reflected in the bank borrowings of reserves (see Chart 1). Recessions are shaded in gray, and data quoted from *The Wall Street Journal* is indicated with an asterisk.

The economic events which began in the early 1970s clearly illustrate these ideas. Do you recall the feverish boom of 1973, when demand for autos and housing was so strong that the United Auto Workers union was complaining of compulsory overtime and there were shortages of lumber? The demand for borrowed funds was very strong; bank lending was heavy; and required reserves grew apace. Accordingly, the Fed instituted a tight money policy, compelling banks to borrow heavily from the Fed in order to maintain adequate reserves. You can see the consequences depicted in Chart 1: net borrowed reserves reached a record $3 billion in 1974. As the Fed applied the brakes, the boom came to a halt.

More than 2 million people were thrown out of work when the full force of recession hit in late 1974 and early 1975. The Fed switched to an easy money policy to stimulate the economy. As a result, bank borrowings of reserves from the Fed dropped sharply, so that for most of the period from 1975 through 1977 the banks had free reserves (excess reserves exceeding borrowing from the Fed).

By 1977 economic expansion was in progress. In response, the Fed reversed itself again, adopting a tight money policy, and the banks' position swung back into net borrowed reserves. First, bank lending to business increased steadily, and with it the level of required reserves. Second, the Fed began to exercise a policy of restraint in order to prevent too rapid an expansion of the economy. As the Fed pursued a restrictive policy, bank reserves became less adequate, which forced the banks to borrow reserves from the Fed.

Now net borrowed reserves grew from 1977 onward, averaging over $2 billion monthly by early 1980. It was 1974 all over again, only inflation was even more severe. While the Fed pursued its traditional tight money policy, President Carter instituted voluntary wage and price controls. By the week of March 12, 1980, net borrowed reserves exceeded $3 billion. The cyclical peak had arrived,

**Chart 1**
**Bank Borrowings of Reserves from Fed, Excess Reserves, Free Reserves, and Net Borrowed Reserves**

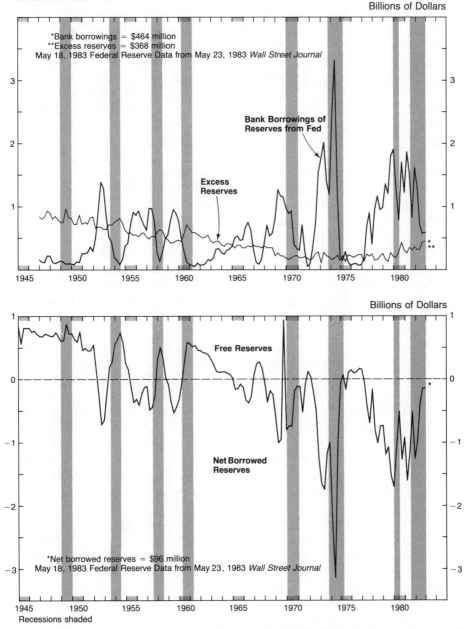

Billions of Dollars

*Bank borrowings = $464 million
**Excess reserves = $368 million
May 18, 1983 Federal Reserve Data from May 23, 1983 *Wall Street Journal*

Bank Borrowings of
Reserves from Fed

Excess
Reserves

Billions of Dollars

Free Reserves

Net Borrowed
Reserves

*Net borrowed reserves = $96 million
May 18, 1983 Federal Reserve Data from May 23, 1983 *Wall Street Journal*

Recessions shaded

Source: U.S. Department of Commerce, *Business Conditions Digest* and *Handbook of Cyclical Indicators*, series 93 and 94.

and downturn was inevitable. When the recession struck, net borrowed reserves plummeted as the Fed's stance eased, until free reserves appeared briefly on July 9, 1980.

In summary, then, the overall aim of the Fed since World War II has been to curb and ultimately reverse the extremes of the cycle: to dampen inflation, to stimulate a depressed economy.

Take another look at the chart of net borrowed and free reserves on page 21. You can see that the Fed's policies contributed to the cycle's severity. Like an inexperienced driver with one foot on the gas and the other on the brake, attempting to achieve a steady speed only to surge forward after screeching to a halt, the Fed alternately stimulated and restrained the economy. Record levels of net borrowed reserves at the cyclical peaks of the late 60s and the middle and late 70s provide evidence of the Fed's desperate attempts to bring inflationary expansion under control. Yet these sudden stops were partly the result of previous attempts, such as those made in 1972 and 1976, to stimulate rapid expansion by providing banks with plentiful free reserves. As the economy accelerated and inflation began to go out of control, the Fed slammed on the brakes.

Meanwhile, the business cycle of the 70s rose higher and higher, with inflation becoming more severe with each boom and unemployment becoming more severe with each bust. The Fed's policies had failed.

Now, although the Fed was unable to control the cycle or inflation in the 70s, it was not solely responsible for the course of events. You can see from Chart 2 that tidal waves of consumer and business borrowing drove demand forward during the expansionary phase of the cycle, creating the inflationary conditions which provoked the Fed's tight money policy and the subsequent crash into recession. The downturn would have occurred in the Fed's absence; the Fed's policies just made it more severe. Unfortunately, the quick shift to an easy money policy once recession took hold fostered the next giant wave of borrowing, spending, and inflation, and this inevitably produced, once the wave's internal energy was spent, a major collapse.

The Fed realized that a new approach was necessary after the 1980 recession. In earlier recessions, the Fed had always permitted a substantial period during which the banks could maintain excess reserves or benefit from a decline in net borrowed reserves. This time, the Fed decided to prevent rapid recovery and expansion by maintaining a very tight money policy during the early phases of recovery. The Fed was convinced that inflation had become so severe that the usual easy-money-aided recovery could not be tolerated. The rate of inflation had risen over each successive cycle and had barely declined during the 1980 recession. Rapid stimulation and recovery of demand would quickly bid prices up once again. This time, tight money was called for, even if it stunted the recovery.

**Chart 2**
**Total Private Borrowing**                                          Billions of Dollars

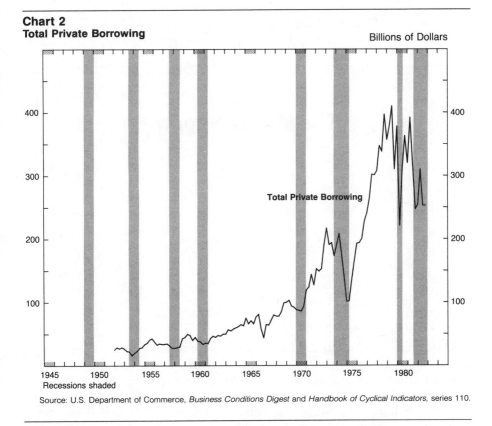

Recessions shaded

Source: U.S. Department of Commerce, *Business Conditions Digest* and *Handbook of Cyclical Indicators,* series 110.

In consequence, the Fed's 1981 tight money policies caused the worst recession since World War II. For the first time, the Fed had stopped a recovery in its tracks and watched the economy slide off into back-to-back recessions. The Fed had made up its mind that restraining demand in order to control inflation was worth the price of economic contraction.

By placing the May 18, 1983 "Federal Reserve Data" covering free reserves on Chart 1 (see page 21), you can see that the Fed's policies have eased. The Fed relaxed its grip, first, because inflation has been wrung out of the economy and unemployment had reached an intolerable level, and second, because there were strong signs that Congress was losing patience with the Fed's restrictive policies. The Fed had accomplished its objective, and there was no need to further antagonize those who had the power to terminate the Fed's independent status. But you should realize that the Fed's 1981 policies marked a major shift in strategy and had significant and far-reaching consequences for our economy. If severe inflation has been eliminated for the foreseeable future, it is no exaggeration to say that the Fed has beaten it back single-handed.

# CHAPTER FOUR

## The Money Supply

One reason so much controversy surrounds the money supply is that many people misunderstand its nature. Currency and coins in circulation together make up only about one quarter of the money supply. Checking accounts (or demand deposits, as they are formally called) constitute the remaining three quarters. The one quarter of the money supply which exists as cash issues from two different sources: the U.S. Treasury mints coins but prints no paper money (currency); the Fed distributes all our paper money but no coins.

These arrangements have an interesting and important history. Before the Civil War, with the exception of the two short-lived attempts at a central bank that were mentioned in Chapter Three, all paper money was issued by private banks and called bank notes. These bank notes resembled modern paper currency and were used to make loans.

The banks' incentive to issue bank notes to borrowers, instead of gold and silver coins, came from the limited supply of gold and silver coins (specie). Each bank kept a specie reserve which was no more than a fraction of its outstanding bank notes. This reserve was used to satisfy those who demanded that a bank redeem its notes with specie; as long as the bank could do so, its notes were accepted at face value and were "good as gold." Bank notes and minted coins circulated together.

After the Civil War, checking accounts replaced bank notes. They were safer and more convenient because the customer (borrower) had to sign them and could write in their exact amount. In modern times, all customers, whether depositors or borrowers, began to make use of checking accounts. The private bank note passed into history.

The U.S. Treasury issued paper money for the first time during the Civil War, and it continued to issue paper money until some time after World War II. During the 20th century, however, most of our paper money has been issued by the Federal Reserve System, and today the Fed has that exclusive responsibility. If you examine a piece of currency, you will see that it is a "Federal Reserve Note." Thus, ironically, bank notes constitute all of our currency today, just as they did before the Civil War. But today the notes are issued by the central bank rather than a host of private banks.

Since the Treasury issues no currency, you can see that the common notion that the federal government prints paper money to finance its deficits has no factual basis. The amount of paper money in circulation has nothing to do with the deficits of the federal government. When the federal government runs a deficit (expenditures exceed revenue), the Treasury borrows by issuing bonds which are bought by investors: the government gets the money, and the investors get the bonds. If a bond is sold to a bank (and banks are the largest purchasers of U.S. Treasury securities), the bank pays for it by crediting the checking account of the U.S. Treasury, thus increasing the total volume of all checking accounts. This is called "monetizing the debt"; it enlarges the money supply but does not affect currency in circulation.

Similarly, the Fed issues paper money in response, not to the budget deficits of the federal government, but to the public's requirements for cash. It supplies banks with cash, and the banks pay for it with a check written on their reserve account. Checks written to "cash" by bank customers then determine the amount of currency circulating outside banks. This demand for cash has no impact upon the money supply because checking accounts decrease by the amount currency increases when the check is "cashed."

But if the total is always the same—if Peter must be robbed in order to pay Paul—then how does the money supply grow? In the same fashion that bank notes outstanding grew in the 19th century. When banks lend, they create demand deposits (checking accounts) or credit an existing demand deposit. The more banks lend, the more the money supply, which is mostly demand deposits, increases. Today, as 100 years ago, bank reserves set the only limit on bank lending and, therefore, on the money supply. The difference is that instead of keeping specie as reserves, the banks must maintain reserves with the Fed.

Keep this in mind: *bank loans create deposits,* not the other way around. As long as the banking system has sufficient reserves, it can make loans in the form of demand deposits (money). You must abandon the notion that depositors' funds provide the wherewithal for bank lending. That may be true for the traditional mortgage lending activity of a savings and loan association, but it is not true for commercial banks. After all, where would depositors get the funds if not by withdrawing them from another checking account? But this actually does not increase deposits for the entire system; it only reshuffles deposits among banks. The total is unchanged.

Thus, demand deposits, and with them the money supply, grow when banks lend, and it makes no difference who the borrower is. When a business borrows from its bank in order to stock goods for the Christmas season, the bank creates a deposit (money) upon which the business writes checks to pay for merchandise. If you borrow from your bank to buy a car, the loan creates a demand deposit which increases the money supply. Therefore, as you can see, it is not just the federal government which "monetizes debt" when it borrows from the banking system; businesses and consumers "monetize" their debt too.

One last point must be made about the nature of bank reserves. A hundred years ago they consisted of gold and silver specie. Today they are deposits which banks maintain with the Federal Reserve System. Of what do these reserves consist, if not specie? They are merely checking accounts which the banks have on deposit with the Fed, very much like the checking account you have at your own bank. Recall, from Chapter Three, that the banks' checking accounts (reserves) increase when the Fed buys securities with a check written on itself (akin to a cashier's check) and the purchaser deposits the Fed's check with his or her bank. The banking system gains reserves when the bank deposits the Fed's check in its reserve account at the Fed.

If it sounds like a house of cards or like bookkeeping entries in a computer's memory, that's because it is. Nothing "backs up" the money supply except our faith in it, expressed every time we accept or write a check. And those checking accounts, and hence the money supply, built on borrowing, *must keep growing* if the economy is to grow over the business cycle. The forward surge of the cycle, when demand grows rapidly and pulls the economy's output with it, is founded on spenders' ability and willingness to borrow, to go into debt.

This, then, is the critical significance of the money supply: it measures the increase in demand made possible by bank lending. With this in mind, turn once again to *The Wall Street Journal's* "Federal Reserve Data."

# THE MONEY SUPPLY (M1)

M1 is demand deposits (checking accounts) and currency in circulation. In the report which appeared on Monday, May 23, 1983, M1 averaged $506.9 billion for the week ending May 11, 1983, and $499.1 billion for the four weeks ending May 11. (See excerpt on page 28.)

The annotation "sa" means seasonally adjusted. All seasonal fluctuations, such as the large increase and subsequent decline in the money supply associated with the Christmas shopping season, have been removed from the data.

You'll see references now and then to a variety of "M's." M2 is M1 plus savings accounts and money market fund shares, and M3 is M2 plus certain other large accounts at financial institutions. All of these have become increasingly volatile in recent years due to the revolution in consumer banking. The public can now use interest-bearing savings accounts as if they were demand deposits, and the distinction between savings and loan associations and commercial banks is rapidly disappearing. As a result, it's difficult to maintain the dividing lines among the "M's."

Use Chart 1 to observe the growth in the money supply (M1) since World War II. (See page 29.)

You can see the money supply's rapid growth in the 1970s. The money supply increased most quickly during the business cycle expansions of the late 60s, 1972–73, and 1977–78, and its growth slowed with the subsequent recessions. This is consistent with the earlier discussion of bank lending over the course of the cycle. Bank lending increased with cyclical expansions, generating a commensurate rise in demand deposits (money supply), and it decreased in the subsequent recessions, restricting money supply growth.

The money supply's rapid growth, and cyclical fluctuation in its rate of growth, fueled a sharp debate which led to an announced change in Federal Reserve policy in October 1979. That debate can be summed up in a few paragraphs.

As you recall from Chapter Three, the Fed was traditionally activist, alternately pursuing easy or tight money policies, depending on the state of the business cycle. During periods of recession and through the recovery stage and the early period of expansion, the Fed's easy money policy contributed to rapid growth in the money supply as banks lent money freely in response to plentiful reserves. As the expansionary phase of the cycle reached its peak, the Fed switched to a tight money policy, restricting the growth of bank reserves and, hence, the money supply.

The Fed's actions may be summarized as shown on page 29.

**KEY ASSETS AND LIABILITIES OF 10 WEEKLY REPORTING MEMBER BANKS IN NEW YORK CITY**
(in millions of dollars)

| ASSETS: | May 11, 1983 | Change from May 4, 1983 |
|---|---|---|
| Total assets | 230,295 | − 3,693 |
| Total loans and investments | 142,079 | − 677 |
| Includes: | | |
| Commercial and industrial loans | 56,364 | − 755 |
| Domestic | 54,856 | − 760 |
| Foreign | 1,508 | + 5 |
| Acceptances, comm'l paper | 1,171 | + 6 |
| Finance company loans | 3,800 | − 64 |
| Personal loans | 11,612 | − 8 |
| Loan loss reserve | 2,537 | + 6 |
| U.S. Treasury securities | 10,485 | + 767 |
| Federal agency securities | 1,450 | − 8 |
| Municipal issues | 11,785 | + 154 |
| Due in one year or less | 1,602 | + 136 |
| Longer term | 10,183 | + 18 |
| LIABILITIES: | | |
| Demand deposits | 118,873 | − 2,426 |
| Demand deposits adjusted (a) | 25,630 | + 11 |
| Time and savings deposits | 72,055 | − 72 |
| Negotiable CDs ($100,000 and up) | 23,639 | − 135 |
| Borrowings | 60,775 | − 467 |

a-Excludes government and bank deposits and cash items being collected.

**MEMBER BANK RESERVE CHANGES**

Changes in weekly averages of reserves and related items during the week and year ended May 18, 1983 were as follows (in millions of dollars)-b

| | May 18 1983 | Chg fm May 11 1983 | wk end May 19 1982 |
|---|---|---|---|
| Reserve bank credit: | | | |
| U.S. Gov't securities: | | | |
| Bought outright | 139,806 | + 1,748 | +10,872 |
| Held under repurch agreemt | .... | .... | − 793 |
| Federal agency issues: | | | |
| Bought outright | 8,908 | .... | − 100 |
| Held under repurch agreemt | .... | .... | − 89 |
| Acceptances—bought outright | | | |
| Held under repurch agreemt | .... | .... | − 233 |
| Borrowings from Fed | 1,074 | + 365 | + 108 |
| Seasonal borrowings | 91 | .... | − 141 |
| Extended credit | 519 | + 13 | + 340 |
| Float | 1,521 | − 673 | − 230 |
| Other Federal Reserve Assets | 8,684 | − 983 | − 322 |
| Total Reserve Bank Credit | 159,993 | + 458 | + 9,213 |
| Gold Stock | 11,132 | − 2 | − 17 |
| SDR certificates | 4,618 | .... | + 800 |
| Treasury currency outstanding | 13,786 | .... | + 30 |
| Total | 189,529 | + 456 | +10,026 |
| Currency in circulation | 157,363 | + 372 | +12,467 |
| Treasury cash holdings | 535 | + 3 | + 47 |
| Treasury dpts with F.R. Bnks | 3,131 | − 681 | + 9 |
| Foreign dpts with F.R. Bnks | 272 | + 49 | + 13 |
| Other deposits with F.R. Bnks | 560 | + 6 | + 60 |
| Other F.R. liabilities & capital | 4,867 | − 27 | − 336 |
| Total | 167,423 | − 272 | +12,769 |
| Reserves | | | |
| With F.R. Banks | 22,105 | + 728 | − 2,744 |
| Total inc. cash | 38,132 | + 129 | − 1,583 |
| Required reserves | 37,764 | + 196 | − 1,511 |
| Excess reserves | 368 | − 67 | − 72 |
| Free reserves | −96 | − 419 | |

b-The figures reflect adjustment for new Federal Reserve rules that impose reserve requirements on most deposit-taking institutions, including non-member commercial banks, mutual savings banks and savings and loan associations.

**MONETARY AND RESERVE AGGREGATES**
(daily average in billions)

| | One week ended: | |
|---|---|---|
| | May 11 | May 4 |
| Money supply (M1) sa | 506.9 | 499.9 |
| Money supply (M1) nsa | 493.6 | 492.2 |
| | May 18 | May 11 |
| Monetary base | 182.86 | 181.87 |
| Total Reserves | 41.12 | 40.82 |
| Nonborrowed Reserves | 40.04 | 40.11 |
| Required Reserves | 40.75 | 40.39 |
| | Four weeks ended: | |
| | May 11 | Apr. 13 |
| Money supply (M1) sa | 499.1 | 496.4 |

sa-Seasonally adjusted. nsa-Not seasonally adjusted.

**KEY INTEREST RATES**
(weekly average)

| | May 18 | May 11 |
|---|---|---|
| Federal funds | 8.59 | 8.48 |
| Treasury bill (90 day) | 8.09 | 8.03 |
| Commercial paper (dealer, 90 day) | 8.26 | 8.17 |
| Certfs of Deposit (resale, 90 day) | 8.41 | 8.31 |
| Eurodollars (90 days) | 8.89 | 8.71 |

**One-Week Money Supply Figure**
M1 averaged $506.9 billion during week ending May 11, 1983

**Four-Week Money Supply Figure**
M1 averaged $499.1 billion during four weeks ending May 11, 1983

**Chart 1**
**The Money Supply** (M1)

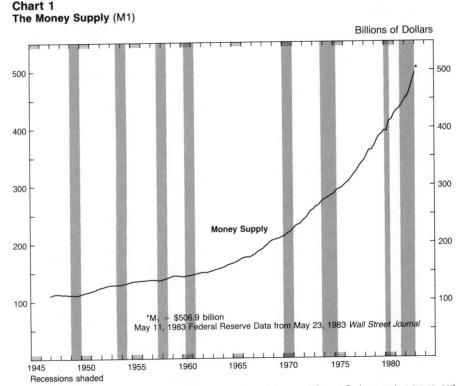

Billions of Dollars

*M₁ = $506.9 billion
May 11, 1983 Federal Reserve Data from May 23, 1983 *Wall Street Journal*

Money Supply

Recessions shaded

Source: U.S. Department of Commerce, *Business Statistics* and *Survey of Current Business*, various issues, and Federal Reserve Board.

**Expansionary policy:** *Fed buys securities → Bank reserves ↑ → Bank lending ↑ → Money supply ↑ → Demand ↑.*

**Contractionary policy:** *Fed sells securities → Bank reserves ↓ → Bank lending ↓ → Money supply ↓ → Demand ↓.*

A growing group of economists began to criticize the Fed's policy. They accused the Fed of contributing to the severity of the business cycle instead of reducing cyclical fluctuations. In their view, the Fed's contractionary policy, applied at the peak of the cycle, only added to the severity of the impending recession, while expansionary policy, during the early stages of recovery, only set the stage for the subsequent inflations.

These economists, known as the *monetarist* school, believe that the rate of increase in the money supply is the most important determinant of business cycle conditions. If the money supply grows rapidly, the economy expands. If the money supply does not grow rapidly, or even contracts, economic activity also contracts. The monetarists also believe that because other forces intrinsic to the economy will lead to normal cyclical activity and fluctuation in the rate of growth in the money supply, the Fed's best course of action is to attempt to keep the money supply's growth on an even keel, preferably at a low rate, reflecting the economy's long-range ability to increase output. According to the monetarists' view, anything beyond that rate will lead to inflation, and attempts to reduce the swings of the cycle will only exacerbate them.

It's as if the monetarists were saying, "If you want a comfortable temperature, set the thermostat and leave it. Don't fiddle with it by alternately raising and lowering it every time you feel a little chilly or a bit too warm, because this will just cause wide swings in temperature which only heighten discomfort, rather than reduce it."

In October 1979, shortly after Paul Volcker began his term of office, the Fed announced an accommodation with the monetarist position. Henceforth, Mr. Volker said, the Fed would set targets for monetary growth which it believed consistent with an acceptable rate of inflation. The monetarists claimed a big victory.

Then, when the Fed tightened the screws in 1981, pursuing a tight money policy and announcing that money supply growth would be constrained until inflation had been brought under control, the monetarists cheered. At long last, the Fed had broken out of its old habit pattern of reflating the economy to aid recovery. After decades of mischief, it had seen the light.

Recently, however, the Fed has emphasized that the money supply is only one of several indicators upon which it bases its policy, and that it feels free to depart from its targeted rate of money supply growth as conditions require. These remarks were greeted by howls of protest from the monetarists, who claimed that the Fed was chickening out just as it was about to drive the stake into inflation's heart.

Whose side should you take? Beware, because much of the theoretical debate is a veneer which thinly disguises ideological differences not always susceptible to common sense. The monetarists are conservatives who believe that government governs best when it governs least. And that includes the Fed. Hence, the monetarists believe that the Fed should not play an activist, interventionist role. The monetarists' opponents advocate an activist, interventionist government. Thus, they believe that the Fed should intercede to control the vicissitudes of the cycle. The emotion which each side brings to the debate is your clue that more than objective analysis is at stake.

In any case, you need not take sides, nor need you permit debate over the money supply's importance to distract your attention from the Fed's policy reversal in 1981. The Fed used its familiar, old-fashioned tight money policy to fight inflation; it was the timing of that policy which was not traditional and thus represented a concession to the monetarists. The Fed conceded that its activities during the 70s had contributed to the cycle's severity and to inflation. Therefore, it took the unprecedented action of flattening the recovery, and the cycle, in order to stop the inflation which the monetarists considered the economy's number one problem. In mid-1982, as inflation subsided and unemployment became severe, the Fed moved to an easy money policy in a pragmatic adjustment to the prevailing economic and political realities.

Now take one last look at M1 in "Federal Reserve Data" and the money supply chart (see pages 28 and 29). As you track this statistic week to week, you will see that it fluctuates severely and erratically. Like many of the statistical series in this book, it is difficult to use in the very short run, and you will need at least a quarter year's data before you can draw firm conclusions regarding significant trends.

# CHAPTER FIVE

## Interest Rates

Every commodity has a price, and the *interest rate* is the price of money. As with any commodity, that price fluctuates according to the laws of supply and demand.

The demand for money increases and interest rates rise during economic expansion as consumers and businesses finance increased spending by drawing upon three sources of funds: current saving, liquidation of financial assets, and borrowing.

During recessions, as the economy moves from trough to recovery, cash becomes plentiful once again. Savings are ample; financial assets accumulate; and debt is repaid. Interest rates fall as the supply of funds exceeds the demand for funds.

This cycle occurs with or without the Federal Reserve System. Yet you can weave the cyclical fluctuation of interest rates into Chapter Three and Four's description of Federal Reserve policy. The Fed traditionally pursued an easy money policy to hold interest rates down and promote easy credit conditions during the recovery phase of the cycle. Eventually, when the expansion was fully under way, the peak of the cycle not far off, and credit conditions becoming tighter, the Fed switched to a tight money policy which reduced the supply of credit even further and drove interest rates higher.

The Fed's actions can be summarized as follows:

**Easy money policy:** *Fed buys securities → Bank reserves ↑ → Bank lending ↑ → Money supply ↑ → Interest rates ↓ → Demand ↑.*

**Tight money policy:** *Fed sells securities* → *Bank reserves* ↓ → *Bank lending* ↓ → *Money supply* ↓ → *Interest rates* ↑ → *Demand* ↓.

The Fed reversed course in 1981 when it clamped its tight money policy on the recovery, sending interest rates to record highs. And as you know, the Fed relaxed its grip in 1982, allowing interest rates to fall.

Thus, whether you observe historical or recent events, interest rates are an important gauge of both Federal Reserve policy and the cycle.

So far, interest rates have been treated collectively, as if they were a single entity. A closer examination of the credit markets, however, reveals a complex scene.

There are a great variety of credit instruments—U.S. Treasury securities, corporate bonds, residential mortgages, and so forth—each with its own market. The market conditions for a particular form of credit determine its rate of interest. Yet the markets for all forms of credit are interrelated. For instance, record federal deficits will require record borrowing in the form of U.S. Treasury security sales. In order to attract lenders and dispose of all securities, the Treasury must offer an increased interest return. This will draw investors away from corporate bonds, requiring business to increase the return on its debt. Thus, the impact of the federal deficit is felt throughout the credit markets.

*The Wall Street Journal* publishes the most important interest rates on a weekly and daily basis.

## KEY INTEREST RATES

A number of important short-term (maturing in less than a year) interest rates are presented at the bottom of **Federal Reserve Data** under the heading **Key Interest Rates** (see page 34).

Our national debt made headlines in 1981 when it passed a trillion dollars, and it continues to mushroom. *Treasury bills* constitute about a quarter of the total, and this huge dollar volume makes them the most important short-term investment instrument, and their return the interest rate to watch.

The U.S. Treasury borrows by selling bills (and notes and bonds, as the longer-term debt instruments are called) at auction (primary market) every Monday in New York. They are sold on a discount basis, which means that buyers pay less than the $10,000 face value they will receive when the bill matures in 90 days (actually, thirteen weeks). If bidding is strong, and the price high, the effective rate of interest will be low, and vice versa.

**KEY ASSETS AND LIABILITIES OF 10 WEEKLY
REPORTING MEMBER BANKS IN NEW YORK CITY**
(in millions of dollars)

| | May 11, 1983 | Change from May 4, 1983 |
|---|---|---|
| ASSETS: | | |
| Total assets | 230,295 | − 3,693 |
| Total loans and investments | 142,079 | − 677 |
| Includes: | | |
| Commercial and industrial loans | 56,364 | − 755 |
| Domestic | 54,856 | − 760 |
| Foreign | 1,508 | + 5 |
| Acceptances, comm'l paper | 1,171 | + 6 |
| Finance company loans | 3,800 | − 64 |
| Personal loans | 11,612 | − 8 |
| Loan loss reserve | 2,537 | + 6 |
| U.S. Treasury securities | 10,485 | + 767 |
| Federal agency securities | 1,450 | − 8 |
| Municipal issues | 11,785 | + 154 |
| Due in one year or less | 1,602 | + 136 |
| Longer term | 10,183 | + 18 |
| LIABILITIES: | | |
| Demand deposits | 118,873 | − 2,426 |
| Demand deposits adjusted (a) | 25,630 | + 11 |
| Time and savings deposits | 72,055 | − 72 |
| Negotiable CDs ($100,000 and up) | 23,639 | − 135 |
| Borrowings | 60,775 | − 467 |

a-Excludes government and bank deposits and cash items being collected.

**MEMBER BANK RESERVE CHANGES**

Changes in weekly averages of reserves and related items during the week and year ended May 18, 1983 were as follows (in millions of dollars)-b

| | May 18 1983 | Chg fm May 11 1983 | wk end May 19 1982 |
|---|---|---|---|
| Reserve bank credit: | | | |
| U.S. Gov't securities: | | | |
| Bought outright | 139,806 | + 1,748 | +10,872 |
| Held under repurch agreemt | .... | .... | − 793 |
| Federal agency issues: | | | |
| Bought outright | 8,908 | .... | − 100 |
| Held under repurch agreemt | .... | .... | − 89 |
| Acceptances−bought outright | .... | .... | − 233 |
| Held under repurch agreemt | .... | | |
| Borrowings from Fed | 1,074 | + 365 | + 108 |
| Seasonal borrowings | 91 | .... | − 141 |
| Extended credit | 519 | + 13 | + 340 |
| Float | 1,521 | − 673 | − 230 |
| Other Federal Reserve Assets | 8,684 | − 983 | − 322 |
| Total Reserve Bank Credit | 159,993 | + 458 | + 9,213 |
| Gold Stock | 11,132 | − 2 | − 17 |
| SDR certificates | 4,618 | .... | + 800 |
| Treasury currency outstanding | 13,786 | .... | + 30 |
| Total | 189,529 | + 456 | +10,026 |
| Currency in circulation | 157,363 | + 372 | +12,467 |
| Treasury cash holdings | 535 | + 3 | + 47 |
| Treasury dpts with F.R. Bnks | 3,131 | − 681 | + 9 |
| Foreign dpts with F.R. Bnks | 272 | + 49 | + 13 |
| Other deposits with F.R. Bnks | 560 | + 6 | + 60 |
| Other F.R. liabilities & capital | 4,867 | − 27 | − 336 |
| Total | 167,423 | − 272 | +12,769 |
| Reserves | | | |
| With F.R. Banks | 22,105 | + 728 | − 2,744 |
| Total inc. cash | 38,132 | + 129 | − 1,583 |
| Required reserves | 37,764 | + 196 | − 1,511 |
| Excess reserves | 368 | − 67 | − 72 |
| Free reserves | −96 | − 419 | .... |

b-The figures reflect adjustment for new Federal Reserve rules that impose reserve requirements on most deposit-taking institutions, including non-member commercial banks, mutual savings banks and savings and loan associations.

**MONETARY AND RESERVE AGGREGATES**
(daily average in billions)

| | One week ended: May 11 | May 4 |
|---|---|---|
| Money supply (M1) sa | 506.9 | 499.9 |
| Money supply (M1) nsa | 493.6 | 492.2 |

| | May 18 | May 11 |
|---|---|---|
| Monetary base | 182.86 | 181.87 |
| Total Reserves | 41.12 | 40.82 |
| Nonborrowed Reserves | 40.04 | 40.11 |
| Required Reserves | 40.75 | 40.39 |

| | Four weeks ended: May 11 | Apr. 13 |
|---|---|---|
| Money supply (M1) sa | 499.1 | 496.4 |

sa-Seasonally adjusted. nsa-Not seasonally adjusted.

**Key Interest Rates** ─────────────────► **KEY INTEREST RATES**
(weekly average)

| | May 18 | May 11 |
|---|---|---|
| Federal funds | 8.59 | 8.48 |
| Treasury bill (90 day) | 8.09 | 8.03 |
| Commercial paper (dealer, 90 day) | 8.26 | 8.17 |
| Certfs of Deposit (resale, 90 day) | 8.41 | 8.31 |
| Eurodollars (90 days) | 8.89 | 8.71 |

Place yourself in the role of buyer. If you pay $9,750 for a bill maturing in 90 days (about a quarter of a year), your effective annual rate of return is approximately 10 percent. Remember, $250 in a quarter year is the equivalent of $1,000 in a year, or 10 percent of a $10,000 base. (Use $10,000 as the base, for ease of calculation, rather than $9,750.) If strong bidding drives the price to $9,875, your return falls to 5 percent. If weak bidding permits the price to fall to $9,500, the effective return rises to 20 percent. Keep in mind that the interest rate varies inversely with the price; the more you pay for the Treasury bill, the lower your rate of return, and vice versa. The examples are summarized below.

| | | | |
|---|---|---|---|
| Face (redemption) value | $10,000 | $10,000 | $10,000 |
| Selling price | 9,875 → | 9,750 → | 9,500 |
| (Note: Prices falling.) | | | |
| Discount (difference) | 125 | 250 | 500 |
| (Note: Interest rate rising.) | 5% → | 10% → | 20% |

Your motivation for buying Treasury bills is probably quite simple: you have idle cash on which you wish to earn an interest return. Therefore, the key question is, "How much will you pay now in order to receive $10,000 in 90 days' time?" If you and all other bidders for Treasury bills have ample funds and are eager to buy, you will drive the price close to $10,000 and earn a low rate of return. If you and all other bidders do not have ample funds, you can be enticed only by a very low price for the right to receive $10,000 in 90 days and you will receive a high rate of interest. The Treasury, which is the seller of the bills, must pay the rate of interest determined by the bidding.

Once you have purchased a Treasury bill, however, you need not wait 90 days to have it redeemed. You can sell it on the open market (secondary market) at any time. Chances are you will have a broker act as your agent, because the daily trading takes place in New York and is reserved for large financial institutions dealing in millions of dollars at a time. The daily trading is called the *money market*, a term which suggests the fact that Treasury bills are the safest, most convenient, and most liquid (marketable) interest-earning alternative to cash. (The term also lets you know where the "money market funds" took their name, though they deal in markets for other financial instruments too.)

The huge volume of outstanding Treasury bills offers a readily available investment vehicle. The Federal Reserve, treasurers of large corporations, state and local governments, pension funds, and banks and other financial institutions can get into and out of the money market on a daily basis as their requirements for cash and their desire for an interest-earning alternative may dictate. This demand for Treasury bills fluctuates with the cycle.

As a general rule, cash holdings accumulate during and immediately after recession as demand and expenditures fall. Businesses, for instance, look for alternative uses for their funds as they curtail expenditures on new factories and machinery. As they enter the money market, seeking a return on idle funds, their demand for Treasury bills drives prices upward and interest rates fall.

At the same time, bank lending falls and loans are repaid, as neither consumers nor businesses have growing levels of expenditures that need financing. Free reserves accumulate, representing the banks' lost opportunity to generate earnings, so the banks invest in Treasury bills, and their purchases also push prices up and interest rates down. And if the Fed pursues an easy money policy at the same time in order to spur the economy, its purchase of bills (securities) will contribute to the interest rate decline. Hence, the general improvement in liquidity brought by the recession generates a growing demand for Treasury bills and a drop in their interest rate. Finally, a decline in Treasury bill rates will prompt investors to switch to other instruments, driving their prices up and their rate of return down.

As the cycle develops from recovery to expansion, the demand for cash increases apace. The process is reversed. Expenditures climb; Treasury bills are liquidated to obtain cash; and so interest rates climb too. As bank lending recovers, free reserves disappear and banks are obliged to sell Treasury bills to generate reserves. If the Fed begins to pursue a tight money policy in order to restrain the growth in demand, its sale of securities (bills) will also contribute to the rise in interest rates. Market forces pull other interest rates along the same cyclical path. Investors are free to sell other instruments and buy Treasury bills when Treasury bill rates rise, thereby depressing the price and raising the return on the other instruments too.

Before you move to the remaining "Key Interest Rates," the Fed's role in the money market should be examined further. Remember that the Fed is not an agency of the U.S. government. The Fed operates in this market like any other investor, buying and selling securities (Treasury bills) for its portfolio. Unlike other investors, however, the Fed does not participate in the money market for ordinary business reasons. The Fed sells Treasury bills when it wishes to drain revenues from banks (the buyers write checks to the Fed, and the banks must pay the Fed with reserves), and the Fed buys Treasury bills when it wishes to supply the banks with reserves (the sellers receive checks from the Fed and deposit them, augmenting bank reserves). The Fed's *Open Market Committee* has the responsibility of overseeing the Fed's actions in the money market.

You know from Chapter Three that the banks pay an interest rate, called the discount rate, when they borrow reserves from the Fed. Banks can borrow reserves from one another too; the interest rate on such loans is called the *federal funds rate.*

Banks that are not located in the main commercial centers of the nation often have more reserves than they need. They are therefore in a position to lend reserves on a day-to-day basis to large banks in the major commercial centers. This practice is profitable for the lenders because they earn interest on funds which would otherwise be idle, and it is profitable for the large city banks because they acquire reserves that enable them to attract and hold borrowers whose loyalty is important. Arrangements for the transfer of funds are made on the telephone by the banks.

*Commercial paper* is unsecured debt issued by the very largest corporations. These giant companies are able to go to investors for short-term funds in much the same manner as the U.S. Treasury. Commercial paper is the private equivalent of the Treasury bill; in order to attract investors, its rate of interest has to be higher than that of the Treasury bill. Corporations issue commercial paper to avoid the higher interest rate (prime rate) levied by banks on business borrowers.

*Certificates of deposit* are issued by large commercial banks in denominations of $100,000. They are like savings accounts for which the investor receives a "certificate of deposit" from the bank. The investor, however, may sell the certificate of deposit to another investor before the 90-day term of maturity is over, and the rate of interest will reflect current market conditions. Banks issue certificates of deposit to compete with Treasury bills and commercial paper for the investor's dollar.

*Eurodollars* are demand deposits, denominated in U.S. dollars, on deposit in Europe. These funds may be borrowed for a short term.

Chart 1 on page 38 presents the relationship between the Treasury bill, federal funds, and prime interest rates since World War II. You can observe the effect of the business cycle on these rates and the impact of Federal Reserve policy. Also note the rise in rates over time as the demand for borrowed funds grew and inflation became more severe. Finally, the impact of the Fed's 1981 tight money policy is self-evident, as is the Fed's recent easing of its grip.


## DAILY INTEREST RATE DATA

You don't have to wait for Monday's "Federal Reserve Data" to assess developments in the money and credit markets. Interest rate data is published daily in The Wall Street Journal under the cap-

**Chart 1**
**Short-Term Interest Rates: The Prime Rate, the Federal Funds Rate, and the Treasury Bills Rate**

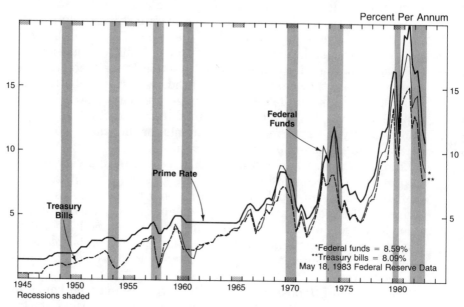

Percent Per Annum

Recessions shaded

Source: U.S. Department of Commerce, *Business Conditions Digest* and *Handbook of Cyclical Indicators,* series 109, 114, and 119.

tions "*Money Rates*" (see page 39) and "*Treasury Issues*" (see page 40). You can find these tables by using the index on the front page.

You can see that a variety of interest rates are reported, but only three (federal funds, certificates of deposit, and Treasury bills) will repay your careful daily attention; these are the most closely watched, and they have already been introduced as "Key Interest Rates." You need very little additional information about them in order to interpret the daily data.

## *Money Rates*

Friday, May 20, 1983

The key U.S. and foreign annual interest rates below are a guide to general levels but don't always represent actual transactions.

**PRIME RATE:** 10½%. The base rate on corporate loans at large U.S. money center commercial banks.

Federal Funds, 8½% ————→ **FEDERAL FUNDS:** 8⅜% high, 8½% low, 8½% near closing bid, 8⅜% offered. Reserves traded among commercial banks for overnight use in amounts of $1 million or more. Source: Mabon, Nugent & Co., N.Y.

**DISCOUNT RATE:** 8½%. The charge on loans to depository institutions by the New York Federal Reserve Bank.

**CALL MONEY:** 9¼% to 9½%. The charge on loans to brokers on stock exchange collateral.

**COMMERCIAL PAPER** placed directly by General Motors Acceptance Corp.: 8⅜% 30 to 179 days; 8¼% 180 to 270 days.

**COMMERCIAL PAPER:** High-grade unsecured notes sold through dealers by major corporations in multiples of $1,000: 8½% 30 days; 8½% 60 days; 8½% 90 days.

90-Day CDs, 8.60% ————→ **CERTIFICATES OF DEPOSIT:** 8.40% one month; 8.50% two months; 8.60% three months; 8.55% six months; 8.625% one year. Typical rates paid by major banks on new issues of negotiable C.D.s, usually on amounts of $1 million and more. The minimum unit is $100,000.

**BANKERS ACCEPTANCES:** 8.45% 30 days; 8.45% 60 days; 8.45% 90 days; 8.50% 120 days; 8.50% 150 days; 8.45% 180 days. Negotiable, bank-backed business credit instruments typically financing an import order.

**LONDON LATE EURODOLLARS:** 9 1/16% to 8 15/16% one month; 9⅛% to 9% two months; 9¼% to 9⅛% three months; 9¼% to 9⅛% four months; 9 5/16% to 9 3/16% five months; 9 7/16% to 9 5/16% six months.

**LONDON INTERBANK OFFERED RATES (LIBOR):** 9¼% three months; 9 ⅜% six months; 9 9/16% one year. The average of interbank offered rates for dollar deposits in the London market based on quotations at five major banks.

**FOREIGN PRIME RATES:** Canada 11%; Germany 7¾%; Japan 6.30%; Switzerland 5½%; Britain 10%. These rate indications aren't directly comparable; lending practices vary widely by location. Source: Morgan Guaranty Trust Co.

**TREASURY BILLS:** Results of the Monday, May 16, 1987, auction of short-term U.S. government bills, sold at a discount from face value in units of $10,000 to $1 million: 8.10% 13 weeks; 8.14% 26 weeks.

**FEDERAL HOME LOAN MORTGAGE CORP.** (Freddie Mac): Posted yields on 30-year mortgage commitments for delivery within 60 days. 12.65%, standard conventional fixed-rate mortgages; 12.15%, adjustable rate mortgages.

**MERRILL LYNCH READY ASSETS TRUST:** 8.15%. Annualized average rate of return after expenses for the past 30 days; not a forecast of future returns.

The Wall Street Journal, *May 23, 1983.*

# Treasury Issues * *Bonds, Notes & Bills*

Friday, May 20, 1983

Mid-afternoon Over-the-Counter quotations supplied by the Federal Reserve Bank of New York City.

Decimals in bid-and-asked and bid changes represent 32nds; 101.1 means 101 1/32. a-Plus 1/64. b-Yield to call date. d-Minus 1/64. n-Treasury notes.

**U.S. TREASURY BONDS**

| Rate | Mat. Date | | Bid | Asked | Bid Chg. | Yld. |
|---|---|---|---|---|---|---|
| 15⅝s, | 1983 | May n | 100.6 | 100.14 | .... | 0.00 |
| 3¼s, | 1978-83 | Jun | 99.15 | 99.23 | – .1 | 7.81 |
| 8⅞s, | 1983 | Jun n | 99.31 | 100.3 | + .3 | 7.68 |
| 14⅝s, | 1983 | Jun n | 100.21 | 100.25 | .... | 6.55 |
| 15⅞s, | 1983 | Jul n | 101.12 | 101.16 | .... | 7.41 |
| 9¼s, | 1983 | Aug n | 100.4 | 100.8 | + .1 | 7.95 |
| 11⅞s, | 1983 | Aug n | 100.22 | 100.26 | .... | 8.01 |
| 16¼s, | 1983 | Aug n | 101.30 | 102.2 | – .2 | 8.11 |
| 9¾s, | 1983 | Sep n | 100.11 | 100.15 | .... | 8.26 |
| 16s, | 1983 | Sep n | 102.17 | 102.25 | – .1 | 7.71 |
| 15½s, | 1983 | Oct n | 102.28 | 103.4 | – .1 | 7.98 |
| 7s, | 1983 | Nov n | 99.8 | 99.16 | .... | 8.08 |
| 9⅞s, | 1983 | Nov n | 100.16 | 100.20 | .... | 8.48 |
| 12⅛s, | 1983 | Nov n | 101.21 | 101.29 | – .1 | 8.30 |
| 10½s, | 1983 | Dec n | 100.29 | 101.1 | .... | 8.71 |
| 13s, | 1983 | Dec n | 102.11 | 102.19 | .... | 8.50 |
| 15s, | 1984 | Jan n | 104.1 | 104.9 | + .1 | 8.49 |
| 7¼s, | 1984 | Feb n | 98.28 | 99 | + .1 | 8.69 |
| 15⅛s, | 1984 | Feb n | 104.16 | 104.24 | – .1 | 8.63 |
| 14⅛s, | 1984 | Mar n | 104.10 | 105.9 | + .4 | 8.82 |
| 14¼s, | 1984 | Mar n | 104.6 | 104.17 | – .4 | 8.72 |
| 13⅞s, | 1984 | Apr n | 104.9 | 104.17 | + .9 | 8.72 |
| 9¼s, | 1984 | May n | 100.9 | 100.11 | .... | 8.87 |
| 13¼s, | 1984 | May n | 104.15 | 105.4 | + .15 | 8.75 |
| 13¾s, | 1984 | May n | 104.15 | 104.23 | – .2 | 8.81 |
| 15¾s, | 1984 | May n | 106.9 | 106.13 | – .1 | 8.76 |
| 8⅞s, | 1984 | Jun n | 99.25 | 100.1 | – .1 | 8.84 |
| 14⅜s, | 1984 | Jun n | 105.13 | 105.21 | – .1 | 8.88 |
| 13⅛s, | 1984 | Jul | 104.10 | 104.26 | – .3 | 8.78 |
| 6⅜s, | 1984 | Aug | 97.15 | 97.31 | + .3 | 8.14 |
| 7¼s, | 1984 | Aug n | 98.8 | 98.16 | + .1 | 8.57 |
| 11⅝s, | 1984 | Aug n | 102.22 | 102.30 | – .2 | 9.13 |
| 13¼s, | 1984 | Aug n | 104.17 | 104.25 | – .1 | 9.06 |
| 12⅛s, | 1984 | Sep n | 103.15 | 103.19 | + .1 | 9.24 |
| 9¾s, | 1984 | Oct | 100.15 | 100.23 | – .2 | 9.20 |
| 9⅞s, | 1984 | Nov n | 100.18 | 100.26 | – .2 | 9.29 |
| 14⅜s, | 1984 | Nov n | 106.22 | 106.26 | – .3 | 9.33 |
| 16s, | 1984 | Nov n | 108.30 | 109.2 | – .3 | 9.29 |
| 9⅜s, | 1984 | Dec n | 99.26 | 99.30 | – .2 | 9.42 |
| 14s, | 1984 | Dec n | 106.20 | 106.28 | – .4 | 9.28 |
| 9¼s, | 1985 | Jan n | 99.18 | 99.26 | – .1 | 9.37 |
| 8s, | 1985 | Feb n | 98 | 98.8 | – .5 | 9.12 |
| 9⅝s, | 1985 | Feb n | 100 | 100.8 | – .3 | 9.47 |
| 14⅝s, | 1985 | Feb n | 107.24 | 108 | – .4 | 9.50 |
| 9⅝s, | 1985 | Mar | 100 | 100.4 | – .4 | 9.55 |
| 13⅜s, | 1985 | Mar n | 106.9 | 106.17 | – .4 | 9.45 |
| 9½s, | 1985 | Apr n | 99.24 | 99.30 | – .2 | 9.50 |
| 3¼s, | 1985 | May | 91.6 | 92.6 | – .8 | 7.58 |
| 4¼s, | 1975-85 | May | 91.21 | 92.21 | – .1 | 8.36 |
| 10⅜s, | 1985 | May n | 101.14 | 101.22 | – .1 | 9.41 |
| 14⅛s, | 1985 | May n | 107.27 | 108.3 | – .7 | 9.54 |
| 14⅜s, | 1985 | May n | 108.10 | 108.18 | – .3 | 9.52 |
| 14s, | 1985 | Jun n | 108.4 | 108.12 | – .4 | 9.61 |
| 8¼s, | 1985 | Aug n | 97.12 | 97.20 | – .4 | 9.45 |
| 9⅝s, | 1985 | Aug n | 99.30 | 100.6 | – .1 | 9.53 |
| 13⅛s, | 1985 | Aug n | 106.20 | 106.28 | – .2 | 9.63 |
| 15⅞s, | 1985 | Sep n | 112.22 | 112.26 | – .4 | 9.67 |
| 9¾s, | 1985 | Nov n | 100.1 | 100.5 | – .1 | 9.69 |
| 11¾s, | 1985 | Nov n | 104.9 | 104.17 | – .5 | 9.65 |
| 14⅛s, | 1985 | Dec n | 109.24 | 110 | – .2 | 9.69 |
| 13½s, | 1986 | Feb n | 108.16 | 108.24 | – .2 | 9.78 |
| 9⅞s, | 1986 | Feb n | 100.4 | 100.8 | – .4 | 9.77 |
| 14s, | 1986 | Mar n | 110.2 | 110.10 | – .2 | 9.77 |
| 7⅞s, | 1986 | May n | 95.5 | 95.9 | – .3 | 9.74 |
| 9⅜s, | 1986 | M | | 30 | – .6 | 9.80 |
| 13¾s, | 1986 | M | | 3 | – .2 | 9.77 |
| 14⅞s, | 1986 | J | | 4 | – .2 | 9.86 |
| 8s, | 1986 | A | | 11 | – .2 | 9.71 |
| 12¼s, | 1986 | S | | 16 | .... | 9.92 |
| 6⅛s, | 1986 | N | | | + .6 | 8.84 |
| 13⅞s, | 1986 | N | | 7 | – .2 | 9.98 |
| 16⅛s, | 1986 | N | | 28 | .... | 9.92 |
| 10s, | 1986 | D | | 12 | – .1 | 9.87 |
| 9s, | 1987 | F | | 12 | – .4 | 9.86 |
| 12¾s, | 1987 | F | | 8 | – .4 | 10.10 |
| 10¼s, | 1987 | Mar n | 100.19 | 100.27 | – .4 | 9.98 |
| 12s, | 1987 | May n | 106.1 | 106.9 | .... | 10.04 |
| 14s, | 1987 | May n | 112.2 | 112.10 | – .2 | 10.16 |
| 13¾s, | 1987 | Aug n | 111.24 | 112 | – .2 | 10.18 |
| 7⅝s, | 1987 | Nov n | 91.30 | 92.6 | – .6 | 9.82 |
| 12⅝s, | 1987 | Nov n | 108.11 | 108.19 | – .6 | 10.19 |
| 12⅜s, | 1988 | Jan n | 107.20 | 107.28 | – .7 | 10.20 |
| 10⅛s, | 1988 | Feb n | 99.25 | 100.1 | – .2 | 10.11 |
| 13¼s, | 1988 | Apr n | 110.30 | 111.6 | – .5 | 10.29 |
| 8¼s, | 1988 | May n | 93.2 | 93.10 | – .3 | 9.98 |
| 9⅞s, | 1988 | May n | 98.26 | 99.2 | – .6 | 10.12 |
| 14s, | 1988 | Jul n | 113.24 | 114 | – .8 | 10.41 |
| 15⅜s, | 1988 | Oct n | 119.28 | 120.4 | – .4 | 10.41 |
| 8¾s, | 1988 | Nov n | 94.11 | 94.19 | – .3 | 10.06 |
| 14⅝s, | 1989 | Jan n | 116.24 | 117 | – .6 | 10.56 |
| 14⅜s, | 1989 | Apr n | 116.1 | 116.9 | – .5 | 10.59 |
| 9¼s, | 1989 | May n | 96.2 | 96.10 | – .6 | 10.09 |
| 14½s, | 1989 | Jul | 116.30 | 117.6 | – .6 | 10.62 |
| 11⅞s, | 1989 | Oct n | 106 | 106.8 | – .5 | 10.51 |
| 10¾s, | 1989 | Nov n | 101.8 | 101.16 | – .6 | 10.43 |
| 10½s, | 1990 | Jan n | 100.4 | 100.12 | – .4 | 10.42 |
| 3½s, | 1990 | Feb | 92.4 | 93.4 | – .4 | 4.71 |
| 10½s, | 1990 | Apr n | 100.5 | 100.9 | – .7 | 10.44 |
| 8¼s, | 1990 | May | 91 | 91.16 | – .6 | 9.96 |
| 10¾s, | 1990 | Aug n | 101.15 | 101.23 | – .3 | 10.41 |
| 13s, | 1990 | Nov n | 111.25 | 112.1 | – .3 | 10.63 |
| 14½s, | 1991 | May n | 119.14 | 119.22 | – .12 | 10.76 |
| 14⅞s, | 1991 | Aug n | 121.24 | 122 | .... | 10.78 |
| 14¼s, | 1991 | Nov n | 118.16 | 119.2 | – .14 | 10.76 |
| 14⅝s, | 1992 | Feb n | 121.9 | 121.17 | – .3 | 10.76 |
| 13¾s, | 1992 | May n | 116.17 | 116.25 | – .4 | 10.79 |
| 4¼s, | 1987-92 | Aug | 91.18 | 92.18 | – .13 | 5.28 |
| 7¼s, | 1992 | Aug | 81.12 | 82.12 | – .2 | 10.25 |
| 10½s, | 1992 | Nov n | 99.19 | 99.27 | – .22 | 10.53 |
| 4s, | 1988-93 | Feb | 91.22 | 92.22 | – .4 | 4.95 |
| 6¾s, | 1993 | Feb | 78.8 | 79.8 | .... | 10.15 |
| 7⅞s, | 1993 | Feb | 84.4 | 84.20 | – .12 | 10.43 |
| 10⅞s, | 1993 | Feb n | 101.25 | 102.1 | – .5 | 10.54 |
| 10⅛s, | 1993 | May n | 97.15 | 97.19 | + .13 | 10.52 |
| 7½s, | 1988-93 | Aug | 81.26 | 82.10 | + .4 | 10.34 |
| 8⅝s, | 1993 | Aug | 88.17 | 88.25 | – .3 | 10.43 |
| 8⅝s, | 1993 | Nov | 88.14 | 88.22 | – .9 | 10.42 |
| 9s, | 1994 | Feb | 90.18 | 90.26 | – .3 | 10.44 |
| 4⅛s, | 1989-94 | May | 91.8 | 92.8 | – .17 | 5.06 |
| 8¾s, | 1994 | Aug | 88.19 | 88.27 | – .4 | 10.46 |
| 10⅛s, | 1994 | Nov | 97.13 | 97.21 | – .4 | 10.48 |
| 3s, | 1995 | Feb | 90.17 | 91.17 | – .9 | 3.90 |
| 10½s, | 1995 | Feb | 99.18 | 99.26 | + .4 | 10.53 |
| 10⅜s, | 1995 | May | 98.10 | 98.18 | – .13 | 10.59 |
| 12⅝s, | 1995 | May | 112.11 | 112.19 | – .1 | 10.73 |
| 11½s, | 1995 | Nov | 105.8 | 105.16 | – .5 | 10.69 |
| 7s, | 1993-98 | May | 73.10 | 73.26 | – .4 | 10.51 |
| 3½s, | 1998 | Nov | 91.6 | 92.6 | – .5 | 4.19 |
| 8½s, | 1994-99 | May | 83.9 | 84.9 | + .9 | 10.56 |
| 7⅞s, | 1995-00 | Feb | 77.28 | 78.4 | – .10 | 10.72 |
| 8⅜s, | 1995-00 | Aug | 81.25 | 82.1 | – .9 | 10.67 |
| 11¾s, | 2001 | Feb | 106.4 | 106.12 | – .8 | 10.93 |
| 13⅛s, | 2001 | May | 116.26 | 117.2 | – .13 | 10.94 |
| 8s, | 1996-01 | Aug | 78.13 | 78.21 | – .8 | 10.69 |
| 13⅜s, | 2001 | Aug | 118.25 | 119.1 | – .15 | 10.94 |
| 15¾s, | 2001 | Nov | 138.20 | 138.28 | –1.5 | 10.84 |
| 14¼s, | 2002 | Feb | 125.27 | 126.3 | – .22 | 10.94 |
| 11⅝s, | 2002 | Nov | 105.8 | 105.16 | – .14 | 10.94 |
| 10¾s, | 2003 | Feb | 98.30 | 99.6 | – .12 | 10.85 |
| 10¾s, | 2003 | May | 98.22 | 98.30 | – .17 | 10.88 |
| 8¼s, | 2000-05 | May | 80.5 | 80.14 | – .5 | 10.55 |
| 7⅝s, | 2002-07 | Feb | 74.30 | 75.6 | – .5 | 10.47 |
| 7⅞s, | 2002-07 | Nov | 75.28 | 77.4 | –1.8 | 10.50 |
| 8⅜s, | 2003-08 | Aug | 80.20 | 80.28 | – .5 | 10.55 |
| 8¾s, | 2003-08 | Nov | 83.6 | 83.14 | – .6 | 10.64 |
| 9⅛s, | 2004-09 | May | 86.8 | 86.16 | – .10 | 10.67 |
| 10⅜s, | 2004-09 | Nov | 95.24 | 97 | –1.11 | 10.74 |
| 11¾s, | 2005-10 | Feb | 106.21 | 106.29 | – .14 | 10.90 |
| 10s, | 2005-10 | May | 93.25 | 94.2 | – .9 | 10.67 |
| 12¾s, | 2005-10 | Nov | 114.12 | 114.20 | – .11 | 10.97 |
| 13⅞s, | 2006-11 | May | 123.24 | 124 | – .11 | 10.99 |
| 14s, | 2006-11 | Nov | 125.2 | 125.10 | – .12 | 10.97 |
| 10⅜s, | 2007-12 | Nov | 97.5 | 97.9 | – .8 | 10.68 |

**U.S. Treas. Bills**

| Mat. date | Bid (Discount) | Asked (Discount) | Yield | Mat. date | Bid (Discount) | Asked (Discount) | Yield |
|---|---|---|---|---|---|---|---|
| -1983- | | | | 9-22 | 8.28 | 8.22 | 8.59 |
| 5-26 | 7.27 | 7.07 | 7.19 | 9-29 | 8.28 | 8.22 | 8.61 |
| 6- 2 | 7.87 | 7.77 | 7.92 | 10- 6 | 8.29 | 8.23 | 8.63 |
| 6- 9 | 7.87 | 7.79 | 7.95 | 10-13 | 8.29 | 8.23 | 8.65 |
| 6-16 | 7.86 | 7.78 | 7.95 | 10-20 | 8.29 | 8.23 | 8.66 |
| 6-23 | 7.89 | 7.81 | 7.99 | 10-27 | 8.29 | 8.23 | 8.68 |
| 6-30 | 7.94 | 7.88 | 8.08 | 11- 3 | 8.30 | 8.24 | 8.70 |
| 7- 7 | 8.11 | 8.07 | 8.29 | 11-10 | 8.29 | 8.23 | 8.71 |
| 7-14 | 8.13 | 8.05 | 8.28 | 11-17 | 8.28 | 8.26 | 8.75 |
| 7-21 | 8.14 | 8.08 | 8.32 | 12- 1 | 8.30 | 8.26 | 8.77 |
| 7-28 | 8.17 | 8.11 | 8.37 | 12-29 | 8.30 | 8.26 | 8.78 |
| 8- 4 | 8.26 | 8.20 | 8.48 | -1984- | | | |
| 8-11 | 8.27 | 8.21 | 8.50 | 1-26 | 8.83 | 8.27 | 8.81 |
| 8-18 | 8.18 | 8.16 | 8.46 | 2-23 | 8.34 | 8.28 | 8.86 |
| 8-25 | 8.31 | 8.25 | 8.57 | 3-22 | 8.33 | 8.27 | 8.88 |
| 9- 1 | 8.28 | 8.22 | 8.55 | 4-19 | 8.35 | 8.29 | 8.95 |
| 9- 8 | 8.30 | 8.24 | 8.59 | 5-17 | 8.33 | 8.31 | 9.01 |
| 9-15 | 8.28 | 8.22 | 8.58 | | | | |

**U.S. Treasury Bills**

**Rate of 90–Day Bills, 8.18%**

The Wall Street Journal, *May 23, 1983.*

For example, notice under **Federal Funds** in the "Money Rates" column on page 39 that four different percentages are listed: 8⅝ percent high, 8½ percent low, 8½ percent near closing bid, and 8⅝ percent offered. These numbers show that during trading on May 20, 1983, 8⅝ percent was the highest interest rate proposed by a potential lender bank and 8½ percent was the lowest interest rate bid by a prospective borrower. The last two percentages describe the state of trading near the end of the day: lender banks were still offering 8⅝ percent, and borrower banks were still bidding 8½ percent. Use the closing bid (8½ percent) when following this interest rate. But beware: sharp fluctuations occur from day to day.

In the case of **Certificates of Deposit** (CDs), which are also on page 39, the reported percentages reflect the interest rates offered by banks on May 20, 1983, for different terms of deposit. Notice that the 90-day CD carried with it an interest rate of 8.60 percent.

---

| U.S. Treas. Bills Mat. date | Bid | Asked | Yield Discount | Mat. date | Bid | Asked | Yield Discount |
|---|---|---|---|---|---|---|---|
| -1983- | | | | 9-22 | 8.28 | 8.22 | 8.59 |
| 5-26 | 7.27 | 7.07 | 7.19 | 9-29 | 8.28 | 8.22 | 8.61 |
| 6- 2 | 7.87 | 7.77 | 7.92 | 10- 6 | 8.29 | 8.23 | 8.63 |
| 6- 9 | 7.87 | 7.79 | 7.95 | 10-13 | 8.29 | 8.23 | 8.65 |
| 6-16 | 7.86 | 7.78 | 7.95 | 10-20 | 8.29 | 8.23 | 8.66 |
| 6-23 | 7.89 | 7.81 | 7.99 | 10-27 | 8.29 | 8.23 | 8.68 |
| 6-30 | 7.94 | 7.88 | 8.08 | 11- 3 | 8.30 | 8.24 | 8.70 |
| 7- 7 | 8.11 | 8.07 | 8.29 | 11-10 | 8.29 | 8.23 | 8.71 |
| 7-14 | 8.13 | 8.05 | 8.28 | 11-17 | 8.28 | 8.26 | 8.75 |
| 7-21 | 8.14 | 8.08 | 8.32 | 12- 1 | 8.30 | 8.26 | 8.77 |
| 7-28 | 8.17 | 8.11 | 8.37 | 12-29 | 8.30 | 8.26 | 8.78 |
| 8- 4 | 8.26 | 8.20 | 8.48 | -1984- | | | |
| 8-11 | 8.27 | 8.21 | 8.50 | 1-26 | 8.83 | 8.27 | 8.81 |
| 8-18 → | 8.18 | 8.16 | 8.46 | 2-23 | 8.34 | 8.28 | 8.86 |
| 8-25 | 8.31 | 8.25 | 8.57 | 3-22 | 8.33 | 8.27 | 8.88 |
| 9- 1 | 8.28 | 8.22 | 8.55 | 4-19 | 8.35 | 8.29 | 8.95 |
| 9- 8 | 8.30 | 8.24 | 8.59 | 5-17 | 8.33 | 8.31 | 9.01 |
| 9-15 | 8.28 | 8.22 | 8.58 | | | | |

On Friday, May 20, 1983, the 90-day Treasury bill rate on the open (secondary) market was 8.18 percent for bills auctioned on May 16 (Monday), issued on May 19 (Thursday), and maturing 13 weeks later on August 18 (Thursday)

---

Turn now to **U.S. Treasury Bills** for the same date (May 20, 1983). These bills are auctioned on Mondays, issued on Thursdays, and, in the case of the 90-day Treasury bill, mature 13 weeks later (also on a Thursday). Thus, using the report for Friday, May 20, 1983, you know that the latest 90-day bill included in the report was auctioned on Monday, May 16, and issued on Thursday, May 19. It will mature 13 weeks later, on August 18 (8–18). On May 20 that bill carried an interest rate (bid) of 8.18 percent (not to be confused with the 8–18 date). This figure is located in the row opposite 8–18 under the column headed "Bid." That is, buyers (bidders) paid a price (less than $10,000) which would yield 8.18 percent if the Treasury bill were held to maturity and cashed in for $10,000. Sellers on May 20 were asking a higher price (lower interest rate), equivalent to 8.16 percent. The last column gives the interest rate on a 366-day (rather than 360-day) basis. (The maturity dates other than 8–18 are for older bills and for bills with maturities of more than 90 days.)

In summary, add 13 weeks to last Thursday's date to find the interest rate on the latest 90-day Treasury bill.

"U.S. Treasury Bills" provides Treasury bill interest rates in the money market (or secondary market), which was described earlier in this chapter. The money market is called the secondary market because it is a daily resale market.

The primary, or issue, market is held each Monday and summarized in Tuesday's *Wall Street Journal*.

You will find this weekly report at the end of Tuesday's "Credit Markets" article. It can be located by using the *Journal's* front page index. The "Credit Markets" article appears daily and reports conditions in credit markets and commentary on those markets. (See page 43.)

Note that 8.46 percent (see blow-up on page 44) was the average interest received on 90-day bills purchased at the Treasury's May 23 auction, and reported in Tuesday's, May 24, 1983, *Journal* article. That is, on the average, the U.S. Treasury received $9,786.20 (97.862 percent of face value) for each $10,000 bill auctioned. The difference between $9,786.20 and $10,000 over 90 days (about $215), calculated over a year (about $860), gives you approximately 8.46 percent of $10,000. If you go to the Federal Reserve bank in your district and buy a $10,000 bill on Monday, you'll receive the rate of interest quoted by the *Journal* at the end of Tuesday's "Credit Markets" article.

## LONG-TERM INTEREST RATES

*Bonds* and *mortgages* are the two principal instruments of long-term credit. Interest rates on the former are reported daily by *The Wall Street Journal* in a chart labeled "Bond Yields" which accompanies the "Credit Markets" article. The May 24, 1983, chart is reproduced on page 44.

The "Bond Yields" chart on page 44 depicts two series. The top line describes the interest rate that financially healthy public utilities must pay on debt instruments maturing in 10 years or more, while the second line describes the interest rate that the federal government must pay on debts that mature in 15 years or more. Public utilities, such as electric, gas, and telephone companies, is-

# *U.S.-Bond Prices Rally in Slow Trading Amid Worry About Money Supply Surge*

By TOM HERMAN
*Staff Reporter of* THE WALL STREET JOURNAL

NEW YORK—Prices of U.S. government bonds rallied yesterday afternoon to post small gains. But trading was sluggish as many investors continue to worry about a recent surge in the nation's money supply.

"The market did a little better but I wouldn't get very excited about it," said Samuel Thorne Jr., senior group vice president of Scudder, Stevens & Clark, an investment management firm. "Trading was deadly dull."

**Credit Markets**

Mr. Thorne and other money managers say they are waiting for the outcome of today's Washington meeting of the Federal Reserve System's 12-member policy-making committee. The Federal Open Market Committee, which consists of the seven members of the Federal Reserve Board and five presidents of regional Reserve banks, meets about eight times a year to review credit policy.

The committee will confront the difficult question of how to interpret a recent burst in the basic money-supply measure, known as M1. This measure, which includes cash held by the public as well as private checking deposits, is running way above the Fed target set earlier this year.

Many economists contend that this statistic has been distorted by special technical factors, and that the committee won't pay much attention to it. Analysts point out that two broader measures of the money supply have been growing much more slowly. And they argue that the Fed's policy makers will decide not to tighten credit conditions because that could send the economy back into recession.

Still, bond traders have been alarmed by M1's huge increase in recent weeks. Some are concerned that the explosive growth will scare inflation-sensitive investors who worry that rapid money growth eventually will translate into another inflationary binge and higher interest rates. Traders say the Fed committee may tighten credit to slow money growth even at the risk of pushing interest rates higher for a brief period.

The enormous $11.4 billion increase in M1 during the past two weeks is "terrible," said Steven L. Edelson, vice president and head of the U.S. government bond department at Chemical Bank. "There isn't any other way to view it."

## *Prices of Recent Issues*

Current quotations are indicated below for recent issues of corporate senior securities that aren't listed on a principal exchange.

| Issue | | Moody's Rating | Bid | Asked | Chg. | Yield % |
|---|---|---|---|---|---|---|
| **UTILITIES** | | | | | | |
| ComwlthEd | 12⅛s '13 | A2 | 97⅜ | 97⅝ | + ⅜ | 12.43 |
| NYTele | 11s '23 | A1 | 94⅛ | 94¼ | − ½ | 11.68 |
| PacG&E | 12s '16 | A1 | 97¼ | 97½ | − ⅛ | 12.31 |
| SoCentBell | 10⅞s '93 | A1 | 99⅛ | 99⅝ | − ⅛ | 10.93 |
| SoCentBell | 11⅞s '23 | A1 | 99⅛ | 99⅝ | − ⅛ | 11.92 |
| **INDUSTRIALS** | | | | | | |
| DiamSham | 11¼s '13 | A2 | 94½ | 95 | − ¼ | 11.86 |
| Sears | 10¾s '13 | Aa2 | 93¾ | 94¼ | − ¼ | 11.43 |
| **FOREIGN** | | | | | | |
| HydroQueb | 11¾s '89 | A1 | 101¼ | 101¾ | − ¾ | 11.32 |
| HydroQueb | 13⅜s '13 | A1 | 108¼ | 109 | − ¾ | 12.23 |
| Ontario | 10½s '89 | Aaa | 99½ | 99¾ | − ¼ | 10.55 |
| Ontario | 11¾s '13 | Aaa | 101 | 101¾ | + ¼ | 11.54 |

Source: Paine Webber, Jackson & Curtis Inc.
(Quotes are for round lots)
n-New listings.

The money supply's rapid growth comes as the U.S. economic recovery appears to be strengthening. That worries some economists who insist that the M1 statistic hasn't been significantly distorted at all this year. They warn that the recovery's accelerating pace, combined with the extremely rapid growth of money, will undermine the progress made against inflation.

## Treasury Bill Auction

Rates are determined by the difference between the purchase price and face value. Thus, higher bidding narrows the investor's return while lower bidding widens it. The percentage rates are calculated on a 360-day year, while the coupon equivalent yield is based on a 366-day year.

| | 13-Week | 26-Week |
|---|---|---|
| Applications | $12,956,495,000 | $14,276,210,000 |
| Accepted bids | $6,208,405,000 | $6,208,150,000 |
| Accepted at low price | 56% | 69% |
| Accepted noncompet'ly | $970,630,000 | $751,105,000 |
| Average price (Rate) | 97.862 (8.46%) | 95.694 (8.47%) |
| High price (Rate) | 97.872 (8.42%) | 95.715 (8.43%) |
| Low price (Rate) | 97.856 (8.48%) | 95.689 (8.48%) |
| Coupon equivalent | 8.79% | 9.00% |

Both issues are dated May 26. The 13-week bills mature Aug. 25, and the 26-week bills mature Nov. 25.

The Wall Street Journal, *May 24, 1983.*

Rates are determined by the difference between the purchase price and face value. Thus, higher bidding narrows the investor's return while lower bidding widens it. The percentage rates are calculated on a 360-day year, while the coupon equivalent yield is based on a 366-day year.

**Treasury Bill Auction**

On Monday, May 23, 1983, the Treasury auctioned bills ⟶ in the primary market which had a yield of 8.46 percent.

|  | 13-Week | 26-Week |
|---|---|---|
| Applications | $12,956,495,000 | $14,276,210,000 |
| Accepted bids | $6,208,405,000 | $6,208,150,000 |
| Accepted at low price | 56% | 69% |
| Accepted noncompet'ly | $970,630,000 | $751,105,000 |
| Average price (Rate) | 97.862 (8.46%) | 95.694 (8.47%) |
| High price (Rate) | 97.872 (8.42%) | 95.715 (8.43%) |
| Low price (Rate) | 97.856 (8.48%) | 95.689 (8.48%) |
| Coupon equivalent | 8.79% | 9.00% |

Both issues are dated May 26. The 13-week bills mature Aug. 25, and the 26-week bills mature Nov. 25.

The Wall Street Journal, *May 24, 1983.*

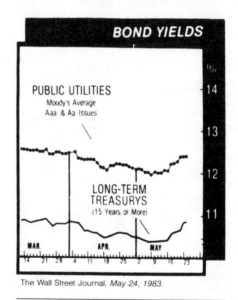

The Wall Street Journal, *May 24, 1983.*

sue substantial amounts of long-term debt to finance their continual capital expansion. Mere profits cannot cover the cost of new generating and switching stations, satellites, and transmission lines, so the difference has to be made up by borrowing. Since the projects of public utility companies are long-term, generating income for these companies over the extensive life of productive assets, it's appropriate that the financing be long-term too. The stretch-out in earnings on these assets will provide for the steady, eventual payment of interest and principal. The federal government sells bonds on a long-term basis too, whenever it anticipates a considerable delay in retiring the debt.

Investors who buy the utility and government bonds wish a secure interest return over several years. The interest earned is usually higher than would be returned on short-term instruments because the borrower is asking the lender to take an extended risk. Long-term rates will move with short-term rates, but at a higher level and with a slight lag as investors in long-term bonds adjust their purchases of these instruments in response to changing short-term rates.

Mortgage rates are watched intensely by everyone involved in buying, selling, and constructing homes and other buildings. The *Journal* devotes a long article, usually appearing toward the beginning of each month, to their discussion. The sample reprinted here was published on May 6, 1983. (See page 46.)

The same forces are at work in the market for mortgage funds. If short-term rates are high, for example, then banks and savings and loan associations must pay their depositors a high rate of return. Otherwise, funds will drain out of these financial intermediaries as depositors buy higher-yielding investments. In order to bear the additional interest expense, the banks and savings and loan associations must charge their mortgage customers more.

Also, many mortgage loans are "passed through" to insurance companies and other investors for which corporate bonds offer an alternative investment vehicle. If mortgages don't offer an attractive yield, investors will buy corporate bonds. These market pressures keep bond and mortgage yields on a parallel course.

Review the record for yourself (see Chart 2, page 47).

You may wish to track the interest rate of a particular bond, or you may wish to purchase a bond. If this bond is traded on the New York Stock Exchange, you will find it listed in *The Wall Street Journal* under "New York Exchange Bonds," a portion of which appears on page 48. Consult the front page index for the daily listing.

From the example on page 48, take the middle listing of Dow Chemical Company, shown below, as an example.

**Example from Page 48** →

| | | | | | | | |
|---|---|---|---|---|---|---|---|
| Divers | 10½91 | 14. | 10 | 73½ | 73½ | 73½ | −3¼ |
| Dow | 7.75s99 | 11. | 15 | 73⅝ | 73⅝ | 73⅝ | − ⅜ |
| Dow | 8⅞2000 | 11. | 5 | 79½ | 79½ | 79½ | + ½ |
| Dow | 7⅞07 | 11. | 4 | 70⅜ | 70⅜ | 70⅜ | −1 |
| duPnt | 8.45s04 | 11. | 24 | 77⅞ | 76½ | 77⅞ | − ⅛ |

| *Bonds* | *Cur Yld* | *Vol* | *High* | *Low* | *Close* | *Net Chg.* |
|---|---|---|---|---|---|---|
| Dow 8⅞ 2000 | 11 | 5 | 79½ | 79½ | 79½ | + ½ |

The interest rate at issue (8⅞ percent) and the year of maturity (2000—the year when the bond is due for redemption) follow the company's name. (You'll find an "s" after the interest rate when a fraction is absent.)

# Home Mortgage Rates Slip to Average 12.73%, Lowest in 33 Months

*By a* WALL STREET JOURNAL *Staff Reporter*
WASHINGTON — Home mortgage rates eased to a 33-month low last week.

Lenders last week asked an average 12.73% basic interest rate, down from 12.75% the week before and 12.82% a month earlier, the Federal Home Loan Mortgage Corp. said. The latest rate is the lowest since the 12.175% average of the week ended July 25, 1980.

The basic weekly figures are for 30-year conventional loans for 80% of the price of a new, single-family house. Conventional loans aren't backed by the government.

Geographically, rates last week averaged 12.64% in the West, 12.68% in the Southeast, 12.79% in the Northeast, 12.80% in the Southwest and 12.86% in the North Central states.

Economists anticipate that home-loan rates will fall further this year.

Separately, the Federal Home Loan Bank Board said lenders in early April were asking a 13.13% average effective interest rate for a standard mortgage, down from 13.34% in early March and the lowest since a 12.52% average in August 1980.

The Bank Board figures apply to 25-year loans for 75% of the price of a new, single-family house. The effective rate includes the basic interest rate stated in the mortgage contract, which averaged 12.7% last month, plus certain initial fees amortized over 10 years.

The Bank Board's monthly survey showed that rates specified on contracts for home loans closed in early April fell to 12.78% from 13.17% a month earlier.

Mortgages averaged 73.1% of the purchase price early last month, up from 72.4% a month earlier. The average term rose to 25.8 years from 24.6 years in March. The average purchase price rose $3,700 to $81,800.

According to the Bank Board's survey of 32 metropolitan areas, rates for new-loan commitments in early April ranged from an average 12.27% in the Los Angeles-Long Beach-Anaheim area to 14.36% in Pittsburgh. The average purchase price ranged from $51,800 in the Louisville area to $144,900 in the San Francisco-Oakland area.

The Wall Street Journal, *May 6, 1983.*

**Chart 2**
**Long-Term Interest Rates: Secondary Market Yields on FHA Mortgages, Yield on New Issues of High-Grade Corporate Bonds, and Yield on Long-Term Treasury Bonds**

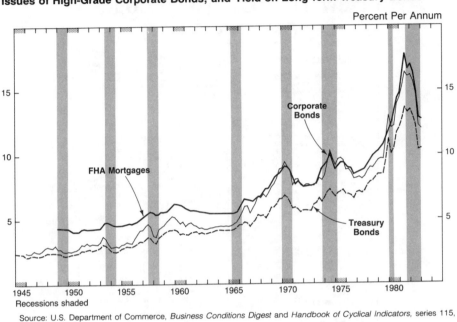

Percent Per Annum

Recessions shaded

Source: U.S. Department of Commerce, *Business Conditions Digest* and *Handbook of Cyclical Indicators*, series 115, 116, and 118.

Corporate bonds are issued in denominations of $1,000, and this particular Dow Chemical bond originally paid an annual fixed-dollar interest return of $88.75 (8⅞ percent of $1,000 = $88.75). That is, Dow Chemical promised to pay the bearer $88.75 a year until the bond matured in the year 2000, at which time Dow would redeem the bond for $1,000.

You can see from the next column that the current yield is 11 percent. Why is the current yield 11 percent when the bonds were issued at 8⅞ percent? Because Dow promised to pay a fixed-dollar return of $88.75 a year until maturity based on an initial value, and a redemption value, of $1,000. If the bond's price varies from $1,000 between issuance and maturity, the current yield will vary from 8⅞ percent, because the fixed annual return of $88.75 would be more than 8⅞ percent if the bond's value dropped below $1,000 and less than 8⅞ percent if it rose above $1,000. As the bond's price falls, the yield (interest rate) rises, and vice versa.

Look at the columns following the "Volume" column. (Volume is reported in thousands of dollars—five bonds with a face value of $1,000 were traded on May 20, 1983.) You can see the high, low, and closing prices for the day. Since bonds are issued in denominations of a thousand dollars, the reported prices are a percentage of

# New York Exchange Bonds

*Friday, May 20, 1983*

**Total Volume $28,320,000**

SALES SINCE JANUARY 1

| 1983 | 1982 | 1981 |
|---|---|---|
| $3,513,201,000 | $2,220,608,000 | $1,823,126,000 |

| | Domestic Fri. | Domestic Thu. | All Issues Fri. | All Issues Thu. |
|---|---|---|---|---|
| Issues traded | 980 | 1082 | 991 | 1094 |
| Advances ...... | 234 | 265 | 238 | 269 |
| Declines ........ | 537 | 634 | 541 | 639 |
| Unchanged .... | 209 | 183 | 212 | 186 |
| New highs .... | 40 | 58 | 42 | 61 |
| New lows ...... | 3 | 5 | 3 | 5 |

## Dow Jones Bond Averages

| −1981− High | −1981− Low | −1982− High | −1982− Low | −1983− High | −1983− Low | | ---Friday--- −1983− | ---Friday--- −1982− | ---Friday--- −1981− |
|---|---|---|---|---|---|---|---|---|---|
| 65.78 | 54.99 | 71.52 | 55.67 | 77.84 | 70.78 | 20 Bonds | 75.51 − .41 | 60.10 − .07 | 58.97 + .17 |
| 66.18 | 53.61 | 72.71 | 53.80 | 78.88 | 69.62 | 10 Utilities | 74.60 − .88 | 58.75 − .03 | 57.98 − .29 |
| 66.15 | 56.32 | 71.23 | 57.36 | 77.13 | 71.51 | 10 Industrial | 76.43 + .07 | 61.45 − .12 | 59.96 + .63 |

| Bonds | Cur Yld | Vol | High | Low | Close | Net Chg. |
|---|---|---|---|---|---|---|
| CnNG 4¾86 | 5.5 | 40 | 86¾ | 86⅝ | 86⅝ | ..... |
| CnNG 7¾94 | 9.9 | 6 | 78⅛ | 78⅛ | 78⅛ | + ⅜ |
| CnNG 8¼94 | 9.7 | 19 | 85 | 85 | 85 | + ⅞ |
| CnPw 4½88 | 6.2 | 2 | 73 | 73 | 73 | +1 |
| CnPw 5⅞96 | 10. | 16 | 59½ | 58¼ | 58¼ | −1⅜ |
| CnPw 6⅞98 | 11. | 5 | 60¾ | 60¾ | 60¾ | −2⅛ |
| CnPw 7⅝99 | 12. | 16 | 65½ | 64¼ | 64¼ | −1¾ |
| CnPw 8⅝00 | 12. | 3 | 71⅜ | 71⅜ | 71⅜ | −1⅜ |
| CnPw 7½2020 | 12. | 5 | 64¼ | 64 | 64 | − ¼ |
| CnPw 8⅝03 | 12. | 32 | 71⅜ | 71¼ | 71¼ | −3¼ |
| CnPw 11⅝94 | 12. | 27 | 96½ | 96 | 96 | −1 |
| CnPw 11½00 | 12. | 15 | 95 | 95 | 95 | −1 |
| CnPw 9s06 | 12. | 13 | 74 | 73⅞ | 74 | ..... |
| CnPw 9s08 | 12. | 20 | 73⅞ | 73⅞ | 73⅞ | −2⅜ |
| CtlAir 3½92 | cv | 2 | 50 | 50 | 50 | + ¾ |
| CtlGp 11⅛89 | 11. | 1 | 100 | 100 | 100 | −1 |
| Ct IICp 9.05s89 | 9.1 | 23 | 99⅛ | 99⅛ | 99⅛ | + ¼ |
| Ct IC 8½85 | 8.9 | 35 | 95 | 95 | 95 | + ¼ |
| CtlDat 5½87 | 6.6 | 2 | 83 | 83 | 83 | − ⅝ |
| Crane 7s94 | 11. | 5 | 66 | 66 | 66 | + ½ |
| CrdF 15½91 | 14. | 15 | 112 | 112 | 112 | − ¼ |
| CrocN 5¾96 | cv | 2 | 77½ | 77½ | 77½ | ..... |
| CrocN 8.6s02 | 12. | 15 | 73 | 73 | 73 | − ⅛ |
| Dana d5⅞06 | cv | 4 | 67¾ | 67¾ | 67¾ | + ¾ |
| Dart 4¼97 | cv | 19 | 93 | 93 | 93 | −1 |
| DatGen 13s05 | 13. | 5 | 104 | 104 | 104 | −1 |
| Datpnt 8⅞06 | cv | 10 | 74 | 73½ | 73½ | + ⅜ |
| Dayc 5¾94 | cv | 22 | 66½ | 66 | 66 | ..... |
| Dayc 6s94 | cv | 19 | 74 | 74 | 74 | ..... |
| DaytP 8⅛01 | 12. | 5 | 70½ | 70⅛ | 70⅛ | ..... |
| Deere 4½83 | 4.6 | 1 | 98⅛ | 98⅛ | 98⅛ | ..... |
| Deere 10½85 | 11. | 15 | 99¾ | 99¾ | 99¾ | − ¼ |
| Deere 9s08 | cv | 72 | 114 | 113 | 113 | −1 |
| DetEd 6s96 | 9.7 | 10 | 62 | 62 | 62 | + ⅞ |
| DetEd 6.4s98 | 11. | 2 | 58½ | 58½ | 58½ | −1¾ |
| DetEd 9s99 | 12. | 8 | 76⅞ | 74 | 74 | −3½ |
| DetEd 9.15s00 | 12. | 21 | 77⅛ | 77⅛ | 77⅛ | −2¼ |
| DetEd 8⅛01 | 12. | 10 | 69⅛ | 69⅛ | 69⅛ | −1⅝ |
| DetEd 7⅝01 | 12. | 27 | 64 | 63⅝ | 64 | −1 |
| DetEd 7½03 | 12. | 1 | 65 | 65 | 65 | − ½ |
| DetEd 9⅞04 | 12. | 15 | 83 | 81⅝ | 81⅝ | + ⅜ |
| DetEd 11⅞00 | 12. | 17 | 96⅜ | 96¼ | 96¼ | − ⅛ |
| DetEd 10⅝06 | 12. | 20 | 88 | 86⅛ | 88 | +1⅞ |
| DialF 8¼s89 | 9.3 | 10 | 89 | 89 | 89 | −1 |
| Divers 10½91 | 14. | 10 | 73½ | 73½ | 73½ | −3¼ |
| Dow 7.75s99 | 11. | 15 | 73⅝ | 73⅝ | 73⅝ | − ⅜ |
| Dow 8⅞2000 | 11. | 5 | 79½ | 79½ | 79½ | + ½ |
| Dow 7⅞07 | 11. | 4 | 70⅜ | 70⅜ | 70⅜ | −1 |
| duPnt 8.45s04 | 11. | 24 | 77⅞ | 76½ | 77⅞ | − ⅛ |
| duPnt 8s86 | 8.4 | 11 | 95 | 95 | 95 | ..... |
| duPnt 8½06 | 11. | 46 | 78⅞ | 77½ | 77½ | −1⅜ |
| duPnt 14s91 | 13. | 35 | 111½ | 111 | 111 | − ½ |
| duPnt 14.15s84 | 14. | 15 | 104½ | 104½ | 104½ | + ½ |
| DukeP 7¾02 | 11. | 5 | 70½ | 70½ | 70½ | −1 |
| DukeP 7⅝02 | 11. | 41 | 67½ | 66⅛ | 66¼ | + ½ |
| DukeP 7¾03 | 11. | 10 | 71 | 70⅜ | 70⅜ | −2 |
| DukeP 8⅛03 | 11. | 5 | 73⅞ | 73⅞ | 73⅞ | + ⅜ |
| DukeP 9¾04 | 11. | 15 | 85¾ | 85 | 85¾ | ..... |
| DukeP 9½05 | 11. | 5 | 85 | 85 | 85 | +1 |
| DukeP 8⅛07 | 11. | 73 | 73 | 73 | 73 | −2 |
| DukeP 10⅞09 | 12. | 19 | 96⅜ | 94 | 94 | − ¾ |
| DukeP 14⅞10 | 13. | 2 | 116⅛ | 116⅛ | 116⅛ | −1⅞ |
| DukeP 14⅝87 | 13. | 25 | 108⅛ | 108 | 108⅛ | −1⅜ |
| DuqL 8¾00 | 12. | 30 | 75 | 74⅝ | 75 | −1 |
| DuqL 9s06 | 12. | 28 | 75⅜ | 74⅛ | 74⅛ | −1⅝ |
| DuqL 8⅝07 | 11. | 2 | 73¼ | 73¼ | 73¼ | + ½ |
| DuqL 12¼10 | 12. | 8 | 100 | 100 | 100 | −2½ |
| InldStl 7.9s07 | 11. | 30 | 69⅞ | 68¼ | 69⅞ | − ⅝ |
| Intrfst 7¾05 | cv | 148 | 96 | 95½ | 95½ | + ¼ |
| IBM 9½86 | 9.6 | 162 | 100 | 98⅝ | 98⅞ | + ¼ |
| IBM 9⅜04 | 11. | 557 | 89¼ | 88⅞ | 88⅞ | − ⅜ |
| IntHrv 4.8s91 | 8.9 | 14 | 54¾ | 53⅞ | 53⅞ | −1⅜ |
| IntHrv 8⅝95 | 15. | 66 | 57 | 56 | 56 | −1⅛ |
| IntHrv 9s04 | 16. | 74 | 57 | 55½ | 56¾ | − ¼ |
| IntHrv 18s02 | 19. | 350 | 98⅞ | 95½ | 95⅝ | −4¼ |
| InHvC 8⅝91 | 13. | 30 | 66 | 66 | 66 | ..... |
| InHvC 9s84 | 9.9 | 46 | 91 | 90¼ | 91 | + ¼ |
| InHvC 8.35s86 | 11. | 43 | 74⅜ | 73⅝ | 74⅜ | − ½ |
| InHvC 13½88 | 16. | 59 | 86¾ | 85⅛ | 85⅞ | −1⅝ |
| InMult 9⅛96 | 12. | 6 | 78⅞ | 78⅞ | 78⅞ | +2⅞ |
| InTT 14¾91 | 13. | 15 | 112 | 111⅛ | 111⅛ | −1⅜ |
| Ipco 5¼89 | cv | 5 | 80¼ | 80¼ | 80¼ | ..... |
| IrvBk 9¾04 | 10. | 50 | 96¾ | 96¾ | 96¾ | ..... |
| JCP 10¼85 | 10. | 25 | 99 | 98⅝ | 99 | + ⅜ |
| JnM 9.7s85f | .. | 27 | 84¼ | 83½ | 84 | − ½ |
| JonsLl 6¾94 | 11. | 30 | 61 | 59¾ | 61 | − ⅛ |
| JoneL 6¾94 | 10. | 5 | 66 | 66 | 66 | +1⅜ |
| K mart 6s99 | cv | 49 | 100 | 99 | 100 | − ⅝ |
| K Mart 9⅞85 | 9.9 | 20 | 100 | 100 | 100 | + ¾ |
| Kaisr 9s05 | cv | 22 | 106 | 105 | 105 | ..... |
| Kane 9½90 | 11. | 5 | 85⅛ | 85⅛ | 85⅛ | ..... |
| KaufB 12¼99 | 13. | 5 | 93⅝ | 93⅝ | 93⅝ | − ¼ |
| Kenn 7⅞01 | 11. | 25 | 72⅜ | 71⅜ | 71⅜ | −3⅝ |
| LFE 10s92 | 13. | 1 | 78 | 78 | 78 | −2 |
| LTV 5s88 | 6.8 | 89 | 74 | 72½ | 74 | + ⅜ |
| LTV 9¼97 | 12. | 2 | 75 | 75 | 75 | ..... |
| LTV 11s07 | 13. | 44 | 84¾ | 83⅜ | 84¾ | +1¼ |
| LaQuin 10s02 | cv | 1 | 127 | 127 | 127 | +7 |
| LearS 10s04 | 12. | 1 | 84¼ | 84¼ | 84¼ | ..... |
| Leucd 13¾99 | 14. | 9 | 101½ | 100¼ | 101½ | − ⅞ |
| Lfemk 11s96 | 12. | 3 | 92 | 92 | 92 | + ⅜ |
| Lfemk 11¾99 | 12. | 30 | 95½ | 95½ | 95½ | − ⅛ |
| Lfemk 13s01 | cv | 20 | 134⅜ | 134 | 134 | ..... |
| Loew 6⅞93 | 9.8 | 144 | 70¾ | 70 | 70 | − ⅜ |
| LomN 9¾08 | cv | 26 | 122 | 120½ | 122 | −1¼ |
| LglsLt 9⅞84 | 9.9 | 9 | 99¼ | 99¼ | 99¼ | ..... |
| Loral 10¾97 | 12. | 10 | 91 | 91 | 91 | −1¾ |
| Lykes 7½94N | 11. | 6 | 66⅞ | 65⅞ | 66⅞ | − ½ |
| Lykes 7½94 | 11. | 115 | 66½ | 64¾ | 66⅜ | − ⅝ |
| MACOM 9¼06 | cv | 164 | 111½ | 110½ | 110½ | .... |
| MCI 15s00 | 14. | 65 | 110⅝ | 110 | 110 | − ¾ |
| MCI d14⅛01 | 13. | 94 | 105⅛ | 105 | 105 | − ⅝ |
| MGIC 8⅝88 | 10. | 15 | 83⅛ | 83⅛ | 83⅛ | ..... |
| MGM 10s93 | 11. | 4 | 88⅛ | 88⅛ | 88⅛ | ..... |
| MGM 10½s96 | 12. | 1 | 86⅜ | 86⅜ | 86⅜ | ..... |
| MGM 9¾s86 | 11. | 10 | 94½ | 92⅝ | 92⅝ | −1⅝ |
| MGM 9½00 | cv | 69 | 92 | 91 | 91 | − ½ |
| MGMUA 10s93 | 11. | 4 | 88⅜ | 88⅜ | 88⅜ | +1⅞ |
| MacMl 4s92 | cv | 5 | 141 | 141 | 141 | ..... |
| MacMl 8¾08 | cv | 35 | 120 | 120 | 120 | −1 |
| MfrH 9¼87 | 9.4 | 37 | 98½ | 98⅜ | 98½ | − ⅛ |
| Mapco 10s05 | cv | 10 | 91¼ | 91 | 91¼ | + ¾ |
| MarO 8½00 | 11. | 30 | 75½ | 75½ | 75½ | − ½ |
| MarO 7.65s83 | 7.7 | 25 | 99 9-32 | 99 9-32 | 99 9-32 | + ⅛ |
| MarO 10¼87 | 10. | 39 | 98½ | 98⅜ | 98½ | ..... |
| MarO 12½94 | 13. | 824 | 99⅝ | 99 | 99⅜ | + ⅜ |
| Marcor 6½88 | 8.2 | 44 | 79⅜ | 79¼ | 79¼ | ..... |
| MarM 7⅝03 | 12. | 5 | 65 | 65 | 65 | −3¾ |
| MaMu 6¾90 | cv | 1 | 90⅛ | 90⅛ | 90⅛ | + ⅛ |
| MaMu 6¼91 | cv | 8 | 72 | 71½ | 71½ | ..... |
| McCro 6½92 | cv | 1 | 61⅝ | 61⅝ | 61⅝ | ..... |
| McCro 7½94 | 12. | 4 | 66⅛ | 64¼ | 64¼ | −3¾ |
| McCro 7½94N | 10. | 16 | 74⅛ | 74 | 74⅛ | + ⅜ |

International Harvester Bond → (IntHrv 8⅝95)

Dow Bond → (Dow 8⅞2000)

Du Pont Bond → (duPnt 14s91)

The Wall Street Journal, *May 23, 1983*.

the face value of $1,000. Thus, 79½ means a price of $795 (79½ percent of $1,000 = $795). This bond was bought and sold for $795 throughout the trading day on May 20. That is why the high, low, and closing prices are all the same. The last column informs you that the May 20 closing price was half a point ($5) higher than the previous close.

Now, if you bought this bond on May 20, your yield would be 11 percent, not 8⅞ percent, because on May 20 the bond had a value of $795, not $1,000. An annual return of $88.75 on an investment of $795 is the equivalent of 11 percent, not 8⅞ percent.

---

**Example from Page 48** ⟶

| | | | | | | | |
|---|---|---|---|---|---|---|---|
| duPnt | 8s86 | 8.4 | 11 | 95 | 95 | 95 | ..... |
| duPnt | 8½06 | 11. | 46 | 78⅞ | 77½ | 77½ | −1⅜ |
| duPnt | 14s91 | 13. | 35 | 111½ | 111 | 111 | − ½ |
| duPnt | 14.15s84 | 14. | 15 | 104½ | 104½ | 104½ | + ½ |

---

When commentators speak of the bond market rising and falling, they mean the price of the bond, not the interest rate. Bondholders want interest rates to fall because then the value of their bonds will rise. For instance, you can see a Du Pont bond with an initial interest rate of 14 percent and a maturity date of 1991 listed five lines below the Dow bond. It closed at $1,110 on May 20. The initial buyer, who paid $1,000, could make a profit of $110 by selling the bond. This gain is in addition to the 14 percent annual interest he or she earned while holding it. Note that the current yield of 13 percent is lower than the initial interest rate of 14 percent because the bond has risen above its face value.

---

**Example from Page 48** ⟶

| | | | | | | | |
|---|---|---|---|---|---|---|---|
| IBM | 9⅜04 | 11. | 557 | 89¼ | 88⅞ | 88⅞ | − ⅜ |
| IntHrv | 4.8s91 | 8.9 | 14 | 54¾ | 53⅞ | 53⅞ | −1⅜ |
| IntHrv | 8⅝95 | 15. | 66 | 57 | 56 | 56 | −1⅛ |
| IntHrv | 9s04 | 16. | 74 | 57 | 55½ | 56¾ | − ¼ |
| IntHrv | 18s02 | 19. | 350 | 98⅞ | 95½ | 95⅝ | −4¼ |
| InHvC | 8⅝91 | 13. | 30 | 66 | 66 | 66 | ..... |

---

Returning to the Dow bond—if you bought it on May 20 and held it to maturity, you would receive $1,000 for your $795 investment as well as an 11 percent annual yield. The second International Harvester (Int Hrv) bond is even more impressive. On May 20 you could have bought this bond for $560, held it for a dozen years (during which you would have received a 15 percent annual interest return), and then cashed it in for $1,000 at a gain of $440 per bond. Substantial capital gains can be made in the bond market.

The relative strengths of these companies affected the quality of their bonds. Dow was investment quality because of its healthy financial condition. Harvester was speculative because it teetered on the edge of bankruptcy. Hence, Harvester had to pay a higher return to attract investors' funds.

*     *     *

To summarize this chapter, Chart 1 on page 38 and Chart 2 on page 47 reconfirm observations made in Chapters Three and Four regarding the 1970s. The sharp rise and extreme fluctuation of interest rates measure the growing severity of the cycle. Ever greater waves of borrowing set off mad scrambles for funds which propelled interest rates to new highs. After the Fed interceded to reinforce the inevitable collapse in borrowing and demand with a tight money policy, the recession provided a breather during which the Fed's easy money policy helped pump liquidity into the system and drive interest rates down. This, of course, set the stage for the next excess.

As you have seen, the Fed forced the system onto a crash diet with its 1981 tight money policy; the staggering interest rates that resulted were the protesting screams of the compulsive eater denied his caloric binges. Now the Fed must maintain a sufficiently tight policy during the current expansion to prevent the runaway credit excess which occurred in the recent past. Every expert will tell you that the key to maintaining the desired weight is moderate intake; it remains to be seen whether our reformed junkie can pass up his monetary chocolate cake.

# CHAPTER SIX

## The Business Cycle
## Phase One: From Trough
## to Recovery

Chapter Two asserted that you cannot scientifically test hypotheses in economics as you can in physics. Yet there is one law of physics which does apply to economics: whatever goes up must come down. Fortunately for us, in economics the reverse is also true. Although boom inevitably goes bust, each recession is also self-correcting and carries with it the seeds of economic recovery.

Why does the business cycle always rebound and return, never falling into an abyss of permanent depression, never sailing a sea of continuous expansion?

Every expansion ends inevitably in recession because every expansion is fueled by credit. Consumers and businesses can borrow to buy new homes, cars, factories, and machinery. The more they borrow and spend, the faster demand grows, and production is pushed into high gear in order to keep pace with demand. But sooner or later, the upward spiral of borrowing and spending comes to an end. Consumers find that their incomes cannot support the burden of additional debt repayment. Businesses, having accomplished their targeted growth in plant and equipment, see that demand will not greatly increase in the near future and cut back or cease their expenditures in this area. Once business and consumer borrowing and spending start to decline, the slump begins and production and income fall.

The recession hits bottom when the components of demand that were financed by credit stop contracting. Remember that these components are a limited, though highly volatile, share of total demand. (The demand for many items that are not financed by credit, such as food and medical care, will hardly decline at all.) As consumers and businesses cease borrowing and turn their attention to liquidating their expansion-generated debts, the price of credit, namely interest rates, falls. A point is finally established where debt burden and interest rates are low enough that consumers can again borrow and spend. At this juncture, auto production, home construction, and business investment in new plant and equipment stop falling, the slide ends, and economic recovery is in sight.

Generally speaking, expansion ceases when consumers are no longer willing to borrow and spend; contraction ends when their confidence returns. In the past decade, these cyclical changes in consumer confidence have been closely tied to the rate of inflation. Rapid economic expansion brought swiftly rising prices with an attendant and sobering drop in real income and consumer confidence. Recession cooled the pace of inflation, encouraging a resurgence of confidence.

Chapters Three, Four, and Five, which examined the Federal Reserve System and the money and credit markets, described the 1970s cycle in financial terms. Look at the cycle now from a different perspective, weaving in the elements of production, income, and consumer demand.

Consumers borrowed heavily in 1972 and 1973 to make record purchases of new homes and automobiles. Business responded by adding plant and equipment to meet the demand and by stockpiling inventory to satisfy customer orders. The sharp growth in consumer and business demand bid prices rapidly upward, and the rate of inflation increased from 4 percent in 1972 to 12 percent in 1974. Interest rates moved in parallel fashion. Soon consumers became discouraged as their incomes failed to keep pace, so their expenditures on homes, autos, and other goods plunged. This led to a general decline in production, and by early 1975 unemployment was at a postwar record. The cycle was complete.

The drop in demand reduced both inflation and interest rates. By 1976 consumers were regaining confidence, and the revival of their willingness to spend brought recovery and expansion. Boom conditions and rising inflation and interest rates returned in 1978, eroding consumer confidence once again. Consumer demand fell, the 1980 recession began, and another cycle had come full circle.

So far, the business cycle has been painted with fairly broad strokes. The time has come to take up a finer brush so that essential details and connections can be clearly drawn. This chapter introduces the statistical series that are particularly useful in charting output, efficiency, and inflation and the relationships among them. Gross national product, industrial production, and capacity utilization measure the economy's output; productivity measures its efficiency. As output increases, efficiency decreases and inflation—as reported by the Producer Price Index—inevitably becomes a problem. The initial connections between output, efficiency, and inflation form this chapter's central theme.

At the peak of the cycle, when output is at its maximum, production facilities are strained to the point where production costs rise sharply. Overburdened equipment fails, accelerating the expense of maintenance and repair. The quantities of labor added to the productive process are relatively greater than the increase in output. Inevitable inefficiencies force up costs, and consequently prices, even though the product itself has not changed. The obvious result: inflation increases rapidly.

With the recession's drop in production, the strain on facilities and labor eases. Costs fall, inflation declines, and the stage is set for a new round of expansion and growth.

This chapter focuses on the earliest phase of recent business cycles, the passage from trough to recovery. Subsequent chapters will examine the remaining three phases of the cycle. Turn now to an examination of the statistical releases which will be of particular importance in charting the course of production and the interaction of efficiency and inflation as the economy moves from trough to recovery.

## GROSS NATIONAL PRODUCT (GNP)

GNP is a good place to start. It is the broadest available measure of economic activity and provides the official scale with which fluctuations in the economy are measured.

*The Wall Street Journal* publishes the U.S. Department of Commerce's quarterly release on the GNP about three weeks after the close of each quarter. The department's "flash" report appears about a month earlier (that is, before the end of the quarter) but necessarily yields a much rougher estimate. Examine the April 21, 1983, article on page 54.

# Economy Grew At a 3.1% Pace In First Quarter

## Prior U.S. Estimate Was 4%; Baldrige Sees More Gains As Slow Recovery Begins

By EILEEN ALT POWELL
*Staff Reporter of* THE WALL STREET JOURNAL

**Constant-Dollar (real) GNP**

WASHINGTON—In a slow start to recovery from 18 months of recession, the U.S. economy expanded at a 3.1% seasonally adjusted annual rate in the first quarter, the Commerce Department said.

The department's preliminary estimate of real gross national product—the value of all goods and services, adjusted for price changes—was applauded by the Reagan administration as a step in the right direction. "We can look forward to further gains in GNP as the year proceeds," Commerce Secretary Malcolm Baldrige told a news conference.

But Mr. Baldrige and private economists expressed concern that the recovery may be constrained by still-high interest rates. Mr. Baldrige said that unless Congress takes action to reduce widening federal deficits, "we cannot expect lower interest rates and enough credit to finance the recovery."

**Profits Estimate Is Cut**

In a related report, the department said revised figures show that after-tax profits of U.S. corporations declined 1.3% in the fourth quarter to a seasonally adjusted annual rate of $117.9 billion. The department earlier estimated that the period's after-tax profits were unchanged from the July-September quarter. Third-quarter profits rose 2.6% to an adjusted $119.4 billion pace.

The department's latest estimate of first-quarter economic performance was slightly lower than its so-called flash estimate released a month ago, which projected a 4% annual rate. Department economists said the difference reflected lower than anticipated government purchases of farm commodities.

But the first-quarter growth was the strongest since the economy expanded at a 7.9% annual rate, after adjusting for inflation, in 1981's first quarter. Inflation-adjusted GNP contracted at an annual rate of 1.1% in 1982's final quarter after expanding at anemic rates of 0.7% in the third period and 2.1% in the second. In 1982's first quarter, the economy contracted at an adjusted 5.1% annual rate.

The department said most of the gain in this year's first quarter reflected increased housing construction, higher production of consumer goods and a slowdown in inventory-cutting by business.

Inventories were reduced at a $12.4 billion annual rate, after adjusting for inflation, in the latest quarter. This was more than expected but slower than the record decline of $20.3 billion, at an adjusted rate, in the fourth quarter.

Many private economists had expected a stronger first-quarter GNP gain. Robert Eggert's "Blue Chip" forecast, reflecting the projections of some 40 business economists, called for 4.4% growth, after adjusting for inflation, in the January-March period.

**Upturn Called 'Modest'**

Robert Gough, director of national forecasting for Data Resources Inc., said the performance "reaffirms initial forecasts that this recovery will be modest by historic standards." He said: "If this were a typical recovery, you would have a heck of a lot more growth than we're seeing."

Mr. Gough expects the economy to grow in this quarter at about the same rate as in the first. The major "risk" to sustaining the recovery, he adds, is a clash between private demand for credit and the government borrowings needed to finance the budget deficit, which he said "could push interest rates up and slow the economy down again."

Mr. Baldrige noted that the Reagan administration and many private economists had expected a recovery by spring of 1982. "It's nice to see it actually begin," he said.

He said the first-quarter performance "is on track" with the administration's most recent forecast that the U.S. economy will grow 4.7% from the fourth quarter of 1982 to the final quarter this year. Last year during the recession, the economy contracted 0.9%. He added that "we expect prices to rise less in 1983 than in 1982."

**Rate of Inflation**

The report showed that prices, measured by a GNP-based index, rose at an annual rate of 5.8% in the first quarter after increasing at a 3.7% pace in the fourth. Most other measures of inflation have shown a smaller price increase in the first quarter than in preceding months. Commerce Department economists said the GNP-based index was reflecting "statistical vagaries" related to the price calculation for inventories, imports and government farm purchases.

A different GNP-based inflation measure, based on a fixed market-basket of goods, showed prices rising at a 3.2% annual rate in the first period following an increase at a 4.9% annual pace in the fourth. The first-quarter rise by this measure was the smallest since a 2.8% annual rate in the second quarter of 1972.

**Current-Dollar (nominal) GNP**

Before adjustment for inflation, GNP expanded at a 9.1% annual rate in the first period after rising at a 2.6% annual rate the preceding quarter. This pushed GNP to $3.177 trillion in the first quarter from $3.108 trillion.

After adjustment for price changes, GNP totaled $1.489 trillion in the first quarter, compared with $1.477 trillion in the fourth.

The report on earnings showed that after-tax corporate profits in 1982 averaged $117.1 billion, the worst performance since profits averaged $102.5 billion in 1976. Profits in 1981 averaged $150.9 billion.

Before-tax earnings declined a revised 2.4% in the final quarter of 1982 to an adjusted $175.9 billion annual rate after rising 5% in the third period to an adjusted $180.3 billion pace. The department earlier had estimated the fourth-quarter decline at 0.8%.

Profits before taxes, but after adjustment for the effects of inflation on inventories and capital, fell 1% in the final quarter last year to a $164.6 billion adjusted annual rate after climbing 7% the preceding period to a $166.2 billion annual pace. The department earlier estimated that inflation-adjusted profits had risen 0.8% in the final quarter.

**Look for the following features: constant-dollar (real) GNP, current-dollar (nominal) GNP, and the rate of inflation.**

*Constant-dollar (real) GNP . . . paragraph 1*

---

WASHINGTON—In a slow start to recovery from 18 months of recession, the U.S. economy expanded at a 3.1% seasonally adjusted annual rate in the first quarter, the Commerce Department said.

---

*Current-dollar (nominal) GNP . . . fifth paragraph from end of article*

---

Before adjustment for inflation, GNP expanded at a 9.1% annual rate in the first period after rising at a 2.6% annual rate the preceding quarter. This pushed GNP to $3.177 trillion in the first quarter from $3.108 trillion.

---

*Rate of inflation . . . seventh paragraph from end of article*

---

The report showed that prices, measured by a GNP-based index, rose at an annual rate of 5.8% in the first quarter after increasing at a 3.7% pace in the fourth. Most other measures of inflation have shown a smaller price increase in the first quarter than in preceding months. Commerce Department economists said the GNP-based index was reflecting "statistical vagaries" related to the price calculation for inventories, imports and government farm purchases.

---

### Constant-Dollar (Real) GNP

Both the headline and the *first paragraph* tell you that "the U.S. economy expanded at a 3.1 percent seasonally adjusted annual rate in the first quarter." What does this mean?

---

WASHINGTON—In a slow start to recovery from 18 months of recession, the U.S. economy expanded at a 3.1% seasonally adjusted annual rate in the first quarter, the Commerce Department said.

---

GNP measures the final output of goods and services produced in the American economy in one year. Note the term *final output:* GNP includes only output which is not further transformed in the productive process. This eliminates measuring the same thing more than once at various stages of its production. For instance, bread purchased by the consumer appears in GNP, but both the flour from which the bread is baked and the wheat from which the flour is milled are omitted because the value of the bread comprises the value of all its ingredients.

Thus, the economy's output of *all* goods and services is far greater than its output of *final* goods and services. We use very little steel, chemicals, or advertising agency services directly. Their value is subsumed in our purchases of well-promoted Chevrolets and Saran Wrap.

Paragraph 1 not only refers to a 3.1 percent increase in final output but also says that this measurement was made at a "seasonally adjusted annual rate in the first quarter." Adjusting for seasonal factors merely means correcting the distortion in the data arising from the fact that the measurement is being taken during January, February, and March rather than any other quarter. Obviously, no seasonal adjustment is required when a whole year's data is measured, but when the year is divided up and data extracted for a run of months, the risk of distortion attributable to the season is great. For instance, retail trade is particularly heavy around Christmas and particularly light immediately after the first of the year; you could not make a useful comparison of the first quarter's retail sales with the last quarter's without first making a seasonal adjustment.

The reference to "annual rate" shows that the data for the second quarter, which of course covers only three months' activity, has been multiplied by four to increase it to a level comparable to annual data.

### Current-Dollar (Nominal) GNP

Nominal or current-dollar GNP includes inflation and is therefore much higher than real or constant-dollar GNP, which does not. Distinguishing clearly between these expressions will help you avoid a good deal of confusion.

The *fifth paragraph from the end of the article* informs you that

> Before adjustment for inflation, GNP ex-
> panded at a 9.1% annual rate in the first pe-
> riod after rising at a 2.6% annual rate the
> preceding quarter. This pushed GNP to
> $3.177 trillion in the first quarter from $3.108
> trillion.

before adjustment for inflation (that is, including inflation), GNP
increased by 9.1 percent, considerably more than the real increase
of 3.1 percent. You can see how rising prices inflate the nominal
value of GNP.

The current-dollar GNP figure of $3.177 trillion reported in this
paragraph is measured in today's high prices. It is therefore more
than double the constant-dollar GNP measurement of $1.489 tril-
lion (reported in the next paragraph) that was calculated in 1972
prices, because prices today are more than twice what they were in
1972. Both measurements calibrate the same level of output, but
the greatly increased value of the current-dollar GNP figure is a direct consequence of the higher level of prices prevailing now.

The constant-dollar or real GNP calculation is made in order to
compare the level of output in one time period with that in another
without inflation's distorting impact. If the inflation factor were
not removed, you would not know whether differences in dollar
value were due to output changes or price changes. Real GNP gives
you a dollar value which measures output changes only.

## Rate of Inflation

The *seventh paragraph from the end of the article* (see top of
page 58) reports that "prices, measured by a GNP-based index, rose
at an annual rate of 5.8 percent in the first quarter." This index,
known as the *implicit price deflator*, yields the broadest measure of
inflation since GNP is the most broadly based measure of economic
activity. The more familiar Consumer Price Index includes consumption expenditures only, while this index includes production
for business and government use as well. The Producer Price Index, which is explained later in this chapter, covers wholesale
prices of goods but not services.

Now you are ready to put GNP's current performance in historical perspective. Compare it with Chart 1 on page 58.

The top graph portrays the actual level of GNP, while the bottom
graph depicts quarterly percentage changes at annual rates. When
the bottom series is above the zero line, GNP has increased; a drop
in GNP is indicated by points below the zero line.

The report showed that prices, measured by a GNP-based index, rose at an annual rate of 5.8% in the first quarter after increasing at a 3.7% pace in the fourth. Most other measures of inflation have shown a smaller price increase in the first quarter than in preceding months. Commerce Department economists said the GNP-based index was reflecting "statistical vagaries" related to the price calculation for inventories, imports and government farm purchases.

**Chart 1**
**Gross National Product (GNP) in Constant (1972) Dollars; Quarterly Change in GNP at Annual Rates**

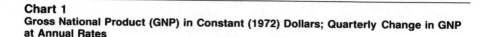

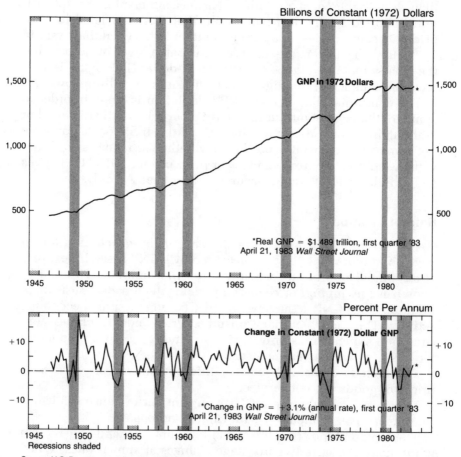

Billions of Constant (1972) Dollars

*Real GNP = $1.489 trillion, first quarter '83
April 21, 1983 *Wall Street Journal*

Percent Per Annum

Change in Constant (1972) Dollar GNP

*Change in GNP = +3.1% (annual rate), first quarter '83
April 21, 1983 *Wall Street Journal*

Recessions shaded

Source: U.S. Department of Commerce, *Business Conditions Digest* and *Handbook of Cyclical Indicators*, series 50 and 50c.

As you look at these graphs, note the unusually brief recovery following the 1980 recession and the quick slide into the 1981–82 recession brought on by the Fed's tight money policy.

The recent rebound in GNP followed the worst recession since World War II. Industrial production and capacity utilization will mirror GNP's performance, and so you should now become acquainted with these series.

## INDUSTRIAL PRODUCTION

The Wall Street Journal reports the Federal Reserve's data on *industrial production* in an article which usually appears midmonth. A typical report was published on May 16, 1983, in conjunction with the report on producer prices. The headline, accompanying chart, and *second paragraph* summarize matters, while the article provides detail and commentary. (See pages 60 and 61.)

# Recovery Advances Without Surge Of Inflation, New U.S. Data Show

## Industrial Production Rose Strong 2.1% Last Month; Producer Prices Fell 0.1%

By LAURIE McGINLEY
*Staff Reporter of* THE WALL STREET JOURNAL

WASHINGTON—Continuing the good economic news, two government reports showed that an acceleration of the nation's recovery isn't being accompanied by a resurgence of inflation.

The Federal Reserve Board said that industrial production in April rose a strong, seasonally adjusted 2.1%. It was the biggest jump since one of 2.2% in August 1975, when the economy also was recovering from a severe recession. Output climbed a revised 1.2% in March and 0.4% in February. The Fed earlier had estimated the March and February increases at 1.1% and 0.3% respectively.

Meanwhile, the Labor Department said that producer prices declined a seasonally adjusted 0.1% last month, matching the 0.1% drop the month before. In February, prices rose 0.1%.

The Reagan administration quickly hailed the new figures. Martin Feldstein, chairman of President Reagan's Council of Economic Advisers, termed the reports "very good news," and said they provided "further evidence that the recovery is on course and, indeed, is shifting into higher gear."

### Economists Encouraged

Private economists also were encouraged. Stephen Roach, a senior economist at Morgan Stanley & Co., said that the industral output figures "are a clear sign that this economy is locked into an expansion with staying power." Given the extensive slack in the economy, he added," inflation probably won't be a major problem for some time."

Some economists cautioned, however, that there is likely to be some acceleration in inflation soon as recent declines in energy prices come to an end.

The economists took particular comfort in the broad-based nature of the rise in industrial production. Led by big increases in the output of appliances, furniture and construction supplies, the increase reflected a robust housing market and a strengthening of consumer demand. Auto production, however, increased only slightly.

The overall increase in output suggests that businesses have begun to rebuild their inventories after an extensive liquidation late last year and early this year, some economists said. The stepped-up production will result in a rise in employment and income, they predicted.

The gains, however, will be modest compared with those of previous recoveries since World War II, contended Robert Scott of Chase Econometrics, a private forecasting company in Bala Cynwyd, Pa. He said he expects the unemployment rate to remain above 10% for the rest of the year as employers hold down the size of their work forces in an effort to rebuild profit margins.

### Consumer Spending

Although subpar by historical standards, the recovery seems on firm footing. Retail sales rose strongly in March and April as consumers became increasingly optimistic about the economic outlook. And consumers have begun to step up their borrowing, which is crucial for a rise in purchases of big-ticket durable goods. Consumers were reluctant to take on debt during the recession.

While the economic recovery is expected to build momentum at a steady pace, inflation may follow an uneven pattern, some economists said.

In April, a sharp, 2.8% drop in energy prices—the fifth consecutive monthly decline—and decreases in car and truck prices more than offset a 1.2% rise in consumer foods. Donald Ratajczak, director of the economic forecasting project at Georgia State University, said that the increase in food prices was an "aberration" caused by abnormally cold, wet weather. This drove up the price of fresh fruits, meat and veal, he said.

He expects the May and June price reports to show increases of 0.7% and 0.5%, respectively, as prices for energy and motor vehicles increase, offsetting a moderation in food prices. Later this year, he anticipates a few months without any increases in producer prices, and then an acceleration in inflation near year-end. Still, Mr. Ratajczak predicted that producer prices this year would rise less than they have in almost two decades.

The Fed's index of the output of the nation's factories, utilities and mines stood in April at 142.6% of the 1967 average, up 1.7% from a year earlier. (See chart on page one.)

Production of business equipment rose an adjusted 1.8% in April after increasing 0.9% in March. Production of consumer goods rose an adjusted 2.1% in April after rising 0.6% in March.

Output of materials increased an adjusted 2.2% in April after rising 1.6% the previous month. Auto assemblies edged up to an adjusted annual rate of 5.9 million units in April from the 5.8 million pace of March.

### Price Report

The Labor Department's price report showed that the cost of non-food items decreased an adjusted 0.5% last month after falling 0.3% the month before. Capital equipment costs fell an adjusted 0.3% in April, after increasing 0.4% in March.

Before seasonal adjustment, the producer price index for finished goods fell 0.1% in April to 283% of its 1967 average and stood 2.1% ahead of the index reading a year earlier.

The index for intermediate goods, which have had some processing, fell a seasonally adjusted 0.2% in April after decreasing an adjusted 0.7% in March. Before seasonal adjustment, this index rose slightly last month and stood at 309.1% of its 1967 average, down 0.3% from a year earlier.

The index for crude goods rose a seasonally adjusted 1.4% in April after increasing an adjusted 0.6% in March. The April rise reflected a sharp, 3% increase in foodstuffs and feedstuffs. Economists suggested that these prices were being driven up by farmers and were holding back their inventories in anticipation of the payment-in-kind program. This is a federal program designed to reduce farm plantings by giving farmers surplus commodities if they reduce their grain and cotton acreage.

Before seasonal adjustment, the index for crude goods rose 1.1% in April and stood at 325.7% of its 1967 average, up 1% from a year earlier.

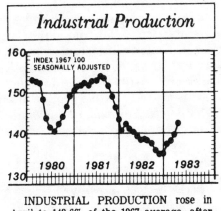

INDUSTRIAL PRODUCTION rose in April to 142.6% of the 1967 average, after seasonal adjustment, from a revised 139.7% in March, the Federal Reserve reports. (See story on page 3.)

*The Wall Street Journal, May 16, 1983.*

*Industrial production . . . second paragraph*

The Federal Reserve Board said that industrial production in April rose a strong, seasonally adjusted 2.1%. It was the biggest jump since one of 2.2% in August 1975, when the economy also was recovering from a severe recession. Output climbed a revised 1.2% in March and 0.4% in February. The Fed earlier had estimated the March and February increases at 1.1% and 0.3% respectively.

The index of industrial production measures changes in the output of the mining, manufacturing, and gas and electric utilities sectors of our economy. Industrial production is a narrower concept than GNP because it omits agriculture, construction, wholesale and retail trade, transportation, communications, services, finance, government, and U.S. activities in the rest of the world. Industrial production is also more volatile than GNP, because GNP, unlike industrial production, includes activities which are largely spared cyclical fluctuation, such as services, finance, and government. The brunt of cyclical fluctuations falls on the mining, manufacturing, and public utilities sectors. Nonetheless, GNP and industrial production move in parallel fashion.

Industrial production is measured by an *index*, a technique that focuses upon the relative size and fluctuation of physical output without concern for its dollar value. To construct the index, a base year (1967) is selected to serve as a benchmark and assigned a value of 100.0. Think of it as 100 percent. Data for all other months and years is then expressed in relative proportion (numerical ratio) to the data for the base year. For example, according to the caption under the "Industrial Production" chart, accompanying the article,

**Chart 2**
**Industrial Production Index** (1967 = 100); **Quarterly Change in Index at Annual Rates**

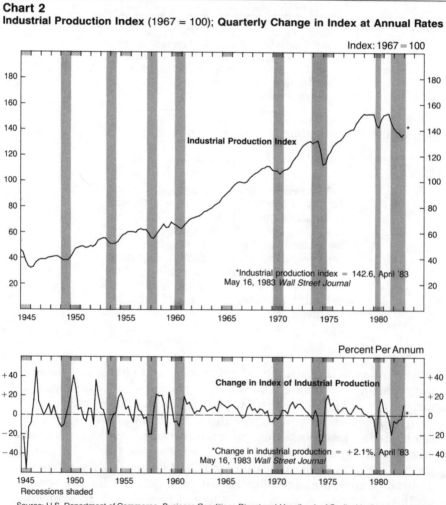

Index: 1967 = 100

**Industrial Production Index**

*Industrial production index = 142.6, April '83
May 16, 1983 *Wall Street Journal*

Percent Per Annum

**Change in Index of Industrial Production**

*Change in industrial production = +2.1%, April '83
May 16, 1983 *Wall Street Journal*

Recessions shaded

Source: U.S. Department of Commerce, *Business Conditions Digest* and *Handbook of Cyclical Indicators*, series 47 and 47c.

industrial production had an index value of 142.6 in April 1982. This means that industrial production in April 1982 was 42.6 percent higher than the average rate of production in 1967.

As with GNP, two graphs are used to illustrate industrial production (see Chart 2). The top graph displays actual index values, and the second illustrates monthly changes.

Now compare the course of industrial production with GNP, and note that both series have rebounded from the long decline of 1981–82 (see Chart 3). These developments will be reflected in the rate of capacity utilization and in the efficiency with which the economy is operated.

**Chart 3**
**GNP and Industrial Production**

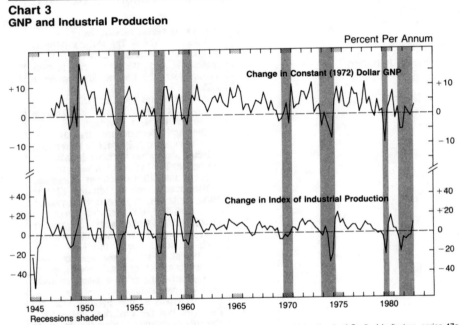

Source: U.S. Department of Commerce, *Business Conditions Digest* and *Handbook of Cyclical Indicators*, series 47c and 50c.

## CAPACITY UTILIZATION

In the third week of each month, *The Wall Street Journal* publishes the Federal Reserve's monthly statistical release on *capacity utilization*, or, as it is often called, the *factory operating rate*. The headline and *first paragraph* of the May 17, 1983, article inform you of April's rate. (See page 64.)

# Factory Rate Of Capacity Rose To 71.1% in April

## Pace Strongest in Over a Year; Continuing Rise Is Seen As Economy Recovers

Capacity Utilization ─────────────►

*By a* WALL STREET JOURNAL *Staff Reporter*

WASHINGTON – The nation's factories operated at a seasonally adjusted 71.1% of capacity in April, the highest rate in more than a year, the Federal Reserve Board said.

Revised figures show that U.S. factories operated at adjusted rates of 69.8% in March and 68.7% in February.

The April performance, the strongest since an adjusted 71.6% pace in March 1982, reflected widespread increases in industrial production. The Fed said last week that the output of the nation's factories, mines and utilities rose a robust, adjusted 2.1% in April, the biggest increase in eight years.

In April 1982, U.S. factories operated at an adjusted 70.8% of capacity. Last month's pace, although higher than the year-ago level, was still far below the 79.8% rate in July 1981 at the start of the recession. Most economists expect the factory operating rate to keep increasing as the economy recovers from the recession.

In its report on the operating rate, the Fed noted that the April rise "included sizable advances among industries that were especially hard-hit in the past few years." For example, the operating rate for auto makers last month rose to an adjusted 60.2% from an adjusted 59.2% in March. Factory rates also rose sharply for the metals and machinery industries, the Fed said.

The latest report showed that advanced-processing industries operated at an adjusted 71.9% in April, up from 70.6% in March, but below 72.6% a year ago. Primary-processing industries operated at an adjusted 69.5% rate in April, up from 67.8% in March and 67.2% a year ago.

For materials industries, the rate increased to 70.7% last month from 69.3% in March and 70.5% a year earlier.

The Wall Street Journal, *May 17, 1983.*

*Capacity utilization . . . first paragraph*

---

WASHINGTON — The nation's factories operated at a seasonally adjusted 71.1% of capacity in April, the highest rate in more than a year, the Federal Reserve Board said.

---

Capacity utilization is the rate at which manufacturing industry operates, expressed as a percentage of the maximum rate at which it could operate under normal conditions. Putting the matter differently, think of capacity utilization as measuring what manufacturing industry is currently producing compared (in percentage terms) to what it could produce. Thus, if an industry produces 80 tons of product in a year, while having plant and equipment at its disposal capable of producing 100 tons a year, that industry is operating at 80 percent of capacity; its capacity utilization is 80 percent.

Capacity utilization is a short-run concept determined by a company's current physical limits; at any moment in which capacity utilization is reported, it is assumed that the company's plant and equipment cannot be increased, although labor and other inputs can. This defines the short run. Although manufacturing industry continually adds new plant and equipment, it is useful to snap a photograph at a particular moment in time to enable measurement and comparison.

What bearing does capacity utilization have on the efficiency or productivity of industry? Consider an analogy. Your car operates more efficiently at 50 miles per hour than at 70 if its maximum speed is 80, for you will obtain better gas mileage at the lower speed. Efficiency is expressed as a relationship between inputs (gas gallons) and outputs (miles driven). Your car's engine operates more efficiently at lower speeds, that is, at lower levels of capacity utilization.

You are therefore confronted with the problem of diminishing returns: as your speed increases, you obtain fewer miles for each additional gallon of gas. At 50 miles per hour, you can go 30 miles on an additional gallon of gas; at 52 miles per hour, 29 miles on an additional gallon; at 54 miles per hour, 28 miles; and so on. Your output (miles) per unit of input (gallon) falls as you push toward full capacity utilization (maximum speed).

As capacity utilization increases, an industry also reaches the point of diminishing returns. This may be at 70 percent, 80 percent, or 90 percent of capacity utilization, depending on the industry, but the point will ultimately be reached where the percentage increases in output will become smaller than the percentage increases in input. For instance, a 15 percent increase in labor input, once we have passed the point of diminishing returns, may provide only a 10 percent increase in output.

This phenomenon does not develop because of some mystical mathematical relationship. Indeed, you probably know many of the commonsense reasons for it.

First, at low levels of capacity utilization, there is ample time to inspect, maintain, and repair equipment; accidental damage can be held to a minimum; and production increases can be achieved easily in a smoothly efficient plant. Above a certain level of capacity utilization, however, it becomes more difficult to inspect, maintain, and repair equipment because of the plant's heavier operating schedule. Perhaps a second shift of workers has been added, or additional overtime scheduled. There is less time for equipment maintenance, and accidental damage becomes inevitable. The labor force is in place and on the payroll, but production does not increase as rapidly as labor input because equipment frequently breaks down.

Second, as production increases and more labor is hired, the last people hired are less experienced and usually less efficient than the older workers; moreover, crowding and fatigue can become a problem if more overtime is scheduled. The result: poor workmanship and accidental damage. All of this ensures that output will not increase as rapidly as labor input.

Third, low levels of capacity utilization occur at the trough of a recession. Business firms have suffered a sharp drop in profit, if not actual losses. Under these circumstances, the employer has reduced the work force as much as possible. Even after output has begun to recover, an extended period of labor reduction may begin as part of a general cost-cutting program. As recovery boosts capacity utilization, however, hiring additional workers becomes inevitable. When full capacity utilization is reached near the peak of a boom, the cost-cutting program will be long forgotten as management scrambles for additional labor in order to meet the barrage of orders. At this point, additions to labor are greater than increments in output.

You can summarize business's decisions regarding labor as follows. During rapid expansion, and into economic boom, when orders are heavy and capacity utilization is strained, business will sacrifice efficiency and short-run profits to maintain customer loyalty. Management adds labor more rapidly than output increases to get the job done. But when the recession hits in earnest, and it becomes apparent that orders will not recover for some time, management cuts labor costs to the bone with layoffs and a freeze on hiring. This is especially true during a prolonged recession, such as that of 1981–82, which followed on the heels of an earlier recession (in 1980) and an incomplete recovery. Even after recovery and expansion begin, as they now have, business will attempt to operate with a reduced labor force in order to reap the benefits of cost-cutting in the form of higher profits. Operating efficiency (productivity) improves rapidly, and it will not be threatened until the expansion heats up and boom conditions develop.

Now compare capacity utilization's historical record with that of GNP and industrial production, noting once again the improvement reported in the May 17, 1983, *Journal* article and comparing it with the 1981–82 figures (see Chart 4 on page 68).

Each of the series examined thus far—GNP, industrial production, capacity utilization—tells the same story. Output has begun to recover after the doldrums of 1981–82. You should expect that the first signs of improved output would have a favorable impact on the economy's efficiency. The next series in this discussion, labor productivity and unit labor costs, will test that expectation.

## LABOR PRODUCTIVITY AND UNIT LABOR COSTS

The *Wall Street Journal* reports the U.S. Department of Labor's release on *labor productivity* about a month after the end of the quarter. Use the April 28, 1983, article on page 69 as an example.

## Chart 4
### GNP, Industrial Production, and Capacity Utilization

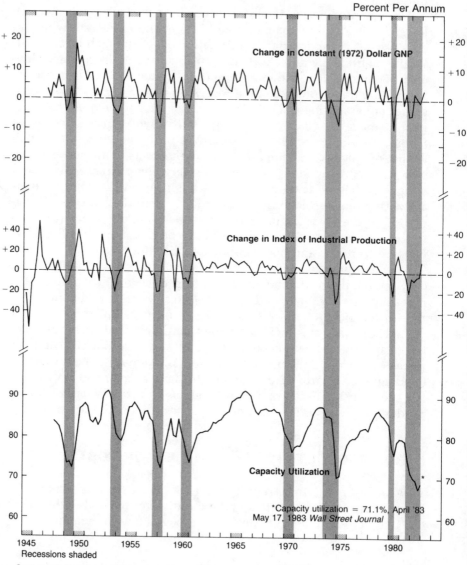

Recessions shaded

Source: U.S. Department of Commerce, *Business Conditions Digest* and *Handbook of Cyclical Indicators*, series 47c, 50c, and 82.

# Productivity Pace Climbed Sharply In the First Quarter

By a WALL STREET JOURNAL Staff Reporter

WASHINGTON — Nonfarm productivity grew at a seasonally adjusted 4.8% annual rate in the 1983 first quarter, far surpassing the 0.4% pace in the fourth quarter of 1982, the Labor Department said.

Labor Productivity

The department said this measurement of output for each paid hour of work was the largest quarterly rise in two years, and it also was the first time in two years that productivity, output and hours all increased.

The productivity gain is in line with economists' earlier projections of steep rises in productivity as the economy begins to improve. Typically, during the early stages of an economic recovery, employers try to step up output without adding workers until they are certain that the recovery will be sustained. Productivity gains are important because they hold down unit costs, thereby keeping a lid on inflation.

In the nonfarm business sector, the Labor Department said, output in the first quarter grew 6.2% and hours rose 1.4%. It said the increased hours reflect a lengthening of the work week, as employment dropped slightly for the sixth consecutive quarter. A department economist called the report "good, strong and pervasive. It's in all sectors. It's about what you'd expect at the turnaround of the economy."

Labor Productivity

Overall business productivity, including farms, rose at an adjusted 2.2% annual rate, after increasing at an 0.3% pace in the 1982 fourth quarter. The department economist said this reflected a "substantial" increase in manufacturing productivity and a decline in farm productivity.

Manufacturing productivity grew at an adjusted 7.1% annual rate in the 1983 first quarter, following an adjusted 1% rise in the final quarter of 1982.

The Wall Street Journal, April 28, 1983.

*Labor productivity . . . first and fourth paragraphs*

---

WASHINGTON — Nonfarm productivity grew at a seasonally adjusted 4.8% annual rate in the 1983 first quarter, far surpassing the 0.4% pace in the fourth quarter of 1982, the Labor Department said.

---

In the nonfarm business sector, the Labor Department said, output in the first quarter grew 6.2% and hours rose 1.4%. It said the increased hours reflect a lengthening of the work week, as employment dropped slightly for the sixth consecutive quarter. A department economist called the report "good, strong and pervasive. It's in all sectors. It's about what you'd expect at the turnaround of the economy."

---

The *first and fourth paragraphs* inform you that a 6.2 percent improvement in output, combined with a 1.4 percent increase in labor input, drove up output per worker 4.8 percent for all *nonfarm* business.

Chart 5 presents the record for all business (including farms). The series are similar.

Labor productivity measures output or production per unit of labor input (for instance, output per hour) and is the most important gauge of our nation's efficiency. Its significance cannot be overemphasized, for per capita real income cannot improve—and thus the country's standard of living cannot rise—without an increase in per capita production.

Unit labor cost measures labor cost per unit of output. Thus, unit labor cost is the inverse of labor productivity, since unit labor costs fall as labor productivity rises, and vice versa. Unit labor cost tells you how much added labor is required to produce an additional unit of output. Because labor is hired for a wage, requiring more labor time to produce each unit of output will raise labor costs per unit of output, and vice versa.

Consider a factory which assembles hand-held calculators. If the production of a calculator has required an hour of labor and a technological innovation permits the production of two calculators per hour, labor productivity has doubled, from one to two calculators per hour. The output per hour of work is twice what it was.

**Chart 5**
**Productivity: Output per Hour, All Persons, Private Business Sector** (1977 = 100);
**Change in Output per Hour** (smoothed)

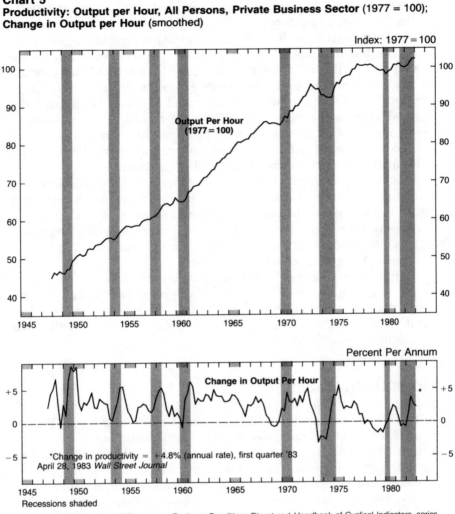

Index: 1977 = 100

Output Per Hour
(1977 = 100)

Percent Per Annum

Change in Output Per Hour

*Change in productivity = +4.8% (annual rate), first quarter '83
April 28, 1983 *Wall Street Journal*

Recessions shaded

Source: U.S. Department of Commerce, *Business Conditions Digest* and *Handbook of Cyclical Indicators*, series 370 and 370c.

If the wage rate is $10 per hour, and before the innovation an hour of work was required to complete a calculator, the labor cost per unit of output was then $10. After the innovation, however, two calculators can be produced in an hour, or one calculator in half an hour, so unit labor cost has fallen to $5. Note that as labor productivity doubled, from one to two calculators per hour, unit labor costs were halved, from $10 to $5 per unit of output. The gain in labor productivity drove down unit labor costs without any change in the wage rate.

Now compare the record of labor productivity and unit labor costs, including the improvement reported in the *Journal* article, with the other indicators examined so far (see Chart 6).

GNP, industrial production, and capacity utilization together define the business cycle. Since 1970 their fluctuations have indicated prosperity and recession. You can also see that labor productivity plunged and unit labor costs soared with the peak of each cycle. Then labor productivity improved and unit labor costs declined with recession and into the next recovery. But as soon as expansion got under way, labor productivity's growth began to weaken and unit labor costs began to rise, until productivity slumped and costs peaked at the end of the boom.

And here you encounter a vital if ironic truth: the economy's efficiency deteriorated with each boom and improved in recession and into recovery. The recent experience is no exception. Productivity grew and unit labor costs declined throughout the recession. The labor productivity gains reported in the April 28, 1983, *Journal* article show the trend continuing.

Since labor costs per unit of output have declined due to recession, you would expect this favorable development to be reflected in a decline in inflation. Take a look at producer prices, the last statistical series to be examined in this chapter, to see whether this expectation was fulfilled.

## PRODUCER PRICES

The *Producer Price Index*, until recently referred to as the *Wholesale Price Index*, is compiled by the U.S. Department of Labor and shows the changes in price charged by producers of finished goods—changes which are, of course, reflected in the prices consumers must pay. The Labor Department's news release on producer prices is usually published by *The Wall Street Journal* on the third Monday of the month. (See page 74.)

The May 16, 1983, article is an example, and the headline and *third paragraph* tell you that the Producer Price Index fell 0.1 percent in April.

**Chart 6**
**GNP, Industrial Production, Capacity Utilization, Labor Productivity, and Unit Labor Costs**

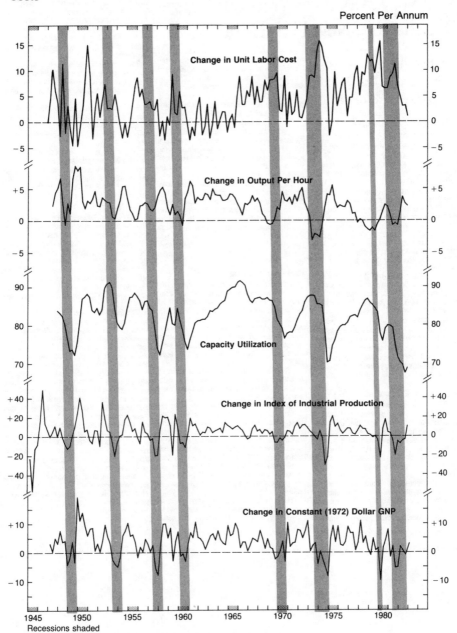

Percent Per Annum

Change in Unit Labor Cost

Change in Output Per Hour

Capacity Utilization

Change in Index of Industrial Production

Change in Constant (1972) Dollar GNP

Recessions shaded

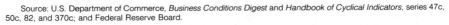

Source: U.S. Department of Commerce, *Business Conditions Digest* and *Handbook of Cyclical Indicators,* series 47c, 50c, 82, and 370c; and Federal Reserve Board.

# Recovery Advances Without Surge Of Inflation, New U.S. Data Show

## Industrial Production Rose Strong 2.1% Last Month; Producer Prices Fell 0.1%

By Laurie McGinley
*Staff Reporter of* The Wall Street Journal

WASHINGTON—Continuing the good economic news, two government reports showed that an acceleration of the nation's recovery isn't being accompanied by a resurgence of inflation.

The Federal Reserve Board said that industrial production in April rose a strong, seasonally adjusted 2.1%. It was the biggest jump since one of 2.2% in August 1975, when the economy also was recovering from a severe recession. Output climbed a revised 1.2% in March and 0.4% in February. The Fed earlier had estimated the March and February increases at 1.1% and 0.3% respectively.

Meanwhile, the Labor Department said that producer prices declined a seasonally adjusted 0.1% last month, matching the 0.1% drop the month before. In February, prices rose 0.1%.

The Reagan administration quickly hailed the new figures. Martin Feldstein, chairman of President Reagan's Council of Economic Advisers, termed the reports "very good news," and said they provided "further evidence that the recovery is on course and, indeed, is shifting into higher gear."

### Economists Encouraged

Private economists also were encouraged. Stephen Roach, a senior economist at Morgan Stanley & Co., said that the industral output figures "are a clear sign that this economy is locked into an expansion with staying power." Given the extensive slack in the economy, he added," inflation probably won't be a major problem for some time."

Some economists cautioned, however, that there is likely to be some acceleration in inflation soon as recent declines in energy prices come to an end.

The economists took particular comfort in the broad-based nature of the rise in industrial production. Led by big increases in the output of appliances, furniture and construction supplies, the increase reflected a robust housing market and a strengthening of consumer demand. Auto production, however, increased only slightly.

The overall increase in output suggests that businesses have begun to rebuild their inventories after an extensive liquidation late last year and early this year, some economists said. The stepped-up production will result in a rise in employment and income, they predicted.

The gains, however, will be modest compared with those of previous recoveries since World War II, contended Robert Scott of Chase Econometrics, a private forecasting company in Bala Cynwyd, Pa. He said he expects the unemployment rate to remain above 10% for the rest of the year as employers hold down the size of their work forces in an effort to rebuild profit margins.

### Consumer Spending

Although subpar by historical standards, the recovery seems on firm footing. Retail sales rose strongly in March and April as consumers became increasingly optimistic about the economic outlook. And consumers have begun to step up their borrowing, which is crucial for a rise in purchases of big-ticket durable goods. Consumers were reluctant to take on debt during the recession.

While the economic recovery is expected to build momentum at a steady pace, inflation may follow an uneven pattern, some economists said.

In April, a sharp, 2.8% drop in energy prices—the fifth consecutive monthly decline—and decreases in car and truck prices more than offset a 1.2% rise in consumer foods. Donald Ratajczak, director of the economic forecasting project at Georgia State University, said that the increase in food prices was an "aberration" caused by abnormally cold, wet weather. This drove up the price of fresh fruits, meat and veal, he said.

He expects the May and June price reports to show increases of 0.7% and 0.5%, respectively, as prices for energy and motor vehicles increase, offsetting a moderation in food prices. Later this year, he anticipates a few months without any increases in producer prices, and then an acceleration in inflation near year-end. Still, Mr. Ratajczak predicted that producer prices this year would rise less than they have in almost two decades.

The Fed's index of the output of the nation's factories, utilities and mines stood in April at 142.6% of the 1967 average, up 1.7% from a year earlier. (See chart on page one.)

Production of business equipment rose an adjusted 1.8% in April after increasing 0.9% in March. Production of consumer goods rose an adjusted 2.1% in April after rising 0.6% in March.

Output of materials increased an adjusted 2.2% in April after rising 1.6% the previous month. Auto assemblies edged up to an adjusted annual rate of 5.9 million units in April from the 5.8 million pace of March.

### Price Report

The Labor Department's price report showed that the cost of non-food items decreased an adjusted 0.5% last month after falling 0.3% the month before. Capital equipment costs fell an adjusted 0.3% in April, after increasing 0.4% in March.

Before seasonal adjustment, the producer price index for finished goods fell 0.1% in April to 283% of its 1967 average and stood 2.1% ahead of the index reading a year earlier.

The index for intermediate goods, which have had some processing, fell a seasonally adjusted 0.2% in April after decreasing an adjusted 0.7% in March. Before seasonal adjustment, this index rose slightly last month and stood at 309.1% of its 1967 average, down 0.3% from a year earlier.

The index for crude goods rose a seasonally adjusted 1.4% in April after increasing an adjusted 0.6% in March. The April rise reflected a sharp, 3% increase in foodstuffs and feedstuffs. Economists suggested that these prices were being driven up by farmers and were holding back their inventories in anticipation of the payment-in-kind program. This is a federal program designed to reduce farm plantings by giving farmers surplus commodities if they reduce their grain and cotton acreage.

Before seasonal adjustment, the index for crude goods rose 1.1% in April and stood at 325.7% of its 1967 average, up 1% from a year earlier.

*Producer prices . . . third paragraph*

---

Meanwhile, the Labor Department said that producer prices declined a seasonally adjusted 0.1% last month, matching the 0.1% drop the month before. In February, prices rose 0.1%.

---

Both the article and Chart 7 (page 76) confirm that inflation, as measured by the Producer Price Index, has been wrung from the economy. The drop since the 1979–80 peak has been dramatic.

You can also see from Chart 8 (page 77) that in the last decade the cyclical trends in producer prices reflected those of unit labor costs. With each boom in output and capacity utilization, productivity dropped and unit labor costs rose, driving producer prices up. Then, when recession hit and output and capacity utilization fell, improved labor productivity and lower unit labor costs were reflected in reduced inflation. The last recession illustrates the principle: inflation's trend followed unit labor costs downward. As the economy's efficiency improved, stable prices followed on the heels of stable costs.

Now the increasing price instability of recent years created problems for all business firms which produce or use commodities. Planning became more difficult as companies attempted to estimate the cost of inputs, or the market price of their output, over the swings of the cycle. For instance, a home builder preparing to develop a subdivision must estimate the future price of lumber before he can advertise home prices to prospective buyers. At the same time, a lumber mill also has to gauge the future price of its product before bidding for the right to log timberland.

As commodity price fluctuations increased, business bought and sold contracts for future delivery in order to protect itself and investors speculated on price changes, buying and selling futures contracts for profit. As interest in commodities increased, the number of commodities traded on futures markets grew.

*The Wall Street Journal* reports *commodity prices* on a daily basis, and each Monday it presents a chart showing indexes of commodity prices over the past year. These indexes cover 12 commodities: wheat, corn, soybeans, cattle, hogs, gold, silver, copper, sugar, coffee, cotton, and lumber. Consult the front-page index for easy reference. (See pages 78, 79, and 80.)

Futures prices provide quotes for future delivery of specified

## Chart 7

**Producer Price Index** (1967 = 100); **Quarterly Change in Index at Annual Rates**
(smoothed)

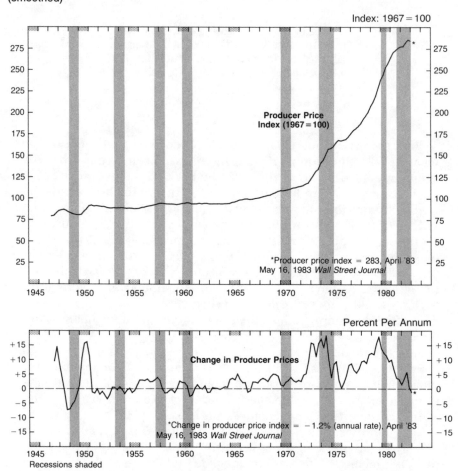

Index: 1967 = 100

*Producer price index = 283, April '83
May 16, 1983 *Wall Street Journal*

Percent Per Annum

Change in Producer Prices

*Change in producer price index = −1.2% (annual rate), April '83
May 16, 1983 *Wall Street Journal*

Recessions shaded

Source: U.S. Department of Commerce, *Business Conditions Digest* and *Handbook of Cyclical Indicators*, series 334
and 334c; Federal Reserve Board.

**Chart 8**
**Changes in Unit Labor Costs and Producer Prices**

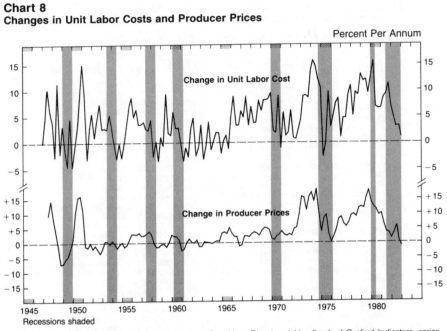

Source: U.S. Department of Commerce, *Business Conditions Digest* and *Handbook of Cyclical Indicators*, series 334c; Federal Reserve Board.

# Lumber Prices Surge to 3½-Year High; Housing Demand, Possible Strike Cited

### By Alan Bayless
*Staff Reporter of The Wall Street Journal*

Lumber prices reached their highest level in 3½ years Friday, spurred by unexpectedly strong demand for wood products from the housing-construction industry. Concern about expiring labor contracts, poor logging weather and low inventories have contributed to the price surge, analysts said.

On the spot market, the benchmark price for softwood lumber reached $230 a thousand board feet Friday, up 2.2% from $225 a week earlier and up 74% from $132 a year ago, according to Random Lengths Publications Inc., a trade paper based in Eugene, Ore. That is the highest level since October 1979, when the price was also $230.

Analysts said further increases are still possible.

"Make no mistake about it, this is a long-term bull market," said Chris Palmer, editor of a Birmingham, Ala.-based lumber and plywood newsletter.

Patrick Hicks, a lumber broker with North Pacific Lumber Co., Portland, Ore., said, "If interest rates remain stable and if a strike occurs in Canada in the next 30 to 45 days, prices could keep rising."

The demand for wood products has surprised many companies over the past few months. A year ago, depressed prices and high carrying costs convinced many producers and retailers to maintain only minimum inventories. According to Mr. Hicks, some lumber companies have been caught short of logs and are unable to replenish supplies because rainy weather has made roads too muddy in California, Montana and Idaho.

He said other companies aren't able to operate at full production because they are having difficulty selling wood chips, a lumber by-product usually taken up by pulp-and-paper mills. The chip market has been affected by continuing weakness in pulp-and-paper demand. "If they can't sell the chips and they have run out of storage space, it's hard to continue high levels of lumber output," he said.

Ross Hay-Roe, president of Vancouver-based consulting firm Papertree Economics Ltd., said that since last October, when lumber sold for $130, the surge in demand has pushed prices up faster than in any other eight-month period in 20 years. Like others, he attributed the gain mostly to higher-than-expected U.S. housing starts.

In the past months alone the benchmark price for Western softwood has risen more than $50. Philip Chiricotti, a Chicago lumber broker, called it "an unprecedented buying spree." He cautioned that the huge volume of purchases could mean that price rises have "run their course for the time being, even though business remains excellent."

More generally, he said "the big picture remains positive as long as the credit outlook holds up."

The labor picture is clouded by negotiations involving close to 100,000 unionized workers, about half of whom are in the western U.S. and the other half in British Columbia. Contracts will start to expire May 31 in the U.S. and in mid- to late June in British Columbia, which alone supplies 20% to 25% of U.S. lumber requirements.

"There is a feeling that a settlement will be reached in the U.S. but British Columbia is less certain," said Mr. Hicks. The British Columbia negotiations, which began in Vancouver last week, quickly led to a shouting match between Jack Munro, regional president of the International Woodworkers of America, and Keith Bennett, negotiating on behalf of most of British Columbia's forest-products companies.

Mr. Bennett said he became upset by the union's opening demands, which include a one-year contract with a wage increase to "maintain and improve the standard of living" of its members, a cost-of-living allowance, improvement in pensions, job security and other provisions.

Although the union hasn't actually specified how large a wage increase it wants, Mr.

Bennett said the demands, as described, could possibly represent a 20% increase in costs for the companies. That, he added, is far more than the companies, which had losses of $1 billion (Canadian) last year, can afford. To recover financially, he said, they must have a three-year labor contract without any cost increases in the first year.

Although the differences between the two sides currently appear great, some observers believe both negotiators may be posturing in advance of real negotiations, which are expected to begin in about a week. In 1981, lumber prices were pushed higher by a five-week strike in British Columbia.

| COMMODITY INDEXES | | | |
|---|---|---|---|
| | Close | Net Chg. | Yr. Ago |
| Dow Jones Futures | 148.90 | − 1.14 | 128.33 |
| Dow Jones Spot | 146.11 | + 0.01 | 126.09 |
| Reuter United Kingdom | 1816.7 | − 5.2 | 1569.3 |

## Cash Prices

Friday, May 20, 1983
(Quotations as of 4 p.m. Eastern time)

| | Fri | Thurs | Yr.Ago |
|---|---|---|---|
| **GRAINS AND FEEDS** | | | |
| **Alfalfa Pellets,** dehy, Neb., ton .... | 112.00 | 112.00 | 82.00 |
| **Barley,** top-quality Mpls., bu ....... | 2.65-2.80 | 2.65-2.80 | 3.05 |
| **Bran,** (Wheat middling) KC ton ... | 70.0-71.0 | 68.00 | 75.00 |
| **Brewer's Grains,** Milw. ton ......... | 96.00 | 96.00 | 92.00 |
| **Corn,** No. 2 yellow Cent-Ill. bu ..... | bp3.05 | 3.10 | 2.63½ |
| **Corn Gluten Feed,** Chgo., ton ...... | 110.00 | 110.00 | 110.33 |
| **Cottnsd Meal,** Clksdle,Miss. ton .. | 155.00 | 155.00 | 137.50 |
| **Flaxseed,** Mpls., bu ..................... | n5.25 | 5.25 | 7.30 |
| **Hominy Feed,** Ill., ton ................. | 108.00 | 108.00 | 82.00 |
| **Linseed Meal,** Mpls., ton ............. | 155.00 | 155.00 | 160.00 |
| **Meat-Bonemeal** 50%-pro, Ill. ton | 202.5-207.5 | 205.0-210.0 | 201.25 |
| **Oats,** No. 2 milling, Mpls., bu ....... | 1.68-1.75 | 1.68-1.75 | 2.11 |
| **Rice,** No. 2 milled fob Ark. cwt ..... | 18.0-19.0 | 18.0-19.0 | 17.25 |
| **Rye,** No. 2 Mpls., bu ..................... | 2.40-2.42 | 2.40-2.42 | 4.05 |
| **Sorghum,** (Milo) No. 2 Gulf cwt ... | 5.96 | 6.07 | 5.41 |
| **Soybean Meal,** Decatur, Ill. ton ... | 180.50 | 184.50 | 191.00 |
| **Soybeans,** No. 1 yel Cent.-Ill. bu ... | bp6.03 | 6.11 | 6.47 |
| **Sunflower Seed,** No 1 Mpls. cwt ... | 10.00 | 9.90 | 12.15 |
| **Wheat,** Spring 14%-pro Mpls. bu .. | r4.44¾ | 4.41¼ | 4.16¾ |
| **Wheat,** amber durum, Mpls. bu ... | 4.74-5.00 | 4.71-5.05 | 4.50 |
| **Wheat,** No. 2 sft red, St.Lou. bu .... | h3.59½ | 3.53½ | 3.24 |
| **Wheat,** No. 2 hard KC, bu ........... | r3.99½ | 4.01 | 4.14½ |
| **FOODS** | | | |
| **Beef,** 700-900 lbs. Mid-U.S.,lb.fob . | 106.00 | 105.00 | 1.16 |
| **Beef,** boxed, gross, Mid-US cwt ... | f109.74 | 109.60 | 120.34 |
| **Broilers,** Dressed "A" NY lb ....... | x.5044 | .5025 | 4806 |
| **Butter,** AA, Chgo., lb. ................. | 1.47 | 1.47 | 1.47 |
| **Cocoa,** Ivory Coast, $metric ton ... | g2,256 | 2,229 | z |
| **Coffee,** Brazilian, NY lb. ............. | n1.28 | 1.28 | 1.38 |
| **Eggs,** Lge white, Chgo doz. ......... | .64½-.65 | .66½-.67 | .59¾ |
| **Flour,** hard winter KC cwt .......... | 10.40 | 10.40 | 10.40 |
| **Hams,** 17-20 lbs, Mid-US lb fob ..... | .66 | .63 | .86 |
| **Hogs,** Iowa-S.Minn. avg. cwt ....... | 46.00 | 46.00 | 59.00 |
| **Hogs,** Omaha avg cwt ................ | e46.85 | 47.50 | 59.80 |
| **Orange Juice,** frz con, NY lb. ....... | b1.14 | 1.13 | 1.13 |
| **Pepper,** black, NY lb. ................. | a.70 | .70 | .67 |
| **Pork Bellies,** 12-14 lbs Mid-US lb .. | .62 | .60 | .81 |
| **Pork Loins,** 14-17 lbs. Mid-US lb ... | .94 | .95½ | 1.16 |
| **Potatoes,** rnd wht, 50 lb., fob ........ | y3.00-3.25 | 3.00-3.25 | 3.25 |
| **Steers,** Omaha choice avg cwt ..... | 68.38 | 68.38 | 74.75 |
| **Steers,** Tex.-Okla. ch avg cwt ...... | e z | 69.50 | 75.00 |
| **Steers, Feeder,** Okl Cty, av cwt ... | 69.50 | 69.50 | 68.50 |
| **Sugar,** beet, ref. Chgo-Wst lb fob .. | .2990 | .2990 | .2740 |
| **Sugar,** cane, raw NY lb. del. ......... | .2264 | .2264 | .1992 |
| **Sugar,** cane, raw, world, lb. fob ... | .0949 | .0931 | .0793 |
| **Sugar,** cane, ref NY lb. fob .......... | .3310 | .3310 | .3060 |
| **FATS AND OILS** | | | |
| **Coconut Oil,** crd, N. Orleans cif ... | a.27½ | .27½ | .23 |
| **Corn Oil,** crd wet mill, Chgo. lb. ... | .22-.22½ | .22½ | .23½ |
| **Corn Oil,** crd dry mill, Chgo. lb. ... | .22½ | .22½ | .23¾ |
| **Cottonseed Oil,** crd Miss Vly lb. ... | n.23½ | .23½ | .22 |
| **Grease,** choice white, Chgo lb. ..... | b.15⅝ | .15⅝ | .17¾ |
| **Lard,** Chgo lb. ........................... | .16¾ | .16¾ | .23 |
| **Linseed Oil,** raw Mpls lb. ........... | .23 | .23 | .28 |
| **Palm Oil,** ref. bl. deod. N.Orl. cif . | a.20¾ | .20¾ | .24½ |
| **Peanut Oil,** crd, Southeast lb. ...... | a.26½ | .26½ | .29½ |
| **Soybean Oil,** crd, Decatur, lb. ...... | .1962 | .1991 | .2148 |
| **Tallow,** bleachable, Chgo lb. ....... | a.16½ | .16½ | .18½ |
| **Tallow,** edible, Chgo lb. .............. | .18¾ | .18¾ | .23½ |
| **FIBERS AND TEXTILES** | | | |
| **Burlap,** 10 oz. 40-in. NY yd ........... | n.2480 | .2470 | .2430 |
| **Cotton** 1 1/16 in str lw-md Mphs lb | .6818 | .6817 | .6272 |
| **Print Cloth,** cotton, 48-in NY yd ... | s.59 | .59 | .63 |
| **Print Cloth,** pol/cot 48-in NY yd ... | t.46½ | .46½ | .47 |
| **Satin Acetate,** NY yd ................. | .66 | .66 | .62 |
| **Sheetings,** 60x60 48-in. NY yd ....... | .79 | .79 | .77 |
| **Wool,** fine staple terr. Boston lb ... | 2.13 | 2.13 | 2.48 |
| **METALS** | | | |
| **Aluminum** ingot lb ..................... | p.76 | .76 | .76 |
| **Copper** cathodes lb ..................... | p.82½-.84 | .82½-.84 | .75½ |
| **Copper Scrap,** No 2 wire NY lb ..... | k z | .62½ | .51½ |
| **Lead,** lb. ........................... | p.20-.23 | .20-.23 | .26½ |
| **Mercury** 76 lb. flask NY ............. | 315.00 | 315.00 | 370.00 |
| **Nickel** plating grade lb ............... | p3.29 | 3.29 | 3.29 |
| **Steel Scrap** 1 hvy mlt Chgo ton ..... | 71.00 | 68.0-69.0 | 70.00 |
| **Tin** Metals Week composite lb. .... | 6.7622 | 6.7526 | 6.5955 |
| **Zinc** High grade lb ..................... | p.38-.40 | .38-.40 | .36½ |
| **MISCELLANEOUS** | | | |
| **Hides,** hvy native strs lb fob ........ | .53 | .52-.52½ | .44½ |
| **Newspapers,** old No. 1 Chgo ton ... | 40.0-45.0 | 40.0-45.0 | 27.50 |
| **Rubber,** smoked sheets, NY lb. .... | n.56¼ | .56½ | .46 |
| **PRECIOUS METALS** | | | |
| **Gold,** troy oz | | | |
| **Engelhard** indust bullion ......... | 438.75 | 442.60 | 338.50 |
| **Engelhard** fabric prods ........... | 460.69 | 464.73 | 355.43 |
| **Handy & Harman** base price .... | 438.75 | 442.60 | 338.50 |
| **London** fixing AM 439.00 PM ... | 438.75 | 442.60 | 338.50 |
| **Krugerrand,** whol ................... | a452.00 | 453.00 | 347.00 |
| **Platinum,** troy ounce ................... | 475.00 | 475.00 | 475.00 |
| **Silver,** troy ounce | | | |
| **Engelhard** indust bullion ......... | 13.275 | 13.475 | 6.645 |
| **Engelhard** fabric prods ........... | 14.204 | 14.418 | 7.164 |
| **Handy & Harman** base price .... | 13.200 | 13.230 | 6.695 |
| **London Fixing** (in pounds) | | | |
| Spot (U.S. equiv. $13.290) ...... | 8.5385 | 8.6265 | 3.7360 |
| 3 months ............................ | 8.7520 | 8.8395 | 3.8570 |
| 6 months ............................ | 8.9655 | 9.0550 | 3.9805 |
| 1 year ................................. | 9.3600 | 9.4520 | 4.2395 |
| **Coins,** whol $1,000 face val ........ | 9,690 | 9,756 | 6,475 |

a-Asked. b-Bid. bp-Country elevator bids to producers. h-Terminal elevator truck bids to producers. c-Corrected. d-Dealer market. e-Estimated. f-Carcass equiv. value. g-Main crop, ex-dock, warehouses, Eastern Seaboard, north of Hatteras. k-Dealer selling prices in lots of 40,000 pounds or more, f.o.b. buyer's works. n-Nominal. p-Producer price. r-Rail bids. s-Thread count 78x76. t-Thread count 78x54. x-Less than truckloads. y-Maine origin; varies seasonally. z-Not quoted.

The Wall Street Journal, *May 23, 1983.*

# Futures Prices

Tuesday, May 24, 1983

**Open Interest Reflects Previous Trading Day.**

**-FOOD & FIBER-**

**COCOA (CSCE)-10 metric tons; $ per ton.**

| | Open | High | Low | Settle | Change | Lifetime High | Lifetime Low | Open Interest |
|---|---|---|---|---|---|---|---|---|
| July | 2,053 | 2,075 | 2,040 | 2,044 | – 38 | 2,095 | 1,475 | 1,385 |
| Sept | 2,086 | 2,104 | 2,076 | 2,083 | – 32 | 2,128 | 1,527 | 7,489 |
| Dec | 2,117 | 2,135 | 2,105 | 2,108 | – 39 | 2,159 | 1,560 | 5,145 |
| Mar84 | 2,135 | 2,155 | 2,130 | 2,133 | – 32 | 2,165 | 1,638 | 2,142 |
| May | .... | .... | .... | 2,154 | – 32 | 2,120 | 1,840 | 311 |
| July | .... | .... | .... | 2,179 | – 32 | 2,020 | 1,894 | 8 |

Est vol 4,805; vol Mon 3,278; open int 29,000, –89.

**COFFEE (CSCE)-37,500 lbs.; cents per lb.**

| | Open | High | Low | Settle | Change | Lifetime High | Lifetime Low | Open Interest |
|---|---|---|---|---|---|---|---|---|
| July | 131.65 | 133.80 | 130.50 | 133.35 | + 2.34 | 133.80 | 102.00 | 5,031 |
| Sept | 128.25 | 129.73 | 127.50 | 129.56 | + 1.81 | 129.73 | 101.00 | 3,379 |
| Dec | 126.00 | 127.70 | 125.75 | 127.70 | + 2.16 | 127.70 | 98.00 | 1,958 |
| Mar84 | 122.75 | 125.00 | 122.75 | 124.80 | + 2.42 | 125.00 | 110.50 | 227 |
| May | 122.50 | 122.50 | 122.00 | 122.33 | + 3.32 | 122.50 | 108.50 | 117 |
| July | 117.25 | 117.25 | 117.25 | 118.50 | + 1.62 | 118.00 | 106.25 | 184 |
| Sept | 117.00 | 117.00 | 116.00 | 117.00 | + 1.75 | 117.00 | 110.50 | 174 |

Est vol 2,410; vol Mon 1,542; open int 11,140, +8.

**COTTON (CTN)-50,000 lbs.; cents per lb.**

| | Open | High | Low | Settle | Change | Lifetime High | Lifetime Low | Open Interest |
|---|---|---|---|---|---|---|---|---|
| July | 74.00 | 74.25 | 73.50 | 73.70 | – .43 | 78.60 | 66.60 | 8,549 |
| Oct | 75.60 | 75.70 | 75.25 | 75.25 | – .52 | 78.50 | 65.65 | 1,302 |
| Dec | 76.10 | 76.15 | 75.55 | 75.72 | – .44 | 77.50 | 65.50 | 22,285 |
| Mar84 | 77.30 | 77.30 | 76.80 | 76.95 | – .55 | 78.40 | 67.10 | 2,339 |
| May | | .... | .... | 77.40 | – .50 | 79.00 | 69.38 | 303 |
| July | 77.60 | 77.60 | 77.60 | 78.00 | – .50 | 79.50 | 71.50 | 207 |
| Oct | 76.75 | 76.75 | 76.60 | 77.00 | – .50 | 78.35 | 74.25 | 18 |

Est vol 6,000; vol Mon 7,589; open int 35,003, –228.

**-WOOD-**

Lumber Futures

**LUMBER (CME)-130,000 bd. ft.; $ per 1,000 bd. ft.**

| | Open | High | Low | Settle | Change | Lifetime High | Lifetime Low | Open Interest |
|---|---|---|---|---|---|---|---|---|
| July | 226.00 | 230.60 | 225.60 | 230.60 | + 5.00 | 231.90 | 158.00 | 5,165 |
| Sept | 223.50 | 227.80 | 222.80 | 227.80 | + 5.00 | 230.10 | 163.80 | 2,179 |
| Nov | 215.50 | 220.40 | 215.00 | 220.40 | + 5.00 | 227.10 | 168.00 | 1,843 |
| Jan84 | 219.30 | 224.30 | 219.00 | 224.30 | + 5.00 | 234.00 | 179.00 | 442 |
| Mar | 221.20 | 226.20 | 221.20 | 226.20 | + 5.00 | 240.50 | 206.50 | 157 |
| May | | .... | .... | 229.00 | + 5.00 | 245.50 | 222.90 | 60 |
| July | 231.50 | 233.00 | 231.50 | 233.00 | + 5.00 | 252.50 | 224.60 | 25 |

Est vol 3,517; vol Mon 2,273; open int 9,871, +55.

**PLYWOOD (CBT)-76,032 sq. ft.; $ per 1,000 sq. ft.**

| | Open | High | Low | Settle | Change | Lifetime High | Lifetime Low | Open Interest |
|---|---|---|---|---|---|---|---|---|
| July | 213.50 | 216.70 | 211.80 | 216.10 | + 4.80 | 221.00 | 170.00 | 1,313 |
| Sept | 211.80 | 216.00 | 211.40 | 215.80 | + 5.60 | 223.90 | 185.00 | 758 |
| Nov | 210.00 | 213.50 | 209.50 | 213.50 | + 5.20 | 226.60 | 201.50 | 223 |
| Jan84 | 212.00 | 214.00 | 211.00 | 214.00 | + 3.80 | 223.00 | 204.50 | 42 |
| Mar | 213.50 | 215.00 | 212.60 | 215.00 | + 2.40 | 225.00 | 208.50 | 21 |
| May | 215.00 | 215.00 | 215.00 | 215.00 | + 1.00 | 219.50 | 215.00 | 0 |

Est vol 263; vol Mon 93; open int 2,357, –57.

**HEATING OIL NO. 2 (NYM)-42,000 gal.; $ per gal.**

| | Open | High | Low | Settle | Change | Lifetime High | Lifetime Low | Open Interest |
|---|---|---|---|---|---|---|---|---|
| June | .7840 | .7880 | .7810 | .7820 | – .0103 | .9220 | .6620 | 2,720 |
| July | .7800 | .7840 | .7750 | .7766 | – .0104 | .9475 | .6650 | 10,431 |
| Aug | .7835 | .7870 | .7770 | .7782 | – .0114 | .8200 | .6760 | 4,938 |
| Sept | .7880 | .7935 | .7870 | .7880 | – .0078 | .8225 | .6850 | 3,876 |
| Oct | .7980 | .8010 | .7950 | .7975 | – .0082 | .8300 | .6950 | 2,619 |
| Nov | .8080 | .8090 | .8075 | .8060 | – .0075 | .8700 | .7050 | 1,478 |
| Dec | .8150 | .8195 | .8130 | .8147 | – .0100 | 1.0090 | .7100 | 1,994 |
| Jan84 | .... | .... | .... | .8200 | – .0100 | .8425 | .7850 | 92 |
| Feb | .... | .... | .... | .8105 | – .0100 | .8300 | .7910 | 23 |
| Mar | .... | .... | .... | .8105 | – .0100 | .... | .... | 10 |
| May | .... | .... | .... | .7860 | – .0100 | .7970 | .6900 | 10 |

Est vol 6,567; vol Mon 9,814; open int 28,191, +474.

**-GRAINS AND OILSEEDS-**

**CORN (CBT) 5,000 bu.; cents per bu.**

| | Open | High | Low | Settle | Change | Lifetime High | Lifetime Low | Open Interest |
|---|---|---|---|---|---|---|---|---|
| May | .... | .... | .... | .... | .... | .... | .... | 181 |
| July | 309 | 310½ | 307¾ | 310¼ | + 3½ | 323¾ | 243 | 59,770 |
| Sept | 296 | 296½ | 294 | 296½ | + 2 | 316¼ | 247 | 13,353 |
| Dec | 284½ | 285 | 280¾ | 284¾ | + 1 | 310¾ | 253 | 61,306 |
| Mar84 | 293¾ | 294 | 288¾ | 292¾ | + ¼ | 319 | 278½ | 15,653 |
| May | 302¾ | 302¾ | 296¼ | 300½ | .... | 325 | 293½ | 4,355 |
| July | 306½ | 306¾ | 301½ | 305½ | – ¼ | 330 | 301½ | 1,689 |

Est vol 47,622; vol Mon 34,504; open int 156,307, –2,906.

**CORN (MCE) 1,000 bu.; cents per bu.**

| | Open | High | Low | Settle | Change | Lifetime High | Lifetime Low | Open Interest |
|---|---|---|---|---|---|---|---|---|
| July | 309¼ | 310¾ | 308 | 310¼ | + 3½ | 323¾ | 243¼ | 6,153 |
| Sept | .... | 296 | 294 | 296½ | + 2 | 316½ | 248 | 259 |
| Dec | 284½ | 285 | 280¾ | 284¾ | + 1 | 310¾ | 253¼ | 2,364 |
| Mar84 | 294¼ | 294¼ | 289 | 292¾ | + ¼ | 319 | 279½ | 1,962 |
| May | .... | .... | .... | 300½ | .... | 398 | 297 | 147 |
| July | 306¾ | 306¾ | 302 | 305½ | – ¼ | 330 | 302 | 49 |

Est vol 750; vol Mon 1,166; open int 10,934, +20.

**OATS (CBT) 5,000 bu.; cents per bu.**

| | Open | High | Low | Settle | Change | Lifetime High | Lifetime Low | Open Interest |
|---|---|---|---|---|---|---|---|---|
| July | 157¼ | 157½ | 155½ | 157½ | + 1½ | 188¾ | 152½ | 4,935 |
| Sept | 159 | 159 | 157 | 159 | + 1½ | 192¼ | 154 | 2,573 |
| Dec | 169¾ | 170¼ | 167¾ | 170 | + 1½ | 201½ | 165¼ | 1,883 |
| Mar84 | 169¾ | 180¼ | 178 | 180¼ | + 1¼ | 204½ | 175½ | 470 |
| May | 185 | 185 | 183½ | 185 | + ½ | 187½ | 183 | 10 |

Est vol 1,181; vol Mon 1,120; open int 9,871, –111.

**SOYBEANS (CBT) 5,000 bu.; cents per bu.**

| | Open | High | Low | Settle | Change | Lifetime High | Lifetime Low | Open Interest |
|---|---|---|---|---|---|---|---|---|
| May | | .... | .... | .... | .... | .... | .... | 1 |
| July | 624½ | 628 | 615½ | 627 | + 3¼ | 731½ | 566½ | 46,359 |
| Aug | 630 | 634 | 621½ | 633¼ | + 5 | 734½ | 566½ | 5,344 |
| Sept | 635 | 637½ | 627 | 636¾ | + 3¾ | 686½ | 567 | 3,970 |
| Nov | 643 | 648 | 636½ | 647¼ | + 5¾ | 696½ | 568½ | 26,637 |
| Jan84 | 655 | 660 | 648½ | 659½ | + 5¾ | 708½ | 594 | 3,780 |
| Mar | 667½ | 672½ | 662 | 672½ | + 6½ | 721 | 616 | 1,253 |
| May | 678½ | 683½ | 674 | 683½ | + 5 | 732 | 644 | 257 |
| July | 690 | 693½ | 683½ | 693½ | + 5 | 740½ | 683 | 170 |
| Aug | .... | .... | .... | 696 | + 6 | 690 | 690 | 1 |

Est vol 51,612; vol Mon 32,340; open int 87,772, –1,556.

**SOYBEANS (MCE) 1,000 bu.; cents per bu.**

| | Open | High | Low | Settle | Change | Lifetime High | Lifetime Low | Open Interest |
|---|---|---|---|---|---|---|---|---|
| May | .... | .... | .... | .... | .... | .... | .... | 4 |
| July | 625 | 628 | 615 | 627 | + 3¼ | 730 | 567 | 8,921 |
| Aug | 629 | 634 | 622 | 633¼ | + 5 | 685 | 575 | 417 |
| Sept | | 637½ | 627 | 636¾ | + 3¾ | 685 | 570⅞ | 150 |
| Nov | 643½ | 648½ | 636 | 647¼ | + 5¾ | 697 | 568 | 2,695 |
| Jan84 | 656 | 659½ | 650½ | 659½ | + 5¾ | 706½ | 596 | 216 |
| Mar | 667½ | 667½ | 664½ | 672½ | + 6½ | 720 | 632 | 130 |
| May | .... | .... | .... | 683½ | + 5 | 724 | 647 | 39 |
| July | 685 | 685 | 685 | 693½ | + 5 | 736 | 682 | 14 |

Est vol 1,400; vol Mon 1,741; open int 12,586. –118.

The Wall Street Journal, *May 25, 1983.*

amounts of each commodity. Take lumber as an example (as shown on the next page).

This commodity (two-by-fours) is traded on the Chicago Mercantile Exchange (CME) in contracts of 130,000 board feet at prices quoted in dollars per thousand board feet (boldface heading). The quotations are for delivery in July, September, and November 1983 and January, March, May, and July 1984.

**Lumber (CME)—130,000 bd. ft.; $ per 1,000 bd. ft.**

| | Open | High | Low | Settle | Change | Lifetime High | Lifetime Low | Open Interest |
|---|---|---|---|---|---|---|---|---|
| July | 226.00 | 230.60 | 225.60 | 230.60 | +5.00 | 231.90 | 158.00 | 5,165 |
| Sept | 223.50 | 227.80 | 222.80 | 227.80 | +5.00 | 230.10 | 163.80 | 2,179 |
| Nov | 215.50 | 220.40 | 215.00 | 220.40 | +5.00 | 227.10 | 168.00 | 1,843 |
| Jan 84 | 219.30 | 224.30 | 219.00 | 224.30 | +5.00 | 234.00 | 179.00 | 442 |
| Mar | 221.20 | 226.20 | 221.20 | 226.20 | +5.00 | 240.50 | 206.50 | 257 |
| May | | | | 229.00 | +5.00 | 245.50 | 222.90 | 60 |
| July | 231.50 | 233.00 | 231.50 | 233.00 | +5.00 | 252.50 | 224.60 | 25 |

Est vol 3,517; vol Mon 2,273; open int 9,871, +55.

The following information is provided by column.

Open—opening price; that is, $226 per thousand board feet for July 83 delivery.

High—highest price for trading day.

Low—lowest price for trading day.

Settle—settlement price, or closing price, for trading day.

Change—difference between the latest settlement price and that of previous trading day (increase of $5 for July 83 delivery).

Lifetime high—highest price ever for the July 83 contract.

Lifetime low—lowest price ever.

Open interest—number of contracts for delivery outstanding for each month.

The bottom line provides the estimated volume (number of contracts) for the day as well as the actual volume for the previous trading day. Finally, the total open interest is given, along with the change in the open interest from the previous trading day.

You can see that on May 24, 1983, you could have bought, or sold, a contract for July 1984 delivery of lumber for $30,290 ($233 × 130). Also, note that the lifetime low price increased over the range of months from July 83 to July 84. At one time, the market was betting that lumber prices would slowly increase with the gradual improvement of economic conditions. But the lifetime high for the same months is much greater, especially in the earlier months, and close to the settlement price on May 24, 1983. Clearly, the demand for lumber improved more quickly than most imagined, and this was reflected in the futures prices.

This means that as producer prices weakened generally during the first phase of the cycle, lumber prices bucked the trend and improved dramatically because of the market's assessment of the strong growth in residential construction (to be discussed in the next chapter). If you had contracted to sell lumber for July 83 delivery at $158, you would have felt foolish. If you had contracted to buy at that price, you would have felt smart. (Note that the settlement price was $230.60 on May 24.) Keep in mind that understanding the basic forces which affect the rate of inflation may not be of any help in understanding an individual commodity market (lumber, for instance).

Finally, Dow Jones announced a revision of its commodities indexes in the January 4, 1982, *Wall Street Journal* (see Chart 9). The article describes the indexes, and the accompanying chart presents them for 1975 through 1981. These indexes are more volatile than the Producer Price Index, and they clearly portray the inflation of the late 1970s, as well as the subsequent deflation. The indexes continued to decline until mid-1982 and then began to improve, as the chart accompanying the May 23, 1983, *Journal* article indicated (see page 78).

*   *   *

To conclude, this chapter has explored the relationship between production, efficiency, and prices, focusing especially on the first phase of the business cycle. We can summarize the cycle's progress from trough to recovery as follows:

GNP ↓ → *Industrial production* ↓ → *Capacity utilization* ↓ →
*Labor productivity* ↑ → *Unit labor costs* ↓ → *Producer prices* ↓.

When GNP and industrial production fall, capacity utilization declines. This leads to an increase in labor productivity and a drop in unit labor costs, driving down the rate of inflation as measured by producer prices.

Like the reveler's hangover, recession grips the economy following the bender of boom and inflation. Rest is the only cure, and recovery is not marked by a renewed round of expansion and growth but by a slack period in which steadiness is restored.

The recession of 1981–82 began prematurely with the Fed's tight money policy. This Mickey Finn produced a malaise which required a long recuperation, during which productivity eventually improved and inflation subsided.

The next chapter will examine the benefits reaped from this cooling-off.

**Chart 9**

# New Indexes of Commodity Futures, Spot Prices With Broader Content Start Today at Dow Jones

By ROBERT D. PRINSKY
*Special to* THE WALL STREET JOURNAL

NEW YORK—Dow Jones & Co. today begins publication of a new commodity futures index and a companion index of spot commodity prices.

The new Dow Jones commodity indexes substantially update the content of these market indicators. They include such active commodities as gold and soybeans, which weren't traded in futures markets when the previous indexes were formulated. All 12 commodities in the new indexes have equal weights, to avoid giving extra influence to any one.

Like the indexes they replace, the new ones will be published daily in The Wall Street Journal. The futures index will be published hourly during the trading day on the Dow Jones News Service, which also will carry the spot index at the close of markets.

## Many Uses

Commodity indexes have a variety of uses. They give an indication of the general trend of futures markets. They enable traders to compare the performance of their own holdings to the general trend. They provide economists with a reading on prices of raw materials generally. Many analysts regard changes in the difference between the futures and spot indexes as an indicator of future price movements.

The hardest part of designing a new index is deciding what it should contain. After consultation with numerous commodity experts, it was determined that the new indexes should be as consistent as possible with the old ones. Thus, they measure prices of 12 widely traded commodities and the futures index calculates prices five months in the future. The spot index measures prices for immediate delivery of the same commodities that are in the futures index.

The old indexes measured only agricultural commodities. The new ones add metals, animals and wood. They don't include financial futures, notably because other indexes of interest and currency rates exist and because financial instruments are of a considerably different nature than raw materials.

The 12 commodities covered are cattle, coffee, copper, corn, cotton, gold, hogs, lumber, silver, soybeans, sugar and wheat.

The base date for the new indexes is Dec. 31, 1974, when gold trading resumed in the U.S.

To give users an immediate history of the indexes, both have been calculated by Drexel Burnham Lambert Inc. for every trading day since the end of 1974, when both were 100.

The accompanying chart and graph give a seven-year history of the indexes for the last trading day of each month. A complete daily history of the indexes is available from Dow Jones (see below).

The weighting of the indexes is neutral. That is, each commodity's price on a given day is divided by its price on the base date

and the results are totaled. The total is divided by 12 and multiplied by 100 to yield the index.

To estimate the price of a commodity five months in the future, two contract months are used, one expiring in fewer than 150 days and one expiring in more than 150 days. It is assumed that each contract expires on the 15th of the month it relates to.

For each commodity, weights are assigned to the two contracts, based on the number of days between the 150th and the theoretical expiration date of the contract. Then, the price of each contract is multiplied by its weight, the results are added and the sum is divided by the number of days between the expiration dates of the two contracts. The result is the estimated price of the commodity for delivery in exactly five months, or 150 days.

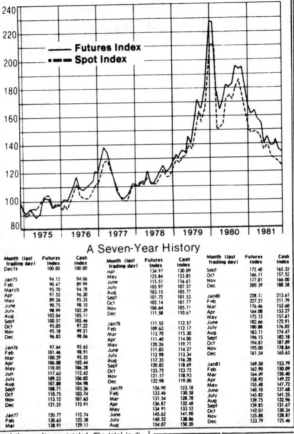

**Futures Index**
**Spot Index**

A Seven-Year History

| Month (last trading day) | Futures Index | Cash Index | Month (last trading day) | Futures Index | Cash Index | Month (last trading day) | Futures Index | Cash Index |
|---|---|---|---|---|---|---|---|---|
| Dec74 | 100.00 | 100.00 | Apr | 134.97 | 130.09 | Sept | 172.40 | 165.32 |
| | | | May | 125.84 | 123.85 | Oct | 166.11 | 157.52 |
| Jan75 | 94.15 | 94.06 | June | 115.51 | 116.61 | Nov | 177.81 | 166.00 |
| Feb | 90.47 | 89.99 | July | 105.97 | 107.57 | Dec | 200.39 | 188.58 |
| March | 95.70 | 94.78 | Aug | 103.15 | 105.77 | | | |
| Apr | 91.52 | 96.30 | Sept | 101.72 | 101.53 | Jan80 | 228.17 | 213.61 |
| May | 89.26 | 95.35 | Oct | 102.14 | 101.77 | Feb | 227.21 | 211.79 |
| June | 90.75 | 98.10 | Nov | 106.64 | 105.71 | Mar | 176.46 | 153.60 |
| July | 98.99 | 102.39 | Dec | 111.58 | 110.67 | Apr | 164.08 | 153.27 |
| Aug | 102.04 | 105.11 | | | | May | 172.12 | 157.61 |
| Sept | 100.57 | 105.46 | Jan78 | 111.55 | 112.57 | June | 182.66 | 172.91 |
| Oct | 95.05 | 97.22 | Feb | 109.63 | 112.17 | July | 180.88 | 176.02 |
| Nov | 95.18 | 99.51 | Mar | 113.70 | 115.30 | Aug | 183.11 | 174.47 |
| Dec | 96.83 | 98.06 | Apr | 111.40 | 114.00 | Sept | 196.15 | 182.18 |
| | | | May | 120.26 | 119.71 | Oct | 194.81 | 187.09 |
| Jan76 | 97.64 | 95.65 | June | 111.85 | 114.27 | Nov | 195.00 | 178.84 |
| Feb | 101.46 | 98.91 | July | 112.98 | 113.34 | Dec | 181.54 | 165.63 |
| Mar | 100.29 | 95.55 | Aug | 117.35 | 116.28 | | | |
| Apr | 106.08 | 102.44 | Sept | 120.82 | 118.69 | Jan81 | 169.50 | 153.79 |
| May | 110.05 | 106.28 | Oct | 125.75 | 123.72 | Feb | 162.90 | 150.09 |
| Jun | 117.63 | 112.42 | Nov | 121.17 | 118.93 | Mar | 164.49 | 150.40 |
| July | 109.23 | 106.02 | Dec | 122.98 | 119.00 | Apr | 158.92 | 149.22 |
| Aug | 107.88 | 104.98 | | | | May | 155.48 | 144.72 |
| Sept | 108.71 | 103.26 | Jan79 | 126.90 | 123.18 | June | 140.10 | 137.68 |
| Oct | 110.75 | 103.74 | Feb | 133.46 | 130.58 | July | 145.82 | 141.25 |
| Nov | 113.12 | 107.63 | Mar | 131.54 | 128.78 | Aug | 139.75 | 132.96 |
| Dec | 121.25 | 112.91 | Apr | 136.87 | 132.48 | Sept | 139.85 | 131.67 |
| | | | May | 134.91 | 133.52 | Oct | 142.01 | 130.34 |
| Jan77 | 120.77 | 112.74 | June | 145.62 | 141.90 | Nov | 135.88 | 128.87 |
| Feb | 130.65 | 122.38 | July | 140.52 | 138.86 | Dec | 133.79 | 125.46 |
| Mar | 138.91 | 129.11 | Aug | 154.07 | 150.20 | | | |

## History Available

A seven-year daily history of both indexes, including a history of the five-month prices for each commodity, will be available later this month, priced at $50 a copy. Orders may be sent to Commodity Index, The Wall Street Journal, 200 Burnett Road, Chicopee, Mass. 01021.

Single copies of this article may be ordered at no charge from Dow Jones Educational Service Bureau, P.O. Box 300, Princeton, N.J. 08540.

The Wall Street Journal, *January 4, 1982.*

# CHAPTER SEVEN

## The Business Cycle
## Phase Two: From Recovery
## to Expansion

Inflation is an increase in prices due to excessive spending financed either by borrowing or by the issue of paper money. "Too many dollars chasing too few goods" is a standard way of putting it. Economists are more formal: "Inflation occurs when demand exceeds supply at current prices, and prices are bid up."

Both explanations conjure up a gigantic auction at which customers bid for both goods and services. The more money the customers have to spend, the higher prices go. Where do they get the money? From banks, which create it.

Although we wait and hope for it to subside, we tend to assume that inflation, like death and taxes, is inevitable. In fact, however, chronic inflation is a recent problem. Before the late 1940s, severe inflation was a temporary phenomenon associated with wars. When the federal government's wartime expenditures overshot tax revenues and the difference was covered by selling bonds to the banking system or by printing paper money, prices increased swiftly.

Except for war-related inflations, prices in America fell more than they rose, until after World War II. As a matter of fact, prices were actually lower in 1914, on the eve of World War I, than they were in 1815, at the end of the Napoleonic Wars and the War of 1812.

Prices dropped during the 19th century because supply grew more rapidly than demand. Business mobilized the technological advances of the industrial revolution to produce standard items of consumption in considerably larger quantities at considerably lower cost. Occasionally, prices rose during the upswing of the business cycle, because investment expenditures were financed by bank borrowing or because there were temporary shortages of agricultural commodities, but these increases were more than offset when prices tumbled in recession years as huge additions in supply were brought to market.

Only the Civil War and World Wars I and II provided great inflationary experiences; even the period between World War I and World War II was a time of deflation (falling prices). War brought inflation, and peace brought deflation, because government borrowed and spent more massively in wartime than business borrowed and spent in peacetime. The difference was more a matter of degree than of kind; peacetime investment expenditures and borrowing by farmers, railroads, and manufacturers, though substantial, were usually not large enough to boost the growth in demand beyond the increase in supply, and thus prices fell.

To summarize, prices fell unless there was a rapid increase in demand (spending) financed by bank borrowing or the printing press. Demand took on a life of its own, and grew more rapidly than supply, only when outside financing provided a boost. It made little difference whether it was government spending for war or business spending for investment, as long as banks printed bank notes or created demand deposits or government printed paper money. Once demand grew more rapidly than supply at current prices, and too many dollars chased too few goods, prices rose.

What was responsible for the post–World War II experience? Why have prices risen steadily? The answers lie in consumer spending. This period marked the first time that consumers borrowed continually and prodigiously to finance purchases of luxury goods. The level of activity grew decade after decade, and with each cycle, so that in the 1970s tidal waves of credit roared through the system, rapidly swelling demand to record levels.

It started in the 1920s, a kind of brief test run for the full-scale activity which followed World War II. At first, following World War I, consumers purchased homes and automobiles, but by modern times demand expanded to include kitchen and laundry appliances, furniture and furnishings, and electronic equipment such as television sets and stereos. All were financed by credit, and the terms became more liberal over time, even as interest rates rose. The American consumer was encouraged—indeed, came to feel obligated—to mortgage the future so that present expenditures could exceed present income, with borrowing covering the difference.

The economy's health thus developed a dependence upon the chronic fix of greater consumer expenditures, financed by borrowing. These circumstances were entirely different from the circumstances of the 19th century, when consumers were largely confined to standard items of consumption purchased with current income (not debt) and economic growth was propelled by increased supply which pushed prices downward. Now the situation is quite different. Full production and employment have become the hostages of ever-larger waves of consumer expenditure on discretionary purchases financed by borrowing.

Unfortunately, these surges in consumer demand always led to their own demise, because expansion brought inflation, which depleted real incomes and generated the downturn of the cycle. Only then did inflation abate, real income recover, and expansion begin anew.

The last chapter examined recession's impact on costs and the attendant decline in the rate of inflation. Now consider the manner in which this decline spurs a recovery in consumer demand. The first statistical series to be examined in this chapter is the Consumer Price Index (CPI), whose fluctuations chart the course of inflation. You'll see that fluctuations in consumer prices are the principal determinant of changes in consumer real income, and that lower inflation means higher real income. This leads to improved consumer sentiment and demand, which drives economic expansion forward. You can gauge the latter through data on auto sales, consumer credit, retail sales, and housing starts, which will serve as the leading indicators of consumer demand.

## CONSUMER PRICE INDEX (CPI)

The Bureau of Labor Statistics' *CPI* release usually appears in *The Wall Street Journal* in the fourth week of the month. In the April 25, 1983, article, the *second paragraph* informs you of the CPI's increase computed at an annual rate. (See pages 87 and 88.)

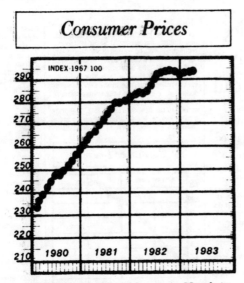

*Consumer Prices*

INDEX 1967 100

CONSUMER PRICES rose in March to 293.4 of the 1967 average from 293.2 in February before seasonal adjustment, the Labor Department reports. (See story on page 2.)

The Wall Street Journal, *April 25, 1983.*

# Consumer-Price Speedup Likely In Months Ahead

## First Period Showed Smallest Rise in 18 Years, but Food, Gasoline to Push Up Rate

By EILEEN ALT POWELL
*Staff Reporter of* THE WALL STREET JOURNAL.

WASHINGTON—Consumer prices in the first quarter registered their smallest increase in nearly 18 years, but economists warn that heftier price rises are in the offing.

The Labor Department reported that consumer prices rose a seasonally adjusted 0.1%, or 1.2% at an annual rate before compounding, in March after falling 0.2%, or 2.4% at an annual rate, in February. Prices also rose 0.2% in January.

The first-quarter performance translates into price increases at a 0.4% annual rate, down slightly from the 0.5% annual pace in the final quarter of 1982 and the smallest since prices were unchanged in the third quarter of 1965, a department economist said.

Economists in and out of government agree, however, that rising gasoline and food prices in coming months are likely to produce quarterly inflation readings closer to annual rates of 5%. While higher than recent readings, such a rate would continue to be a sharp slowdown from the double-digit inflation pace at the start of the decade.

In a White House news conference, President Reagan called the recent price performance "welcome relief for every American." But he warned that such a low inflation rate "can't last forever" and suggested that congressional approval of his administration's budget proposals would help keep prices in check.

Martin Feldstein, chairman of the president's Council of Economic Advisers, told the Joint Economic Committee of Congress that the March report contains "very positive figures." He called for continuing federal policies aimed at slow growth in the nation's monetary policy and reduced federal spending.

The slower pace of inflation through March also means that the annual increase in benefit checks for the nation's 36 million Social Security recipients will be the smallest since benefits were tied to consumer prices in 1975.

Government officials calculate that Social Security benefits, along with those for four million Supplemental Security Income recipients, will be raised 3.5% this year, compared with a cost-of-living adjustment of 7.4% in 1982. The only smaller adjustment was a 5.9% increase in 1977. The latest increase reflects the rise in the separate consumer price index for urban wage earners and clerical workers from the first quarter of 1982 to the first quarter of 1983. The principal measure, the all-urban consumer price index, covers about 80% of the population.

## Consumer Prices

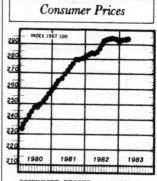

CONSUMER PRICES rose in March to 293.4 of the 1967 average from 293.2 in February before seasonal adjustment, the Labor Department reports. (See story on page 2.)

In most recent years, the cost-of-living increases went into effect in June and were reflected in July benefit checks. But legislation passed by Congress this year to ensure solvency of the Social Security system will delay this year's adjustment to December.

Jim Brown, a spokesman for the Social Security Administration, said the average monthly benefit for a single retiree will rise to $425 from $411. The benefit for a retired couple, both of whom receive benefits, will go to $733 from $709.

The inflation report showed that most of the price increase in March stemmed from a sharp rise in fresh vegetable prices, reflecting bad weather in growing areas, and a smaller decline in gasoline prices than in earlier months. Gasoline prices fell an adjusted 1% in March after plunging a record 6.7% the month before.

Donald Ratajczak, director of the Georgia State University Economic Forecasting Project, said that "the numbers looked pretty good" in March but that April's reading could be as high as an adjusted 0.7%. Contributing to the rise will be the gasoline-tax boost of five cents a gallon, which took

effect April 1, higher fuel prices and rising vegetable prices.

Mr. Ratajczak predicts that prices will rise at an annual rate of about 5% in the current quarter, slightly less than 5% in the third period and at an annual rate of about 6% in the final quarter. Some of the increase starting late this summer will reflect higher meat prices, he said, as the Reagan administration's program of paying farmers with grain to reduce planting this year boosts cattle-feed prices.

This year's consumer-price performance won't compare exactly with last year's, because in January the department changed the way it calculates the price index. But both Mr. Ratajczak and Susan Lakatos, an economist at Washington Analysis Corp., expect the consumer price increase for all of this year to be less than the 5% registered for 1982 on an experimental measure that is similar to the current index. "Given the performance in the first quarter, I think we can expect about 4.6% to 4.7% for all of 1983," Miss Lakatos said.

The report showed that food prices rose an adjusted 0.6% in March after holding unchanged in February from January. Housing costs declined an adjusted 0.1% last month after holding unchanged the month before. Clothing costs fell an adjusted 0.1% in March after rising an adjusted 0.5% the month before. Transportation costs, reflecting a smaller drop in gasoline prices, were unchanged last month after falling an adjusted 1.6% in February. And medical-care costs increased an adjusted 0.5% in March after rising an adjusted 0.8% in February.

Before seasonal adjustment, the price index for all urban consumers rose 0.1% in March to 293.4% of its 1967 average and was up 3.6% from a year earlier. (See chart on page one.)

The index for urban wage earners and clerical workers rose a seasonally adjusted 0.3% in March after falling 0.2% in the previous month. Before adjustment, this index increased 0.2% last month to 293% of its 1967 average and was up 3.7% from a year earlier.

In a related report, the Labor Department said the gross weekly earnings of U.S. workers rose 0.9% in March after adjustment for both inflation and seasonal factors. These earnings had fallen 1.5% in February after rising 1.6% in January.

The department said that in March, a 1.5% increase in average weekly hours was partly offset by a 0.1% decrease in average hourly earnings and the rise in the consumer price index for urban wage earners and clerical workers.

Gross weekly earnings in March were $274.57, up from $270.52 in February, the department said. After seasonal adjustment, March earnings were $275.01, compared with $271.42 the months before.

*CPI . . . second paragraph*

---

The Labor Department reported that consumer prices rose a seasonally adjusted 0.1%, or 1.2% at an annual rate before compounding, in March after falling 0.2%, or 2.4% at an annual rate, in February. Prices also rose 0.2% in January.

---

The CPI is designed to compare relative price changes over time. An index must be constructed because consumers purchase such a wide variety of goods and services that no single item could accurately reflect the situation. (See Chart 1 on page 90.)

A base year (1967) is selected and assigned an index number of 100.0; and prices for other periods are then reported as percentage changes from this base. For instance, if prices rose 5 percent from this base, the index would be 105.0. If prices fell by 10 percent, the index would be 90.0.

The Bureau of Labor Statistics (BLS) calculates the CPI by compiling a list of the goods and services purchased by the typical consumer, including such items as food, clothing, shelter, public utilities, and medical care. These make up the "market basket." The base year price of each item is recorded and assigned a weight according to its importance in the basket. Changes in the price of each item are noted, and the percentage change in the total price is reflected in the change of the index number. For example, if clothing represented 5 percent of the market basket and gasoline 10 percent (their weights), and if clothing prices fell by 3 percent and gas prices rose by 10 percent, and if the prices of all other items remained unchanged, the CPI would fall by 0.15 percent and rise by 1 percent, for a net increase of 0.85 percent. If this happened the year after the base year, the index would be at 100.85.

The ways consumers spend are continuously shifting because tastes change, as do incomes and the relative prices of goods. New goods and services are frequently introduced. It would be impossible, however, to generate a consistent index of consumer prices if the components of the market basket were constantly changed. A balance must be struck between the need for consistency and the need for an accurate reflection of consumer buying patterns. Therefore, the BLS revises the contents of the market basket only occasionally, after conducting a survey of consumer expenditure patterns.

Contrary to the popular image, the CPI is not really a "cost of living" index. The BLS's market basket is fixed; the individual

**Chart 1**
**Consumer Price Index** (CPI) (1967 = 100); **Quarterly Change in Index at Annual Rates** (smoothed)

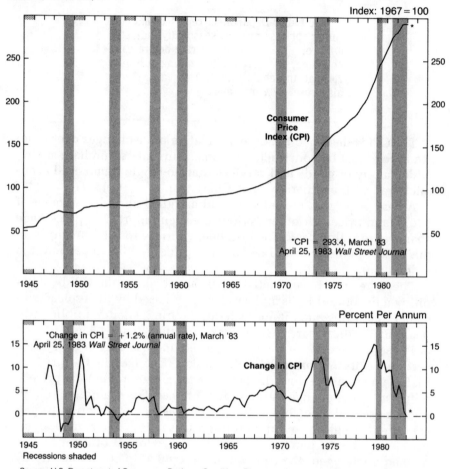

Index: 1967 = 100

Consumer Price Index (CPI)

*CPI = 293.4, March '83
April 25, 1983 *Wall Street Journal*

Percent Per Annum

*Change in CPI = +1.2% (annual rate), March '83
April 25, 1983 *Wall Street Journal*

Change in CPI

Recessions shaded

Source: U.S. Department of Commerce, *Business Conditions Digest* and *Handbook of Cyclical Indicators*, series 320 and 320c.

consumer's is not. Substitutions are made with changes in prices and with changes in income. Your "cost of living" can vary (or can be made to vary) independently of any change in the CPI.

A final point should be made. The Bureau of Labor Statistics recently replaced the cost of homeownership with an imputation (or estimate) of the rental value of owner-occupied homes. The cost of homeownership, which includes mortgage interest rates and home purchase prices, swiftly escalated in the late 1970s, so that this component of the CPI grew rapidly and pulled the entire index upward. Many found this an unjustified upward bias. Accordingly, the Bureau of Labor Statistics adjusted the shelter component to estimate the increase in the rental value of an owner-occupied home, which more closely approximates its usage value than does actual appreciation in price. Ironically, interest rates and home prices have fallen lately, so that the old index, were it now in use, would have a downward bias and rise less rapidly than the new index.

Now compare the CPI's recent record to that of the Producer Price Index, making a mental note that the *Journal's* April 25, 1983, report updates Chart 2 and confirms inflation's continued abatement. You can see from Chart 2 that the CPI's trends have followed the Producer Price Index since World War II.

**Chart 2**
**Change in Producer Prices and in Consumer Prices** (smoothed)

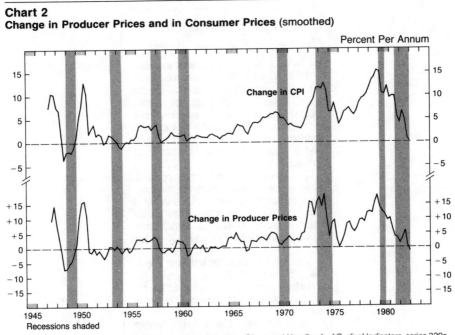

Source: U.S. Department of Commerce, *Business Conditions Digest* and *Handbook of Cyclical Indicators*, series 320c and 334c.

## CONSUMER REAL INCOME AND CONSUMER SENTIMENT

The Fed's tight money policies and the natural run of the business cycle forced the rate of inflation down to a moderate level in 1982. What impact did that have on economic recovery in general and on the consumer's leading role in particular?

The Survey Research Center of the University of Michigan compiles the *Index of Consumer Sentiment*. Consumers are asked a variety of questions regarding their personal financial circumstances and their outlook for the future. Responses are tabulated according to whether conditions are perceived as better or worse, and an index is constructed comparing the outcome to that for a base year (1966). *The Wall Street Journal* does not report this index, although it occasionally publishes the Conference Board's index, which is similar.

Compare the CPI with the Survey Research Center's index (see Chart 3).

---

## Consumer Confidence 'Inched Ahead' in April

*By a* WALL STREET JOURNAL *Staff Reporter*

NEW YORK—The Conference Board said its consumer-confidence index posted another small gain last month, indicating that "while consumers have yet to shed their concern about current economic conditions, they continue to be highly optimistic" about the future of the economy.

The board, an industry-supported, nonprofit economic research institute, said its survey of 5,000 U.S. households showed that consumer confidence "inched ahead" to 77.3 last month from 77.1 in March (1969-70 equals 100 on the scale).

"About 38% look for business conditions to improve during the next six months, compared with less than 7% expecting conditions to worsen," the board said.

However, the board said, buying plans, "which tend to show volatile swings," fell back in April after a substantial gain in March." The board said its buying-plans index, with 1969-70 as 100, registered 77.2 last month, down from 87.9 in March.

But home-buying plans appear to remain strong, with 2.6% of those questioned last month saying they planned to buy homes, only slightly below the 2.7% figure registered in March and up from 2.1% in April 1982.

The Wall Street Journal, *May 10, 1983.*

---

**Chart 3**
**Index of Consumer Sentiment and Quarterly Change in CPI**

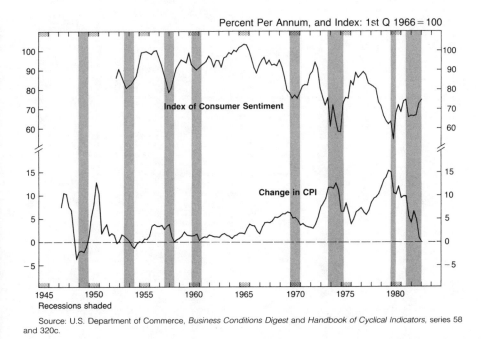

Percent Per Annum, and Index: 1st Q 1966 = 100

Recessions shaded

Source: U.S. Department of Commerce, *Business Conditions Digest* and *Handbook of Cyclical Indicators*, series 58 and 320c.

Consumers are influenced by more than inflation. Employment opportunities, interest rates, and current events all play a role. Consumer psychology is complicated. Yet you can see that the singular impact of inflation has been too strong to overlook since the early 1970s.

There's good reason that inflation and consumer sentiment have moved in opposite fashion in recent years: cyclical swings in inflation have infallibly determined cyclical swings in consumer real income (see Chart 4 on page 94). Gains in current-dollar compensation were wiped out by cyclical increases in inflation, driving real compensation down as the peak of the cycle approached. Real compensation improved only after recession hit, as inflation eased and began to decline. Note the steady improvement in real compensation and consumer sentiment since 1980 as inflation slackened.

Since consumer real income and the Index of Consumer Sentiment are not reported regularly in *The Wall Street Journal*, you will have to base your estimate of changes in consumer sentiment on your observations of the CPI.

Other influences on consumer sentiment, such as interest rates, were alluded to just a few paragraphs earlier. You can compare the

**Chart 4**
**Index of Consumer Sentiment, Change in Real Average Hourly Compensation, and Change in CPI**

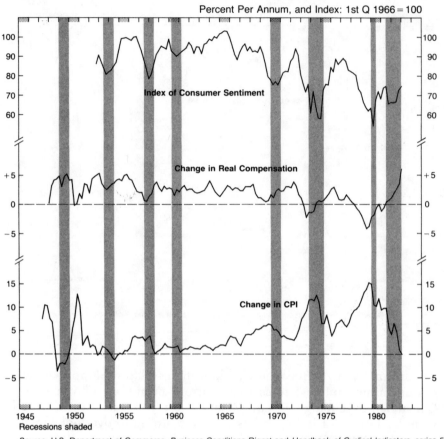

Percent Per Annum, and Index: 1st Q 1966 = 100

Recessions shaded

Source: U.S. Department of Commerce, *Business Conditions Digest* and *Handbook of Cyclical Indicators*, series 58, 320c, and 346c.

chart on home mortgage interest rates on page 47 with the change in the CPI on page 93 and see that the two moved together. That's not surprising, because interest rates and prices were subject to the same cyclical forces, rising in boom periods and falling with recession. Thus, rising interest rates were part of inflation's dampening impact on consumer sentiment, while falling interest rates were one of the benefits of deflation which turned consumer sentiment upward. Consumer sentiment benefited when the Fed relaxed its grip and permitted interest rates to fall in the summer of 1982.

*Marginal employment adjustments* also affect consumer sentiment. This is a fancy term for workers' opportunity to bolster their paychecks by stretching the workweek and putting in overtime.

The Labor Department reports *workweek* and *overtime* data with its monthly *employment report,* which *The Wall Street Journal* usually publishes on Monday of the second week. These figures appear at the end of the article and were in the *last paragraph* of the May 9, 1983, story.

# Jobless Figure Shows Recovery Is Gaining Speed

## But High Unemployment Seen Into '84 Despite Fall In April's Rate to 10.2%

By EILEEN ALT POWELL
*Staff Reporter of THE WALL STREET JOURNAL*

WASHINGTON—The further decline in the nation's unemployment rate in April to 10.2% of the work force shows that the economic recovery is gaining momentum.

But economists in and out of government caution that the upturn's pace will be slow by historical standards and that high unemployment will continue to be a problem into 1984.

The Labor Department's latest report shows that the U.S. civilian jobless rate fell last month from 10.3% of the work force in March and 10.4% in both February and January. The figures are seasonally adjusted. (See chart on page one.)

While the jobless rate is down from the recession peak of an adjusted 10.8% last December, it remains much higher than the adjusted 7.2% rate of July 1981, when the 18-month recession began.

By another measure, which includes the armed forces stationed in the U.S. as part of the work force, the U.S. unemployment rate in April was unchanged from March at 10.1%. This rate had been 10.2% in both February and January.

Janet Norwood, the Department's commissioner of statistics, says the April figures "show considerable improvement in the overall labor market," with employment and hours of work registering strong gains.

But Mrs. Norwood noted in an appearance before Congress's Joint Economic Committee that "the unemployment rate tends to decline very slowly" as recoveries get under way because improving conditions tend to lure people back into the labor force

faster than the market can absorb them. And she said that businesses, hit hard by both the 1980 and 1981-82 recessions, may remain cautious about hiring additional workers until the economy improves further.

In fact, Allen Gutheim, an economist at Wharton Econometric Forecasting Associates in Philadelphia, contends the jobless rate "could take an upward bounce" in the next several months, which he said isn't "an uncommon occurrence at the early stages of recovery." As the year progresses, he expects the unemployment rate to decline gradually, reaching about 9.5% of the work force by December. "I think employment will really accelerate in 1984 after the recovery is well in place," Mr. Gutheim concludes.

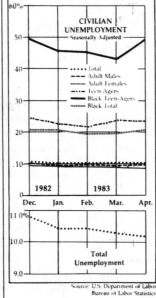

1982    1983

Dec.   Jan.   Feb.   Mar.   Apr.

Total Unemployment

Source: U.S. Department of Labor
Bureau of Labor Statistics

The Help-Wanted Advertising Index maintained by the Conference Board in New York was unchanged in March for the fourth consecutive month. Kenneth Goldstein, an economist with the business group, says this

gauge of the demand for workers suggest that "things aren't moving very fast at all" and that the unemployment rate could hold at 10% or higher through the summer.

The latest unemployment report also drew a rare comment from Labor Secretary Raymond Donovan. "We are on the road to development of the healthy economy with steady job growth and the lower prices to which this administration is committed," he said in a statement.

Reagan administration economists expect the U.S. jobless rate to fall below 10% by year-end and decline further in 1984.

The latest report showed that total civilian employment in April rose 0.4%, or 355,000, to an adjusted 99.5 million after rising less than 0.1%, or 40,000, in March to an adjusted 99.1 million.

The department said that employment gains last month were widespread, with nearly three-quarters of 186 different industry groupings reporting gains.

The number of unemployed people decreased 0.5%, or 53,000, last month to an adjusted 11,328,000 after falling 0.9%, or 109,000, in March to an adjusted 11,381,000.

Almost all of April's employment gains were made by adult women, for whom the unemployment rate declined to 8.4% from 8.8% in March.

The unemployment rate for adult men rose to an adjusted 9.8% in April from 9.6% in March. Jack Bregger, chief of the department's employment analysis division, said he "wouldn't place any great significance" in a one-month rise in this reading. More troublesome, he added, is that while the jobless rate for whites continue to fall, the rate for blacks continues to increase.

The report showed that the unemployment rate for whites declined in April to an adjusted 8.9% from 9% a month before, while the rate for blacks rose to an adjusted 20.8% last month from 19.9% in March. For all teen-agers, unemployment edged down to an adjusted 23.4% in April from 23.5% in March.

Non-farm payrolls rose 0.3%, or 258,000, in April to an adjusted 89.2 million after rising 0.2%, or 196,000, in March to an adjusted 89 million.

The average workweek for non-farm workers rose to 35 hours in April from 34.8 hours in March. The average manufacturing workweek increased to 40.1 hours last month from 39.6 hours a month before. And average factory overtime rose to three hours in April from 2½ hours in March.

## Unemployment Rate

Percent of Labor Force
Seasonally Adjusted

1980   1981   1982   1983

UNEMPLOYMENT in April fell to a seasonally adjusted rate of 10.2% of the labor force from 10.3% the preceding month, the Labor Department reports. (See story on page 3.)

The Wall Street Journal, *May 9, 1983.*

*Marginal employment adjustments . . . last paragraph*

The average workweek for non-farm workers rose to 35 hours in April from 34.8 hours in March. The average manufacturing workweek increased to 40.1 hours last month from 39.6 hours a month before. And average factory overtime rose to three hours in April from 2½ hours in March.

Compare the latest data to Charts 5a and 5b on pages 97 and 98, and note that both the workweek and overtime have picked up since their recession lows. You should also observe that these indicators improve during expansion, flatten with boom conditions, and plummet in recession. Manufacturing production workers typically have no say over how long their workweek will be or whether they will work overtime. Their employer makes those decisions. Yet the extra income afforded by overtime is welcome and bolsters consumer sentiment early in the expansion, although its effect is exhausted by the time boom conditions develop. Therefore, marginal employment adjustments are a reinforcing element of the business cycle through their impact on consumer sentiment.

**Chart 5a**
**Average Workweek of Production Workers, Manufacturing**

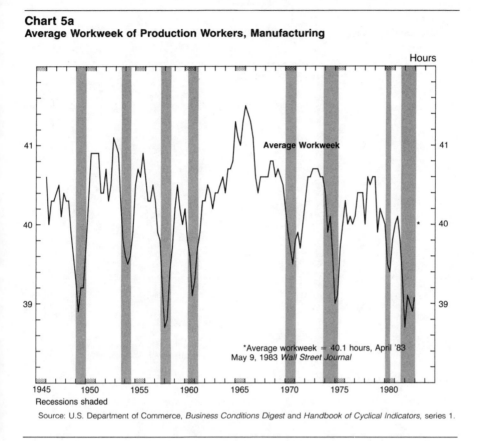

Hours

*Average workweek = 40.1 hours, April '83
May 9, 1983 *Wall Street Journal*

1945    1950    1955    1960    1965    1970    1975    1980
Recessions shaded

Source: U.S. Department of Commerce, *Business Conditions Digest* and *Handbook of Cyclical Indicators*, series 1.

One further comment before you turn from the employment data. The continued high level of unemployment and its slow decline yield further evidence that business needs relatively less labor during recovery and expansion. Output will therefore improve much faster than employment, boosting productivity and holding costs down.

The Commerce Department's monthly *personal income* report appears in *The Wall Street Journal* during the third week. The headline and *first paragraph* of the April 20, 1983, article informs you that personal income grew by 0.6 percent in March 1983, and the caption under the "Personal Income" chart accompanying the article puts the current figure at $2.659 trillion. (See pages 99 and 100.)

**Chart 5b**
**Average Weekly Overtime of Production Workers, Manufacturing**

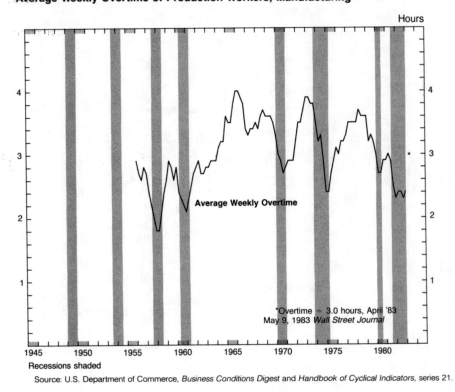

Hours

Average Weekly Overtime

*Overtime = 3.0 hours, April '83
May 9, 1983 *Wall Street Journal*

Recessions shaded

Source: U.S. Department of Commerce, *Business Conditions Digest* and *Handbook of Cyclical Indicators*, series 21.

# Personal Income Increased 0.6% During March

## Monthly Gain Was Biggest Since November, Points To Stronger Retail Sales

By EILEEN ALT POWELL
*Staff Reporter of* THE WALL STREET JOURNAL

WASHINGTON—The personal income of Americans grew 0.6% in March, the largest monthly gain since November, suggesting that retail sales may begin to strengthen in coming months.

The Commerce Department said personal income rose $14.6 billion last month to a seasonally adjusted $2.659 trillion annual rate after rising 0.1%, or $2.6 billion, in February to an adjusted $2.644 trillion pace. (See chart on page one.) More than 60% of the March increase, which was the strongest since a 0.7% rise in November, reflected rising income from wages and salaries, the report showed.

As payroll income grew last month, Americans stepped up spending and saving. Economists in and out of government expect additional income gains in the current quarter to lead to stronger retail sales as the economy continues to recover from the 1981-1982 recession.

And the current moderate pace of inflation means that consumer buying power isn't being eroded significantly by rapidly rising prices. Robert Ortner, the department's chief economist, said: "The income figures are even better than they look given the noninflationary environment we've got."

Mr. Ortner described the March improvement in wages and salaries as "a healthy sign" that could lead to spending gains, and thus stronger economic growth, in the current quarter.

The department is scheduled today to issue its preliminary report on the nation's real gross national product—the value of all goods and services produced, adjusted for inflation—for the first quarter. Mr. Ortner said the reading "may be slightly higher" than the 4% annual rate of growth the department projected from sketchy information a month ago, in part because "consumer spending has held up fairly well."

Sandra Shaber, an economist at Chase Econometrics in Bala-Cynwyd, Pa., termed the March income growth "a nice increase compared with what we had been seeing" and agreed that the rise "should give a boost to consumer spending."

Still, Mrs. Shaber expects that inflation-adjusted consumer spending will show growth of a modest 3.3%, at an annual rate, in the current quarter following expansion at about a 2.5% pace in the first period. "Consumer interest rates still remain high," she said. She added that some people also may continue to step up saving in the current quarter, taking advantage of the tax breaks associated with individual retirement accounts. Higher federal tax refunds stemming from last year's tax-rate cut also could prompt more saving, she concluded.

The report showed that consumer spending increased 0.4%, or $7.6 billion, in March to an adjusted $2.059 trillion annual rate after holding unchanged in February from January at an adjusted $2.051 trillion pace.

An inflation measure linked to spending, but reported after a one-month lag, rose 0.1% in February after rising 0.4% in January.

Savings rose 3.8% last month to an adjusted $134.6 billion annual pace after falling 1.1% in February to an adjusted $129.7 billion rate. For March, savings represented 6% of Americans' after-tax income, up from 5.8% the month before.

The income statistics showed that private wages and salaries rose 0.6% in March to an adjusted annual rate of $1.603 trillion after falling 0.1% in February to an adjusted $1.594 trillion pace. Factory payrolls increased 0.7% last month to an adjusted $385.6 billion annual rate after climbing 0.6% in February to an adjusted $382.9 billion pace.

Government transfer payments, which include unemployment and Social Security benefits, increased 0.4% in March to an adjusted $396.4 billion annual rate after rising 0.1% in February to an adjusted $394.9 billion pace.

Interest income rose 0.7% last month to an adjusted $380 billion annual rate after increasing 0.6% the month before to an adjusted $377.4 billion pace. Dividend income was unchanged in March from February at an adjusted $69.8 billion annual rate after rising 0.1% the month before.

The Wall Street Journal, *April 20, 1983.*

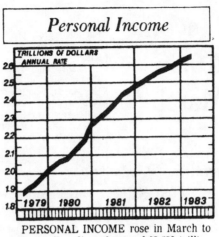

*Personal Income*

PERSONAL INCOME rose in March to a seasonally adjusted rate of $2.659 trillion from a revised $2.644 trillion a month earlier, the Commerce Department reports. (See story on page 3.)

The Wall Street Journal, *April 20, 1983.*

*Personal income . . . first paragraph*

WASHINGTON – The personal income of Americans grew 0.6% in March, the largest monthly gain since November, suggesting that retail sales may begin to strengthen in coming months.

Personal income is all the income we earn (wages, salaries, fringe benefits, profit, rent, interest, and so on) plus the transfer payments we receive (such as veterans' benefits, social security, unemployment compensation, and welfare), less the personal income taxes, social security taxes, and other taxes we pay to government. Therefore, the federal government's ability to borrow, and pay out to us in transfer payments more than it receives from us in taxes, gives it a cushion which keeps personal income growing even in recession when earned income is down. The huge federal deficits, due to the recent tax cuts, have helped maintain personal income's growth trend despite heavy unemployment. This has kept a floor under personal consumption expenditures.

For this reason, as you can see from the chart accompanying the *Journal* article, and from the historical data too (Chart 6 on page 101), personal income has grown so steadily that it is difficult to

**Chart 6**
**Personal Income**

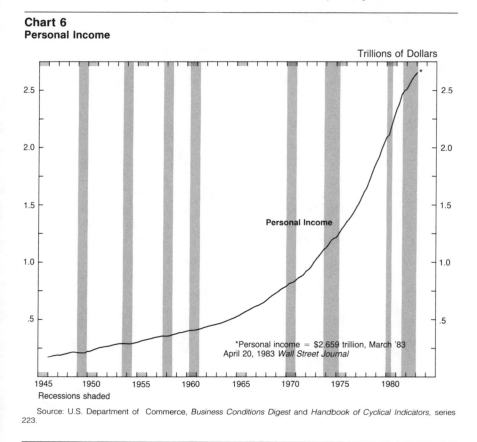

Trillions of Dollars

*Personal income = $2.659 trillion, March '83
April 20, 1983 *Wall Street Journal*

1945    1950    1955    1960    1965    1970    1975    1980
Recessions shaded

Source: U.S. Department of  Commerce, *Business Conditions Digest* and *Handbook of Cyclical Indicators,* series 223.

use as a cyclical indicator. As a first step in improving its usefulness, you would have to adjust it for inflation in order to ascertain
trends in real income. But this brings the analysis back to the earlier discussion about the CPI and real income's impact on consumer sentiment. Use the CPI as your test for consumer sentiment,
because the two series move in opposite directions.

The relationship between the CPI, real income, and consumer
sentiment is the mechanism linking the recession's reduced inflation rate to the subsequent economic recovery. You know from the
previous chapter's discussion of the first phase of the business cycle
(from trough to recovery) that productivity improves in recession
and that declining costs drive down the inflation rate as measured
by the Producer Price Index. This decline is reflected in the CPI, and
consumer real income improves, lifting consumer sentiment. What
an irony that the consumer must wait for recession (and hope not to
join the unemployed) to boost his or her purchasing power, and only
then regains the confidence to resume spending.

Consumer spending's resurgence propels the cycle's second phase (from recovery to expansion). Once the consumer resumes borrowing and spending, all components of demand will eventually advance, propelling the economy's expansion. Therefore, it's time to consider the most important indicators of consumer demand.

## CONSUMER DEMAND

Each month *The Wall Street Journal* publishes articles on four indicators of consumer demand: auto sales, consumer credit, retail sales, and housing starts. Examine each in turn.

Around the fifth of each month, *The Wall Street Journal* publishes *automobile sales* data compiled by the manufacturers, such as this May 5, 1983, report.

# Auto Sales Rose By 14.3% in April From a Slow '82

## Chrysler Big-Car Deliveries Helped Domestic Makers Register a 15.7% Advance

*By a* WALL STREET JOURNAL *Staff Reporter*

DETROIT—Aided by a surge in big-car deliveries by Chrysler Corp., auto sales rose 14.3% in April to 763,188 units from an anemic 667,630 a year earlier. April 1982 was one of the poorest months of the recession for car sales.

Sales of domestic cars rose 15.7% to 576,688 units, and a Wall Street Journal survey of leading importers indicated a 10% rise in sales of imported cars to about 186,500 units. The increases were about what Detroit's industry observers expected.

Among domestic auto makers, Chrysler reported a 32.6% sales increase in April to 78,355 units. General Motors Corp. sales rose 15.4% to 354,804; Ford Motor Co. sales were up 3% to 117,282; and American Motors Corp. sales advanced 132.5% to 19,518. Volkswagen of America Inc.'s domestic sales declined 31.3% to 6,725 units.

### Late Chrysler Surge

Chrysler's sales appeared even stronger for the final third of April. The No. 3 U.S. auto maker sold 33,596 cars in late April, a 63.6% gain from a year earlier and an unusually strong 15% of the domestic market. Total domestic sales rose 11.7% in late April to 229,446 units. Chrysler attributed much of its increase to a 70% rise in April deliveries of its New Yorker Fifth Avenue model, a luxury car based on an old rear-drive design.

"We can't get enough of that car," said William Stone, sales manager at a Houston Chrysler dealership. "I've more than doubled the inventory of all the cars I carry over what I've had during the last two or three years" to keep up with orders, he said.

Chrysler's success with the model reflects a recent resurgence in big-car popularity. Lower gasoline prices removed the compulsion many car-buyers felt the past few years to buy smaller, more fuel-efficient models. In addition, growing signs of economic recovery are starting to bring more of the traditional buyers of large American cars back into the market, observers say.

### Off the Sidelines

"The people who were standing on the sidelines were your domestic-type buyers," who tend to prefer bigger cars built by U.S.

auto companies, said J. David Power, head of a Los Angeles market-research firm. As the economy has begun to improve, such buyers have begun to return to dealer showrooms, Mr. Power said recent surveys show.

This is particularly helping Chrysler, he said, because the No. 3 auto maker's reputation recently has soared relative to the reputations of its domestic competitors. Chrysler Chairman Lee A. Iacocca's aggressive television ads also have helped, Mr. Power said.

Chrysler added that sales of its new E-cars, a group of luxury front-drive models that it didn't have last year, augmented its April comparisons with 1982. The company further pointed out that the addition of 48 dealers this year accounted for about 4,000 April deliveries, or about 5% of the total.

Chrysler's second-quarter production plans indicate that managers believe its sales successes will continue. While the total domestic industry scheduled a 15% production increase for the current quarter, Chrysler set a 69% increase from a conservative production schedule a year ago.

Much of Chrysler's sales gain in April seemed to come at Ford's expense. A Ford spokesman pointed out that the No. 2 auto maker's dealers essentially have run out of compact Fairmont and Zephyr models, which are being discontinued. Tempo and Topaz models, the front-drive compact replacements, don't go on sale until late this month.

Overall, domestic sales in April were up only slightly from the relatively sluggish pace of recent months. On a seasonally adjusted basis, April sales were equivalent to an annual rate of about 6.3 million units. In the first quarter, the annual sales rate was about six million units. Last April, domestic cars sold at an annual rate of 5.4 million units.

Import sales were equivalent to an annual rate of about 2.1 million units, down slightly from a March pace of about 2.2 million. Total industry sales in April were at an annual rate of 8.4 million units, up slightly from March's 8.2 million-unit rate.

Detroit observers generally expect deliveries this month to continue at about the same 6.3 million-unit annual pace. If they prove right, May sales will be about even with year-earlier sales or perhaps down slightly. After last April's plunge, the industry bolstered May sales a year ago with a round of price promotions. Industry observers currently are predicting a slow, steady recovery in car sales for the next several months as the economy strengthens.

In late April, GM reported a 4.9% sales increase to 136,175 units; Ford, a 2.6% increase to 48,285; and AMC had an estimated 139.9% increase to 7,668. AMC's surge reflects the addition of the popular subcompact front-drive Renault Alliance and the phasing out of its outmoded rear-drive products. VW's sales of domestic units in late April declined 22.6% to 3,722 units.

## Auto Sales Statistics

### Percentage of Total U.S. Market

| | April 1983 | April 1982 |
|---|---|---|
| xGeneral Motors | 46.5 | 46.1 |
| xFord | 15.3 | 17.0 |
| xChrysler | 10.3 | 8.0 |
| American Motors | 2.5 | 1.3 |
| Toyota | 5.2 | 6.1 |
| Datsun | 5.4 | 4.3 |
| xVolkswagen | 0.9 | 1.5 |
| Honda | 4.0 | 4.6 |
| Other imports | 9.9 | 10.3 |
| Total domestic | 75.6 | 74.7 |
| Total imported | 24.4 | 25.3 |

x-Excludes foreign cars sold by these makers.

| | April 21-30 1983 | April 21-30 1982 | %Chg. |
|---|---|---|---|
| **GENERAL MOTORS CORP.** | | | |
| Chevrolet Div. | 47,634 | 45,209 | + 5.4 |
| Pontiac Div. | 16,126 | 15,687 | + 2.8 |
| Oldsmobile Div. | 33,225 | 32,704 | + 1.6 |
| Buick Div. | 30,047 | 27,909 | + 7.7 |
| Cadillac Div. | 9,143 | 8,285 | + 10.4 |
| Total cars | 136,175 | 129,796 | + 4.9 |
| **FORD MOTOR CO.** | | | |
| Ford Div. | 30,668 | 29,976 | + 2.3 |
| Lincoln-Mercury Div. | 17,617 | 17,093 | + 3.1 |
| Total cars | 48,285 | 47,069 | + 2.6 |
| **CHRYSLER CORP.** | | | |
| Chry-Plym Div. | 20,610 | 13,129 | + 57.0 |
| Dodge Div. | 12,986 | 7,406 | + 75.3 |
| Total cars | 33,596 | 20,535 | + 63.6 |
| **VOLKSWAGEN** | | | |
| Total cars | 3,722 | 4,810 | − 22.6 |
| **AMERICAN MOTORS CORP.** | | | |
| Total cars | e7,668 | e3,196 | + 139.9 |
| **U.S. INDUSTRY** | | | |
| Total cars | e229,446 | e205,404 | + 11.7 |

### Percentage of market (excluding imports)

| | 1983 Period | 1982 Period |
|---|---|---|
| General Motors | 59.4 | 63.2 |
| Ford Motor | 21.1 | 22.9 |
| Chrysler | 14.6 | 10.0 |
| Volkswagen | 1.6 | 2.3 |
| American Motors | 3.3 | 1.6 |

e-Estimate.

| | April 1983 | 1982 | %Chg. |
|---|---|---|---|
| **GENERAL MOTORS CORP.** | | | |
| Chevrolet Div. | 120,221 | 107,229 | + 12.1 |
| Pontiac Div. | 41,766 | 40,542 | + 3.0 |
| Oldsmobile Div. | 87,588 | 75,307 | + 16.3 |
| Buick Div. | 80,646 | 63,965 | + 26.1 |
| Cadillac Div. | 24,583 | 20,488 | + 20.0 |
| Total cars | 354,804 | 307,531 | + 15.4 |
| **FORD MOTOR CO.** | | | |
| Ford Div. | 76,897 | 76,097 | + 1.1 |
| Lincoln-Mercury Div. | 40,385 | 37,718 | + 7.1 |
| Total cars | 117,282 | 113,815 | + 3.0 |
| **CHRYSLER CORP.** | | | |
| Chry-Plym Div. | 49,974 | 37,779 | + 32.3 |
| Dodge Div. | 28,381 | 21,322 | + 33.1 |
| Total cars | 78,355 | 59,101 | + 32.6 |
| **VOLKSWAGEN** | | | |
| Total cars | 6,725 | 9,787 | − 31.3 |
| **AMERICAN MOTORS CORP.** | | | |
| Total cars | e19,518 | e8,396 | + 132.5 |
| **U.S. INDUSTRY** | | | |
| Total cars | e576,688 | e498,630 | + 15.7 |

### Percentage of market (excluding imports)

| | 1983 Period | 1982 Period |
|---|---|---|
| General Motors | 61.5 | 61.7 |
| Ford Motor | 20.3 | 22.8 |
| Chrysler | 13.6 | 11.8 |
| Volkswagen | 1.2 | 2.0 |
| American Motors | 3.4 | 1.7 |

e-Estimate.

### Retail Sales of Leading Imports

| | | Apr. '83 | Apr. '82 | % Chg. | 4 Mos. 1983 | 4 Mos. 1982 |
|---|---|---|---|---|---|---|
| a-Make | | | | | | |
| Toyota | | 39,530 | 40,964 | − 3.5 | 175,484 | 167,117 |
| Datsun | | 41,111 | 28,448 | + 44.5 | 174,844 | 144,113 |
| Honda | | 30,503 | 30,936 | − 1.4 | 124,017 | 125,196 |
| Mazda | | 13,817 | 12,448 | + 11.0 | 59,200 | 50,854 |
| Subaru | | 13,452 | 11,667 | + 15.3 | 52,094 | 49,319 |
| Chrysler | | 6,913 | 5,411 | + 27.8 | 29,893 | 23,636 |
| Volvo | | 7,909 | 7,247 | + 9.1 | 30,410 | 27,013 |
| Volkswagen | | 5,870 | 5,680 | + 3.3 | 26,603 | 21,293 |
| Mercedes | | 6,100 | 5,685 | + 8.8 | 21,788 | 19,933 |
| Porsche-Audi | | 5,757 | 5,166 | + 11.4 | 19,994 | 19,210 |
| BMW | | 3,334 | 4,234 | − 21.3 | 15,941 | 15,788 |
| Renault | | 3,602 | 4,482 | − 31.2 | 9,012 | 11,933 |
| Saab | | 2,744 | 1,513 | + 81.4 | 8,486 | 5,417 |
| Isuzu | | 989 | 1,020 | − 3.0 | 6,657 | 6,467 |
| Fiat | | 1,093 | 1,953 | − 68.4 | 2,541 | 6,824 |
| Peugeot | | 1,092 | 1,383 | − 14.8 | 4,817 | 4,599 |
| Jaguar | | 1,536 | 933 | + 64.6 | 4,494 | 2,778 |
| Mitsubishi | | 1,858 | | | 7,091 | |

a-Ranked by sales for the year to date.

*Comparison with same month, one year ago . . . first paragraph*

DETROIT—Aided by a surge in big-car deliveries by Chrysler Corp., auto sales rose 14.3% in April to 763,188 units from an anemic 667,630 a year earlier. April 1982 was one of the poorest months of the recession for car sales.

*Seasonally adjusted annual data . . . third and fourth paragraphs from end of article*

Overall, domestic sales in April were up only slightly from the relatively sluggish pace of recent months. On a seasonally adjusted basis, April sales were equivalent to an annual rate of about 6.3 million units. In the first quarter, the annual sales rate was about six million units. Last April, domestic cars sold at an annual rate of 5.4 million units.

Import sales were equivalent to an annual rate of about 2.1 million units, down slightly from a March pace of about 2.2 million. Total industry sales in April were at an annual rate of 8.4 million units, up slightly from March's 8.2 million-unit rate.

The 14.3 percent increase reported in the headline and *first paragraph* compares all auto sales with auto sales the same month one year ago. But you need *seasonally adjusted data at an annual rate* to make a comparison with recent months as well as years past. Thus, the *fourth paragraph from the end of the article* reports the April rate of 6.3 million domestically produced automobiles as substantially higher than the previous April's 5.4 million figure. By using the figures on imports and total sales in the *third paragraph from the end*, you can calculate that the 6.3 million figure for April was slightly better than the 6.0 million total for March (8.2 million less 2.2 million). Picture this number on Chart 7. (See Chart 7 on page 105 and Chart 8 on page 106.)

The well-equipped auto, like the well-equipped home, has been a symbol of the American consumer economy since the 1920s. Other countries have copied it, and have even outdone us in some

**Chart 7**
**New Auto Sales, Domestic Type** (excluding imports)

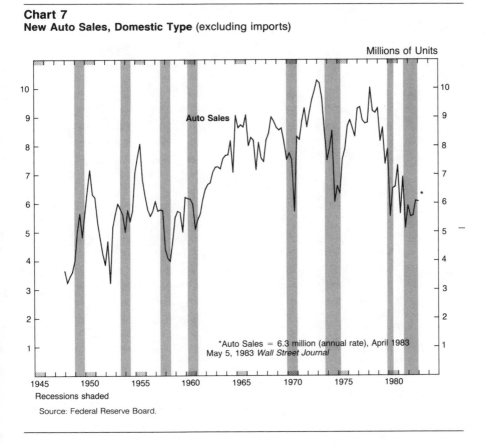

Millions of Units

*Auto Sales = 6.3 million (annual rate), April 1983
May 5, 1983 *Wall Street Journal*

Recessions shaded

Source: Federal Reserve Board.

respects, but we were first. In the effort to mass-merchandise this new convenience, Henry Ford reduced the price of a Model T to $300 in the early 1920s, and provided customers with any color they wanted, as long as it was black. It was General Motors that saw the profit potential in continually inflating the product by offering colors, options, and model changes and increased size, weight, and speed. GM took the sales lead from Ford, and from then on, competition in autos meant more (and different) car for more money, not the same car for a lower price. The option of less car for less money was eliminated until the German and Japanese imports arrived.

Ford had grafted 20th-century technology onto 19th-century marketing techniques, driven the price down as far as it could go, and seen sales go flat in the mid-1920s as the market was saturated. GM pioneered the 20th-century marketing technique of product inflation on a mass scale and gambled that the consumer would borrow ever more in order to buy next year's model.

**Chart 8**
**Personal Consumption Expenditures on Automobiles**

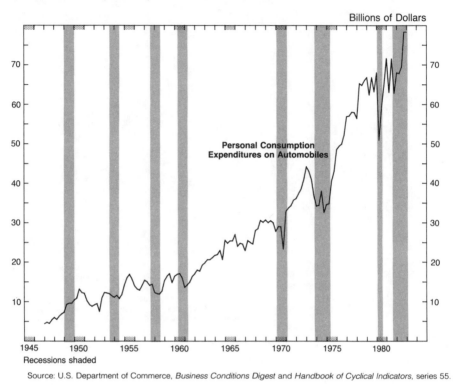

Source: U.S. Department of Commerce, *Business Conditions Digest* and *Handbook of Cyclical Indicators,* series 55.

Product inflation boosts sales by cajoling the consumer into buying something new at a higher price. The customer isn't swindled, just convinced by marketing and advertising techniques that he or she needs an improved product for more money. Planned obsolescence is a corollary, because style and model changes, as well as product improvement, aid in persuading the consumer that the present (and still serviceable) model should be replaced with a better, more expensive model, not a lower-cost repeat of the old model.

That set the pattern for American marketing of consumer goods. You can see it in your kitchen, laundry room, and living room, not just your driveway. TV replaced radio, color TV replaced black-and-white TV, and videotape recorders and video-game hookups are now required accessories for many. Price went up, and so did debt.

Glance at the auto sales charts. You can see the record sales volume of the 1970s, which looks even more impressive in dollar terms. Part of the growth since the 1950s was pure price inflation, but some was product inflation.

You can also see that auto sales were a leading indicator of economic activity, turning down as soon as escalating inflation eroded consumer sentiment and recovering quickly when inflation subsided and consumer sentiment improved. The figures reported in the May 5, 1983 *Journal* article confirm this.

However, auto sales are expanding far more slowly this time than after earlier recessions, and some say the American automobile industry will not recover. Product inflation was pushed too far; the love affair is over; fuel is too expensive; the Japanese and Germans do a better job; and so forth. Perhaps. Yet it was not until after World War II that auto sales surpassed rates achieved in the 1920s. The American auto industry has been counted out before, and then revived. It remains to be seen whether this is a mature industry with no further prospects of expansion.

*The Wall Street Journal* publishes the Commerce Department's release on *consumer installment debt* in the second week of the month. The headline and *first paragraph* of the April 12, 1983, *Journal* article provides the figure you need. Changes in consumer credit are an important barometer of consumer activity because consumers borrow heavily to finance purchases of autos and other expensive and postponable items, such as household appliances, furniture, and furnishings. (See page 108.)

# Consumer Debt Expanded $1.74 Billion In February, Weakest Gain Since October

*By a* WALL STREET JOURNAL *Staff Reporter*

Consumer Credit {

WASHINGTON — Consumer installment credit expanded a seasonally adjusted $1.74 billion in February, or at a 6.1% annual rate, the Federal Reserve Board reported.

The February increase followed a rise of an adjusted $2.93 billion, or 10.4% at an annual rate, in January, the Fed said.

The February performance was the weakest since October, when consumer credit contracted an adjusted $131 million. A Fed analyst called the February rise "moderate, at best."

Still, he contended that it wasn't "particularly significant" that the February increase was smaller than the January rise, which was unusually robust. And he noted that the performance for the November-February period was "considerably stronger" than that of the previous four months.

The Fed has stopped providing information on new credit extended or on repayments, so it isn't possible to determine what caused the debt expansion or contraction in any given month.

The report showed that auto credit outstanding rose an adjusted $185 million in February after increasing $233 million in January. Revolving credit outstanding, which includes retail, gasoline and bank credit cards, fell an adjusted $6 million in February after rising $68 million in January. Mobile-home credit outstanding expanded an adjusted $215 million in February after increasing $444 million in January.

For the second consecutive month, the Fed said, the miscellaneous credit category showed the strongest rate of growth. Miscellaneous credit, which covers other consumer debt, increased an adjusted $1.35 billion in February after rising $2.18 billion in January. The Fed attributed the February increase to personal cash loans and to sales finance contracts for goods such as furniture and large appliances.

At the end of February, consumer installment debt stood at $344 billion, up 4.6% from a year earlier.

The Wall Street Journal, *April 12, 1983.*

*Consumer credit . . . first paragraph*

WASHINGTON — Consumer installment credit expanded a seasonally adjusted $1.74 billion in February, or at a 6.1% annual rate, the Federal Reserve Board reported.

Now multiply the $1.74 billion reported in the *first paragraph* of the *Journal* article by 12 (slightly more than $20 billion) to determine the annual rate and update Chart 9 on page 109 with that figure.

Consumer credit rose gradually and cyclically until the 1970s. Then it exploded. You can see the cyclical maximum of $10 billion in the late 60s, $20 billion in the early 70s, and $50 billion in the

## Chart 9
### Change in Consumer Installment Credit

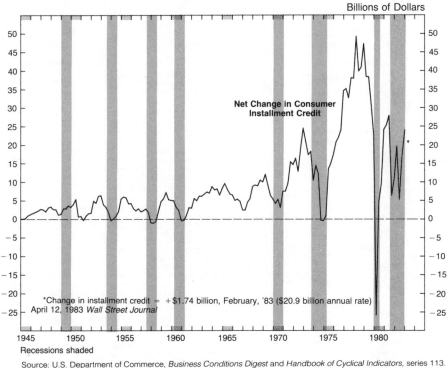

Billions of Dollars

Net Change in Consumer
Installment Credit

*Change in installment credit = +$1.74 billion, February, '83 ($20.9 billion annual rate)
April 12, 1983 *Wall Street Journal*

Recessions shaded

Source: U.S. Department of Commerce, *Business Conditions Digest* and *Handbook of Cyclical Indicators,* series 113.

late 70s. It's amazing that inflation was not more severe in the face of this stimulus to demand.

You can also see the cyclical sensitivity of consumer credit and its reaction to changes in consumer sentiment. Increases in consumer credit trailed off with the surge of inflation in the late 60s and 1973–74. It remained surprisingly strong in the late 1970s, though the pace of growth stalled during the severe inflation of 1979. Then, with each recession and the return of consumer confidence, consumer credit rebounded.

Until recently, consumer credit was notoriously impervious to the long-run rise in interest rates since World War II. Consumers were primarily concerned with the size of monthly payments, and stretching out the term of the loan was usually regarded as sufficient to mitigate the steady rise in the interest rate. But this piece of conventional wisdom went out the window with the Fed's 1981 tight money policy. Monthly payments became so large that many consumers were forced to forsake consumer credit and postpone purchases of autos and other expensive items. Only recently have lowered interest rates and reduced inflation contributed to the resurgence of consumer sentiment and the increased use of credit.

The U.S. Department of Commerce's monthly release on *retail sales* appears in *The Wall Street Journal* around the second week. You can see from the headline, *first paragraph*, and accompanying chart of the May 12, 1983, article that retail sales began to recover around the beginning of 1982. This series was one of the earliest indicators of recovery.

---

# Retail Sales Rose Strong 1.6% in April

## Gain Is Best Evidence Yet Of a Stronger Recovery; Consumer Credit Expands

By Eileen Alt Powell
*Staff Reporter of* The Wall Street Journal

etail
ales
WASHINGTON — U.S. retail sales increased a strong 1.6% last month after a 1.7% rise in March, providing the best evidence to date that the recovery will gain strength through the summer.

The Commerce Department said sales rose to a seasonally adjusted $94.22 billion in April from a revised $92.74 billion in March. (See chart on Page 1.) The March increase earlier had been estimated as 0.3%, but was raised to reflect greater strength in sales of building materials, automotive products and home furnishings.

The two strong advances in retail sales followed three consecutive monthly declines that had led some economists to worry that sluggish consumer spending would inhibit the nation's recovery from the 1981-82 recession. In fact, the improved sales picture suggests that the nation can expect further increases in factory production and employment in the current quarter, resulting in higher overall economic growth than in the first period.

Separately, the Federal Reserve Board said that consumer installment debt expanded an adjusted $2.58 billion, or 9% at an annual rate, in March after rising $735 mil-

lion, or 2.6% at an annual rate, the month before. The report said that credit expanded at a 7% annual pace in the January-March quarter, considerably stronger than the 4% growth for all of 1982.

**Vigor in Consumer Sector**

Robert Dederick, commerce undersecretary for economic affairs, hailed the latest retail sales figures as "clear evidence of renewed vigor in the consumer sector." He attributed the strength to recent gains in employment and after-tax income and suggested that these, along with the scheduled July 1 cut in income tax rates, will create a "highly favorable" climate for further spending gains.

Private economists were equally enthusiastic.

James Fralick, a vice president for economics at Morgan Guaranty Trust Co. of New York, called the latest reports "just super." Although Mr. Fralick expects sales to be stronger in the current quarter than in the first period, he argues that the tax-rate cut scheduled for July "remains necessary to keep sales going into the second half of the year." Some in Congress have suggested eliminating or reducing the tax-rate cut to help hold down federal budget deficits.

At Chase Econometrics in Bala Cynwyd, Pa., economist Ralph Semprevio says that "the sales figures are telling us that the economy is turning around much better than we would have thought a month ago." But while he expects industries to respond by increasing production to rebuild inventories, he expects a slower buildup than in previous recoveries because of still-high interest rates and business caution in the wake of two recessions.

The latest retail sales report shows that the April gains were broad-based. The figures aren't adjusted for inflation but would show increases even if price changes were taken into account, economists said.

Excluding autos, total retail sales in April increased 0.7% to an adjusted $76.61 billion after rising 0.5% in March to an ad-

justed $76.05 billion. Sales by automotive dealers rose 5.5% in April to an adjusted $17.61 billion after increasing 7.7% the month before to an adjusted $16.69 billion.

**Durable Goods**

Sales at stores specializing in durable goods, which are items such as construction materials and home furnishings that last more than three years, rose 4% last month to an adjusted $29.99 billion after increasing 4.9% in March to an adjusted $28.84 billion.

Sales at stores specializing in nondurables, which are items such as food and apparel that have a usefulness of less than three years, rose 0.5% in April to an adjusted $64.23 billion after increasing 0.4% the month before to an adjusted $63.9 billion.

Total sales last month were up 6.5% from April 1982, with durable goods up 12.2% and nondurables sales up 4%.

The Fed's report showed that the March expansion in consumer installment debt approached the January debt increase of $2.73 billion, or 9.6% at an annual rate. January's rise was the largest since the increase of $2.89 billion in September 1981.

The report doesn't provide information on new credit extended or on repayments. Thus, it isn't possible to determine the reason for debt expansion or contraction in any given month.

Auto credit outstanding increased an adjusted $1.22 billion in March after falling $233 million in the previous month. Revolving credit, which includes retail and bank-card borrowing, rose an adjusted $1.18 billion in March after declining $135 million in February.

Mobile-home credit contracted an adjusted $61 million in March after increasing $204 million in February. And the miscellaneous credit category, which covers cash loans and certain retail financial contracts, expanded an adjusted $245 million in March after rising $899 million in February.

At the end of March, consumer installment debt stood at $342.57 billion, up 5% from a year earlier.

The Wall Street Journal, *May 12, 1983.*

## Retail Sales

BILLIONS OF DOLLARS

RETAIL SALES rose in April to a seasonally adjusted $94.22 billion from a revised $92.74 billion in March, the Commerce Department reports. (See story on page 3)

The Wall Street Journal, *May 12, 1983.*

*Retail sales . . . first paragraph*

WASHINGTON — U.S. retail sales increased a strong 1.6% last month after a 1.7% rise in March, providing the best evidence to date that the recovery will gain strength through the summer.

However, you can see from the historical chart (Chart 10, page 112) that retail sales has not been a volatile series and that using retail sales to trace the course of the business cycle is not as easy as using auto sales or consumer credit.

The Commerce Department's monthly release on *housing starts* is usually published in *The Wall Street Journal* between the 17th and the 20th of the month. Always direct your attention to the seasonally adjusted monthly figure, presented at an annual rate. The *second paragraph* and the chart accompanying the May 18, 1983, story tells you that there were 1.5 million home and apartment unit construction starts in March. (See pages 113 and 114.)

**Chart 10**
**Retail Sales**

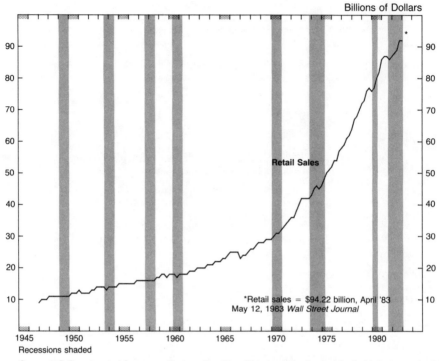

Billions of Dollars

*Retail sales = $94.22 billion, April '83
May 12, 1983 *Wall Street Journal*

Retail Sales

Recessions shaded

Source: U.S. Department of Commerce, *Business Conditions Digest* and *Handbook of Cyclical Indicators*, series 54.

# Housing Starts Fell 8.4% in April, But Permits Rose

## Weather Cited in Second Drop In Row; Builders, Realtors Say Recovery Continuing

*By a* WALL STREET JOURNAL *Staff Reporter*

WASHINGTON—Housing starts declined for the second month in a row in April as wet weather hampered construction. But building permits—a sign of future home construction—reached a 43-month high.

Work began on new houses last month at a seasonally adjusted annual rate of 1,490,000 units, down 8.4% from the annual pace of 1,627,000 (Chart on Page 1). Starts in March were down 8.8% from February. The April rate was 63.6% above the recession level of 911,000 units of a year earlier, the Commerce Department said. Last month's decline occurred in every region of the country.

Referring to the widespread heavy rainfall, Michael Sumichrast, chief economist of the National Association of Home Builders, said, "The most expensive thing for a builder is to push mud." He said he considers the April figure a "good" number despite the further decline.

Despite the two-month-long dropoff, housing starts this year have surged 76% from a

year earlier, to 458,000 units from 260,800. Kenneth Kerin, economist at the National Association of Realtors, said the recent decline in activity wasn't surprising and noted that analysts thought the big leap earlier in the year wasn't sustainable. Starts rose 32.3% in January from December and by a further 5% in February.

"The housing recovery is still in pretty good shape," he said.

One reason for the optimism is the 6.5% increase in April building permits, to an adjusted annual rate of 1,563,000 units. That is the highest level since September 1979, when permits were issued at a 1,638,000-unit annual pace. The April level was 89% above a year earlier.

Last month's level of permits, said Mr. Kerin, "makes us feel comfortable that we'll still see the housing recovery unfold." Mr. Sumichrast said the figure suggests that housing starts could reach the 1.8 million annual level soon.

However, analysts are concerned about several things. Mr. Kerin said he is "worried" that interest rates may begin to rise late in the year as demands for credit for purposes other than housing "start to pinch upon the mortgage market."

Michael Berliner, a senior economist with Chase Econometrics, said he is disturbed by an apparent drop in the number of households forming, which could hurt housing activity, and by a decline in demand for apartments.

In April, starts of multifamily units plunged 16.1% to a 507,000-unit annual rate. Starts for single-family houses fell 3.9% to 983,000 a year. Most economists predict that starts this year will be in the 1.5 million to 1.6 million range, up from 1,062,200 last year.

The Wall Street Journal, *May 18, 1983.*

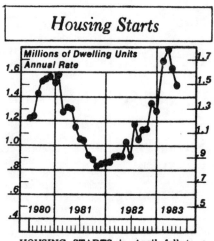

## Housing Starts

Millions of Dwelling Units
Annual Rate

1980   1981   1982   1983

HOUSING STARTS in April fell to a seasonally adjusted annual rate of 1,490,000 units from a revised 1,627,000 units in March, the Commerce Department reports. (See story on Page 6)

The Wall Street Journal, *May 18, 1983.*

*Housing starts . . . second paragraph*

Work began on new houses last month at a seasonally adjusted annual rate of 1,490,-000 units, down 8.4% from the annual pace of 1,627,000 (Chart on Page 1). Starts in March were down 8.8% from February. The April rate was 63.6% above the recession level of 911,000 units of a year earlier, the Commerce Department said. Last month's decline occurred in every region of the country.

You can see the record levels of housing starts in the 1970s (Chart 11 on page 115), but the growth of mortgage borrowing is even more impressive (see Chart 12 on page 116). That growth reflects the increased dollar volume of building activity due to the steep rise in housing prices. It also demonstrates the crucial role of credit in sustaining recent levels of housing activity. In the 1950s and 1960s, anything over $20 billion was a good year. Then mortgage borrowing reached $60 billion in the boom of the early 70s and $100 billion in the late 70s. Inflation, propelled by these record levels of borrowing, became an irresistible force.

**Chart 11**
**Housing Starts**

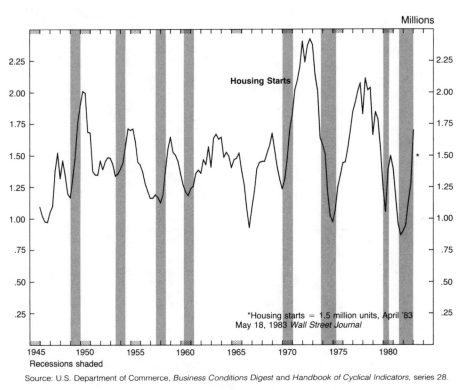

Millions

*Housing starts = 1.5 million units, April '83
May 18, 1983 *Wall Street Journal*

1945    1950    1955    1960    1965    1970    1975    1980
Recessions shaded

Source: U.S. Department of Commerce, *Business Conditions Digest* and *Handbook of Cyclical Indicators*, series 28.

The cyclical sensitivity of housing starts to consumer sentiment and the availability of mortgage credit is equally striking. Housing starts turned down well before the onset of recession, as soon as rising inflation reduced consumer confidence and the Fed slammed on the brakes, drying up mortgage credit. But you can see that they turned up even before the recession ended as consumer confidence returned with the decline of inflation and the Fed's switch to an easy money policy.

The impact of the Fed's recent tight money policy on mortgage rates has been equally dramatic. The Fed's policy put a new home beyond the reach of most consumers, and mortgage borrowing and housing starts plunged. Although housing starts and mortgage borrowing have risen once again since the Fed's policies have eased and consumer sentiment has improved, it remains to be seen whether both figures will soon reach the heights of the 1970s. If the Fed maintains restraint and mortgage interest rates stay in double digits, it may be a long time before 1972's record level of housing starts is broken.

**Chart 12**
**Net Change in Mortgage Debt**

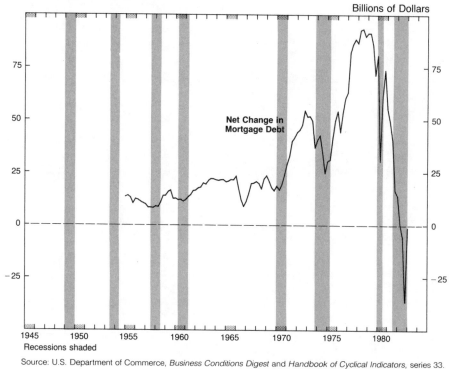

Billions of Dollars

Net Change in
Mortgage Debt

1945    1950    1955    1960    1965    1970    1975    1980
Recessions shaded

Source: U.S. Department of Commerce, *Business Conditions Digest* and *Handbook of Cyclical Indicators*, series 33.

In conclusion, the modern American economy has come to depend on product inflation and ever-larger volumes of debt. These
sustain the growth in demand required to maintain production and
income at adequate levels. Moreover, consumer debt and consumer
demand have been the leading edge of the post–World War II business cycle. Ironically, their strong growth led to cyclical problems
with inflation, which eventually became chronic, and tended to
choke off credit, demand, and economic expansion.

The business cycle resumed its course after each recession, because of the temporary reduction in the rate of inflation. Reduced
inflation encouraged consumers to indulge in a new wave of borrowing and spending, launching another cycle and another round
of inflation.

In this chapter, you have observed the outlines of this process
and you have followed the cycle's second phase (from recovery to
expansion) as a chain of events leading from lowered rates of inflation to the expansion of consumer demand.

*CPI* ↓ → *Consumer real income* ↑ → *Consumer sentiment* ↑ →
*Consumer demand* ↑ *(Auto sales* ↑ + *Consumer credit* ↑ + *Re-tail sales* ↑ + *Housing starts* ↑*).*

The 1970s epitomized the process, encouraged by the Fed's alternating tight and easy money policies. Following each recession, the Fed permitted the banks to pump huge amounts of credit into the system, encouraging an explosion of borrowing and demand. Then, as the economy overheated and inflation raced ahead, the Fed slammed on the brakes, contributing to the next recession.

The latest data on auto sales, consumer credit, retail sales, and housing starts provides evidence that the second phase of the cycle has begun, that the economy is moving from recovery to expansion. Since inflation has fallen sharply and consumers were restrained for two years by the Fed's 1981–82 tight money policy, the potential is present for explosive growth in consumer demand. Only if the Fed maintains a firm rein during this expansion can the excesses of the 1970s be avoided.

The economy is at an ironic turning point. The irony exists because so many want the Fed to open the floodgates and irrigate the expansion with abundant credit. Under these circumstances, demand will grow too quickly and too soon, and collapse under its own weight before its time. It would be far better to avoid the rapid growth of demand and the resurrection of inflation which killed all previous booms. If demand grows slowly because credit is restrained, the expansion will last longer and not be set back so severely by the next recession.

# CHAPTER EIGHT

## The Business Cycle
## Phase Three: From Expansion
## to Peak

If you ask a businessperson why prices rise, he or she will answer, "Rising costs," probably referring to personal experience. When you ask an economist the same question, the response will be, "Demand exceeds supply at current prices, and therefore prices rise," probably referring to the textbook case. These points of view seem to have nothing in common. Yet an analysis of economic expansion shows that they meld into a single explanation.

Currently, all the indicators of economic expansion—auto sales, consumer credit, retail sales, housing starts—are showing improvement. This will initiate broad-based growth as incomes increase in the construction, auto, and other durable goods industries, spilling over and boosting demand for other consumer goods. Boom conditions will intensify as business invests in additional factories and machinery to meet the rush in orders.

As the expansion unfolds, capacity utilization increases with the growth in demand and production. Soon factories move from, say, 70 percent to 90 percent of their rated maximum. Productive facilities strain to meet the demands and retain the loyalty of customers.

Next, high levels of capacity utilization drive labor productivity down and unit labor costs up as efficiency is sacrificed in the name of increased output. Machinery which is always in use cannot be adequately maintained and breaks down. Inexperienced workers cannot make the same contribution as old hands. The amount of labor employed increases more rapidly than output, and as output per worker falls, the labor cost per unit of output rises. This generates a surge in production costs.

Third, rapidly increasing costs are translated into rapidly increasing prices, and a renewed round of inflation begins.

This third phase of the cycle (from expansion to peak) is the inverse of the first. All the forces which led to a reduction in the rate of inflation are now reversed.

GNP ↑ → Industrial production ↑ → Capacity utilization ↑ → Labor productivity ↓ → Unit labor costs ↑ → Producer price index ↑.

So the practical (businessperson's) and the theoretical (economist's) explanations of inflation are not at odds. During expansion, demand bids production to a level which is inefficient and costly. The businessperson experiences the increased cost and attributes inflation directly to that experience. The economist sees increased demand as the ultimate cause of the production gain which drives costs up. Each explanation covers different aspects of the single phenomenon, economic expansion.

The late 1970s illuminates the process graphically. You will need the same statistical series employed in Chapter Six ("Phase One: From Trough to Recovery") to serve as illustrations because this phase of the cycle is the reverse of the first. Since this phase will occur in the future of the present cycle, however, you must return to an earlier cycle to find your examples. To illustrate expansion's impact on inflation, look at GNP, industrial production, capacity utilization, labor productivity and unit labor costs, and the Producer Price Index. Each of these statistical series has already been introduced, so clippings from The Wall Street Journal will not be presented again.


## THE 1975–1979 ECONOMIC EXPANSION

The 1974 recession set a record. GNP declined for four quarters, and industrial production tumbled 15 percent. By the spring of 1975 the unemployment rate was over 9 percent. Though recently eclipsed, it was a postwar record at the time.

Like all recessions, however, this one too prepared the way for the subsequent recovery. Capacity utilization fell to a postwar low, and labor productivity began to rise immediately. The resulting decline in unit labor costs cut the rate of inflation.

At the same time, the Federal Reserve System switched from a tight to easy money policy, reducing interest rates and providing ample credit. A sharp recovery and strong expansion began as the decline in the rate of inflation dramatically improved consumer real income and boosted consumer sentiment. At long last, consumers were pulling ahead of inflation; their pleasure was reflected in demand's rapid increase.

By 1977–78 new housing starts were 2 million annually and domestic automobile sales peaked at over 10 million. Retail sales and consumer credit provided further evidence of the escalating boom. Consumer installment borrowing hit annual rates of $50 billion, a record which has yet to be equaled.

The evidence of a robust economic expansion was all around as GNP and industrial production surged ahead. Rapid growth in demand, production, and capacity utilization had its inevitable result. The nation's factories and other productive facilities were strained. Increases in the labor force no longer made a proportional contribution to output. (See Chart 1 on page 121.)

In 1979 labor productivity stopped improving and began to fall. As a result, unit labor costs increased steadily, and by early 1980 the rate of inflation, as measured by the Producer Price Index, had reached 15 percent (see Chart 2 on page 122).

Declining labor productivity is the focal point of this analysis. Once output is pushed past the point of diminishing returns, unit labor costs become an inevitable problem. This has little to do with the wage rate. Unit labor costs will rise swiftly even if wage gains are well below the rate of inflation (that is, real wages are falling).

Falling real wages, coupled with the forward surge in labor costs, create one of the cruelest features of inflation. Because labor productivity has declined, there is less per capita output, and therefore less real income per person. Declining real income pits one segment of American society against another, fighting over a shrinking pie. Labor-management relations become especially bitter in this period of boom without prosperity. Employers blame workers' wages for rising labor costs and shrinking profits, while workers blame employers' profits for shrinking real wages, though neither is actually to blame for the other's misfortune.

In these times, the public's support for wage and price controls becomes insistent (although management has a greater interest in controlling wages and labor has a greater interest in controlling prices). Yet you can see from this chapter's analysis that rising costs due to reduced efficiency (falling labor productivity) are responsible for the increase in prices that captures everyone's attention. No one's greed is to blame. And therefore controls designed to limit greed are bound to be ineffective.

There have been two recent attempts at wage and price controls: the first under President Nixon in 1971–72 and the second under President Carter in 1979–80.

President Nixon's controls were certain to "succeed" because they were implemented during the transition from recovery to ex-

## Chart 1
**GNP, Industrial Production, Capacity Utilization, Labor Productivity, and Unit Labor Costs**

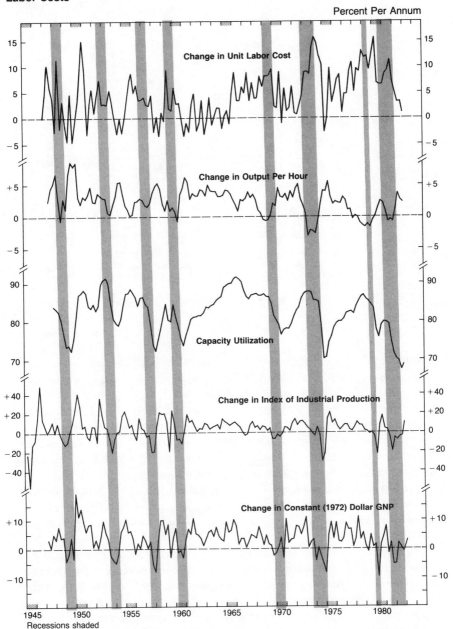

Percent Per Annum

Change in Unit Labor Cost

Change in Output Per Hour

Capacity Utilization

Change in Index of Industrial Production

Change in Constant (1972) Dollar GNP

Recessions shaded

Source: U.S. Department of Commerce, *Business Conditions Digest* and *Handbook of Cyclical Indicators*, series 47c, 50c, 82, and 370c; and Federal Reserve Board.

**Chart 2**
**Changes in Unit Labor Costs and Producer Prices**

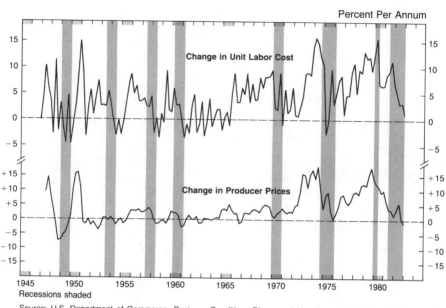

Source: U.S. Department of Commerce, *Business Conditions Digest* and *Handbook of Cyclical Indicators*, series 334c; and Federal Reserve Board.

pansion while capacity utilization was low and labor productivity high. As a result, the rate of inflation was still falling from its 1970 cyclical peak. It would have continued to decline in any event, and remained low until the expansion gained strength. The controls did slightly dampen inflation, but their impact was marginal.

President Carter's controls were bound to "fail," just as President Nixon's were bound to "succeed," because President Carter's were implemented during the virulent expansion of 1977–79. As labor productivity fell, and unit labor costs climbed, business merely passed its increased costs on to the consumer. Rising prices reflected rising costs, not greed, and business did not earn excess profits.

Keep in mind also that more stringent wage controls could not have restrained business costs. Some of the increase in unit labor costs was due to the increase in wage rates, but most of it was due to declining productivity caused by high capacity utilization. Workers were no more culpable than their employers.

This is an important point. We really can't blame the recent declines in labor productivity on the American worker, as some are prone to do. Lapses in productivity in the past decade occurred cyclically, when the economy overheated. Thus, these lapses really reflect the limitations of plant and equipment under extreme conditions rather than failures of diligence in the labor force.

And harking back to World War II for a workable example of wage and price controls is not the answer, either. Wage and price (and profit) controls worked then because the economy was on a war footing. About half of the economy's output was devoted to the war effort, much of it under a system of planning and direct resource allocation which operated outside ordinary market relationships. You couldn't bid up the price of a car (none were produced because the auto plants were converted to war production) or buy all the gasoline and steak you wanted (because these were rationed). And it's important to note that black markets arose to subvert the controls despite the patriotism aroused by the war effort. Therefore, it's doubtful whether such a system could work to contain peacetime inflation for which, unlike war-induced inflation, there is no end in sight.

Imposing wage and price controls during the expansionary phase of the business cycle is a little like trying to stop the rattle of a boiling kettle by taping down the lid. Demand heats the expansion, and inflation is the natural result. Turning down the heat is the only practical solution.

Finally, there's the question of "supply-side shocks." These are sudden increases in the price of important commodities (imposed by the sellers) or reductions in supply due to forces beyond our control. Some believe that much of our recent inflation is due to these shocks. This argument should be taken with a grain of salt. First, any explanation which places the blame on others should be suspect. If you wish to find fault, it is always best to look in the mirror. Second, neither OPEC, nor the Russian wheat deal, nor the failure of the Peruvian anchovy harvest can explain the price explosions of the 70s. If demand had been weak, prices would have remained stable. After all, prices stopped climbing as soon as recession hit.

Whether or not the current expansion will generate inflation as virulent as that of 1977–79 remains to be seen. It depends on the strength of the expansion. If demand increases rapidly, generating explosive growth in output and capacity utilization, be prepared for a sharp increase in costs and prices. On the other hand, leisurely growth in demand will prevent such a strain and limit inflation.

This chapter examined expansion's impact on costs and prices during the third phase of the business cycle. Now turn to the cycle's last phase, when expansion and inflation lead to the inevitable contraction.

# CHAPTER NINE

## The Business Cycle
## Phase Four: From Peak
## to Contraction

Is the next recession inevitable? Yes, because all economic expansions end in recession. Will the recession be mild or severe? That depends on the expansion. A strong and rapid expansion, driven by large increases in consumer and business borrowing, which ends in virulent inflation will produce a sharp and severe recession. A mild and gradual expansion, without excessive borrowing, which ends with only slight inflation will produce a mild recession.

Recall from the last chapter that economic expansion generates reduced efficiency and heightened inflation. As production grows, and with it capacity utilization, labor productivity falls. Labor costs increase, driving prices upward. The economy has reached a level of activity which cannot be sustained.

The fourth phase of the business cycle is the inverse of the second. In that phase of the cycle, from recovery to expansion, a declining rate of inflation pushed consumer real income upward, prompting consumers to borrow and spend, thus fueling the economic expansion. Now, in the last phase of the cycle, a rising rate of inflation has the opposite impact on the consumer. Real income falls, and consumer sentiment erodes. Consumers become pessimistic when their paychecks don't keep up with inflation, giving them less and less real buying power. They respond by restricting their purchase of deferrable items, especially those which require heavy borrowing. The downturn in consumer activity will lead to a general contraction in demand which will continue until the trough of the cycle is reached.

The root cause of the recession, declining productivity, which depressed real wages because rising costs spurred inflation, demands emphasis. It's an important point because some, as the last chapter noted, have incorrectly blamed rapidly rising wages for recent bouts of inflation. As a matter of fact, the charts demonstrate that real wages suffered, rather than improved, whenever inflation heated up. If rising wages had been responsible for inflation, real wages would have increased.

The 1980 recession is a good example. You will need the same statistical series developed in Chapter Seven to follow it. Inflation's impact on the consumer will be measured by the *Consumer Price Index (CPI)*, *real compensation*, and the *Index of Consumer Sentiment*. The contraction in consumer expenditures will be measured by the decline in *automobile sales, consumer credit, retail sales,* and *housing starts*.

As you know from Chapter Seven, with the exception of real compensation and consumer sentiment, which are reported only occasionally, articles covering all of these series appear regularly in *The Wall Street Journal*. Representative articles were treated in Chapter Seven; they need not be reproduced here. This discussion will be limited to an outline of the behavior of these series during the cycle's final phase, as summarized below.

CPI ↑ → *Consumer real income* ↓ → *Consumer sentiment* ↓ →
    *Consumer expenditures* ↓ *(Auto sales* ↓ + *Consumer credit* ↓
    + *Retail sales* ↓ + *Housing starts* ↓*).*

By late 1979 rapid increases in the Producer Price Index had pushed the rate of inflation, as measured by the Consumer Price Index, to 15 percent at an annual rate (see Chart 1, page 126).

Employee compensation was growing at 10 percent a year, but that was hardly enough to offset the effect of inflation. As you can see, real compensation fell by 5 percent, an even worse decline than in 1974 (see Chart 2, page 127).

The Index of Consumer Sentiment had fallen steadily through 1978 and 1979 as inflation surged upward. In late 1979 it matched 1974's dismal performance. Consumers were discouraged. Their take-home pay was losing the race with inflation, interest rates were high and rising, and relief was nowhere in sight. There was no cause for anything but pessimism.

Slumping auto sales and housing starts were the first omens of recession. Both declined throughout 1979. Housing starts fell from a 1.8 million annual rate to 1.4 million, and auto sales declined from 9 million to 7 million (see Chart 3, page 128, and Chart 4, page 129).

In the face of all this, consumer credit remained remarkably

**Chart 1**
**Change in Producer Prices and in Consumer Prices** (smoothed)

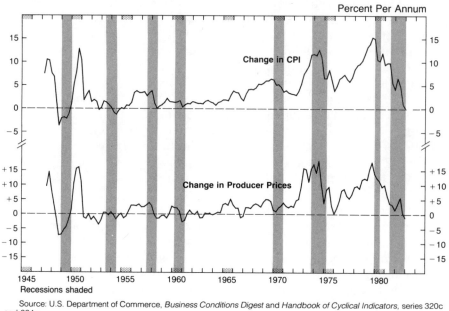

Percent Per Annum

Recessions shaded

Source: U.S. Department of Commerce, *Business Conditions Digest* and *Handbook of Cyclical Indicators*, series 320c and 334c.

strong in 1979, declining somewhat, but only slightly (see Chart 5, page 130). Retail sales continued to grow (see Chart 6, page 131).

Thus, 1980 began with most of the important leading indicators of consumer activity heading downward or showing weakness. They were beginning to drag the rest of the economy with them.

Interest rates and inflation hit record postwar highs in the first quarter of 1980. The Federal Reserve System clamped down hard on consumer credit, restricting its availability and raising interest rates even higher. This was the proverbial last straw, and in the second quarter consumer credit fell more steeply than at any other time in the postwar period. All consumer activities which had come to depend on consumer credit were affected. Auto sales, retail sales, and housing starts plunged. The Fed's action had brought the entire process to a head and hastened the recession that had been inevitable for over a year.

In summary, the developments were typical of the cycle's fourth phase (from peak to contraction). Rapidly rising inflation depressed consumer real income and consumer sentiment, bringing on a collapse in consumer demand.

There was no human villain in this drama. Blame the inanimate

**Chart 2**
**Index of Consumer Sentiment, Change in Real Average Hourly Compensation, and Change in CPI**

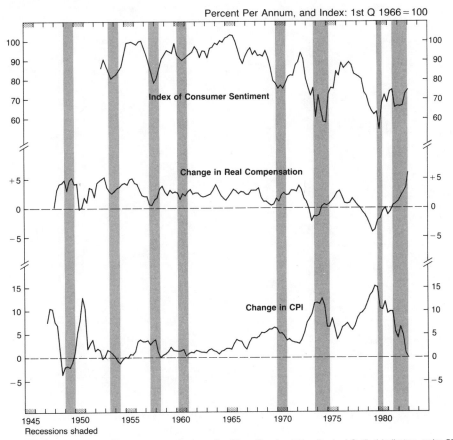

Percent Per Annum, and Index: 1st Q 1966 = 100

Index of Consumer Sentiment

Change in Real Compensation

Change in CPI

1945   1950   1955   1960   1965   1970   1975   1980
Recessions shaded

Source: U.S. Department of Commerce, *Business Conditions Digest* and *Handbook of Cyclical Indicators*, series 58, 320c, and 346c.

forces of credit and inflation, which periodically swept over the economy to leave recession's wreckage behind. The Fed finally came to grips with the problem in 1981, when in its attempt to bring inflation under control, it tightened credit sufficiently to turn recovery into recession. That is why the 1980 recession, rather than the 1981–82 experience, was used as an illustration of the cycle's fourth phase. The most recent recession was engineered by the Fed to reduce inflation, while the recession of 1980 was a more natural outcome of cyclical developments.

Although all factors of production bore the burden of inflation in

**Chart 3**
**New Auto Sales, Domestic Type** (excluding imports)

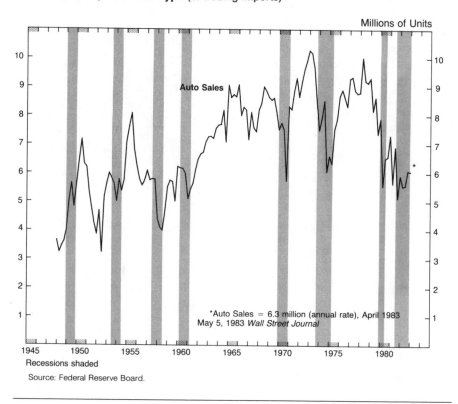

Millions of Units

Auto Sales

*Auto Sales = 6.3 million (annual rate), April 1983
May 5, 1983 *Wall Street Journal*

1945    1950    1955    1960    1965    1970    1975    1980

Recessions shaded

Source: Federal Reserve Board.

the form of declining real income, there is no doubt who bore the burden of recession: the unemployed. Their loss of income is not shared equally as the economy contracts. Moreover, unemployment hits those industries hardest which depend heavily on big-ticket consumer expenditures financed by borrowing. It is worst in construction, autos, and other durable goods industries, and in the steel and nonferrous metal industries. Workers in agriculture, communications, public utilities, services, finance, and government are largely spared.

Through no fault of their own, workers (and their families) in a narrow band of industries must bear most of the cycle's burden. They are not responsible for the economy's fluctuations, but they are the chief victims in every downturn. Someone must build the homes and cars, and mill the lumber and steel. Yet, as if caught in a perverse game of musical chairs, those who do are always left without a seat when the music stops.

This chapter completes the analysis of the four phases of the

**Chart 4**
**Housing Starts**

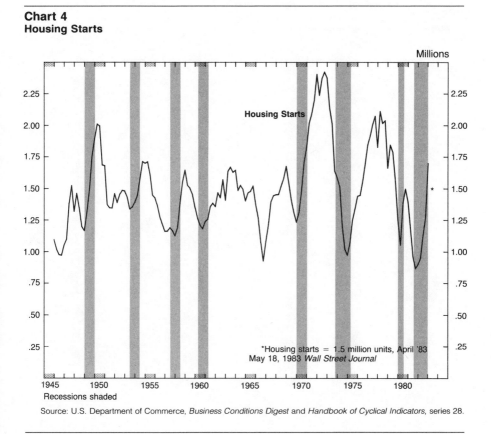

Millions

*Housing starts = 1.5 million units, April '83
May 18, 1983 *Wall Street Journal*

Recessions shaded

Source: U.S. Department of Commerce, *Business Conditions Digest* and *Handbook of Cyclical Indicators*, series 28.

business cycle. The statistical series which are particularly useful in charting the persistent rise and fall of the cycle's course are now familiar to you.

Now it's time to examine the cycle's impact on other economic indicators, such as inventory accumulation, business capital expenditures, profits and the stock market, and America's international transactions.

## Chart 5
**Change in Consumer Installment Credit**

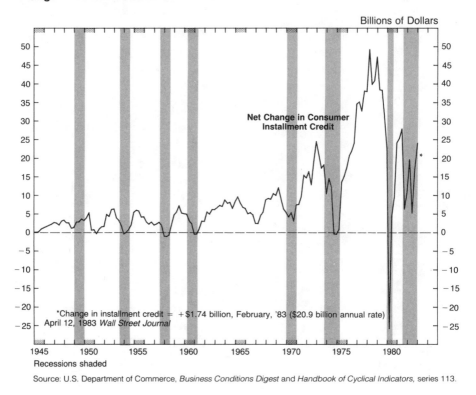

Billions of Dollars

Net Change in Consumer
Installment Credit

*Change in installment credit = +$1.74 billion, February, '83 ($20.9 billion annual rate)
April 12, 1983 *Wall Street Journal*

Recessions shaded

Source: U.S. Department of Commerce, *Business Conditions Digest* and *Handbook of Cyclical Indicators,* series 113.

**Chart 6**
**Retail Sales**

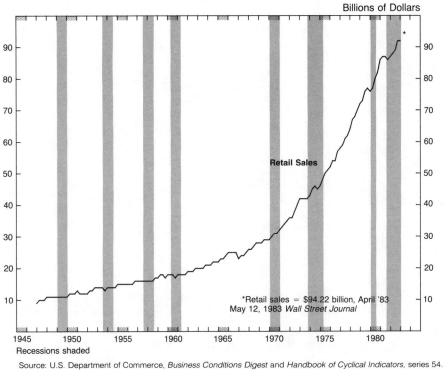

Billions of Dollars

*Retail sales = $94.22 billion, April '83
May 12, 1983 *Wall Street Journal*

Recessions shaded

Source: U.S. Department of Commerce, *Business Conditions Digest* and *Handbook of Cyclical Indicators,* series 54.

# CHAPTER TEN

## Inventories

Inventories are stocks of goods on hand—raw materials, goods in process, or finished products. Individual businesses use them to bring stability to their operations, yet you'll see that they actually have a destabilizing effect on the business cycle.

Businesses view inventories as a necessary evil. Business cannot live from hand to mouth, continually filling sales orders from current production. Stocks of goods "on the shelf" are a cushion against unexpected orders and slowdowns in production. On the other hand, inventories are an investment in working capital and incur an interest cost. If the firm borrows capital to maintain inventories, the direct interest cost is obvious. Even if the firm need not borrow, however, working capital tied up in inventories represents an interest cost. Any funds invested in inventories could have earned the going interest rate in the money market, and this loss can crimp profits substantially.

Therefore, business attempts to keep inventories at an absolute minimum consistent with smooth operations. For a very large business, literally millions of dollars are at stake. This is why you see modern automated cash registers in large chain supermarkets and retail establishments. These cash registers not only ring up your purchase; they also tie into a computer network which keeps track of inventories of thousands of items on a daily basis.

But why do inventories exacerbate the business cycle?

Consider the upswing of the cycle first. As demand increases rapidly, businesses must boost production to meet the growing volume of orders. If they are not quick enough, and sales grow more rapidly than output, an unplanned drawdown of inventories will occur as orders are filled. This is known as involuntary inventory depletion. If inventories are severely depleted, shortages can result and sales may be jeopardized. To protect itself against such developments once it is confident of the unfolding expansion, business will expand output and defensively accumulate inventories more rapidly than the growth in sales. Since all firms are stockpiling to prevent shortages, industrial production increases more vigorously than it otherwise would, accentuating the cyclical expansion and the swift rise in capacity utilization. This, of course, hastens the inevitable decrease in labor productivity and increase in unit labor costs associated with this phase of the cycle. Hence, inventory accumulation adds to the inflationary pressures.

Now consider the downswing of the cycle. No firm willingly maintains production in a sales slump, because unsold goods would pile up on the shelf. As sales weaken and fall, business curtails production in order to prevent involuntary inventory accumulation. Indeed, once business recognizes the severity of the slump, it will begin to liquidate the large volume of (now unnecessary) inventories built up during the previous expansion. These stockpiles of goods are no longer needed and can be disposed of. But as goods are sold from inventories, output and employment are reduced more than sales, since orders can be filled from inventories rather than current production. This aggravates the cycle's downturn.

Thus, inventories play an important destabilizing role in the cycle through their influence on industrial production, boosting production in expansion and depressing it during slump. Now this destabilizing influence is compounded by inventory's impact on inflation. When rapid expansion is heightened by inventory accumulation, contributing to inflationary pressures, business firms increase their inventory buildup to take advantage of rising prices. And when inventory liquidation in a recession contributes to deflationary pressures, falling prices can trigger a panic sell-off which drives prices down even more steeply.

Here's how it works. Business stockpiles goods during the expansionary phase of the cycle to prevent involuntary inventory depletion and shortages, and prices start to rise. Firms quickly discover that goods held in inventory increase in value along with the general rise in prices. They have an incentive to buy now while prices are low, hold the goods in inventory, and sell them later at higher prices and profits. If prices are rising rapidly enough, widespread speculation can set in, which adds to the general increase in production and reinforces the inflation.

Recall, for example, the rapid increase in sugar prices in 1973–

74. Sugar manufacturers and industrial users of sugar (canners, soft drink bottlers, confectioners, and bakers) produced sugar and sweetened products and held them in inventory while their prices were low, hoping to make large profits from sales when their prices increased. This speculative stockpiling contributed to the price increase.

Of course, when the inevitable contraction comes, liquidation of the inventory overhang helps halt the inflationary spiral. Businesses panic when faced with the prospect of selling at a price which will not recoup interest costs. If sufficiently severe, the sell-off can force prices down. More important, output plummets and layoffs mount as orders are filled from the shelf. Liquidation continues until inventories are in proper relation to sales.

Thus, speculative inventory accumulation and liquidation become a self-fulfilling prophecy. Firms pile up inventories in anticipation of a price increase, and the large volume of orders bids prices upward. When the recession begins, firms sell inventories in haste, afraid of a drop in prices, and the sell-off forces prices downward.

Now you understand why inventories, and their relationship to sales, are such an important economic indicator. They not only confirm the stage of the cycle; they also provide advance warning of turning points and of the strength or severity of impending boom and bust.

The cyclical experience of the early 1970s will serve as an illustration. This will be followed by an examination of recent developments.

To begin with, *The Wall Street Journal* publishes the Commerce Department's *inventory and sales data* around the middle of each month. The May 13, 1983, article is representative. (See page 135.)

# Inventories Fell By 1.1% in March At U.S. Concerns

## Recent Sales Gains Expected To Spur a Rebuilding; Output Seen Up in April

By Eileen Alt Powell
*Staff Reporter of* The Wall Street Journal

WASHINGTON—U.S. businesses reduced inventories 1.1% in March, but economists inside and outside of government expect the recent strengthening in sales to lead to inventory rebuilding.

The Commerce Department said business inventories in March fell $5.54 billion from the previous month to a seasonally adjusted $502.91 billion, after rising a revised $893 million, or 0.2%, in February to an adjusted $508.45 billion. February's increase, which followed four consecutive monthly declines, was earlier estimated at 0.1%.

Businesses cut inventories at a record rate in 1982's final quarter, to eliminate overstocks stemming from sluggish sales during the 1981-1982 recession. Although inventory liquidation slowed in this year's first quarter, businesses apparently have been waiting for evidence of a sustained sales rebound to resume building inventories.

### Upturn Seen Close

The ratio of inventories to sales suggests a turnaround is near. Total business inventories in March fell to 1.45 months' supply at the March sales rate, down sharply from 1.5 the month before. That is the lowest reading since last October and is close to the 1.44 level that prevailed in late 1979 before two recessions.

Robert Orther, the Commerce Department's chief economist, suggested that "if retail sales keep growing as they did in March and April, businesses will have to lift production pretty quickly to end the inventory declines." Mr. Ortner said he expects evidence of this trend today with a "smart increase" in the Federal Reserve Board's report on industrial production for April.

Mr. Ortner said inventory reduction in March was larger than expected. This could result in a lower first-quarter estimate of growth in the nation's real gross national product, the value of all goods and services produced, adjusted for inflation. But he added that the sharper inventory decline could have been "about offset" by higher-than-expected sales, resulting in "a wash" in GNP statistics. The department's preliminary estimate put first-quarter real GNP growth at a 3.1% annual rate.

Richard Rippe, an economist at Dean Witter Reynolds Inc., New York, said the latest report "shows that we are quite far along in the inventory liquidation process." Although retail sales began strengthening in March, Mr. Rippe said he doesn't expect to see much inventory rebuilding before this year's second half. "It takes time for businesses to be confident that sales are going to be sustained," he said, adding: "It takes time, too, to gear up production."

### Strong Gain in Volume

The latest report showed that overall business sales in March increased a strong $6.23 billion, or 1.8%, to an adjusted $346 billion, after falling $3.92 billion, or 1.1%, the month before to an adjusted $339.78 billion.

Retail inventories fell 1% in March to an adjusted $129.05 billion after increasing 2% in February to an adjusted $130.39 billion. Wholesale inventories declined 0.3% in March to an adjusted $116.06 billion, after contracting 1% the month before to an adjusted $116.42 billion. And manufacturers' inventories fell 1.5% in March to an adjusted $257.81 billion, after falling 0.2% in February to an adjusted $261.64 billion.

Before-seasonal adjustment, overall business inventories fell 0.3% in March to $505.88 billion from the previous month's $507.5 billion and were down 3.5% from a year earlier.

The Wall Street Journal, *May 13, 1983.*

Look for the following: *inventories, sales,* and *the inventory-sales ratio.*

*Inventories . . . paragraph 2*

The Commerce Department said business inventories in March fell $5.54 billion from the previous month to a seasonally adjusted $502.91 billion, after rising a revised $893 million, or 0.2%, in February to an adjusted $508.45 billion. February's increase, which followed four consecutive monthly declines, was earlier estimated at 0.1%.

*Sales . . . third paragraph from end of article*

The latest report showed that overall business sales in March increased a strong $6.23 billion, or 1.8%, to an adjusted $346 billion, after falling $3.92 billion, or 1.1%, the month before to an adjusted $339.78 billion.

*Inventory-sales ratio . . . paragraph 4*

The ratio of inventories to sales suggests a turnaround is near. Total business inventories in March fell to 1.45 months' supply at the March sales rate, down sharply from 1.5 the month before. That is the lowest reading since last October and is close to the 1.44 level that prevailed in late 1979 before two recessions.

Inventories and sales are straightforward concepts. The inventory-sales ratio tells you how many months it would take to sell off inventories at the prevailing sales pace. Calculate the ratio by dividing monthly inventory by monthly sales. Typically, inventories are roughly 1½ times sales over the cycle. A rise in the ratio indicates that inventories are growing out of proportion to sales and that inventory liquidation and recession are imminent. A fall in the ratio informs you that sales are outpacing inventory growth and that economic expansion is under way. This is a key indicator; you should follow it closely.

Return to this article after examining the inventory cycle of the early 1970s. This cycle concluded with a good example of inventory accumulation and speculation followed by severe inventory liquidation. To trace these events, follow the steep rise in inventories from 1972 through 1974 and the 1975 liquidation; and note the decline in the inventory-sales ratio in 1971–72 and the increase in 1973 and 1974 (see Chart 1).

Trace the decline of the inventory-sales ratio as the business cycle

## Chart 1
**Manufacturing and Trade Sales and Inventories, Inventory-Sales Ratio** (monthly basis), **and Change in Book Value of Manufacturing, and Trade Inventories**

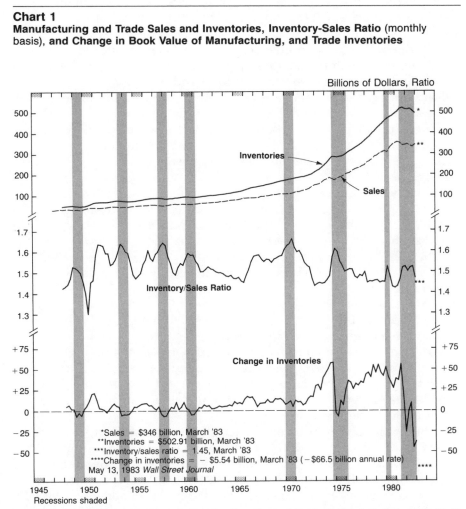

Billions of Dollars, Ratio

*Sales = $346 billion, March '83
**Inventories = $502.91 billion, March '83
***Inventory/sales ratio = 1.45, March '83
****Change in inventories = − $5.54 billion, March '83 (− $66.5 billion annual rate)
May 13, 1983 Wall Street Journal

Recessions shaded

Source: U.S. Department of Commerce, Business Conditions Digest and Handbook of Cyclical Indicators, series 31, 56, and 71; and Federal Reserve Board.

moved from recovery to expansion in 1971–72. Sales were expanding, but it was still too early for business to rebuild inventories.

As increasing demand boosted sales, 1973 displayed all the symptoms of the expansion-to-peak phase of the cycle: strong and rapidly growing sales, strained capacity utilization and slower deliveries, and a rising rate of inflation. Under these circumstances, business sought to defend itself against possible shortages by adding to inventories more rapidly than sales grew. The long decline in the inventory-sales ratio was reversed, and speculation began. Business boosted inventories in the expectation of rising prices, hoping to make a profit as goods increased in value. This intensified inflationary pressures (recall sugar) as a share of production went on the shelf instead of satisfying consumer demand. You can see that the inventory run-up dwarfed all other postwar experiences.

As the cycle's peak approached, in 1974, sales stopped growing. Unplanned inventory accumulation became a problem; the inventory-sales ratio rose even more rapidly; and business firms had to deal with ever-larger stockpiles of goods. They had a premonition that a sell-off was around the corner and that inventories had to be brought under control. Unfortunately, this was more easily said than done. Orders had to be canceled and production curtailed more than once because business underestimated the situation's severity.

Finally, beginning in late 1974 and continuing into 1975, inventory liquidation began. Under panic conditions, business desperately dumped goods on the market. Despite the sell-off, you'll notice that the inventory-sales ratio remained high until early 1975. This is evidence of the collapse in sales, the recession's severity, and the reason business went to such lengths to unload its stocks of goods.

Other postwar recessions had been mild by comparison. Industrial production plunged as business firms cut output severely and filled the meager volume of orders from their overstocked inventories. Two million workers were laid off between the fall of 1974 and the spring of 1975, and the unemployment rate brushed 10 percent. It was the worst recession since World War II. There is no doubt that inventory accumulation and liquidation played a key role in the cycle's severity.

Unlike the cycle of the early 70s, the recent recession can't be used as a typical example of inventory accumulation and liquidation, because of the Fed's role in aborting the 1981 recovery. Sales were doing well and the inventory-sales ratio was low when the Fed's tight money policy clamped a vise on the economy in 1981.

The twin peaks in the inventory-sales ratio during 1982 attest to the virulence of the Fed's tight money policy. Sales fell in 81, forcing the ratio up and compelling business to liquidate inventories at the end of the year. This inventory correction drove down the inventory-sales ratio. Sales turned up in early 1982, so it seemed that business had brought matters under control. But sales began to slump again in midyear (due to the Fed's continued restrictive policies) and the ratio rose once more, goading business into a renewed round of inventory liquidation which was even sharper than the liquidation in the early months of 82.

As you can tell from the May 13, 1983, *Journal* article, the second inventory liquidation continued into the spring of 1983. Yet sales began to recover, so that the inventory-sales ratio fell to 1.45. As the expansion unfolds and the sales pace accelerates, the inventory-sales ratio should continue to fall despite the end of the inventory liquidation and renewed inventory buildup.

But what does the future hold in store? In answering this question, remember two things.

First, the severe inflation of the past decade contributed to the cyclical volatility of inventory accumulation and liquidation. Inflation provided an incentive for business firms to accumulate stockpiles of goods, and recession forced them to sell off those stockpiles. This compounded production's cyclical volatility. However, since it appears that inflation has been wrung from the economy and that the Fed intends to keep inflation under control, inventory accumulation and liquidation should be less severe than they were in the recent past. This will aid cyclical stability.

Second, follow the inventory-sales ratio closely. It should fall as the expansion gains strength. As long as the decline continues and the ratio remains low, there should be no threat of recession. But when the ratio begins to climb, expect the worst, because inventories are growing while the pace of sales is slipping. That's the surest sign that the next (inevitable) recession is not far away.

How long will the decline in the inventory-sales ratio continue, and how long will it be before inventory accumulation exacerbates the expansion and contributes to the next recession? That depends on the strength of the expansion as determined by the growth in consumer demand. If demand grows too quickly and inflation speeds up, business will begin stockpiling for self-protection and speculation and the inventory-sales ratio will reverse its downward trend and start to climb. This will be a dead giveaway that inventory accumulation is contributing to boom conditions and that the peak of the cycle cannot be far off. On the other hand, if the expansion is restrained, the decline in the inventory-sales ratio should continue and the ratio should remain flat for a long time. In that case, inventory accumulation will not aggravate the expansion and the business cycle will not be brought to a peak prematurely.

# CHAPTER ELEVEN

---

## Business Capital Expenditures

---

Business's expenditures on factories, warehouses, offices, machinery, and equipment, like its accumulation of inventories, reinforce the business cycle; they do not lead it. Business waits for its signal from the economy before committing its capital. Similarly, only after the expansion is over does business begin to cut back on capital expenditures in anticipation of reduced sales.

There are five principal factors influencing business decisions to spend on new plant and equipment.

First, the rate of capacity utilization must be high. Putting it simply, if sales are strong, business will invest in new machinery and equipment in order to have the capacity necessary to fill the orders. During a recession, however, the rate of capacity utilization is low and business has more than enough plant and equipment on hand to satisfy the low volume of orders. Why add to plant and equipment when the existing level is already more than adequate?

Second, old facilities, whether fully utilized or not, will be scrapped and replaced by new if operating costs can be reduced through innovation in the process of production. Competition leaves business no choice. If equipment is no longer cost-effective, it must be replaced even though it can still be used.

Third, new plant and equipment may be required to produce a new or redesigned product even if existing facilities are operating at full capacity and have a continued useful life. Model and style changes have forced the automobile industry to spend billions replacing still functional equipment.

Fourth, spending on plant and equipment is sensitive to current and anticipated profits. Business will invest in additional facilities if it expects long-range profit growth beyond any short-run cyclical fluctuation. In addition, profits plowed back into the business provide the cash flow necessary to finance capital expenditures. A recession will limit business's ability to finance capital expenditures; an expansion will generate the necessary cash flow.

The final factor is interest rates. Business must borrow to finance plant and equipment expenditures if internally generated funds are not adequate. When interest rates are very high, the cost of borrowing may be prohibitive, and so business firms postpone or cancel their capital expenditure plans. Or they may feel that for the time being they can get a better return by investing their own funds at high rates of interest than by making expenditures on new productive facilities.

Keep these factors in mind when evaluating business's capital expansion plans and their role in the current cycle. You can keep abreast of capital expenditures by following three series published monthly in *The Wall Street Journal*: the Commerce Department report on new orders for nondefense capital goods, the National Machine Tool Builders' Association report on machine tool orders, and the F. W. Dodge report on building awards.

*The Wall Street Journal* publishes preliminary data for *nondefense capital goods*, such as the April 22, 1983, release below, around the 22d or 23d of the month, and the final report appears about a week later. You will have to keep your eyes open for these figures because they are part of an overall report on *durable goods*. (See page 142.)

The *revised data*, appearing a week later, is included with a general release on *factory orders*. The May 3, 1983, article is a good example. (See page 143.)

# Durable-Goods Orders Rose 0.3% in March

---

## Gain, Fourth in Five Months, Reflects Greater Strength In Machinery and Defense

---

*By a WALL STREET JOURNAL Staff Reporter*

WASHINGTON—Factory orders for durable goods rose 0.3% in March, reflecting strength in orders for machinery and defense products.

The Commerce Department said that new orders for durables increased to a seasonally adjusted $78.34 billion last month after declining a revised 3.5% in February to an adjusted $78.08 billion. The February decline initially was estimated as 4% but was revised to 3.2%. (See chart on page one.)

It was the fourth increase in the past five months in orders for durable goods, which are items such as machinery and household furnishings that have a usefulness of three years or more.

Despite the recent improvement, factory orders for durable items remain nearly 11% below the peak of an adjusted $87.6 billion in July 1981, when the 1981-82 recession began. The latest orders figures confirm the prediction of most economists that the recovery, which began in the first quarter this year, will be modest by historical standards.

Commerce Secretary Malcolm Baldrige said in a statement that the March increases in orders for machinery and household goods "are key indicators suggesting further gains in production during the second quarter."

In fact, new orders for machinery rose a strong 8% last month to an adjusted $26.65 billion, the largest one-month gain since a 10.1% increase in January 1980. Machinery orders had declined 2.5% in February to an adjusted $24.68 billion.

Richard Berner, an economist at Morgan Guaranty Trust Co. of New York, noted that orders for nondefense capital goods "rebounded nicely in March." This, he added, is "consistent with a modest rebound in economic activity and a modest turnaround in capital spending." Still, he doesn't look for much improvement in capital investment before the second half of the year because factory utilization rates remain low and interest rates high.

The report showed that factory orders for nondefense capital goods, considered a barometer of future plant and equipment spending, increased 4.1% last month to an adjusted $19.53 billion after falling 8.3% the month before to an adjusted $18.77 billion.

Nondefense Capital Goods

New orders for defense-related goods rose 13% in March to an adjusted $6.94 billion after falling 30.9% in February to an adjusted $6.14 billion.

Durable-goods shipments in March rose 1.9% to an adjusted $79.11 billion after rising 0.5% in February to an adjusted $77.62 billion.

The backlog of orders last month fell 0.3% to an adjusted $288.45 billion after increasing 0.2% in February to an adjusted $289.21 billion.

The Wall Street Journal, *April 22, 1983.*

# Factory Orders In March Rose A Sturdy 3.2%

## Gain From February Suggests Jobs, Output Will Grow; Recovery Still Seen as Mild

By EILEEN ALT POWELL
*Staff Reporter of* THE WALL STREET JOURNAL.

WASHINGTON—New factory orders rose a sturdy 3.2% in March, suggesting that industrial production and employment will continue to rise in the months ahead.

The Commerce Department reported that new orders rose to a seasonally adjusted $161.75 billion in March after falling 2.2% in February, to an adjusted $156.68 billion. New orders had risen 2.5% in January, to an adjusted $160.21 billion.

Commerce Secretary Malcolm Baldrige noted that orders in March were more than 8% ahead of the recession low of $149.7 billion in October. Mr. Baldrige termed March "a sound month of recovery for the nation's manufacturing sector," adding that the rise in orders should lead to "further increases in production."

Still, the rise in orders—coupled with further weakness in construction in March as shown in a separate Commerce Department report—supports the prediction that the nation's recovery this year from the recession will be uneven and less robust than most. "Both numbers are consistent with recovery, but with one that doesn't have the kind of momentum that usually typifies the first few quarters of a recovery," said Edward Yardeni, director of economics for Prudential-Bache Securities in New York.

Economists said that the most encouraging sign in the March report was the sharp

The Wall Street Journal, *May 3, 1983.*

upward revision in factory orders for durable goods, which are items such as machinery and household furnishings that have an estimated usefulness of at least three years. New orders for durables rose a revised 3.5% in March, to an adjusted $80.79 billion, after falling 3.5% in February, to an adjusted $78.08 billion. A preliminary report had put the March rise at 0.3%.

New orders for nondurable items, such as apparel and other goods that have an expected usefulness of less than three years, increased 3% in March, to an adjusted $80.96 billion, after falling 0.9% in February, to an adjusted $78.6 billion.

Mr. Yardeni said the durable-goods revision "suggests that the recovery is occurring very much on track and is benefiting both durable and nondurable goods sectors."

Stephen Roach, a senior economist at Morgan Stanley & Co. in New York, said the durable-goods revision "is consistent with an economy that is beginning to turn up." He also points to the strong March rise in non-defense capital-goods orders as "the best barometer of near-term capital-spending prospects" for the economy. Further liquidation of inventories in March, Mr. Roach adds, "should be very constructive for production in the second and third quarters."

The report showed that March orders for nondefense capital goods increased 11% to an adjusted $20.77 billion, following a decrease of 8.3% in February to an adjusted $18.77 billion. Orders in the volatile defense category soared 25% in March, to an adjusted $7.68 billion, after declining 31% the month earlier, to an adjusted $6.14 billion.

*Nondefense Capital Goods*

Factory inventories in March contracted 1.5%, to an adjusted $257.81 billion, after decreasing 0.2% in February, to an adjusted $261.64 billion. The department noted that except for a 0.2% rise in February 1982, inventories have been declining since November 1981.

Factory shipments in March rose 2.4% to an adjusted $160.17 billion, after falling 0.1% in February to $156.37 billion.

Order backlogs rose 0.5% in March to an adjusted $300.1 billion, after rising 0.1% in February, to an adjusted $298.51 billion.

*April 22, 1983 . . . fourth paragraph from end of article . . . preliminary data*

---

> The report showed that factory orders for nondefense capital goods, considered a barometer of future plant and equipment spending, increased 4.1% last month to an adjusted $19.53 billion after falling 8.3% the month before to an adjusted $18.77 billion.

---

*May 3, 1983 . . . fourth paragraph from end of article . . . final report*

---

> The report showed that March orders for nondefense capital goods increased 11% to an adjusted $20.77 billion, following a decrease of 8.3% in February to an adjusted $18.77 billion. Orders in the volatile defense category soared 25% in March, to an adjusted $7.68 billion, after declining 31% the month earlier, to an adjusted $6.14 billion.

---

Whether you use the preliminary or final report, you are looking for a single sentence buried at the end of the article. In both the April 22 and May 3 articles, the data appears in the *fourth paragraph from the end.*

This series presents new orders received by manufacturers of durable goods other than military equipment. Durable goods are defined as having a useful life of more than three years. Nondefense capital goods represent approximately one fifth to one third of all durable goods production. The series includes engines; construction, mining, and materials handling equipment, office and store machinery; electrical transmission and distribution equipment and other electrical machinery (excluding household appliances and electronic equipment); and railroad, ship, and aircraft transportation equipment. Military equipment is excluded because new orders for such equipment do not respond directly to the business cycle.

Returning to the key paragraph in the April 22 *Journal* report, note that the March figure was $19.53 billion, which was revised to $20.77 billion on May 3. Both the revised and the preliminary re-

**Chart 1**
**Nondefense Orders of Capital Goods**

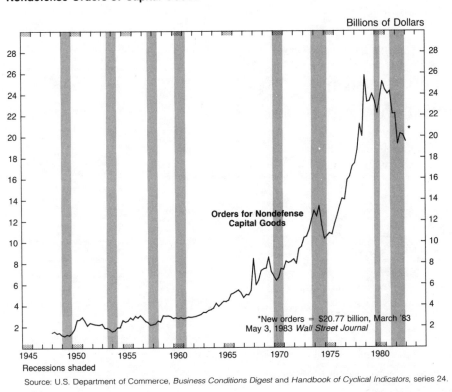

Billions of Dollars

Orders for Nondefense
Capital Goods

*New orders = $20.77 billion, March '83
May 3, 1983 *Wall Street Journal*

1945    1950    1955    1960    1965    1970    1975    1980
Recessions shaded

Source: U.S. Department of Commerce, *Business Conditions Digest* and *Handbook of Cyclical Indicators*, series 24.

ports tell you that the March figure was an increase from the figure for the preceding month.

These figures, together with Chart 1, provide a good illustration of the earlier observation. Despite evidence that a strong expansion had begun, nondefense capital goods orders were still languishing at their recession lows. At approximately $20 billion, the level of orders in March 1983 was about 20 percent less than the previous peak of $25 billion. The record postwar slump in capacity utilization continued to discourage many businesses from adding to their facilities.

*Machine tools* are used to shape parts for all durable goods; therefore, orders for new machine tools reliably herald industry's plans to add to plant and equipment. The National Machine Tool Builders' Association reports data for *new machine tool orders*, which is published by *The Wall Street Journal* around the last Monday of each month, just after the Commerce Department's preliminary release on new orders for nondefense capital goods. Take a look at the April 25, 1983, *Journal* article.

---

# Machine-Tool Orders Are Seen Bottoming Out

## Last Month Saw Jump of 29% From February, but Drop Of 8.9% From Year Ago

By RALPH E. WINTER
*Staff Reporter of* THE WALL STREET JOURNAL

Manufacturers are still ordering machinery and equipment very cautiously, but orders probably have passed their low point, machine-tool producers say.

March orders for machine tools, which are used by durable goods manufacturers to shape most metal parts, rose to $125.6 million, a 29% rise from February's $97.5 million. However. orders remained 8.9% below the $137.8 million of March 1982, the National Machine Tool Builders' Association reported.

"We are seeing the leaves starting to come out, but we aren't sure that they won't be frosted," cautioned Glenn S. Babbitt, president, Oerlikon Motch Corp., a machine-tool producer that also distributes machines made by other companies. "Requests for quotes on prices are growing in number," he said, and, for the first time in months, there is an indication that all three major auto producers are going to make sizable orders

during the second quarter.

Machine-tool orders in the last half of 1982 and first quarter of 1983, when adjusted for inflation, were at the lowest level in 50 years, said James A. Gray, president of the association. "Things can't get much worse for our industry. The one ray of hope is that the decline seems to be leveling off."

Producers of other capital goods appear to be experiencing the same trend. Non-defense capital goods orders in March rose 4.1% from February, to $19.53 billion, the Commerce Department reported last week. However, capital goods orders remained 12% below the $22.17 billion of a year earlier.

"We have a lot of bids out, and by the time companies ask for bids they're usually reasonably serious about buying," said Frederick W. Searby, president of Bendix Industrial Group, a unit of Allied Corp. He said Bendix has been pleased by the number of companies asking for bids on flexible manufacturing systems, which make a number of different parts. The inquiries are coming from a wide range of different industries, including aerospace. defense, automotive and job shops.

As another indication of increased willingness to buy, Mr. Searby said Bendix received nine orders for a new $200,000-plus machine that automatically punches holes in sheet metal within two weeks of the machine's introduction.

March orders for lathes, machining centers, milling machines, grinders, boring mills and other machines to shape metal parts by cutting were $89.7 million, a 16% rise from $77.4 million in February, but down 15% from $105.8 million in March of last year, the machine-tool association reported.

Orders for metal-forming presses and other machines to shape metal parts with pressure jumped to $35.9 million in March, a 79% rise from $20.1 million in February and 12% above the $32.1 million of a year earlier.

Despite the March order gain, machine-tool orders continue to run below shipments, depleting the industry's backlog. Shipments in March were $176.5 million, a 57% drop from $411.1 million a year earlier, but up 11% from $158.4 million in February.

The industry's backlog of unshipped orders at the end of the quarter was $1.02 billion, less than half the $2.65 billion of a year earlier.

"This is going to be a tough year," said Mr. Searby. "We expect orders to exceed shipments by the end of the second quarter, but it will take time to complete engineering on those new orders" before the equipment can go into production.

In the meantime, shipments will remain at extremely depressed levels, and layoffs and plant closings will continue, industry executives said.

| Comparative new orders for metal-cutting machines: | | | |
|---|---|---|---|
| | March 1983 | Feb. 198 | March 1982 |
| Domestic | $84,950,000 | $69,550,000 | $90,200,000 |
| Foreign | 4,700,000 | 7,850,000 | 15,550,000 |
| Total | 89,650,000 | 77,400,000 | 105,740,000 |
| Three-month total for 1983: $205,850,000; for 1982: $384,850,000. | | | |

| Metal-forming machine orders: | | | |
|---|---|---|---|
| Domestic | $32,100,000 | $18,700,000 | $26,750,000 |
| Foreign | 3,800,000 | 1,400,000 | 5,300,000 |
| Total | 35,900,000 | 20,100,000 | 32,050,000 |
| Three-month total for 1983: $90,800,000; for 1982: $121,950,000. | | | |

| Comparative shipment figures for metal-cutting machines: | | | |
|---|---|---|---|
| Domestic | $119,850,000 | $116,700,000 | $303,050,000 |
| Foreign | 14,700,000 | 12,100,000 | 29,700,000 |
| Total | 134,500,000 | 128,800,000 | 332,750,000 |
| Three-month total for 1983: $370,750,000; for 1982: $933,050,000. | | | |

| Metal-forming machine shipments: | | | |
|---|---|---|---|
| Domestic | $36,450,000 | $26,450,000 | $73,150,000 |
| Foreign | 5,450,000 | 3,000,000 | 5,150,000 |
| Total | 41,900,000 | 29,550,000 | 78,300,000 |
| Three-month total for 1983: $116,900,000; for 1982: $221,150,000. | | | |

---

*New orders for machine tools . . . second paragraph*

---

March orders for machine tools, which are used by durable goods manufacturers to shape most metal parts, rose to $125.6 million, a 29% rise from February's $97.5 million. However, orders remained 8.9% below the $137.8 million of March 1982, the National Machine Tool Builders' Association reported.

You can see from the *second paragraph* that new machine tool orders were $125.6 million in March 1983, 8.9 percent less than new machine tool orders a year earlier. Compare these figures with the data in Chart 2. There will be no recovery in business capital expenditures until these depressed levels of machine tool orders improve.

You have examined two sources of data on equipment expenditures. Turn now to a series on plant expenditures. F. W. Dodge's report on *building awards* is published by *The Wall Street Journal* at the turn of the month, as in the May 3, 1983, article. (See page 148.)

**Chart 2**
**Machine Tool Orders**

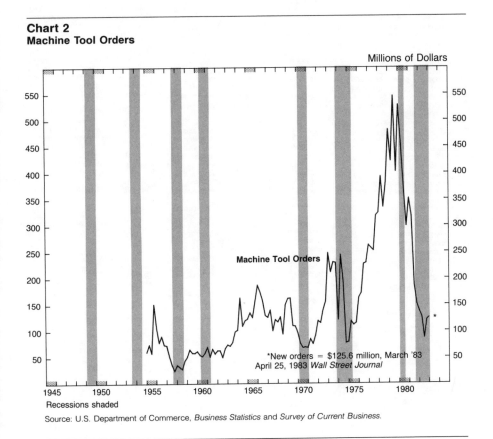

Millions of Dollars

*New orders = $125.6 million, March '83
April 25, 1983 *Wall Street Journal*

Recessions shaded

Source: U.S. Department of Commerce, *Business Statistics* and *Survey of Current Business*.

# Construction Outlays Slipped By 1.6% in March

## Commercial, Public Building Cited; F.W. Dodge Says New Awards Rose 10%

*By a WALL STREET JOURNAL Staff Reporter*

WASHINGTON — Construction spending fell 1.6% in March, reflecting weakness in both commercial and public building, the Commerce Department said.

But the latest report on construction outlays also shows that residential building continued to advance in March, as interest-rate declines since last fall made mortgages more affordable.

The March decline in construction spending to a seasonally adjusted $245.4 billion, at an annual rate, followed a revised 2.6% drop in February to an adjusted $249.3 billion annual pace. The February decline earlier had been estimated as 2%. Construction spending rose 7.1% in January to an adjusted $256 billion annual rate.

Despite the two consecutive monthly declines, construction spending in March was 9.3% higher than the pace a year earlier, the report showed.

Meanwhile, F.W. Dodge Co. said new construction contracts rose a seasonally adjusted 10% in March over the previous month on the strength of home building and public works.

In its monthly survey of construction activity, the forecasting unit of McGraw-Hill Inc. said new contracts totaled $16.17 billion in March, bringing the quarterly total to $38.78 billion, an 8% gain from the first quarter of 1982.

George Roff Jr., a Commerce Department economist, noted that F.W. Dodge tallies new contract awards, while the department tracks the value of construction work actually under way. Rises in new contracts generally are reflected in the department's construction-spending figures after several months' lag, he added.

### New Residential Construction

Robert Gough, vice president for national forecasting at Data Resources Inc., Lexington, Mass., says he expects nonresidential construction to decline about 2% this year, after rising nearly 3% in 1982 and 6.3% in 1981. "We'll see nonresidential construction pick up after the recovery leads to filling the office space already out there," he said.

On the residential side, Mr. Gough said "mortgage rates will have to come down a little more if we are going to maintain the level of housing activity we saw in the first quarter this year."

The Commerce Department report showed that private construction fell 0.3% in March to an adjusted $198.6 billion annual rate, after declining 0.5% in February to an adjusted $199.1 billion pace. Still, the March pace was 14.4% higher than in March 1982, largely because of strengthening housing construction.

Residential construction increased 1.6% in March to an adjusted $97.8 billion annual rate, after rising 3.1% the month before to an adjusted $96.3 billion pace, and was up 39.7% from a year earlier. But nonresidential construction fell 2.4% in March to an adjusted $62.1 billion annual rate, after declining 4.4% in February to an adjusted $63.6 billion pace, and was down 4.3% from a year earlier.

Public construction, including highway and other public-works projects, fell 6.8% in March to an adjusted $46.8 billion annual rate, after falling 10.2% in February to an adjusted $50.2 billion annual pace, and was down 8.2% from a year earlier.

Measured in 1977 dollars to eliminate the effects of inflation, construction spending decreased 1.8% in March to a $154.1 billion annual rate, after falling 2.9% in February to a $156.9 billion pace, but was up 7.2% from a year earlier.

### Dodge Index

As for the F.W. Dodge report, its March total boosted the seasonally adjusted Dodge Index of construction-contract value 10% to 131 from February's 119. For January, the index was 127. The company uses 1977 as its 100 base.

For the quarter, the index averaged 126, a 5% gain from last year's fourth quarter. "The building industry was a major force in the economy's turnaround during the first quarter," said George A. Christie, chief economist for F.W. Dodge. Public-works contracting rose sharply, he said, mostly because of replacement construction of a bridge in Tampa Bay that was damaged by a ship collision in 1980.

Contracting for residential building totaled $7.76 billion in March, an 11% rise over February. Non-building construction—which includes bridges and roads—rose 12% to $2.97 billion, after seasonal adjustments.

Nonresidential building contracts totaled $5.44 billion in March, a 2% improvement from February. The month's small gain was confined to institutional buildings, as post-recession excess capacity inhibited the construction of business-related facilities," Mr. Christie said.

In the first quarter, commercial and industrial building contracts, at $8.8 billion, fell 19% below the total for the 1982 quarter, with most of the decline in commercial building.

Contracts for institutional buildings—schools, hospitals, and such—totaled $5.2 billion in 1983's first quarter, an 11% rise from the 1982 quarter.

The following is Dodge's summary of construction contracts:

| | March '83 Construction Contract Val. (000,000) | Seasonally Adjusted % Change From Prev. Month |
|---|---|---|
| Nonresidential bldg. | $5,437.8 | + 2 |
| Residential building | 7,762.2 | + 11 |
| Nonbuilding constr. | 2,970.7 | + 12 |
| Total construction | $16,170.7 | + 10 |

| | 3 Mos. 1983 (000,000) | 3 Mos. 1982 (000,000) | Cumulative % Change |
|---|---|---|---|
| Nonresidential bldg. | $13,976.6 | $15,502.4 | − 10 |
| Residential building | 17,581.1 | 10,620.2 | + 66 |
| Nonbuilding constr. | 7,222.2 | 9,940.3 | − 27 |
| Total construction | $38,779.9 | $36,062.9 | + 8 |

The Wall Street Journal, *May 3, 1983.*

*Nonresidential building . . . fourth paragraph from end of article*

---

Nonresidential building contracts totaled
$5.44 billion in March, a 2% improvement
from February. "The month's small gain
was confined to institutional buildings, as
post-recession excess capacity inhibited the
construction of business-related facilities,"
Mr. Christie said.

---

Focus on the *fourth paragraph from the end of the article*, which
reports *nonresidential building*, including factories, offices, and
retail and wholesale establishments. Ignore the data on residential
building, because this refers to home construction, which has already been covered in Chapters Seven and Nine, and on nonbuild-
ing construction, because this covers projects such as roads and
bridges rather than business plant.

Note that March's figure was only a slight improvement over
February's.

You can use the *Journal* article in tandem with Chart 3 on page
150. Both reinforce earlier observations that expansion will have to
be well under way before business contracts for additional factories, offices, and warehouses.

In conclusion, the data in the *Journal* articles, along with Charts
1–3, illustrate the point that capital expenditures, like inventory
accumulation, reinforce the cycle rather than initiate it. Business
responds to consumer orders by adding plant and equipment. As
the expansion develops into the peak of the cycle and productive
capacity is strained, business adds facilities and equipment. Their
completion swells the level of demand and contributes to generally
inflationary conditions.

After recession begins, some of the investment projects are canceled, but most are completed, and these expenditures ease the
downturn. Time elapses before a new cycle's expansionary phase
encourages another round of capital expenditures. Until this occurs, the depressed level of plant and equipment expenditures
holds demand down and prevents the economy from heating up
too quickly. When capital expenditures do recover, the economy is
once again approaching the cycle's peak.

Returning one last time to the articles and charts for an overview

**Chart 3**
**Nonresidential Building**

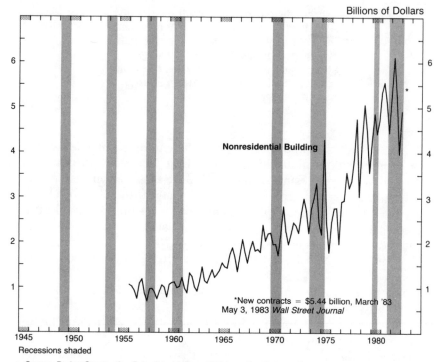

Billions of Dollars

Nonresidential Building

*New contracts = $5.44 billion, March '83
May 3, 1983 *Wall Street Journal*

1945   1950   1955   1960   1965   1970   1975   1980
Recessions shaded

Source: Dodge Construction Potentials, McGraw-Hill Information Systems Company; and U.S. Department of Commerce, *Business Statistics* and *Survey of Current Business.*

of the process, note that low levels of capacity utilization are depressing capital expenditures. That's why, despite the other evidence of expansion, nondefense orders for capital equipment, machine tool orders, and nonresidential construction have not yet recovered. As capacity utilization improves, however, they will improve, contributing to the general expansion of demand and economic activity.

# CHAPTER TWELVE

## Profits and the Stock Market

The *Dow Jones Industrial Average* provides an excellent leading economic indicator: the rise or fall in its value precedes corresponding movements in the business cycle.

The Dow represents share prices of 30 blue-chip industrial corporations, chosen because their operations cover the broad spectrum of industrial America. The names of all 30 of these corporations are familiar to every American. The list includes three of the "Generals" (General Electric, General Foods, and General Motors), as well as Du Pont, Kodak, Exxon, IBM, Procter & Gamble, and U.S. Steel. Some of these corporations produce basic commodities, such as food, forest products, steel and nonferrous metals, petroleum, glass, and chemicals. Others manufacture more complex products, such as transportation equipment, tires, electrical equipment, computers, photographic equipment, and drugs. And four (American Express, Sears, Woolworth, and AT&T) are not primarily engaged in mining or manufacturing, the activities ordinarily described as industrial.

Dow Jones also publishes indexes for public utilities and transportation, and there are broader stock market barometers that measure changes in the average price of 500 shares, or even all of the shares traded on the New York Stock Exchange (NYSE). Yet the Dow Industrials is the most closely followed average because it was first and because its handful of blue-chip companies do reflect stock market activity with surprising precision.

Finally, the firms which make up the Dow are the "crème de la crème" by virtue of their size and public interest in their shares. A corporation must meet minimum qualifications, such as capital invested and trading activity in its shares, to be listed on the NYSE. Companies engaged in agriculture, services, construction, trade, and finance are usually too small to be publicly traded on the New York Stock Exchange. Industrial corporations make up the majority of the companies traded there, and the companies in the Dow are the biggest and most widely traded of these.

Corporations issue stock to raise capital. Investors buy shares of stock in order to earn dividends and to enjoy a capital gain if the stock goes up in price. The ability of a corporation to pay dividends and the potential for increase in the value of a share of stock depend directly on the profits earned by the corporation. The greater the flow of profit, the higher the price investors will pay for that share of stock. Fluctuations in the Dow precede those in the economy because investors buy shares of stock in order to take advantage of future profit potential and will bid up stock prices when that potential looks promising.

That's how you would expect the capitalist system to operate. The ownership value of assets depends on the income they generate, because potential buyers will pay a higher price for them if they engender a rising stream of income. The value of farmland reflects profits which can be reaped by raising crops on it, and the value of an apartment building reflects rents that can be collected. Similarly, the value of a share in the ownership of a corporation ultimately depends on the ability of that corporation to create profits. Note that the value of an asset depends not only on the income it is currently earning but also on its potential for earning more and on the willingness of buyers to pay for those prospective earnings.

The broad line of industrial companies represented by the Dow enjoys an improvement in earnings during the expansionary phases of the cycle and suffers a decline in earnings when the economy slips into recession. Because these companies represent the backbone of industrial America, their fortunes are intimately tied to the swings of the business cycle. Thus, the Dow moves in anticipation of the cycle as investors gauge not only the profit potential of these corporations but also future cyclical prospects for the economy as a whole.

A corporation's profit is the most important measure of its success because profit indicates the effectiveness and efficiency with which its assets are managed and employed. Profits calibrate the ability of a firm to make and sell its product for more than the cost of production. Profit means that the firm has efficiently combined the labor, material, and capital necessary to produce and market its product at a price which society is willing to pay and which provides the owners with the financial incentive to expand the operation. When costs exceed revenues and the firm takes a loss, the amount society is willing to pay for the firm's product no longer justifies the cost of producing it.

Therefore, you should now explore the various statistical series on profits and profitability and the stock market averages so that you can understand their role in the business cycle.

## PROFITS AND PROFITABILITY

*The Wall Street Journal survey of corporate profits* for over 500 corporations appears about a month after the close of the quarter. The *second paragraph* of the May 9, 1983, report for the first quarter of 1983 states that profits fell 8 percent from the same period a year earlier. (See page 154.)

# *Staying Soft*

## Corporate Profits Fell 8% in the First Quarter For Sixth Drop in Row

### Despite Economic Recovery, Many Sectors Are Weak; Steel, Oil and Airlines Hit

### But Autos Rebound Sharply

A WALL STREET JOURNAL *News Roundup*

Despite the economic recovery, corporate profits continued to sink in the first quarter.

**Corporate Profits**

After-tax profits of 569 major corporations fell 8% from a year earlier, a Wall Street Journal survey finds. Although the drop wasn't nearly as steep as the 30% year-to-year plunge in the fourth quarter of 1982, the latest period's earnings—like those in the previous quarter—were lower even though they were being compared with another weak quarter. Profits last scored a year-to-year gain in the 1981 third period.

Many industries struggled through a difficult three months. Most steelmakers posted either wider losses or deficits that contrasted with slim profits in the 1982 first period. Oil-industry earnings fell, once again because of an oversupply of crude and of refined products. Railroads, airlines, aluminum producers and machine-tool makers also fared poorly.

### Some Bright Spots

But some industries did better. Sharply higher auto production helped the three major U.S. car makers report combined net income of $1.04 billion, for the most profitable first quarter since the Big Three posted combined earnings of $1.8 billion in the 1979 period. Banks also generally reported profit gains, and many housing-related sectors showed a turnaround from their dismal year-earlier performance.

Although the year-to-year comparison of overall corporate profits was weak, earnings generally strengthened from the 1982 fourth quarter, and most analysts expect them to keep rising as the economic recovery continues. The analysts are optimistic even though the recovery so far is unusually slow in comparison with past periods. The Commerce Department late last month reported that inflation-adjusted gross national product rose at an annual rate of 3.1% in the first quarter, and analysts generally expect only modest gains in GNP in later quarters this year.

"Because firms are remaining so cautious and not rehiring labor, rebuilding inventory stocks or ordering new capital goods, their profit margins are increasing much faster than would ordinarily be expected for this sluggish an upturn," says Michael K. Evans, an economic consultant to the American Production and Inventory Control Society.

The recession, which most economists believe ended last November or December, was so prolonged that many businesses did a thorough job of weeding out inefficient plants and equipment and paring work forces. The aggressive cost-cutting has contributed to gains in productivity, and rising output per man-hour helps hold down unit labor costs and bolsters profits.

### Productivity Gain

Although first-quarter GNP increased only modestly, "productivity in the nonfarm business sector rose at a healthy 4.8% annual rate," says Frank Mastrapasqua, an economist for the brokerage firm of Smith Barney, Harris Upham & Co. He believes that this sizable gain reinforces expectations of "a strong rebound in corporate profits."

In addition, compensation per hour has risen moderately; it increased at a 5.7% annual rate in the first quarter, down from a 7.2% rate in all 1982. Compensation gains can be expected to grow as the recovery continues, but some analysts predict that they will be mostly offset by higher productivity. As a result, Edward S. Hyman, an economist for the brokerage firm of Cyrus J. Lawrence, expects unit labor costs to be unchanged over the next 12 months.

Corporate after-tax profits, as reported by the Commerce Department, reached a record $165.1 billion in 1979 and have declined each year since then. Last year, they totaled less than $118 billion. Analysts expect the total to rise sharply this year, though not back to the 1979 level. For example, Lacy H. Hunt, the chief economist at the brokerage firm of Marroll, McEntee & McGinley, sees 1983 profits at $154.9 billion.

However, the declining rate of inflation and the increased depreciation allowances permitted by the 1981 tax legislation make the profit numbers look much better than those in 1979. Adjusted to remove the "inventory profits" produced by inflation and to add depreciation allowances, 1979 profits came to only $107.2 billion.

*First-quarter profits . . . second paragraph*

---

After-tax profits of 569 major corporations fell 8% from a year earlier, a Wall
Street Journal survey finds. Although the
drop wasn't nearly as steep as the 30% year-
to-year plunge in the fourth quarter of 1982,
the latest period's earnings—like those in
the previous quarter—were lower even
though they were being compared with another weak quarter. Profits last scored a
year-to-year gain in the 1981 third period.

---

The *Commerce Department's quarterly survey of profits* appears
about 20 days later and covers a much larger sample. Examine the
May 20, 1983, report, especially the *first two paragraphs*. (See
page 156.)

Don't be confused by different comparisons. Profits were 4.6
percent lower in the first quarter of 1983 than in the last quarter of
1982, but only 2.2 percent lower than in the same quarter one year
earlier.

# Corporate Profits After Taxes Fell 4.6% in 1st Period

## Data Show Recovery Got Off To Weak Start, but Sharp Increases Are Predicted

By LAURIE McGINLEY
*Staff Reporter of* THE WALL STREET JOURNAL

WASHINGTON – First-quarter after-tax profits of U.S. corporations declined 4.6% from the fourth quarter as the economic recovery got off to a weaker start than previously thought.

The Commerce Department said after-tax profits decreased to a seasonally adjusted annual rate of $112.5 billion in the January-March quarter, after falling 1.3% in the fourth quarter of last year to an adjusted $117.9 billion pace. The latest quarter's decline left profits 2.2% below the $115 billion pace of the first quarter of 1982 and 3.9% below the $117.1 billion average for all of last year.

Meanwhile, the department said revised figures show that the nation's real gross national product, the value of all goods and services adjusted for inflation, expanded a modest 2.5% at an adjusted annual rate in the first quarter. That was less than the department's preliminary growth estimate of 3.1%, which was made a month ago. The revision reflected a sharper-than-expected decline in inventories, the department said. Residential investment and consumer spending were revised upward.

Several economists said the decline in after-tax profits, which was the steepest since a 20.7% decrease in the first quarter of last year, reflected the lingering effects of the 18-month recession, as well as the tax law passed last summer, which increased corporate liabilities.

The Wall Street Journal, *May 20, 1983.*

## Sharp Rises Predicted

The analysts predicted, however, that profits will increase sharply in the current quarter and throughout the rest of the year, as the economic recovery gathers momentum. Allen Gutheim, senior economist at Wharton Econometric Forecasting Associates in Philadelphia, predicted that after-tax profits in the April-June quarter would rise 32% at an adjusted annual rate from the first quarter. He expects profits to increase 37% in the third quarter and 28% in the fourth quarter.

Other economists noted that another measure of corporate profits painted a far healthier picture. Profits before tax, but after adjustment for the effects of inflation on inventories and capital, rose 12.6% in the first quarter to an adjusted annual rate of $185.4 billion. That followed a decrease of 1% to a $164.6 billion pace in the fourth quarter of last year.

The downward revision in the economy's first-quarter performance wasn't surprising after a recent report that business inventories fell a sharp 1.1% in March. The preliminary GNP estimate was prepared before the March inventory data were available.

Because the revision in GNP reflected extensive inventory liquidation, economists didn't interpret it as bad news. Many analysts, in fact, contend that inventory levels have become so low that any rise in demand quickly will be translated into stepped-up orders and production.

Allen Sinai, senior vice president of Data Resources Inc., a Lexington, Mass., economics consulting firm, predicted that the economy would expand at a robust 5% to 7% adjusted annual rate in the current quarter, as inventory liquidation slows sharply and consumer spending rises.

## Powerful Advance

"This quarter looks very much like the first quarter of previous recoveries," he said. "It's shaping up as a powerful advance." He predicted that the economy would increase at a 5% to 6% pace in the second half of the year.

Maury Harris, chief economist for Paine Webber Inc., a New York securities firm, made a similar prediction. He anticipates growth of "at least" 6% at an annual rate in the current quarter, and possibly as high as 7.5%, followed by growth at a 5% rate in the second half of the year.

Robert Dederick, undersecretary of commerce for economic affairs, agreed that "the odds favor a significant acceleration in the GNP growth rate" in the current quarter. "With inflation in check, monetary policy accommodative and an income-tax cut in store for July," he said, "the economy should continue to roll along during the second half of the year."

The economy contracted 1.1% at an adjusted annual rate in the fourth quarter of last year, after increasing at a weak 0.7% pace in the third quarter. The latest quarter's performance, despite the downward revision, still was the strongest since the economy expanded at a 7.9% pace in the first quarter of 1981.

The department's report showed that prices, measured by a GNP-based index, rose at a revised annual rate of 5.7% in the first quarter after increasing at a 3.7% pace in the fourth quarter of last year. The department earlier had put the first-quarter inflation rate at 5.8%.

Most other price measures have shown a slowing of inflation in the first quarter from preceding months. Another GNP-based inflation measure, based on a fixed market-basket of goods, has been more consistent with these other inflation gauges. This measure showed prices rising at a 3.2% rate in the first quarter, following an increase at a 4.9% pace in the final quarter of last year.

Before adjustment for inflation, GNP rose to a $3.171 trillion annual rate in the first quarter from a $3.108 trillion pace in the previous period. Calculated in 1972 dollars, to adjust for the effects of inflation, GNP increased to a $1.486 trillion pace in the first quarter, after declining to a $1.477 trillion rate in the final quarter of last year.

The profits report showed that before-tax profits rose an adjusted 1.4% in the first quarter to $178.3 billion at an adjusted annual rate after declining 2.4% in the fourth quarter of last year to an adjusted $175.9 billion pace.

*Corporate profits . . . first two paragraphs*

---

WASHINGTON – First-quarter after-tax profits of U.S. corporations declined 4.6% from the fourth quarter as the economic recovery got off to a weaker start than previously thought.

The Commerce Department said after-tax profits decreased to a seasonally adjusted annual rate of $112.5 billion in the January-March quarter, after falling 1.3% in the fourth quarter of last year to an adjusted $117.9 billion pace. The latest quarter's decline left profits 2.2% below the $115 billion pace of the first quarter of 1982 and 3.9% below the $117.1 billion average for all of last year.

---

Compare first-quarter 83 profits of $112.5 billion with the postwar record of profits in Chart 1. (See page 158.) You can see that profits deteriorated in the 1981–82 recession, following a meager recovery from the 1980 recession. How will profits perform during the current recovery and expansion? Will they rebound to record highs? The answers to these questions are found in an examination of profits over the business cycle.

Profits measure efficiency by comparing revenues to costs. Recall that the economy's efficiency improves during the early phases of the cycle and deteriorates during the latter phases. Thus, profits grow during recovery and expansion and deteriorate during peak and contraction.

What is the relationship between general changes in economic efficiency over the cycle and the specific measurement of profit? Efficiency improves early in the cycle because factories are operating with excess capacity and producing less than maximum output. The general reduction in costs due to improved productivity increases the spread between prices and costs, known as the profit rate or profit per unit of output. As sales improve, total profit grows because of both higher output and higher profits per unit of output.

Efficiency deteriorates late in the cycle as factories strain to produce maximum output. Costs rise as productivity falls, and industry is forced into a "profit squeeze," meaning that costs push up against prices. Total profits fall as sales volume stops growing, or actually contracts, and profit per unit of output (the profit rate) falls.

**Chart 1**
**Corporate Profits after Taxes**

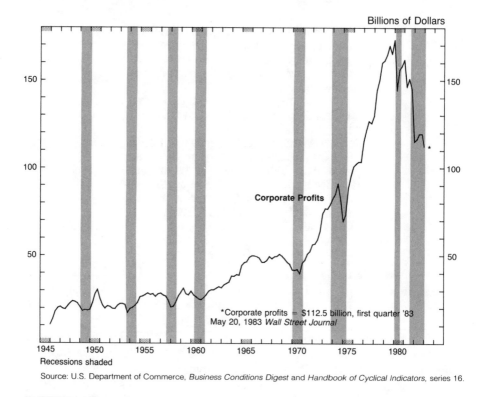

Billions of Dollars

150

100

50

Corporate Profits

*Corporate profits = $112.5 billion, first quarter '83
May 20, 1983 *Wall Street Journal*

1945    1950    1955    1960    1965    1970    1975    1980
Recessions shaded

Source: U.S. Department of Commerce, *Business Conditions Digest* and *Handbook of Cyclical Indicators*, series 16.

The top graph in Chart 2 on page 159 is a bedrock picture of real profits, stripped of inflationary gains. It portrays the quality of profits by removing inventory profits swollen by inflation and by taking into account the replacement cost of depreciating plant and equipment (rather than the unrealistically low original cost). The bottom graph portrays the ratio of price to unit labor costs, that is, the relative strength of prices and unit labor costs. This informs you of the extent to which labor costs are encroaching on prices and of business's ability to hold down labor costs in relation to the prices received.

Each of the cycles in the past decade demonstrates the same sequence of events. Start with a typical recovery and expansion such as the recovery and expansion of 1971–72 or 1975–77. Unit labor costs were kept down by good gains in labor productivity due to modest levels of capacity utilization. As a result, the ratio of price to unit labor costs (our proxy for the term *profit margins*) improved and held up well. Since sales volume and output were growing, total real profits grew sharply.

**Chart 2**
**Corporate Profits in 1972 Dollars with Inventory Valuation and Capital Consumption Adjustment; and Ratio, Price to Unit Labor Cost, Nonfarm Business**

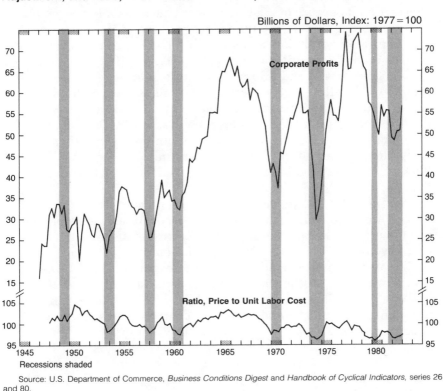

Billions of Dollars, Index: 1977 = 100

Recessions shaded

Source: U.S. Department of Commerce, *Business Conditions Digest* and *Handbook of Cyclical Indicators*, series 26 and 80.

Then, in 1973 and 1978–79, as production and capacity utilization peaked, labor productivity declined and unit labor costs increased. As a result, the ratio of price to unit labor costs fell as profit margins were squeezed. Since, at the peak of the cycle, sales and output had also stalled, real profits tumbled and continued to fall throughout the ensuing recessions of 1974–75 and 1980.

Note that after the mid-1960s, real profits suffered from the same malaise as real wages. All improvements were eroded in the course of the cycle. This serves to further underscore the point made in earlier chapters that both real wages and profits were hurt by the steep inflation and cyclical instability of the past 15 years. Profits' poor performance cannot be blamed on workers' wages, nor can wages' poor performance be blamed on profits. Both were victims of the cycle's debilitating impact on productivity.

Recall Chapter Eight's discussion of wage and price controls. Chart 2 in this chapter illustrates the foolishness of this adventure. The rate of inflation declined in 1971–72, during President Nixon's controls, despite rising real wages, a rising ratio of price to unit labor costs, and rising real profits. Since real wages and profits were rising, what use were the wage and price controls? Inflation subsided, not because of the controls, but because of improved productivity brought about by the recovery phase of the business cycle. The rate of inflation increased in 1979–80, during President Carter's controls, despite falling real wages, a falling ratio of price to unit labor costs, and falling real profits. Since real wages and profits were falling, why weren't controls effective in limiting greed? Because the inflation was due to cyclical expansion's negative impact on productivity, which boosted costs. Controls could not stem the rising spiral of prices. To summarize, profits, when calculated for the entire economy, measure efficiency, not greed. It's a mistake to think that prices can be controlled by limiting profits.

Looking to the future, you can predict with confidence that profits will improve during this economic recovery and expansion as profit margins and sales volume grow. Low rates of capacity utilization have boosted labor productivity and cut unit labor costs, providing an increased spread between prices and costs. As production grows, total profits should improve substantially.

If the expansion is mild and gradual, and capacity utilization does not rise quickly and intensify cost pressures, real profits should continue to grow over a number of years and, like real wages, break out of the low range of the past 15 years.

But suppose you wish to monitor the earnings of a particular company rather than all corporations? You can do so by using The Wall Street Journal's "Digest of Earnings Reports," listed as "Earnings Digest" in the front-page index. (See page 161.)

Take Velcro Industries as an example (last column, second from the bottom). Note that the statement is broken out into a report for the quarter and the six-month period ending March 31 and that both reports are compared with figures for the same period one year earlier (see page 162). Three figures are given: revenues, net income (profit), and net income (earnings) per share (that is, total earnings divided by total shares of stock outstanding).

Velcro Industries swam against the tide, increasing its profits despite the recession.

# Digest of Earnings Reports

**AMERICAN GUARANTY FIN'L (O)**

| Quar Mar 31: | 1983 | 1982 |
|---|---|---|
| Loss | $1,052,000 | a$359,000 |
| Cap loss | 16,000 | 16,000 |
| Net loss | 1,068,000 | a343,000 |
| Shr earns: | | |
| Loss | .... | b.09 |
| Net loss | .... | b.09 |

a-Income. b-Income; adjusted for a 5% stock dividend payable in June 1983.

**ANGELES CORP. (O)**

| Quar Mar 31: | 1983 | 1982 |
|---|---|---|
| Net loss | $866,000 | $61,000 |

**BETHLEHEM CORP. (A)**

| Quar Mar 31: | 1983 | 1982 |
|---|---|---|
| Sales | $3,446,000 | $4,599,000 |
| Net income | 7,000 | 192,000 |
| Shr earns: | | |
| Net income | .01 | a.18 |

a-Adjusted for a 10% stock dividend paid in April 1983.

**C 3 INC. (N)**

| Year Mar 31: | 1983 | 1982 |
|---|---|---|
| Revenues | $62,500,000 | $48,600,000 |
| Net income | 8,900,000 | 8,400,000 |
| Shr earns: | | |
| Net income | 1.05 | .98 |
| Quarter: | | |
| Revenues | 22,800,000 | 13,500,000 |
| Net income | 3,600,00 | 2,400,000 |
| Shr earns: | | |
| Net income | .42 | .28 |

**CADILLAC FAIRVIEW CORP. (T)**

| Year Feb 28: | 1983 | a1982 |
|---|---|---|
| Revenues | $272,457,000 | $258,453,000 |
| Inco cnt op | 12,615,000 | 42,058,000 |
| Loss dis op | .... | 16,035,000 |
| Net income | 12,615,000 | 26,023,000 |
| Shr earns: | | |
| Inco cnt op | .02 | .39 |
| Net income | .02 | .19 |

a-Restated. Amounts in Canadian dollars.

**CIRCLE K CORP. (A)**

| Year Apr 30: | 1983 | 1982 |
|---|---|---|
| Sales | $747,844,000 | $726,792,000 |
| Net income | 15,164,000 | d15,278,000 |
| Shr earns: | | |
| Net income | 1.37 | .... |
| Quarter: | | |
| Sales | 182,325,000 | 174,245,000 |
| Net income | 3,665,000 | d26,479,000 |
| Shr earns: | | |
| Net income | .33 | .... |

d-Loss.

**CNL FINANCIAL CORP. (O)**

| Quar Mar 31: | 1983 | 1982 |
|---|---|---|
| Income | $316,702 | $235,735 |
| Cap loss | .... | 414 |
| Net income | 318,702 | 235,321 |
| Shr earns: | | |
| Income | .13 | .10 |
| Net income | .13 | .10 |

**COURTAULDS PLC. (A)**

| Year Mar 31: | 1983 | 1982 |
|---|---|---|
| Sales | $2,965,900,000 | $2,793,000,000 |
| Income | 49,000,000 | 29,400,000 |
| Extrd chg | 43,900,000 | 1,500,000 |
| Net income | 5,100,000 | 27,900,000 |

The above results have been computed at the pound's current rate.

**DONALDSON CO. (N)**

| Quar Apr 30: | 1983 | 1982 |
|---|---|---|
| Sales | $52,114,000 | $69,482,000 |
| Net loss | 1,892,000 | c2,083,000 |
| Shr earns: | | |
| Net income | .... | c.40 |
| 9 months: | | |
| Sales | 151,491,000 | 206,252,000 |
| Net loss | 2,972,000 | c7,411,000 |
| Shr earns: | | |
| Net loss | .... | c1.43 |

c-Income.

**DUNES HOTELS & CASINOS (A)**

| Quar Mar 31: | 1983 | a1982 |
|---|---|---|
| Revenues | $3,034,000 | $3,701,000 |
| Loss cnt op | 2,651,000 | 349,000 |
| Inco dis op | .... | 2,162,000 |
| Net loss | 2,651,000 | c1,813,000 |
| Shr earns: | | |
| Net loss | .... | c.38 |

a-Restated to reflect discontinued operations. c-Income.

(N) New York Stock Exchange (A) American Exchange (O) Over-the-Counter (Pa) Pacific (M) Midwest (P) Philadelphia (B) Boston (T) Toronto (Mo) Montreal (F) Foreign.

**ABBREVIATIONS**

**A partial list of frequently used abbreviations: Net inv inc (net investment income); Loss dis op (Loss from discontinued operations); Inco cnt op (Income from continuing operations.)**

**DYNATECH CORP. (O)**

| Year Mar 31: | 1983 | a1982 |
|---|---|---|
| Sales | $99,096,000 | $76,428,000 |
| Net income | 7,378,000 | 4,962,000 |
| Avg shrs | 5,209,000 | 5,064,000 |
| Shr earns: | | |
| Net income | 1.42 | .98 |
| Quarter: | | |
| Sales | 25,629,000 | 21,342,000 |
| Net income | 1,935,000 | 1,126,000 |
| Avg shrs | 5,236,000 | 5,118,000 |
| Shr earns: | | |
| Net income | .37 | .22 |

a-Restated to reflect current year acquisitions on a pooling of interests basis.

**JAMESWAY CORP. (N)**

| 13 wk Apr 30: | 1983 | 1982 |
|---|---|---|
| aSales | $75,725,000 | $63,631,000 |
| Net income | 862,000 | d216,000 |
| Shr earns (primary): | | |
| Net income | .30 | .... |

a-Excludes leased departments. d-Loss.

**KEY CO. (A)**

| 13 wk Apr 29: | 1983 | 1982 |
|---|---|---|
| Revenues | $4,363,911 | a$3,015,324 |
| Net income | 188,041 | d4,666 |
| Shr earns: | | |
| Net income | .32 | .... |
| 26 weeks: | | |
| Revenues | 7,860,555 | a5,828,670 |
| Net income | 361,850 | d981 |
| Shr earns: | | |
| Net income | .62 | .... |

a-Restated. d-Loss.

**LANE WOOD INC. (O)**

| Quar Mar 31: | 1983 | 1982 |
|---|---|---|
| Revenues | $10,798,000 | a$11,878,000 |
| Net loss | 34,000 | c73,000 |
| Shr earns: | | |
| Net loss | .... | c.04 |

a-Income. a-Restated.

**LONGVIEW FIBRE CO. (O)**

| Quar Apr 30: | 1983 | 1982 |
|---|---|---|
| Sales | $84,647,000 | $96,058,000 |
| Net income | 921,000 | 5,423,000 |
| Avg shares | 1,104,686 | 11,180,517 |
| Shr earns: | | |
| Net income | .08 | .49 |
| 6 months: | | |
| Sales | 165,384,000 | 188,970,000 |
| Loss | 1,851,00 | a2,375,000 |
| Acctg adj | .... | b39,087,000 |
| Net loss | 1,851,000 | a41,462,000 |
| Shr earns: | | |
| Loss | .... | a.21 |
| Net loss | .... | a3.69 |

a-Income. b-Credit; cumulative effect on prior periods of an acounting change.

**MAGIC CIRCLE ENERGY (O)**

| Quar Mar 31: | 1983 | a1982 |
|---|---|---|
| Revenues | $8,904,000 | $8,559,000 |
| Net income | 404,000 | 343,000 |
| Shr earns: | | |
| Net income | .03 | .03 |

a-Restated.

**MATERIALS RESEARCH (A)**

| 13 wk Apr 30: | 1983 | 1982 |
|---|---|---|
| Sales | $15,726,000 | $16,469,000 |
| Net income | 36,000 | 236,000 |
| Avg shares | 3,669,000 | 3,461,000 |
| Shr earns: | | |
| Net income | .01 | .07 |
| 26 weeks: | | |
| Sales | 30,186,000 | 31,727,000 |
| Net income | 92,000 | 437,000 |
| Avg shares | 3,572,000 | 3,457,000 |
| Shr earns: | | |
| Net income | .03 | .13 |

**MECHANICAL TECHNOLOGY (O)**

| Quar Mar 26: | 1983 | 1982 |
|---|---|---|
| Sales | $14,117,000 | $13,006,000 |
| Loss cnt op | 45,000 | c49,000 |
| Loss dis op | .... | 7,000 |
| Net loss | 45,000 | c42,000 |
| Shr earns: | | |
| Loss cnt op | .... | c.02 |
| Net loss | .... | c.02 |
| 6 months: | | |
| Sales | 27,322,000 | 24,896,000 |
| Inco cnt op | 31,000 | 305,000 |
| Loss dis op | .... | 200,000 |
| Net income | 31,000 | 305,000 |
| Shr earns: | | |
| Inco cnt op | .01 | .11 |
| Net income | .01 | .04 |

c-Income.

**MICC INVESTMENTS LTD. (T)**

| Quar Mar 31: | 1983 | a1982 |
|---|---|---|
| Net income | $3,825,000 | $5,102,000 |
| Shr earns: | | |
| Net income | .06 | .30 |

a-Restated.
Amounts in Canadian dollars.

**OMEGA OPTICAL CO. (O)**

| Quar Apr 30: | 1983 | 1982 |
|---|---|---|
| Sales | $9,426,060 | $9,717,275 |
| Net income | 194,891 | 361,095 |
| Shr earns: | | |
| Net income | .05 | .10 |
| 6 months: | | |
| Sales | 17,413,224 | 18,008,456 |
| Net income | 188,661 | 305,960 |
| Shr earns: | | |
| Net income | .05 | .08 |

**OPTICAL COATING LABS (O)**

| Quar Apr 30: | 1983 | 1982 |
|---|---|---|
| Revenues | $19,402,000 | $16,711,000 |
| Income | 1,410,000 | 507,000 |
| Extrd cred | a164,000 | .... |
| Net income | 1,574,000 | 507,000 |
| bAvg shares | 4,949,000 | 3,116,000 |
| bShr earns: (primary): | | |
| Income | .28 | .16 |
| Net income | .31 | .16 |
| bShr earns (fully diluted): | | |
| Income | .27 | .15 |
| Net income | .30 | .15 |
| 6 months: | | |
| Revenues | 35,160,000 | 30,746,000 |
| Income | 2,306,000 | 541,000 |
| Extrd cred | a248,000 | .... |
| Net income | 2,554,000 | 541,000 |
| bAvg shares | 4,784,000 | 3,100,000 |
| bShr earns (primary): | | |
| Income | .50 | .17 |
| Net income | .55 | .17 |
| bShr earns (fully diluted): | | |
| Income | .49 | .... |
| Net income | .54 | .... |

a-Tax-loss carry-forward. b-Adjusted for a two-for-one stock split paid May 16, 1983.

**PENGO INDUSTRIES INC. (N)**

| Quar Mar 31: | 1983 | a1982 |
|---|---|---|
| Revenues | $29,161,000 | $39,574,000 |
| Loss cnt op | 32,814,000 | 2,223,000 |
| Loss dis op | 5,749,000 | c4,103,000 |
| Net loss | 38,563,000 | c1,880,000 |
| Shr earns (com & com equiv): | | |
| Net loss | .... | c.20 |
| 6 months: | | |
| Revenues | 58,447,000 | 76,079,000 |
| Loss ctn op | 43,999,000 | 1,193,000 |
| Loss dis op | 7,410,000 | c7,527,000 |
| Net loss | 51,409,000 | c6,334,000 |
| Shr earns (com & com equiv): | | |
| Net loss | .... | c.67 |

a-Restated for discontinued operations. c-Income.

**PROPERTY CAPITAL TRUST (A)**

| Quar Apr 30: | 1983 | 1982 |
|---|---|---|
| Net income | $2,829,000 | a$3,631,000 |
| Avg shares | 4,252,000 | 3,160,000 |
| Shr earns: | | |
| Net income | .67 | 1.15 |
| 9 months: | | |
| Net income | 7,754,000 | a7,292,000 |
| Avg shares | 3,807,000 | 3,146,000 |
| Shr earns: | | |
| Net income | 1.98 | 2.31 |

a-Includes a gain of $1,700,000 from sale of investment.

**RAVEN INDUSTRIES INC. (A)**

| Quar Apr 30: | 1983 | 1982 |
|---|---|---|
| Sales | $6,846,042 | $7,048,310 |
| Net income | 215,369 | 175,523 |
| Avg shares | 1,539,153 | a1,494,093 |
| Shr earns (primary): | | |
| Net income | .14 | a.12 |

a-Adjusted for stock dividends.

**SAGE DRILLING CO. (O)**

| Quar Mar 31: | 1983 | 1982 |
|---|---|---|
| Revenues | $2,171,000 | $6,731,000 |
| Net loss | 65,000 | c807,000 |
| Shr earns: | | |
| Net loss | .... | c.46 |
| 9 months: | | |
| Revenues | 7,586,000 | 17,944,000 |
| Net income | 15,000 | 2,624,000 |
| Shr earns: | | |
| Net income | .01 | 1.50 |

c-Income.

**SANDERS ASSOCIATES INC. (N)**

| 13 wk Apr 29: | 1983 | 1982 |
|---|---|---|
| Sales | $152,343,000 | $111,337,000 |
| Net income | 10,999,000 | 7,116,000 |
| Avg shares | 9,030,000 | 7,995,000 |
| Shr earns: | | |
| Net income | 1.22 | .89 |
| 39 weeks: | | |
| Sales | 406,652,000 | 314,055,000 |
| Net income | 25,598,000 | 18,596,000 |
| Avg shares | 8,930,000 | 7,993,000 |
| Shr earns: | | |
| Net income | 2.87 | 2.33 |

**STEINBERG INC. (Mo)**

| 12 wk Apr 9: | 1983 | 1982 |
|---|---|---|
| Sales | $754,540,000 | a$742,509,000 |
| Net loss | 2,101,000 | c7,260,000 |
| Shr earns: | | |
| Net loss | .... | c.87 |
| 36 weeks: | | |
| Sales | 2,335,257,000 | a2,248,858,000 |
| Net income | 12,568,000 | 22,505,000 |
| Shr earns: | | |
| Net income | 1.01 | 2.69 |

c-Income. a-Restated. Amounts in Canadian dollars.

**TELECONCEPTS CORP. (A)**

| Quar Mar 31: | 1983 | 1982 |
|---|---|---|
| Sales | $6,399,081 | $3,010,834 |
| Net income | 340,032 | 160,740 |
| Shr earns: | | |
| Net income | .12 | .07 |

**TIPPERARY CORP. (O)**

| Quar Mar 31: | 1983 | 1982 |
|---|---|---|
| Revenues | $12,983,000 | $11,859,000 |
| Loss | 1,032,000 | 2,262,000 |
| aExtrd cred | 790,000 | .... |
| Net loss | 242,000 | 2,262,000 |
| Avg shrs | 6,244,000 | 6,015,000 |
| 6 months: | | |
| Revenues | 31,410,000 | 33,970,000 |
| Loss | 271,000 | b1,632,000 |
| aExtrd cred | 790,000 | .... |
| Net income | 519,000 | d1,632,000 |
| Avg shrs | 6,099,000 | 6,034,000 |
| Shr earns: | | |
| Net income | .09 | .... |

a-Gain from extinguishment of debt. b-Includes gain of $1,391,000 from sale of assets. d-Loss.

**TRANS-WESTERN EXPLOR (O)**

| Quar Mar 31: | 1983 | a1982 |
|---|---|---|
| Revenues | $768,000 | $955,000 |
| Net loss | 819,000 | c286,000 |
| Shr earns: | | |
| Net loss | .... | c.04 |

a-Restated. c-Income.

**TRANSTECHNOLOGY CORP. (A)**

| Year Mar 31: | 1983 | 1982 |
|---|---|---|
| Revenues | $71,665,000 | $51,007,000 |
| Net income | 5,766,000 | 3,723,000 |
| Avg shares | 3,037,000 | 2,628,000 |
| Shr earns (primary): | | |
| Net income | 1.90 | 1.42 |
| Shr earns (fully diluted): | | |
| Net income | 1.62 | 1.26 |

**TWIN FAIR INC. (A)**

| Quar Mar 31: | 1983 | a1982 |
|---|---|---|
| Revenues | $697,000 | $995,000 |
| Loss cnt op | 587,000 | 553,000 |
| Inco dis op | .... | 42,000 |
| Net loss | 587,000 | 511,000 |

a-Restated to reflect discontinued operations.

**U.S. TELEPHONE INC. (O)**

| Quar Apr 30: | 1983 | 1982 |
|---|---|---|
| Revenues | $31,453,000 | $18,214,000 |
| Net income | 477,000 | 1,516,000 |
| Avg shares | 16,022,000 | 12,879,000 |
| Shr earns: | | |
| Net income | .03 | .12 |
| 6 months: | | |
| Revenues | 60,191,000 | 32,270,000 |
| Net loss | 899,000 | c1,657,000 |
| Avg shares | 15,377,000 | 12,620,000 |
| Shr earns: | | |
| Net loss | .... | c.14 |

c-Income.

**VELCRO INDUSTRIES N.V. (O)**

| Quar Mar 31: | 1983 | a1982 |
|---|---|---|
| Revenues | $14,354,000 | $11,869,000 |
| Net income | 1,759,000 | 1,486,000 |
| Shr earns: | | |
| Net income | .59 | .49 |
| 6 months: | | |
| Revenues | 26,870,000 | 23,118,000 |
| Net income | 3,518,000 | 3,235,000 |
| Shr earns: | | |
| Net income | 1.17 | 1.07 |

a-Restated.

Velcro Industries

**YARDNEY CORP. (B)**

| Quar Apr 30: | 1983 | 1982 |
|---|---|---|
| Sales | $5,712,000 | $6,436,000 |
| Net income | 431,000 | 412,000 |
| Shr earns: | | |
| Net income | .09 | .08 |
| 6 months: | | |
| Sales | 9,845,000 | 11,772,000 |
| Net income | 650,000 | 639,000 |
| Shr earns: | | |
| Net income | 13 | 13 |

The Wall Street Journal, *May 23, 1983.*

```
VELCRO INDUSTRIES N.V. (O)
    Quar Mar 31:    1983        a 1982
Revenues .......  $14,354,000  $11,869,000
Net income ....    1,759,000    1,486,000
Shr earns:
    Net income .        .59          .49
    6 months:
Revenues .......  26,870,000   23,118,000
Net income ....    3,518,000    3,235,000
Shr earns:
    Net income .       1.17         1.07
    a-Restated.
```

## STOCK MARKET AVERAGES

On the next to the last page of the second section, *The Wall Street Journal* publishes detailed information on the Dow Jones Industrial Average in tabular and chart form, as well as other stock market news, every business day, and on Mondays it presents a chart of activity over the past year. Take a look at the May 23, 1983, edition shown on the following page.

If you want, you can "buy the Dow." All you need do is purchase a share of stock of each of the 30 corporations in the Industrial Average. The value of your investment would fluctuate with the average.

But you may wish to purchase other shares of stock and follow their progress on your own. Here's how you do it.

Suppose you own some shares of Dow Jones & Co. Turn to the daily listing of "*NYSE-Composite Transactions*" in *The Wall Street Journal*. You'll find a reference to all exchanges in the index on the front page.

Dow Jones & Co. is sandwiched between Dow Chemical and Dravo in the accompanying reprint for May 20, 1983, on page 164.

Columns 1 and 2 tell you the highest and lowest value of the

| (1) | (2) | | (3) | (4) | (5) | (6) | (7) | (8) | (9) | (10) |
|-----|-----|---|-----|-----|-----|-----|-----|-----|-----|------|
| 52 Weeks | | | | Yld | P-E | Sales | | | | Net |
| High | Low | Stock | Div. | % | Ratio | 100s | High | Low | Close | Chg. |
| 51½ | 17⅞ | DowJn | s .60 | 1.2 | 34 | 48 | 50¼ | 49¾ | 50 | − ½ |

stock in the past 52 weeks, expressed in dollars and fractions of a dollar. Thus, Dow Jones & Co. stock was as low as 17⅞ dollars and as high as 51½ dollars in the year preceding May 20, 1983.

Footnotes are listed next to the company name. In this case, the "s" indicates that there has been a stock split or stock dividend. That is, shareholders received additional shares in some fixed ratio (say, two for one or three for two) with the appropriate adjustment

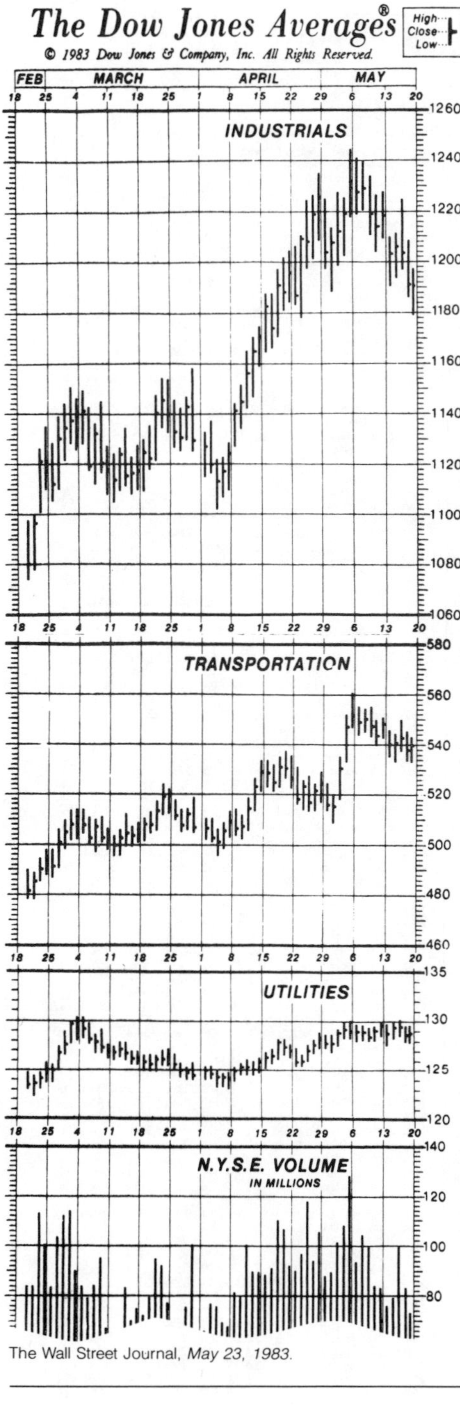


The Wall Street Journal, *May 23, 1983.*

## *An Appraisal*

# Industrials Expected to Continue To Post Gains, but at a Slower Pace

By Victor J. Hillery

Although the bull market has had a dazzling run during the past nine months, some investment officers think it still has further to go, but in a more plodding and halting manner.

From its 1982 low last August, the Dow Jones Industrial Average soared 455 points, or more than 58%, to a record 1232.59 on May 6. Since then, it has retreated, closing at 1190.02 Friday.

"In contrast to the experience of the past 15 years, we're in a major bull market and we're closer to its beginning than to the end of the line," asserts Robert L. Kemp, president of Loomis, Sayles & Co., Boston. "However, over the short term the market may rest until interest rates move to lower levels."

Meanwhile, he adds, "We aren't inclined to focus on whether the market will have a major pullback. We prefer to take the long view and seek out attractive issues and stay with them as long as the fundamentals remain intact."

As for the fundamentals, Mr. Kemp thinks the economy will continue in "a slow recovery of business activity with only modest inflation." Over the next 12 months he expects "long-term interest rates to decline at least 1 to 1½ percentage points and the industrial average to rise to the 1500 area."

He is optimistic about the inflation outlook because of the favorable trend in commodity prices, including energy; productivity gains, and prospects of holding wage increases this year to about 5%. "We still believe the disinflation-type strategy is correct," says Mr. Kemp. Loomis Sayles, which manages more than $10 billion of assets, including $5.5 billion in equities, favors stocks such as autos, textile-apparel, banks, brokerage houses, housing, office equipment, retail and savings-and-loan association issues.

**Abreast of the Market**

"We're in a sustained bull market rather than a cyclical bull market," contends David R. Geis, senior vice president and senior investment officer at Northern Trust Co., Chicago. But he also says: "The easy-money phase, when the whole market went from an undervalued to a moderate-valued level, is over. Now it's a stock-selection and earnings game."

At its current level, the market needs only improved earnings to sustain it, he asserts. "The earnings forecasts for 1984, coupled with moderate inflation, should allow stocks' price-earnings multiples to expand as we go into 1984."

However, Mr. Geis also thinks the strength in the equity indexes "belie a number of undercurrents." He thinks "the economic recovery is less robust and more selective than anticipated" and that "earnings disappointments are more prevalent" than expected. He notes the worrisome "froth" or overspeculation, in the new-issues market, but sees it being offset by the corporate liquidity the equity markets are providing, thus strengthening balance sheets.

Northern Trust, which handles $2.6 billion in pension and profit-sharing funds, has cash reserves of about 10%-15% in its equity portfolios. It would prefer to have a little higher reserves but notes that the market is "providing attractive investment opportunities," Mr. Geis says. The company favors technology issues that enhance productivity and disinflation beneficiaries. It's avoiding capital-intensive cyclicals.

"We think the market gains will slow somewhat, but we also look for the industrial average to hit 1400 sometime this year and 1700 by the middle of 1984," asserts Cabanne C. Smith, vice president of Provident Capital Management Inc., Philadelphia.

He also says that "a correction of 8% to 10% could occur at any time over a period of about 10 trading days." Any such setback, he adds, "likely would come prior to July 1—before the market feels the impact of the 10% tax cut scheduled for that date."

Mr. Smith isn't overly concerned about money-supply gyrations. He also thinks interest rates will drift lower, with the prime rate, currently 10½%, "possibly becoming a single-digit figure in the next 60 days." The most significant problem facing the economy, he contends, is the exposure of money-center banks to the problems of Mexico, Brazil and Argentina.

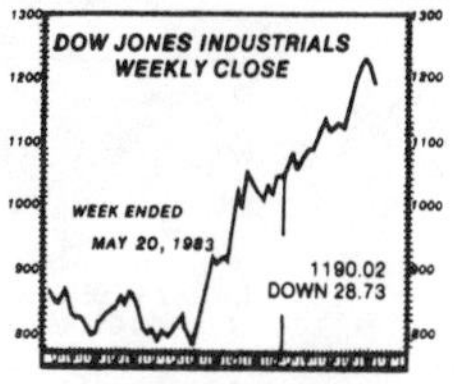


### MARKET DIARY

| | Fri. | Thu. | Wed. | Tue. | (a) | (b) |
|---|---|---|---|---|---|---|
| Issues traded | 1,968 | 2,022 | 1,997 | 1,994 | 2,215 | 2,211 |
| Advances | 733 | 561 | 987 | 974 | 1,304 | 821 |
| Declines | 845 | 1,080 | 663 | 662 | 833 | 1,174 |
| Unchanged | 390 | 361 | 347 | 358 | 178 | 216 |
| New highs | 81 | 113 | 210 | 130 | 616 | 384 |
| New lows | 2 | 2 | 1 | 3 | 10 | 10 |

(a)-Summary for the week ended May 13, 1983.
(b)-Summary for the week ended May 20, 1983.

### DOW JONES CLOSING AVERAGES

| | ----Friday---- | | | Yr. Ago | | --Since-- | |
|---|---|---|---|---|---|---|---|
| | 1983 | Change | % | 1982 | % Chg. | Dec. 31 | % |
| Ind | 1190.02 | − 1.35 | − 0.11 | 835.90 | + 42.36 | +143.48 | +13.71 |
| Trn | 539.62 | + 1.55 | + 0.29 | 333.56 | + 61.78 | + 91.24 | +20.35 |
| Utl | 128.88 | + 0.14 | + 0.11 | 113.78 | + 13.27 | + 9.42 | + 7.89 |
| Cmp | 470.14 | + 0.17 | + 0.04 | 328.36 | + 43.18 | + 60.99 | +14.91 |

### OTHER MARKET INDICATORS

| | 1983 | −Change− | | 1982 |
|---|---|---|---|---|
| N.Y.S.E. Composite ..... | 93.71 | + 0.04 | + 0.04% | 66.26 |
| Industrial ...... | 108.33 | + 0.08 | + 0.07% | 74.97 |
| Utility ........... | 47.43 | + 0.01 | + 0.02% | 39.33 |
| Transp. .......... | 88.31 | + 0.21 | + 0.24% | 55.75 |
| Financial ....... | 101.03 | − 0.31 | − 0.31% | 67.86 |
| Am. Ex. Mkt Val Index | 449.61 | + 0.36 | + 0.08% | 270.06 |
| Nasdaq OTC Composite | 303.56 | + 0.74 | + 0.24% | 182.40 |
| Industrial ...... | 366.38 | + 1.40 | + 0.38% | 209.99 |
| Insurance ...... | 278.92 | + 1.60 | + 0.58% | 188.41 |
| Banks ............ | 185.04 | − 0.04 | − 0.02% | 137.31 |
| Standard & Poor's 500 . | 162.14 | + 0.15 | + 0.09% | 114.89 |
| 400 Industrial | 181.78 | + 0.19 | + 0.10% | 128.13 |
| Value Line Index ......... | 195.66 | + 0.03 | + 0.01% | 127.67 |
| Wilshire 5000 Equity .. | 1,719.446 | + 1.480 | + 0.09% | 1,185.006 |

Market value, in billions of dollars, of N.Y.S.E., Amex and actively traded OTC issues.

### TRADING ACTIVITY

Volume of advancing stocks on N.Y.S.E., 31,235,200 shares; volume of declining stocks, 31,150,900. On American S.E., volume of advancing stocks, 8,587,400; volume of declining stocks, 3,304,300. Nasdaq volume of advancing stocks, 24,578,700; volume of declining stocks, 17,620,600.

## Friday's Market Activity

Several technology issues scored big gains but the general market retreated Friday for the third consecutive session in moderately active trading.

The industrial average finished at 1190.02, off 1.35 points, as losers exceeded gainers 845 to 733.

In the technology sector, Texas Instruments climbed 4⅛ to 152½; Motorola, 3¼ to 119; Honeywell, 1¾ to 117⅛; NCR, 1⅛ to 119; National Semiconductor, 1¾ to 39¾, and Teledyne, 1 to 148.

Communications Satellite spurted 3¾ to 75½; it moved up to the fall of 1984 the planned start of satellite-to-home broadcasts and increased to five the channels of pay-television service it will offer.

For all of last week, the industrial average slipped 28.73 points, or 2.36%. The transportation index slid 8.27 points, or 1.51%, to 539.62. And the utility indicator eased 0.73 point, or 0.56%, to 128.88. For all of last week, Big Board volume fell to 412,062,060 shares from 464,717,880 shares the prior week but exceeded the 237,019,302 total of the comparable 1982 week.

# NYSE-Composite Transactions

*Friday, May 20, 1983*

**Quotations include trades on the Midwest, Pacific, Philadelphia, Boston and Cincinnati stock exchanges and reported by the National Association of Securities Dealers and Instinet**

| 52 Weeks High | 52 Weeks Low | Stock | Div. | Yld % | P-E Ratio | Sales 100s | High | Low | Close | Net Chg. |
|---|---|---|---|---|---|---|---|---|---|---|
| 49½ | 31 | CrZel pf | 4.63 | 9.6 | .. | 19 | 48¼ | 47⅞ | 48 | − ¼ |
| 44¼ | 23⅝ | Culbro | 1 | 2.3 | 14 | 22 | 43¾ | 43 | 43¾ | + ¾ |
| 43¾ | 12 | Cullin s | | .. | 65 | 795 | 43⅛ | 41½ | 42⅞ | + 1¼ |
| 64¼ | 26 | CumEn | 2 | 3.8 | .. | 406 | 53⅜ | 51¼ | 53¼ | − ½ |
| 9⅞ | 7½ | CurrInc | 1.10 | 11. | .. | 9 | 9¾ | 9⅝ | 9⅝ | ..... |
| 52 | 32⅜ | CurtW | 1.20 | 2.4 | 11 | 49 | 49 | 48 | 49 | + 1 |
| 34 | 13⅝ | Cyclops | 1.10 | 3.7 | .. | 161 | 30 | 29⅞ | 29⅞ | ..... |
| | | – D–D–D – | | | | | | | | |
| 4⅛ | 2⅛ | DMG | | .. | .. | 236 | 4 | 3⅞ | 3⅞ | ..... |
| 39⅞ | 5¾ | Damon | .20 | .5 | .. | 246 | 37¾ | 37⅛ | 37¾ | + ⅛ |
| 22⅜ | 10½ | DanRiv | .56 | 2.5 | .. | 111 | 22¼ | 22¼ | 22¼ | ..... |
| 39½ | 21⅞ | DanaCp | 1.60 | 4.2 | 28 | x85 | 37⅞ | 37¼ | 37⅞ | + ⅜ |
| 15¾ | 8⅝ | Daniel | .18b | 1.6 | 8 | 309 | 11⅜ | 11 | 11⅛ | ..... |
| 77¼ | 50½ | DartKr | 3.84 | 5.6 | 11 | 1370 | 69½ | 68½ | 69⅛ | − ⅞ |
| 73¼ | 20¼ | DataGn | | .. | 54 | 1620 | 57¾ | 56⅜ | 57 | + ¼ |
| 10⅝ | 4½ | DatTer | | .. | .. | 26 | 7¼ | 7⅛ | 7¼ | + ⅛ |
| 25⅝ | 10⅞ | Datpnt | | .. | .. | 762 | 20⅜ | 19⅞ | 20⅛ | − ⅛ |
| 13⅛ | 6¼ | Dayco | .16 | 1.3 | 156 | 33 | 12¾ | 12½ | 12½ | − ⅛ |
| 74¾ | 33½ | DayHud | 1.20 | 1.7 | 17 | 1389 | 72¾ | 71¾ | 72½ | − ¼ |
| 19 | 14⅜ | DaytPL | 2 | 11. | 7 | 331 | 17⅞ | 17¾ | 17⅞ | + ⅛ |
| 64 | 49 | DPL pf | 7.70 | 12. | .. | z220 | 62¾ | 62¾ | 62¾ | + 2½ |
| 101½ | 81 | DPL pf | 11.60 | 12. | .. | 270 | 100¾ | 100⅝ | 100¾ | + ¾ |
| 36⅝ | 14½ | DeanF s | .60 | 1.6 | 18 | 87 | u37⅞ | 36⅝ | 37½ | + ⅞ |
| 39½ | 22 | Deere | 1 | 2.6 | .. | 858 | 37¾ | 37⅜ | 37¾ | + ¼ |
| 17 | 13¼ | DelmP | 1.64 | 9.8 | 8 | 135 | 16⅞ | 16¾ | 16¾ | ..... |
| 51 | 25⅜ | DeltaAr | 1 | 2.3 | .. | 1013 | 44 | 43¼ | 44 | + ½ |
| 13⅜ | 4¾ | Deltona | | .. | .. | 49 | 11¼ | 11 | 11⅛ | + ⅛ |
| 47¾ | 22¼ | DixChk | 1.12 | 2.7 | 14 | 625 | 42 | 41 | 41½ | − ⅛ |
| 35¼ | 16¼ | DenMfg | 1.44 | 4.3 | 15 | 30 | 33⅜ | 33⅛ | 33¼ | − ⅛ |
| 36⅞ | 22⅜ | Dennys | .64 | 1.9 | 13 | 412 | 34 | 33¼ | 33⅜ | − ⅝ |
| 37¼ | 13⅜ | DeSoto | 1.24 | 4.1 | 16 | 88 | 30⅞ | 30¼ | 30¼ | − ¾ |
| 15¼ | 11 | DetEd | 1.68 | 11. | 8 | 1198 | 15⅛ | 14⅞ | 15 | + ⅛ |
| 81½ | 59 | DetE pf | 5.50 | 6.9 | .. | 1 | 80 | 80 | 80 | − ¼ |
| 74 | 57 | DetE pf | 9.32 | 13. | .. | z200 | 74 | 72¼ | 74 | ..... |
| 61 | 46½ | DetE pf | 7.68 | 13. | .. | z100 | 61 | 59⅞ | 59⅞ | + ⅛ |
| 60⅜ | 44½ | DetE pf | 7.36 | 13. | .. | z520 | 59 | 58⅛ | 58⅛ | − 1⅞ |
| 23¼ | 17½ | DE pfF | 2.75 | 12. | .. | 5 | 23⅛ | 23⅛ | 23⅛ | ..... |
| 27 | 23½ | DE pfP | 3.12 | 12. | .. | 5 | 25 | 25 | 25 | ..... |
| 23½ | 18⅜ | DE pfB | 2.75 | 12. | .. | 7 | 23⅛ | 23 | 23 | − ⅛ |
| 27⅜ | 23⅞ | DE pfO | 3.40 | 13. | .. | 8 | 27⅛ | 27 | 27 | − ⅛ |
| 27⅞ | 24 | DE pfM | 3.42 | 13. | .. | 80 | 27⅞ | 27⅛ | 27⅛ | − ⅛ |
| 32¼ | 24⅝ | DE prL | 4 | 13. | .. | 14 | 31⅞ | 31¼ | 31½ | ..... |
| 33 | 24¾ | DE pfK | 4.12 | 13. | .. | 8 | 32⅞ | 32¼ | 32¼ | − ¼ |
| 19 | 14 | DetE pr | 2.28 | 12. | .. | 3 | 18½ | 18½ | 18½ | + ⅛ |
| 48⅝ | 21⅜ | Dexter | 1.10 | 2.5 | 17 | 54 | 44⅞ | 44½ | 44⅞ | + ⅝ |
| 15¾ | 8⅜ | DiGior | .64 | 4.4 | 17 | 255 | 14⅝ | 14⅜ | 14⅝ | + ⅛ |
| 29¾ | 19⅝ | DiGio pf | 2.25 | 8.0 | .. | 2 | 28⅛ | 28 | 28⅛ | + ⅛ |
| 26⅜ | 16½ | DiamS | 1.76 | 7.0 | 13 | 1732 | 25 | 24¾ | 25 | + ⅛ |
| 102 | 42½ | Diebld | 1 | 1.1 | 19 | 236 | 91 | 89¾ | 90⅜ | − ¼ |
| 132⅛ | 61¾ | Digital | | .. | 19 | 6410 | 109⅞ | 108 | 108½ | − 1 |
| 84¾ | 49⅝ | Disney | 1.20 | 1.6 | 23 | 586 | 75⅛ | 74⅛ | 74¼ | ..... |
| 28 | 19⅛ | DEI | 2.28 | 8.6 | 7 | 6 | 26¾ | 26½ | 26½ | − ¼ |
| 4⅞ | 1⅞ | Divrsin | | .. | .. | 66 | 4⅜ | 4¼ | 4⅜ | ..... |
| 16⅝ | 11⅝ | DrPepp | .84 | 5.7 | 35 | 955 | 15 | 14¾ | 14¾ | − ¼ |
| 22¼ | 5 | Dome g | .10 | .. | .. | 1843 | 20¼ | 19⅞ | 20⅛ | + ⅛ |
| 23⅞ | 18 | DomRs | | .. | 8 | 1447 | 22⅝ | 22⅛ | 22⅜ | ..... |
| 23½ | 12¾ | Donald | .66 | 3.2 | 67 | 30 | 21⅛ | 20¾ | 20¾ | − ¾ |
| 24⅞ | 8⅜ | DonLJ | .24 | 1.2 | 14 | 228 | 21⅛ | 20¼ | 20½ | − ½ |
| 84 | 38½ | Donnly | 1.60 | 2.0 | 16 | 159 | 80½ | 80 | 80¼ | − 1½ |
| 44⅝ | 20 | Dorsey | 1.10 | 3.4 | .. | 45 | 32 | 32 | 32 | − ¼ |
| 37 | 17¾ | Dover | .70 | 2.0 | 15 | 600 | 35⅝ | 35 | 35⅝ | + ⅜ |
| 34⅛ | 19⅝ | DowCh | 1.80 | 5.6 | 21 | 2582 | 32⅜ | 31⅝ | 32¼ | + ⅛ |
| Dow Jones → 51½ | 17⅞ | DowJn s | .60 | 1.2 | 34 | 48 | 50¼ | 49¾ | 50 | − ½ |
| 16⅞ | 9¼ | Dravo | .50 | 3.2 | .. | 155 | 15½ | 15⅜ | 15½ | − ⅜ |
| 23⅝ | 12¼ | Dresr | .80 | 4.1 | 103 | 1150 | 19⅝ | 19 | 19⅝ | + ½ |
| 19⅝ | 14¼ | DrexB | 2 | 10. | .. | 12 | 19⅛ | 18⅞ | 19⅛ | + ⅛ |
| 64 | 24¼ | Dreyfus | .80 | 1.3 | 9 | 61 | 62⅜ | 60⅞ | 60⅞ | − 1¾ |
| 48⅞ | 30 | duPont | 2.40 | 5.3 | 13 | 1433 | 46 | 44⅞ | 45⅜ | − ¾ |
| 37 | 27⅝ | duPnt pf | 3.50 | 10. | .. | 4 | 35 | 35 | 35 | + ¼ |
| 47⅜ | 36½ | duPnt pf | 4.50 | 10. | .. | 10 | 44½ | 44 | 44 | − ½ |
| 24 | 20¼ | DukeP | 2.28 | 10. | 7 | 1278 | 22⅞ | 22¾ | 22⅞ | ..... |
| 77⅜ | 59 | Duke pf | 8.70 | 11. | .. | z200 | u77½ | 77 | 77 | + 1 |
| 73½ | 55 | Duke pf | 8.20 | 12. | .. | z200 | 71⅜ | 71 | 71 | − 1¼ |
| 71½ | 52 | Duke pf | 7.80 | 11. | .. | z270 | 69 | 69 | 69 | − ⅜ |
| 26 | 20⅛ | Duke pf | 2.69 | 11. | .. | 4 | 25⅜ | 25¼ | 25¼ | + ⅛ |
| 34⅛ | 25½ | Duke pf | 3.85 | 12. | .. | 19 | 32⅞ | 32 | 32⅛ | + ⅛ |
| 103 | 79 | Duke pf | 11 | 11. | .. | 230 | 102¾ | 101½ | 102¾ | + 4¼ |
| 83¼ | 65 | Duk pfN | 8.84 | 11. | .. | z10 | 80 | 80 | 80 | + 5¼ |
| 135¼ | 66 | DunBr | 3.20 | 2.5 | 24 | 642 | 131¼ | 126½ | 128 | − 3½ |
| 18¼ | 13 | DuqLt | 2 | 11. | 10 | 237 | 17⅞ | 17¾ | 17¾ | ..... |
| 15¾ | 11¾ | Duq pf | 1.87 | 13. | .. | z330 | 15 | 14⅞ | 14⅞ | − ⅛ |
| 17 | 12¾ | Duq pf | 2 | 12. | .. | z250 | 16⅝ | 16½ | 16½ | ..... |
| 17 | 12¾ | Duq pf | 2.05 | 12. | .. | z1700 | 16¾ | 16¼ | 16¾ | + ¾ |
| 20 | 14⅜ | Duq pr | 2.31 | 12. | .. | z800 | 19¼ | 19 | 19 | − 1 |
| 20⅝ | 11½ | DycoPt | .24 | 1.7 | 8 | 48 | 14⅝ | 14½ | 14½ | ..... |
| 20¾ | 5⅝ | DynAm | .15 | .8 | 16 | 65 | 19⅜ | 18⅝ | 18¾ | − ¾ |
| 27¾ | 7⅜ | GnHous | .20 | .8 | 14 | 75 | 25½ | 24⅝ | 25 | − ⅜ |
| 66⅞ | 26⅝ | GnInst | .50 | 1.0 | 15 | 1532 | 49⅜ | 47¾ | 48⅞ | + ⅞ |
| 56½ | 38⅝ | GnMills | 1.84 | 3.3 | 13 | 625 | 55⅞ | 55⅜ | 55⅞ | + ⅛ |
| 71⅝ | 39⅝ | GMot | 2.40e | 3.7 | 14 | 3211 | 66⅜ | 65¼ | 65¼ | − 1 |
| 40 | 28½ | GMot pf | 3.75 | 9.6 | .. | 2 | 39⅛ | 39 | 39 | − ⅜ |
| 52⅛ | 38¼ | GMot pf | 5 | 9.8 | .. | 1 | 51 | 51 | 51 | + ¼ |
| 29⅝ | 5 | GNC s | .12 | .4 | 39 | 82 | 29 | 28½ | 29 | + ¼ |
| 9⅝ | 4⅝ | GPU | | .. | 16 | 389 | 9 | 8¾ | 8⅞ | ..... |
| 73 | 33⅞ | GenRe s | 1.28 | 2.0 | 13 | 387 | 62¾ | 61⅝ | 62¾ | + 1⅝ |
| 6¾ | 2¾ | GnRefr | | .. | .. | 58 | 6 | 5⅞ | 5⅞ | ..... |
| 48½ | 28 | GnSignl | 1.68 | 3.9 | 12 | 159 | 43⅜ | 42⅝ | 43 | − ¼ |
| 12½ | 9¼ | GTFI pf | 1.30 | 11. | .. | z200 | 11¾ | 11¾ | 11¾ | ..... |
| 37½ | 19½ | GTire | 1.50b | 4.0 | 17 | 124 | 37⅜ | 36¾ | 37⅜ | + ⅝ |
| 8⅞ | 3⅝ | Gensco | | .. | .. | 862 | 8⅝ | 8¼ | 8⅜ | − ¼ |
| 39⅜ | 11 | GnRad s | .08 | .2 | 53 | 234 | 36¼ | 35¼ | 35⅜ | − ¼ |
| 25⅛ | 7⅛ | Genst g | .60 | .. | .. | 392 | 24⅝ | 24⅜ | 24⅝ | + ⅛ |
| 47⅜ | 29¾ | GenuPt | 1.38 | 3.2 | 15 | 1091 | 42¾ | 41⅝ | 42½ | ..... |
| 30¾ | 13¼ | GaPac | .60 | 2.1 | .. | 1235 | 29 | 28¼ | 29 | + ⅜ |
| 35¼ | 25¾ | GaPc pf | 2.24 | 6.4 | .. | 1 | 35 | 35 | 35 | ..... |
| 29½ | 25⅜ | GaPw pf | 3.44 | 12. | .. | 388 | 29⅛ | 28½ | 28¾ | ..... |
| 31¾ | 24 | GaPw pf | 3.76 | 12. | .. | 320 | 31½ | 30¾ | 31½ | + ¼ |
| 22¼ | 16⅛ | GaPw pf | 2.56 | 12. | .. | 54 | 22¼ | 21¾ | 22 | − ⅛ |
| 21⅜ | 15½ | GaPw pf | 2.52 | 12. | .. | 11 | 21⅜ | 21 | 21⅜ | + ⅜ |
| 25¼ | 19¼ | GaPw pf | 2.75 | 11. | .. | 2 | 24¾ | 24¾ | 24¾ | ..... |
| 67⅞ | 48⅜ | GaPw pf | 7.80 | 12. | .. | z120 | 65¼ | 65¼ | 65¼ | ..... |
| 65 | 49 | GaPw pf | 7.72 | 12. | .. | z310 | 64 | 62½ | 64 | + 1½ |
| 31½ | 19⅜ | GerbPd s | 1.48 | 5.1 | 10 | 149 | 29¾ | 29 | 29⅛ | − ⅝ |
| 25⅝ | 6½ | GerbSc | .12 | .5 | 44 | 195 | 24½ | 24¼ | 24¼ | − ⅛ |
| 72½ | 43 | Getty | 2.60e | 3.9 | 8 | 1435 | 68 | 66 | 66¾ | − 1¼ |
| 9½ | 4½ | GiantP | | .. | .. | 2 | 8¾ | 8¾ | 8¾ | ..... |
| 16 | 2¾ | GibrFn | | .. | .. | 855 | 14½ | 13¾ | 14½ | + ¼ |
| 22¼ | 10 | GiffHill | .52 | 2.6 | .. | 33 | 19⅞ | 19¾ | 19⅞ | − ⅛ |
| 51⅜ | 30¾ | Gillette | 2.30 | 5.3 | 10 | 885 | 43¾ | 42⅜ | 43¾ | + 1¼ |
| 15⅛ | 8⅛ | GleasW | | .. | .. | 27 | 13⅝ | 13¼ | 13⅜ | + ⅛ |
| 14⅛ | 7¼ | GlobIM | .24 | 2.4 | 4 | 1108 | 10¼ | 9¾ | 10 | − ⅛ |
| 60½ | 21½ | GldNug | | .. | 14 | 109 | 57½ | 56¼ | 57⅛ | − ⅜ |
| 30½ | 4½ | GldWF | | .. | 40 | 324 | 27¾ | 27¼ | 27⅜ | − ½ |
| 43⅞ | 16⅝ | Gdrich | 1.56 | 3.9 | .. | 529 | 40⅜ | 40 | 40¼ | − ⅛ |
| 38¼ | 21⅝ | Gdrch pf | 3.12 | 9.4 | .. | 976 | 33⅜ | 33 | 33¼ | − ⅛ |
| 36⅞ | 21⅜ | Goodyr | 1.40 | 4.3 | 10 | 4375 | 33 | 32⅝ | 32¾ | − ¼ |
| 29¾ | 13⅛ | GordnJ | .56 | 2.1 | 11 | 33 | 27¾ | 27¼ | 27¼ | + ¼ |
| 39¾ | 20 | Gould | 1.72 | 4.5 | 19 | 1939 | 39 | 38 | 38⅝ | − ⅝ |
| 38 | 20½ | Gould pf | 1.35 | 3.6 | .. | 1 | 38 | 38 | 38 | ..... |
| 48¾ | 28½ | Grace | 2.80 | 5.9 | 11 | 579 | 47½ | 47 | 47⅛ | − ½ |
| 56 | 33⅞ | Graingr | 1.20 | 2.2 | 17 | 25 | 54¼ | 53⅞ | 54 | − ¼ |
| 16¾ | 8½ | Granitv | | .. | .. | 401 | 16¼ | 15⅝ | 16⅛ | ..... |
| 12½ | 5⅝ | GtAtPc | | .. | 20 | 258 | 11⅝ | 11 | 11½ | + ⅛ |
| 38⅝ | 17⅛ | GtLkIn | .80a | 2.3 | 13 | 43 | 35½ | 35 | 35¼ | − ⅜ |
| 27¾ | 15¾ | GNIrn | 1.50e | 7.6 | 11 | 2 | 19⅞ | 19⅝ | 19⅝ | ..... |
| 49 | 29 | GtNoNk | 2 | 4.4 | 10 | 213 | 45¼ | 45 | 45 | + ¼ |
| 31½ | 10½ | GtWFin | .40 | 1.4 | 33 | 2569 | 28¼ | 27½ | 27¾ | − ¾ |
| 17⅜ | 7 | GWHsp | | .. | 40 | 468 | 16½ | 15¾ | 16½ | + ½ |
| 15 | 11⅞ | GMP | 1.56 | 11. | 11 | 13 | 13⅝ | 13¼ | 13⅝ | + ¼ |
| 25⅜ | 12⅝ | Greyh | 1.20 | 5.3 | 9 | 920 | 22⅞ | 22½ | 22¾ | + ¼ |
| 7¾ | 1⅞ | Groler n | | .. | 16 | 496 | 6¾ | 6⅜ | 6½ | + ⅛ |
| 15 | 7 | GrowG | .36b | 2.8 | 16 | 97 | 12⅞ | 12¾ | 12⅞ | ..... |
| 5 | 2¼ | GthRty | | .. | .. | 76 | 4⅞ | 4¾ | 4¾ | ..... |
| 11½ | 3 | GrubEl | | .. | 49 | 91 | 9¾ | 9¼ | 9¼ | − ¼ |
| 62¾ | 26⅝ | Grumm | 1.60 | 2.8 | 17 | 421 | 57⅜ | 57 | 57¼ | + ¼ |
| 25¼ | 19⅛ | Grum pf | 2.80 | 11. | .. | 11 | 24½ | 24½ | 24½ | − ⅛ |
| 44¾ | 12⅝ | Guardl | .42 | 1.0 | 17 | 86 | 40¾ | 40⅜ | 40⅝ | − ¼ |
| 27¾ | 11½ | GlfWst | .75 | 2.9 | 13 | 1411 | 26¾ | 25¾ | 26 | + ¼ |
| 36½ | 24¼ | GulfOil | 2.80 | 7.8 | 7 | 1389 | 35⅞ | 35⅜ | 35⅞ | ..... |
| 19 | 11⅞ | GulfRs | | 2.1 | .. | 182 | 18⅛ | 17⅜ | 17¾ | + ⅜ |
| 15¼ | 11¼ | GlfStUt | 1.64 | 11. | 7 | 547 | 14½ | 14¼ | 14⅜ | − ⅛ |
| 32⅜ | 27½ | GlfSU pr | 3.85 | 13. | .. | 3 | 30⅝ | 30⅝ | 30⅝ | + ¼ |
| 35¾ | 27¼ | GlfSU pr | 4.40 | 13. | .. | 25 | 34⅝ | 34¼ | 34¼ | − ⅛ |
| 79 | 57¼ | GlfSU pf | 8.80 | 11. | .. | z30 | 77¼ | 77¼ | 77¼ | − 1¾ |
| 29¾ | 16¾ | GulfUtd | 1.32 | 4.7 | 9 | 425 | 28⅛ | 27⅞ | 28⅛ | ..... |
| 21½ | 16½ | GAero n | | .. | 13 | 437 | 21 | 20¼ | 20⅜ | − ½ |
| 19⅞ | 7½ | Gulton | .60 | 3.3 | 14 | 65 | 18⅞ | 18⅜ | 18⅜ | − ½ |
| | | – H–H–H – | | | | | | | | |
| 14⅞ | 7 | HMW | | .. | 46 | 67 | 14¼ | 13¾ | 14¼ | + ¼ |
| 10⅜ | 2¼ | vjHRT | | .. | .. | 224 | 6⅛ | 5½ | 5½ | − ½ |
| 22⅞ | 15⅝ | HackW s | 1.84 | 7.5 | 12 | 164 | u25 | 23 | 24⅜ | + 1⅝ |
| 35⅜ | 23⅛ | HallFB | 1.70 | 5.3 | 18 | 292 | 32½ | 31⅛ | 32¼ | + ⅞ |
| 39½ | 21 | Halbtn | 1.60 | 4.5 | 10 | 2102 | 36 | 35½ | 35⅞ | + ¼ |
| 36½ | 21½ | HamrP | 1.84 | 5.2 | 14 | 64 | 35⅝ | 35¼ | 35⅝ | ..... |
| 13⅞ | 11 | HanJS | 1.47a | 11. | .. | 234 | 13¾ | 13⅝ | 13¾ | ..... |
| 18⅜ | 14¼ | HanJI | 1.84a | 10. | .. | 98 | 18 | 17½ | 18 | + ½ |
| 30¼ | 12 | Hndlmn | 1 | 3.6 | 14 | 42 | 27⅞ | 27½ | 27½ | − ⅜ |
| 24 | 12¼ | HandH | .60 | 3.1 | 36 | 208 | 20 | 19⅝ | 19⅝ | − ¾ |
| 32⅝ | 16½ | Hanna | .40 | 1.6 | .. | 71 | 25⅛ | 25 | 25⅛ | ..... |
| 27¾ | 12⅝ | HarBrJ | 1 | 3.8 | 13 | 263 | 26⅝ | 25¾ | 26½ | + ½ |
| 47⅞ | 19½ | HarInd | .76 | 2.0 | 18 | 266 | 38¾ | 37¾ | 38½ | + ¼ |
| 9¾ | 5½ | Harnish | | .. | .. | 102 | 9⅜ | 9⅛ | 9⅛ | − ⅛ |

The Wall Street Journal, *May 23, 1983*.

| | | | | | | | | | | | |
|---|---|---|---|---|---|---|---|---|---|---|---|
| | 23½ | 12¾ | Donald | .66 | 3.2 | 67 | 30 | 21⅛ | 20¾ | 20¾ | – ¾ |
| | 24⅞ | 8⅜ | DonLJ | .24 | 1.2 | 14 | 228 | 21⅛ | 20¼ | 20½ | – ½ |
| | 84 | 38½ | Donnly | 1.60 | 2.0 | 16 | 159 | 80½ | 80 | 80¼ | –1½ |
| | 44⅝ | 20 | Dorsey | 1.10 | 3.4 | .. | 45 | 32 | 32 | 32 | – ¼ |
| | 37 | 17¾ | Dover | .70 | 2.0 | 15 | 600 | 35⅝ | 35 | 35⅝ | + ⅜ |
| | 34⅛ | 19⅝ | DowCh | 1.80 | 5.6 | 21 | 2582 | 32⅜ | 31⅝ | 32¼ | + ⅛ |
| Dow Jones → | 51½ | 17⅞ | DowJn | s .60 | 1.2 | 34 | 48 | 50¼ | 49¾ | 50 | – ½ |
| | 16⅞ | 9¼ | Dravo | .50 | 3.2 | .. | 155 | 15½ | 15⅜ | 15½ | – ⅜ |
| | 23⅝ | 12¼ | Dresr | .80 | 4.1 | 103 | 1150 | 19⅝ | 19 | 19⅝ | + ½ |
| | 19⅜ | 14¼ | DrexB | 2 | 10. | .. | 12 | 19⅛ | 18⅞ | 19⅛ | + ⅛ |
| | 64 | 24¼ | Dreyfus | .80 | 1.3 | 9 | 61 | 62⅜ | 60⅞ | 60⅞ | –1¾ |
| | 48⅞ | 30 | duPont | 2.40 | 5.3 | 13 | 1433 | 46 | 44⅞ | 45⅜ | – ¾ |
| | 37 | 27⅝ | duPnt | pf3.50 | 10. | .. | 4 | 35 | 35 | 35 | + ¼ |

in the stock's price, or else a dividend was paid to shareholders in the form of more stock rather than cash, usually without any price adjustment.

The third column of data reports the latest quarterly cash dividend (of 60 cents). The dividend is expressed as a percentage of the closing price in the following column ($0.60/$50.00 = 1.2 percent).

Column 5 reports the price-earnings (P-E) ratio, which is obtained by dividing the price of the stock by earnings per share. This important statistic is discussed in detail later in this chapter. On May 20, 1983, Dow Jones & Co.'s stock was worth 34 times the profits per share of stock.

The sixth column informs you of the number of shares traded that day, expressed in hundreds of shares. Thus, on May 20, 1983, 4,800 shares of Dow Jones & Co. stock were traded. If a "z" appears before the number in this column, the figure represents the actual number (not hundreds) of shares traded.

Columns 7, 8, and 9 tell you the stock's highest, lowest, and closing (last) price for the trading day. (Note in the caption under the date in the illustration that these quotes are a composite of transactions on the NYSE and the other exchanges listed. The closing price on the Pacific Stock Exchange in San Francisco rather than the closing price on the NYSE may be listed because trading ends later in San Francisco than in New York due to the time zone difference.) Thus, on May 20 Dow Jones & Co.'s stock traded as high as 50¼ and as low as 49¾ before closing at 50.

The last column provides the change in the closing price of the stock from the price at the previous close. You can see that this stock closed on May 20 at a price half a dollar less than the previous closing price.

Shares of other, usually smaller companies than those traded on the NYSE are traded on the *American Stock Exchange (AMEX)*. Information on that exchange is published by *The Wall Street Journal* in a form identical to the information on the NYSE, as you can see from the May 26, 1983, listing, which is reprinted on page 166.

# Amex-Composite Transactions

*Thursday, May 26, 1983*

Quotations include trades on the Midwest, Pacific, Philadelphia, Boston and Cincinnati stock exchanges and reported by the National Association of Securities Dealers and Instinet

| 52 Weeks High | Low | Stock | Div. | Yld % | P-E Ratio | Sales 100s | High | low | Close | Net Chg. |
|---|---|---|---|---|---|---|---|---|---|---|
| 9⅛ | 5 | Friedm | .24 | 2.8 | 14 | 4 | 8⅝ | 8½ | 8½ | – ⅛ |
| 13⅞ | 5⅜ | FriendF | | .. | 4 | 5 | 11¾ | 11¾ | 11¾ | – ⅛ |
| 12¾ | 6½ | Friona | .40 | 3.5 | 6 | 41 | 11⅝ | 11⅜ | 11½ | + ⅛ |
| 18½ | 8¼ | Frischs | .40b | 2.2 | 11 | 5 | 18 | 18 | 18 | ..... |
| 30½ | 16 | FronfHd | .20b | 1.0 | 47 | 163 | 20 | 19⅝ | 19⅝ | + ⅛ |
| 20¾ | 9½ | FrtA wt | .36t | 2.7 | .. | 4 | 13¼ | 13⅛ | 13¼ | ..... |
| | | – G–G–G – | | | | | | | | |
| 9¼ | 2⅞ | GNC En | | .. | .. | 200 | 6¼ | 5⅞ | 6 | ..... |
| 6½ | 3½ | GIExpt | | .. | 20 | 29 | 5⅞ | 5¾ | 5¾ | – ⅛ |
| 8½ | 4½ | GRI | | .. | 13 | 89 | 8⅛ | 7½ | 7½ | – ½ |
| 7⅝ | 2⅞ | GTI | | .. | .. | 247 | u 8 | 7⅛ | 8 | +1 |
| 27 | 4¾ | GalaxC s | | .. | 12 | 15 | 24½ | 24⅜ | 24⅜ | – ⅜ |
| 5⅞ | 1⅜ | GalxyO | | .. | .. | 1026 | 3¼ | 2⅞ | 3⅛ | – ⅛ |
| 34¼ | 13⅛ | Garan | 1.20 | 3.4 | 10 | 46 | u35 | 34½ | 35 | + ¾ |
| 19 | 10⅞ | GatLit | .20 | 1.2 | 14 | 22 | 17 | 16¾ | 16¾ | ..... |
| 10 | 2⅜ | Gaylrd | | .. | .. | 84 | 10 | 9⅜ | 9⅝ | – ⅜ |
| 16⅛ | 8 | GelmS | | .. | 23 | 208 | 16⅛ | 15½ | 15½ | – ⅛ |
| 6⅝ | 3 | Gemco | | .. | 35 | 166 | 6⅝ | 6⅜ | 6⅜ | ..... |
| 21¼ | 8¾ | GDefn s | | .. | 16 | 141 | 18⅝ | 18¼ | 18½ | ..... |
| 6¼ | 3¼ | GnEmp | | .. | .. | 28 | 5¾ | 5⅝ | 5¾ | ..... |
| 15¾ | 6⅞ | Genisco | | .. | 18 | 66 | 13⅝ | 13⅛ | 13⅛ | – ⅜ |
| 22⅜ | 6½ | GenvDr | .28b | 1.3 | 15 | 28 | 22 | 21¾ | 21⅞ | + ¼ |
| 12⅞ | 8⅜ | GeoRes | | .. | 7 | 40 | 12¼ | 12 | 12¼ | – ¼ |
| 22¾ | 7¾ | GiantF S | .60 | 2.8 | 8 | 93 | 22 | 21¼ | 21¼ | – ½ |
| 23⅝ | 5 | GntYl g | | .. | .. | 59 | 22¾ | 22½ | 22½ | + ¼ |
| 36¼ | 16½ | Glnmr | 1b | 3.0 | 17 | 26 | 34 | 33⅛ | 33¼ | – ¾ |
| 25 | 7½ | Glosser | .50 | 2.0 | 12 | 137 | u25⅝ | 24⅝ | 25½ | +1 |
| 16¾ | 6⅞ | GoldW | | .. | .. | 186 | 16½ | 16¼ | 16½ | ..... |
| 2¾ | ¾ | GldFld | | .. | .. | 333 | 2⅜ | 2¼ | 2¼ | ..... |
| 20⅝ | 19⅞ | Goldme | pf2.50 | 12. | .. | 605 | 20¼ | 19⅞ | 20⅛ | + ⅛ |
| 14 | 1⅛ | Gdrch wt | | .. | .. | 486 | 12⅞ | 11¾ | 12¼ | + ⅝ |
| 26 | 13⅞ | GouldT | 1.40 | 5.5 | 9 | 2 | 25½ | 25½ | 25½ | + ¼ |
| 13⅝ | 7½ | GrahMf | .32 | 2.7 | 6 | 1 | 11¾ | 11¾ | 11¾ | – ⅛ |
| 56⅜ | 17¾ | GrndAu | .60 | 1.2 | 14 | 40 | 54¾ | 50⅜ | 51⅛ | – 3⅞ |
| 14⅞ | 8⅛ | GrndCtl | | .. | .. | 77 | 10 | 9⅝ | 9⅝ | – ¼ |
| 42¼ | 12 | Grang s | | .. | 43 | 83 | u42¾ | 42⅛ | 42⅜ | + 1⅛ |
| 14⅝ | 7¼ | Grant | .51t | 3.7 | 16 | 75 | 14⅛ | 13⅞ | 13⅞ | + ¼ |
| 5¼ | 1⅛ | Grant wt | | .. | .. | 18 | 5 | 4⅞ | 5 | ..... |
| 23⅜ | 11 | GtAml | | .. | 9 | 8 | 21½ | 21¼ | 21¼ | – ⅛ |
| 53¼ | 24⅞ | GtLkCh | .60 | 1.1 | 23 | 157 | u54 | 53¾ | 54 | +1 |
| 19⅝ | 5 | Grenm | | .. | 10 | 101 | u20⅛ | 19¾ | 19⅞ | + ½ |
| 61 | 23¼ | GrossT | 2 | 3.7 | 13 | 5 | 55½ | 54½ | 54½ | – 1¼ |
| 7⅞ | 2⅝ | GuarBk | | .. | 13 | 51 | 7⅝ | 7⅝ | 7⅝ | ..... |
| 16⅛ | 8¼ | GuardC | .60 | 4.0 | 21 | 17 | 15⅛ | 15 | 15 | ..... |
| 33 | 16½ | Guilfrd | .72 | 2.3 | 16 | 22 | 31½ | 31 | 31½ | ..... |
| 14½ | 10⅛ | GlfCd g | .44 | .. | .. | 143 | 13¼ | 13 | 13⅛ | ..... |
| 32⅛ | 10⅜ | Glfstr | .10e | .3 | 20 | 108 | u32⅜ | 32 | 32⅜ | + ½ |
| | | – H–H–H – | | | | | | | | |
| 23⅞ | 11 | HMG | .60 | 2.6 | 20 | 4 | 23¼ | 23¼ | 23¼ | + ¼ |
| 11 | 4⅞ | Hamptl | .57t | 5.8 | 8 | 9 | 9⅞ | 9¾ | 9¾ | ..... |
| 27⅛ | 10⅝ | Hanfd s | .80 | 3.0 | 9 | 18 | 26⅝ | 26⅜ | 26⅜ | – ½ |
| 5½ | 2 | Harvey | | .. | .. | 22 | 4 | 3⅞ | 3⅞ | ..... |
| 29⅛ | 7 | Hasbro | s.28 | 1.0 | 13 | 23 | 27½ | 27¼ | 27½ | ..... |
| 28¾ | 11⅜ | Hasting | .40a | 1.4 | 12 | 37 | u30 | 29 | 29⅛ | + ⅜ |
| 7 | 3⅞ | HawaiA | | .. | .. | 3 | 4⅝ | 4½ | 4½ | ..... |
| 13¼ | 5⅛ | HlthCh | | .. | 210 | 156 | 10¾ | 10⅜ | 10½ | – ⅛ |
| 14 | 5 | HlthE n | | .. | 87 | 161 | 12½ | 11½ | 12⅛ | – ⅜ |
| 14¼ | 6⅝ | HelthM | .44 | 3.1 | 17 | 32 | 14⅛ | 13½ | 14⅛ | + ½ |
| 8½ | 2⅞ | HeinWr | | .. | 92 | 41 | 7⅜ | 7¼ | 7⅜ | + ⅛ |
| 12 | 5 | Heinick | .10 | .9 | 18 | 66 | 11¾ | 11 | 11½ | + ⅛ |
| 17 | 7 | Heizer | | .. | .. | 937 | 16⅛ | 15 | 15¾ | – ⅜ |
| 5⅞ | 1¼ | Heldor | | .. | .. | 95 | 5⅛ | 4⅞ | 5⅛ | + ⅜ |
| 3⅞ | 2 | HelmR | | .. | .. | 88 | 3½ | 3¼ | 3⅜ | ..... |
| 8⅞ | 4¼ | HershO | | .. | 43 | 71 | 8½ | 8¼ | 8¼ | – ¼ |
| 10⅞ | 4⅜ | HiGInc | | .. | .. | 94 | 9⅜ | 9⅛ | 9⅜ | ..... |
| 13⅞ | 7 | Highld | 3e | 22. | .. | 3 | 13¾ | 13⅝ | 13⅝ | – ¼ |
| 7⅜ | 3⅞ | HilrAv | .52t | 9.9 | .. | 9 | 5¼ | 5¼ | 5¼ | – ⅛ |
| 5¼ | 2⅞ | Hindrl | .12 | 2.2 | 60 | 187 | u 5½ | 5¼ | 5⅜ | + ⅛ |
| 21⅛ | 11⅛ | Hiptron | .16 | 1.0 | 20 | 28 | 16¾ | 16½ | 16¾ | ..... |
| 4 | 1¼ | Hofman | | .. | 18 | 52 | 4 | 3⅞ | 4 | ..... |
| 13¼ | 5⅝ | HollyCp | .24 | 1.8 | 13 | 207 | 13 | 12¾ | 13 | + ⅛ |
| 30¾ | 17½ | Horml | 1 | 3.8 | 12 | 32 | 26⅞ | 26¼ | 26⅝ | + ⅝ |
| 39⅜ | 14⅜ | HornHr | 1.84t | 4.7 | 30 | 298 | u39½ | 38⅞ | 39 | + ⅜ |
| 18¼ | 8 | HornH wt | | .. | .. | 44 | 18⅛ | 17⅞ | 18⅛ | + ⅜ |
| 15⅞ | 10¼ | HouOTr | 2.32e | 16. | .. | 456 | 14⅝ | 14⅜ | 14½ | – ⅛ |
| 7⅛ | 2 | Howell | | .. | 68 | 2 | 6¾ | 6¾ | 6¾ | ..... |
| 34⅛ | 17¼ | HubelA | 1.16 | 3.6 | 11 | 1 | 31⅞ | 31⅞ | 31⅞ | + ¼ |
| 35½ | 17 | HubelB | 1.16 | 3.6 | 11 | 7 | 32⅞ | 32⅜ | 32⅜ | – ⅝ |
| 46 | 25½ | Hubbl | pf2.06 | 4.7 | .. | 5 | 44 | 43½ | 43½ | – 1½ |
| 16⅛ | 7⅛ | HudGn | .30 | 1.9 | 11 | 25 | 16 | 15¾ | 16 | + ⅜ |
| 20½ | 12 | HuntMfg | .38 | 1.9 | 17 | 18 | 20¼ | 19¾ | 19¾ | – ¼ |
| 12¾ | 5¾ | HuntH | .12 | 1.0 | 19 | 23 | 11⅝ | 11⅜ | 11½ | ..... |
| 10 | 3 11-16 | Husky g | .15 | .. | .. | 42 | 9⅝ | 9⅜ | 9½ | – ⅛ |
| | | – I–I–I – | | | | | | | | |
| 12¾ | 8¾ | PGEpfB | 1.37 | 12. | .. | 19 | 11¾ | 11½ | 11½ | – ½ |
| 11½ | 8⅛ | PGEpfC | 1.25 | 12. | .. | 6 | 10¾ | 10¾ | 10¾ | – ⅛ |
| 11⅜ | 7⅜ | PGEpfD | 1.25 | 12. | .. | 10 | 10⅞ | 10⅜ | 10⅝ | + ⅛ |
| 11 | 7¾ | PGEpfE | 1.25 | 12. | .. | 30 | 10¾ | 10½ | 10½ | ..... |
| 10¾ | 7½ | PGEpfG | 1.20 | 12. | .. | 60 | 10¼ | 10 | 10¼ | + ¼ |
| 36 | 27⅜ | PGEpfF | 4.34 | 13. | .. | 89 | 34¼ | 33⅞ | 33⅞ | – ⅜ |
| 34 | 25¼ | PGEpfZ | 4.06 | 12. | .. | 81 | 33 | 32½ | 32¾ | – ¼ |
| 28¼ | 20 | PGEpfY | 3.20 | 12. | .. | 77 | 28 | 27 | 27 | ..... |
| 22⅜ | 16⅛ | PGEpfW | 2.57 | 12. | .. | 7 | 21¾ | 21½ | 21¾ | + ¼ |
| 20¼ | 14⅝ | PGEpfV | 2.32 | 12. | .. | 4 | 19⅝ | 19⅝ | 19⅝ | – ⅜ |
| 22⅜ | 16 | PGEpfT | 2.54 | 12. | .. | 12 | 21⅝ | 21⅜ | 21⅜ | – ¼ |
| 23 | 16½ | PGEpfS | 2.62 | 12. | .. | 37 | 22 | 21¾ | 21⅞ | – ⅛ |
| 10⅜ | 7⅛ | PGEpfH | 1.12 | 12. | .. | 23 | 9½ | 9½ | 9½ | – ¼ |
| 21 | 14¾ | PGEpfR | 2.37 | 11. | .. | 61 | 20¾ | 20¼ | 20¾ | + ⅛ |
| 18½ | 13 | PGEpfP | 2.05 | 12. | .. | 12 | 17⅝ | 17⅝ | 17⅝ | – ⅛ |
| 17½ | 12¾ | PGEpfO | 2 | 12. | .. | 2 | 17⅛ | 17⅛ | 17⅛ | ..... |
| 17⅛ | 12½ | PGEpfM | 1.96 | 12. | .. | 29 | 17 | 16¾ | 16¾ | ..... |
| 19½ | 14 | PGEpfL | 2.25 | 12. | .. | 16 | 18¾ | 18¾ | 18¾ | – ¼ |
| 18⅝ | 12⅝ | PGEpfK | 2.04 | 12. | .. | 32 | 17¾ | 17½ | 17½ | ..... |
| 19⅞ | 14¾ | PGEpfJ | 2.32 | 12. | .. | 6 | 19¼ | 19¼ | 19¼ | ..... |
| 9⅞ | 6¾ | PGEpfI | 1.09 | 12. | .. | 1 | 9 | 9 | 9 | ..... |
| 19½ | 11¾ | PGTrn | 1 | 5.6 | 5 | 337 | 18 | 17⅝ | 17¾ | ..... |
| 38⅝ | 28 | PacLt | pf4.40 | 12. | .. | z60 | 36 | 36 | 36 | –1¼ |
| 45 | 33¼ | PacPLpf | 5 | 13. | .. | z650 | 42 | 39¾ | 39¾ | –2¼ |
| 10¼ | 2⅝ | Page g | | .. | .. | 249 | 4⅛ | 3⅞ | 4 | + ¼ |
| 39¾ | 18⅜ | PallCp s | .36 | .9 | 26 | 105 | 39 | 38 | 38 | –1 |
| 6¼ | 1½ | PalmrF | | .. | 11 | 83 | 5⅞ | 5⅝ | 5¾ | + ⅛ |
| 5 | 2½ | Pantast | | .. | .. | 39 | u 5⅛ | 5 | 5 | ..... |
| 32 | 13 | ParkCh | .60a | 1.9 | 16 | 5 | 32 | 32 | 32 | + ⅛ |
| 44½ | 15¼ | ParkEl | | .. | 28 | 33 | 40¾ | 38¾ | 40⅝ | + 1⅝ |
| 6¼ | 2⅛ | PayFon | | .. | 63 | 7 | 5⅛ | 5 | 5 | – ⅛ |
| 6⅝ | 4¼ | PUMG | | .. | .. | 28 | u 7 | 6⅝ | 7 | + ⅜ |
| 9¾ | 5½ | PeerTu | .40b | 4.7 | 21 | 3 | 8½ | 8½ | 8½ | ..... |
| 6 | 1⅝ | Penin | | .. | .. | 62 | 3¼ | 2⅞ | 3 | ..... |
| 30⅜ | 17 | PenEM | 1 | 3.7 | 14 | 46 | 27¼ | 27 | 27 | – ⅛ |
| 23¼ | 11⅝ | PenTr | 1.20 | 5.3 | 9 | 28 | 23 | 22¾ | 22¾ | + ⅛ |
| 2⅞ | 1¼ | PECp | .19t | 7.2 | 6 | 157 | 2⅝ | 2½ | 2⅝ | ..... |
| 39¾ | 21⅛ | PenRE | 2.50 | 6.5 | 12 | 6 | 38½ | 38½ | 38½ | ..... |
| 12½ | 7⅛ | PenobS | .40 | 3.4 | 12 | 4 | 11¾ | 11¾ | 11¾ | – ⅛ |
| 13¼ | 7¼ | Penril | .17 | 1.4 | 16 | 79 | 11⅞ | 11½ | 11⅞ | + ⅜ |
| 1⅞ | ⅜ | Pentron | | .. | .. | 121 | 1⅜ | 1⅜ | 1⅜ | + ⅛ |
| 28⅝ | 11½ | PepB s | .30 | 1.3 | 15 | 80 | 24⅝ | 24 | 24 | – ⅛ |
| 40¼ | 15½ | Perini | .80 | 2.1 | 8 | 20 | 38¼ | 38 | 38 | + ¼ |
| 12¾ | 7¼ | PetLew | | .. | 9 | 280 | 12 | 11½ | 11⅝ | – ⅜ |
| 4½ | 2⅜ | PetLw wt | | .. | .. | 319 | 3⅞ | 3¾ | 3¾ | – ¼ |
| 12⅝ | 9⅝ | PetLe | pf1.65 | 14. | .. | 19 | 12 | 11¾ | 12 | ..... |
| 16¼ | 13¼ | PetLe | pf2.28 | 14. | .. | 35 | 15⅞ | 15¾ | 15⅞ | + ⅛ |
| 4⅜ | 3⅜ | PhilLD | .57r | 15. | 8 | 47 | 3⅞ | 3¾ | 3⅞ | ..... |
| 3½ | 1⅛ | Phoenix | | .. | .. | 101 | 3⅜ | 3⅛ | 3¼ | ..... |
| 20⅜ | 5 | PicoPd | | .. | 64 | 53 | 18⅝ | 17⅝ | 18⅝ | + 1⅛ |
| 9¾ | 2⅞ | PionrSy | | .. | 86 | 102 | 8⅝ | 8⅜ | 8⅝ | + ⅜ |
| 8⅛ | 4⅞ | PitWVa | .56a | 8.1 | 9 | 14 | 7 | 6⅞ | 6⅞ | – ⅛ |
| 21⅜ | 11⅞ | PitDM | .40 | 2.3 | 196 | 15 | 18⅛ | 17⅝ | 17⅝ | – ¾ |
| 53½ | 41⅜ | Pittway | 1.65 | 3.2 | 10 | 16 | 51¼ | 51¼ | 51¼ | + ¼ |
| 14 | 4½ | Pizzaln | .02e | .1 | 17 | 101 | 13¾ | 13¼ | 13½ | – ⅛ |
| 21 | 9⅛ | PlcrD g | .20 | .. | .. | 31 | 20½ | 20⅜ | 20⅜ | + ⅛ |
| 4⅛ | 2⅛ | Plantln | | .. | .. | 155 | 3⅜ | 3⅜ | 3½ | ..... |
| 13 | 4 | PlyGm s | .20 | 1.7 | 20 | 34 | 11⅞ | 11⅝ | 11¾ | + ⅛ |
| 4⅜ | 2 | PlyR A | | .. | .. | 12 | 3⅞ | 3⅞ | 3⅞ | + ⅛ |
| 4⅛ | 1⅞ | PlyR B | | .. | .. | 5 | 3⅞ | 3⅞ | 3⅞ | + ⅛ |
| 20¼ | 14 | PneuSc | .80 | 4.4 | 33 | 3 | 18 | 18 | 18 | ..... |
| 16¾ | 6⅜ | PopeE s | | .. | 11 | 154 | 14⅞ | 14⅜ | 14⅝ | ..... |
| 29¼ | 8¼ | PortSy | | .. | 30 | 339 | 28⅞ | 27⅛ | 28¾ | + 1¾ |
| 44½ | 26 | PostCp | .60 | 1.4 | 19 | 13 | 43¼ | 42⅞ | 42⅞ | – ⅝ |
| 21¼ | 10⅝ | PostlPr | .20 | .9 | 18 | 106 | u23 | 21⅛ | 22⅝ | + 1¾ |
| 13⅝ | 9¾ | PowerT | .30b | 2.4 | 32 | 15 | 13¼ | 12¾ | 12¾ | – ½ |
| 24 | 11⅝ | PrairO g | | .. | .. | 7 | 22 | 21⅞ | 21⅞ | – ½ |
| 30¾ | 15⅜ | PratLm | 1.22 | 4.3 | 9 | 8 | 28¼ | 28⅛ | 28⅛ | – ¼ |
| 9¼ | 5⅞ | PrattRd | .30 | 3.5 | 15 | 22 | 8⅝ | 8½ | 8½ | – ¼ |
| 3 | 1 | PremRs | | .. | .. | 210 | 2⅛ | 1⅞ | 2⅛ | + ¼ |
| 54⅞ | 24 | PrenHa | 1.76 | 3.3 | 15 | 390 | 54 | 53¼ | 54 | + 1⅛ |
| 9 | 2¼ | PresR B | .50 | 6.3 | 9 | 41 | 8 | 7¾ | 8 | – ⅛ |
| 5¼ | 2⅝ | Presid | | .. | 50 | 34 | 5 | 4¾ | 5 | – ⅛ |
| 36 | 23⅛ | PrpCT | 2.61e | 7.7 | 13 | 13 | 34⅛ | 34 | 34 | ..... |
| 19¾ | 10⅞ | ProvEn | 1.60 | 8.5 | 4 | 5 | 19 | 18¾ | 18¾ | + ⅛ |
| 38 | 27½ | PSCol | pf4.25 | 12. | .. | z300 | 35¾ | 35½ | 35½ | – ½ |
| 20⅜ | 15⅛ | Pgt | pfC 2.34 | 12. | .. | 20 | 19⅝ | 19⅛ | 19⅛ | – ⅜ |
| 36 | 27 | Pgt | pfE4.38 | 13. | .. | 25 | 33⅞ | 33⅜ | 33⅜ | ..... |
| 73⅜ | 7⅝ | PulteH s | .14 | .2 | 31 | 187 | 71¾ | 70 | 71⅝ | + 1⅜ |
| 37 | 34½ | Pulte wi | | .. | .. | 11 | 36 | 36 | 36 | + ½ |
| 13⅞ | 4⅞ | PuntaG | | .. | .. | 14 | 11½ | 11⅛ | 11⅛ | – ⅛ |
| 16⅝ | 9¼ | Punta | pf.87e | 6.6 | .. | 23 | 13⅝ | 13¼ | 13¼ | – ⅝ |
| | | – R–R–R – | | | | | | | | |

The Wall Street Journal, *May 27, 1983.*

*Over-the-counter stocks,* issued by even smaller or newer companies, are not traded on an exchange. Instead, dealers make a market for them with a computer network referred to as *Nasdaq,* which is an acronym for the *National Association of Securities Dealers Automated Quotation* system. As of May 20, 1983, some of these stocks were quoted in Nasdaq's *National Market* in a fashion similar to the listings of the New York and American Exchanges. Take a look at the reprint, using Apple Computer as an example. (See pages 168 and 169.)

# Over-the-Counter Markets

***Quotations From the Nasdaq System***

4:00 p.m. Eastern Time Prices, Friday, May 20, 1983

## Volume, All Issues, 69,582,000

**SINCE JANUARY 1**

| | 1983 | 1982 | 1981 |
|---|---|---|---|
| Total sales ....... | 5,959,965,145 | 2,709,550,530 | 3,165,409,295 |

**MARKET DIARY**

| | Fri | Thu | Wed | Tue | Mon |
|---|---|---|---|---|---|
| Issues traded ....... | 3,458 | 3,453 | 3,452 | 3,452 | 3,452 |
| Advances ............ | 658 | 583 | 1,034 | 923 | 358 |
| Declines .............. | 734 | 819 | 488 | 559 | 1,267 |
| Unchanged .......... | 2,066 | 2,051 | 1,930 | 1,970 | 1,827 |
| xNew highs ......... | 171 | 195 | 311 | 207 | 142 |
| xNew lows ........... | 16 | 18 | 21 | 23 | 31 |

x-Based on 4 p.m. Eastern time bid quote.

**ACTIVE STOCKS**

| | Dollar Volume | 4:00 Bid | Chg. |
|---|---|---|---|
| Apple Computer .................. | $37,093,000 | 56⅞ | + 2⅞ |
| MCI Communications ......... | 25,601,000 | 44⅛ | − ⅞ |
| Cosmo Commun Cp ............ | 18,745,000 | 22 | .... |
| Intel Cp ................................ | 17,793,000 | 57¼ | + 2¾ |
| Convergent Tech ................ | 12,879,000 | 33⅛ | − ⅛ |
| Digital Switch ..................... | 11,898,000 | 139 | + 4 |
| Philips Gloeilamp ............... | 10,092,000 | 16½ | + ½ |
| Ericsson (LM) Tel ADR ..... | 9,675,000 | 59¾ | − 1½ |
| L S I Logic ......................... | 8,572,000 | 29¾ | + 2 |
| Systems Assoc .................... | 8,291,000 | 20¾ | .... |

## Nasdaq National Market

Apple Computer →

| 1983- High | Low | | Sales (hds) | High | Low | Last | Net Chg. |
|---|---|---|---|---|---|---|---|
| 29 | 19 | Academy Insu | 421 | 28¾ | 27⅜ | 27⅜ | − ⅞ |
| 27⅜ | 18 | Adac Labs | 497 | 22¼ | 21⅞ | 22 | ... |
| (H) | 13¾ | AGS Computr | 240 | 24½ | 22¾ | 24 | + ¼ |
| 16¼ | 12¼ | Air Wisconsin | 124 | 16 | 15¾ | 15¾ | − ¼ |
| 40¾ | 28½ | Alex&Baldn 2 | 11 | 38¼ | 37⅞ | 38 | + ¼ |
| 25⅞ | 20⅞ | AlliedBcsh .80 | 489 | 24⅞ | 24½ | 24¾ | ... |
| 28½ | 19⅜ | Altos Comptr | 308 | 20 | 19½ | 19⅞ | − ⅛ |
| 2⅞ | ⅞ | qAmarexInc p | 609 | 2⅜ | 2¼ | 2⅜ | + ⅛ |
| 16⅛ | 10¼ | ABnkrs Ins .50 | 72 | 14⅞ | 14⅝ | 14¾ | − ⅛ |
| 24⅜ | 17⅜ | AmGreetg .34 | 1023 | 22⅞ | 22⅜ | 22⅝ | ... |
| 17 | 10⅞ | Am Income Lf | 834 | 15⅜ | 14¾ | 15¼ | + ¼ |
| 77¾ | 52¼ | AmIntlGrp .44 | 482 | 76½ | 75¾ | 76½ | + ¾ |
| 22 | 15 | AmNatlIns .84 | 70 | 19⅜ | 19⅛ | 19⅜ | + ⅛ |
| 33 | 11¼ | AmSolar King | 479 | 33 | 31½ | 33 | + ¾ |
| 41¾ | 33½ | Andrew Corpn | 95 | 39½ | 39¼ | 39½ | − ⅛ |
| 49½ | 25¼ | Apollo Cmptr | 110 | 47 | 46¼ | 46¾ | + ½ |
| (H) | 27¼ | Apple Comptr | 6522 | 57 | 53⅜ | 56⅞ | + 2¾ |
| 40¼ | 21¾ | Applied Matrl | 660 | 39 | 38½ | 39 | + ¼ |
| 36¼ | 22½ | AskCmptr Sys | 48 | 33¾ | 33⅜ | 33½ | + ⅛ |
| 13⅜ | 10¼ | Astrosystms | 659 | 12⅝ | 12 | 12½ | + ⅜ |
| 55¾ | 35½ | Atl Research | 28 | 52½ | 52¼ | 52½ | ... |
| 27⅞ | 20 | Avantek Inc | 115 | 26¾ | 26⅜ | 26½ | − ¼ |
| 39 | 32¾ | BancOne 1.36 | 150 | 35½ | 34¾ | 35 | − ¼ |
| 35¾ | 26⅛ | BayBanks 2 | 84 | 34⅜ | 34 | 34⅛ | − ¼ |
| 24½ | 14½ | Bekins Co .60 | 417 | 23 | 22¾ | 22¾ | − ⅛ |
| 44¾ | 32¾ | Betz Labs .88 | 161 | 40½ | 40¼ | 40¼ | − ¼ |
| 40¾ | 9⅞ | Bliss AT Co | 159 | 18½ | 17¾ | 18 | ... |
| 30 | 24¼ | Bob Evans .30 | 102 | 26¾ | 25¾ | 25¾ | − ¼ |
| 19¼ | 13¼ | Brunos Inc .20 | 158 | 19⅛ | 18¾ | 19 | + ⅛ |
| 22¼ | 14¾ | C Cor Electrn | 481 | 19½ | 19 | 19¼ | + ¼ |
| 34⅛ | 21 | Cal Mcrowave | 149 | 32 | 31⅝ | 31⅞ | + ⅛ |
| 30¼ | 20¾ | Carl Karcher | 120 | 29½ | 29 | 29½ | + ¼ |
| 19 | 11⅝ | Cetus Corptn | 1178 | 17⅜ | 17⅛ | 17⅜ | ... |
| 14½ | 8 | CGA Assc Inc | 796 | 14⅛ | 13¾ | 14 | + ⅛ |
| 23¼ | 13⅜ | Char Shops .25 | 79 | 22½ | 22¼ | 22⅜ | − ⅛ |
| 34¼ | 20⅝ | ChartHous .60 | 798 | 32½ | 31¾ | 32 | − ⅝ |
| 32⅝ | 20⅞ | ChiChis Incrp | 543 | 31⅝ | 30¼ | 31¼ | − ⅝ |
| 60½ | 45 | Chubb Cp 2.92 | 129 | 56¾ | 55⅞ | 56¾ | + ¾ |
| 48¼ | 22 | Cipher DataP | 125 | 45½ | 43½ | 44 | − 2 |
| 15⅞ | 10¼ | CitznSoGa .56 | 232 | 14⅞ | 14⅝ | 14¾ | ... |
| 31½ | 16 | CityFedSL 5i | 133 | 27¾ | 27 | 27¾ | + ½ |
| 50¾ | 30¼ | Cobe Labrator | 79 | 45¼ | 43¾ | 45¼ | + ¾ |
| 27⅝ | 20½ | Color Tile Inc | 1038 | 22¼ | 22 | 22 | − ¼ |
| 28⅜ | 17⅝ | Comdial Corp | 152 | 25¾ | 25½ | 25⅝ | ... |
| 13⅝ | 6⅜ | Comm CpAm | 210 | 7⅞ | 7⅜ | 7¾ | ... |
| 34¼ | 29¼ | Comun Ind .32 | 134 | 33 | 32¾ | 32¾ | − ¼ |
| 37 | 18 | Comprh Cr .24 | 713 | 36½ | 36 | 36⅛ | − ⅜ |
| 21⅛ | 10¾ | Compucorp | 388 | 12⅞ | 12⅝ | 12¾ | ... |
| 24¼ | 14¾ | C C T Corp | 287 | 22½ | 21¾ | 22¼ | ... |
| 16⅝ | 10¾ | Cmptr Device | 236 | 14⅛ | 13⅜ | 13¾ | − ¼ |
| 18¾ | 10 | Comserv Corp | 263 | 14½ | 14 | 14½ | ... |
| 17⅞ | 12⅝ | Concept Inc | 622 | 14⅜ | 13⅞ | 14 | − ⅜ |
| 30¾ | 27⅝ | CnCapIn 3.36a | 237 | 29½ | 29¼ | 29½ | ... |
| 34⅞ | 21½ | Convergnt Tec | 3888 | 33⅝ | 33⅛ | 33⅜ | + ⅛ |
| 25½ | 20¾ | Cooprvisn Inc | 217 | 22¼ | 22 | 22 | − ¼ |
| 20½ | 11⅞ | CoorsCo B .30 | 3989 | 20⅛ | 18¾ | 19⅞ | + ⅝ |
| 22½ | 16¼ | Corvus Systm | 216 | 20⅝ | 20⅛ | 20½ | + ¼ |
| 21½ | 12⅝ | CP Rehab Cp | 49 | 20 | 19½ | 19½ | − ⅛ |
| 26⅞ | 17¼ | C P T Corp | 347 | 25⅜ | 25 | 25⅛ | ... |
| 27⅜ | 18¼ | Cross Trck .80 | 351 | 24⅛ | 23¾ | 24 | − ⅛ |
| 17¼ | 12¼ | Data Card .24 | 191 | 16 | 15¾ | 16 | + ⅛ |
| 29¾ | 13 | Data I-O | 321 | 28¾ | 27¾ | 28 | − ½ |
| 14½ | 5 | Datum Inc | 69 | 13⅜ | 13 | 13⅛ | − ¼ |
| (H) | 10⅛ | Decision Data | 1625 | 15½ | 15 | 15⅛ | + ⅛ |
| 21¾ | 16⅛ | Dekalb Ag .72 | 492 | 21½ | 21¼ | 21½ | − ⅛ |
| 29¾ | 18 | Diasonics Inc | 1112 | 21¼ | 20⅝ | 21¼ | + ⅛ |
| 144 | 38¼ | Digital Switch | 856 | 140½ | 134½ | 140 | + 4 |
| 33⅞ | 19⅞ | Docutel Olivet | 465 | 33 | 31¾ | 31⅞ | − 1⅜ |

| 1983- High | Low | | Sales (hds) | High | Low | Last | Net Chg. |
|---|---|---|---|---|---|---|---|
| 25¼ | 16½ | Kasler Cp .30e | 47 | 22¼ | 21¾ | 21¾ | − ¼ |
| 51⅝ | 37¼ | Kemper C 1.80 | 23 | 49½ | 49½ | 49½ | − ¼ |
| 28⅝ | 18⅜ | KindrCLrn .10 | 358 | 27¼ | 26⅝ | 26¾ | − ⅝ |
| 15¾ | 12¾ | LndmBFI .50g | 832 | 14⅝ | 14⅜ | 14½ | + ⅛ |
| 14 | 7½ | LD Brinkman | 587 | 13⅝ | 12⅝ | 13½ | − ¼ |
| 33 | 25½ | Lee Data Corp | 331 | 26¾ | 26¼ | 26⅝ | + ¼ |
| 28 | 19½ | Liebert Corp | 219 | 22 | 21½ | 21½ | ... |
| 32½ | 28¼ | LifeInvestr .24 | 5 | 31¾ | 31¾ | 31¾ | ... |
| (H) | 31¾ | Lin Broadcast | 289 | 43⅛ | 42 | 42¾ | + ½ |
| 28 | 19¾ | LngviewF 1.20 | 112 | 27½ | 27 | 27¼ | ... |
| 21¼ | 17 | Manitowoc .80 | 87 | 20⅜ | 20 | 20¼ | − ⅛ |
| 11¼ | 7½ | May Petrolm | 197 | 9⅝ | 9⅜ | 9⅝ | + ⅛ |
| 48⅜ | 33⅝ | MCI Communi | 5802 | 45⅛ | 43⅝ | 44⅛ | − ¾ |
| 31⅞ | 24⅝ | McCormk .88a | 167 | 30⅝ | 30¼ | 30⅜ | + ⅛ |
| 11⅛ | 6⅞ | McCorm OlGs | 84 | 9⅝ | 9⅜ | 9½ | + ⅛ |
| 14½ | 9 | McRaeCn Oil | 221 | 10⅜ | 10 | 10¼ | − ⅛ |
| 19⅝ | 11⅛ | MDC Corp .16 | 2763 | 18¾ | 17½ | 18¾ | + 1⅛ |
| 46 | 24⅞ | Micom Systm | 93 | 43¼ | 42½ | 42½ | ... |
| 15⅞ | 10¾ | Microdyne .06 | 207 | 15⅛ | 14⅝ | 14¾ | + ⅛ |
| 19¼ | 13½ | Midway Airln | 174 | 14¼ | 13⅝ | 14⅛ | + ⅛ |
| 33½ | 24⅝ | MilliporeCp .40 | 297 | 29⅞ | 29½ | 29½ | − ⅜ |
| 12⅛ | 8½ | Mobile Com B | 93 | 11⅜ | 11 | 11¼ | ... |
| 32¾ | 23¾ | MonrchCp 1.36 | 307 | 32¾ | 32½ | 32½ | − ¼ |
| 46⅝ | 18¼ | Monlithc Mem | 554 | 41⅜ | 39¼ | 41⅛ | + 1⅝ |
| 20¼ | 16¾ | Morrison .40 | 822 | 18⅜ | 17¾ | 17⅞ | − ⅝ |
| 25⅝ | 17 | Natl Data .36 | 200 | 23⅛ | 22⅝ | 23⅛ | ... |
| 30⅛ | 16⅜ | Nat Microntcs | 312 | 29 | 28½ | 28⅝ | − ¼ |
| 27 | 22⅜ | Netwrk Systm | 301 | 24⅝ | 24¼ | 24⅝ | + ⅛ |
| 35¾ | 22 | NewportCp .12 | 365 | 34¾ | 34 | 34¼ | + ¾ |
| 6 | 3⅝ | Nicklos Oil Gs | 240 | 5½ | 5⅛ | 5½ | + ¼ |
| 23¾ | 15⅛ | Nike Inc B | 939 | 19¾ | 19½ | 19⅝ | − ¼ |
| 75¾ | 45¾ | Nordstrom .56 | 476 | 74¼ | 73¾ | 74¼ | ... |
| 13¼ | 11⅛ | NowstNG 1.28 | 84 | 13¼ | 13 | 13 | ... |
| 16¾ | 10½ | Nuclear Phar | 1477 | 13 | 11⅝ | 13 | + 1¼ |
| 16⅝ | 10⅛ | Oceanrg Intl | 325 | 12¾ | 12⅝ | 12⅝ | + ⅛ |
| 15⅜ | 7⅝ | OCG Technolg | 200 | 11¼ | 10⅞ | 11 | − ⅛ |
| 16 | 8¾ | Onyx IMI | 1210 | 15 | 14 | 14¾ | + ⅝ |
| 11⅜ | 7¾ | OXOCO Inc | 421 | 10 | 9¾ | 9⅞ | ... |
| 66½ | 20⅝ | PabstBrw .10b | 279 | 60½ | 59½ | 60½ | ... |
| 35⅝ | 22⅛ | PandickPr .20 | 65 | 35⅛ | 34⅝ | 34⅝ | − ½ |
| 49 | 30⅞ | Pay'nSave .56 | 171 | 47¼ | 47 | 47¼ | − ⅛ |
| 40½ | 18⅛ | People Exprss | 491 | 38¾ | 36⅝ | 38¼ | ... |
| 11 | 6⅞ | Peoples Rest | 401 | 11 | 10¾ | 11 | + ¼ |
| 33¾ | 27¾ | Petrolite Cp 1 | 57 | 31¼ | 30¾ | 31¼ | + ⅛ |
| 47¾ | 33⅜ | Pic N Save Cp | 701 | 46⅜ | 46 | 46⅜ | + ⅛ |
| 27¾ | 21½ | Pionr Hibr .72 | 138 | 26 | 25⅝ | 26 | + ¼ |
| 26 | 14½ | PizzaTime Th | 477 | 23½ | 23 | 23½ | + ¼ |
| 43½ | 31½ | P N C F 1.92 | 79 | 40½ | 40 | 40 | − ¼ |
| 62½ | 38¼ | Price Comony | 116 | 61 | 59½ | 61 | + 1¼ |
| 34 | 26¼ | Printronix Inc | 78 | 28¼ | 27¾ | 28¼ | ... |
| 7⅞ | 5¼ | QuadrexCp .24 | 1092 | 6¼ | 5⅜ | 6 | + ½ |
| 33½ | 20 | Quantum Corp | 65 | 29 | 28¾ | 28¾ | − ⅛ |
| 55⅛ | 34 | Quotron Sysm | 939 | 52½ | 51 | 51¼ | − 1¼ |
| 34¾ | 26 | RainierBc 1.60 | 131 | 33 | 32⅜ | 32½ | − ¾ |
| 26¼ | 15¼ | Ramtek Corp | 90 | 24 | 23½ | 23¾ | − ¼ |
| 22¼ | 15½ | Reeves Comm | 693 | 22¼ | 21½ | 22 | + ½ |
| 32⅜ | 16½ | RegencyEl .40 | 184 | 31⅛ | 30½ | 30½ | − ⅝ |
| 14½ | 11 | Rival Mfg .80 | 483 | 14¼ | 13⅞ | 14¼ | + ¼ |
| 68½ | 57 | RdwaySv 1.60 | 154 | 65 | 64¼ | 64¾ | − ¼ |
| 16⅛ | 10¾ | Rockcor Incrp | 139 | 13⅞ | 13⅝ | 13¾ | − ⅛ |
| 33¾ | 25⅞ | Rouse Co .72 | 71 | 32¾ | 32⅜ | 32⅝ | + ⅛ |
| 19 | 14½ | R P M Inc .56 | 136 | 18 | 17¾ | 17¾ | ... |
| 59⅞ | 45¾ | Safeco Cp 2.40 | 69 | 57¾ | 57½ | 57⅝ | − ⅛ |
| 70¾ | 54⅜ | StPaulCos 2.80 | 600 | 65⅛ | 64½ | 65⅛ | + ⅜ |
| 23¼ | 12½ | SaveWayIn .10 | 280 | 22½ | 22 | 22½ | ... |
| 16¾ | 8⅛ | Scan Optics | 804 | 15⅞ | 14⅛ | 15⅝ | + 1½ |
| 25½ | 16¾ | SchererRP .30 | 206 | 24¾ | 24⅜ | 24½ | − ¼ |
| 47¾ | 28½ | SCI SystemsIn | 195 | 43 | 42½ | 43 | + ¼ |

The Wall Street Journal, *May 23, 1983.*

| | | | | | | | | | |
|---|---|---|---|---|---|---|---|---|---|
| | $16\frac{1}{8}$ | $10\frac{1}{4}$ | ABnkrs Ins | .50 | 72 | $14\frac{7}{8}$ | $14\frac{5}{8}$ | $14\frac{3}{4}$ | $-\frac{1}{8}$ |
| | $24\frac{3}{8}$ | $17\frac{3}{8}$ | AmGreetg | .34 | 1023 | $22\frac{7}{8}$ | $22\frac{3}{8}$ | $22\frac{5}{8}$ | ... |
| | 17 | $10\frac{7}{8}$ | Am Income | Lf | 834 | $15\frac{3}{8}$ | $14\frac{3}{4}$ | $15\frac{1}{4}$ | $+\frac{1}{4}$ |
| | $77\frac{3}{4}$ | $52\frac{1}{4}$ | AmIntlGrp | .44 | 482 | $76\frac{1}{2}$ | $75\frac{3}{4}$ | $76\frac{1}{2}$ | $+\frac{3}{4}$ |
| | 22 | 15 | AmNatlIns | .84 | 70 | $19\frac{3}{8}$ | $19\frac{1}{8}$ | $19\frac{3}{8}$ | $+\frac{1}{8}$ |
| | 33 | $11\frac{1}{4}$ | AmSolar | King | 479 | 33 | $31\frac{1}{2}$ | 33 | $+\frac{3}{4}$ |
| | $41\frac{3}{4}$ | $33\frac{1}{2}$ | Andrew | Corpn | 95 | $39\frac{1}{2}$ | $39\frac{1}{4}$ | $39\frac{1}{2}$ | $-\frac{1}{8}$ |
| | $49\frac{1}{2}$ | $25\frac{1}{4}$ | Apollo | Cmptr | 110 | 47 | $46\frac{1}{4}$ | $46\frac{3}{4}$ | $+\frac{1}{2}$ |
| **Apple Computer** → | (H) | $27\frac{1}{4}$ | Apple | Comptr | 6522 | 57 | $53\frac{3}{8}$ | $56\frac{7}{8}$ | $+2\frac{3}{4}$ |
| | $40\frac{1}{4}$ | $21\frac{3}{4}$ | Applied | Matrl | 660 | 39 | $38\frac{1}{2}$ | 39 | $+\frac{1}{4}$ |
| | $36\frac{1}{4}$ | $22\frac{1}{2}$ | AskCmptr | Sys | 48 | $33\frac{3}{4}$ | $33\frac{3}{8}$ | $33\frac{1}{2}$ | $+\frac{1}{8}$ |
| | $13\frac{3}{8}$ | $10\frac{1}{4}$ | Astrosystms | | 659 | $12\frac{5}{8}$ | 12 | $12\frac{1}{2}$ | $+\frac{3}{8}$ |
| | $55\frac{3}{4}$ | $35\frac{1}{2}$ | Atl | Research | 28 | $52\frac{1}{2}$ | $52\frac{1}{4}$ | $52\frac{1}{2}$ | ... |
| | $27\frac{7}{8}$ | 20 | Avantek | Inc | 115 | $26\frac{3}{4}$ | $26\frac{3}{8}$ | $26\frac{1}{2}$ | $-\frac{1}{4}$ |

| 1983 | | | | | | | |
|---|---|---|---|---|---|---|---|
| High | Low | | Sales (hds) | High | Low | Last | Net Chg. |
| (H) | $27\frac{1}{4}$ | Apple Computer | 6522 | 57 | $53\frac{3}{8}$ | $56\frac{7}{8}$ | $+2\frac{3}{4}$ |

The first two columns give the high and low for the calendar year. The "(H)" indicates that the May 20 price was the high for the year.

The column after the company name lists sales in hundreds, informing you that 652,200 shares of Apple Computer traded on May 20.

The next three columns provide the high (57) low ($53\frac{3}{8}$), and last price of the day ($56\frac{7}{8}$).

The final column tells you that Apple's stock closed $2\frac{3}{4}$ dollars higher than its price at the previous close.

The remainder of the over-the-counter (OTC) stocks are quoted currently with bid and asked prices (although all OTC stocks will eventually be quoted with closing prices). Take the Addison-Wesley Publishing Company as an example. (See pages 170 and 171.)

Addison-Wesley →

| Stock & Div | Sales 100s | Bid | Asked | Net Chg. |
|---|---|---|---|---|
| - - A A - - | | | | |
| Aaron Rents | 65 | 28 | 28¾ | - ¼ |
| Acapulco Rest | 28 | 6⅛ | 6⅜ | ... |
| AcclrtnCp .05d | 62 | 8 | 8¼ | ... |
| AccurayCp .14 | 79 | 19⅛ | 19¼ | ... |
| AcetoChem 3k | 2 | 22 | 22½ | ... |
| ACMAT Corp | 18 | 11 | 11½ | ... |
| Acme Genl .20 | 2 | 16¾ | 17¼ | ... |
| Adage Incorp | 178 | 50¼ | 50½ | - 3 |
| AddWesley .50 | 28 | 24½ | 25 | ¾ |
| Advance Ross | 130 | 4⅞ | 5 | ... |
| AdvSemi Mat | 69 | 24 | 24½ | ... |
| Advn Syst .15f | 76 | 27¾ | 28½ | ... |
| AEC Inc .40 | 5 | 10¾ | 11½ | + ¼ |
| AEICOR Inc | 1093 | 2 | 2⅛ | ... |
| Aero Services | 133 | 3½ | 3⅝ | ... |
| Aero Syst Inc | 356 | 6⅝ | 6¾ | ... |
| AffilBkCp 1.56 | 2 | 27 | 29¾ | ... |
| AffiBkshrs 1 | 12 | 22 | 22½ | ... |
| A F G Indust | 143 | 28½ | 28¾ | - 1 |
| Agnico Eagle | 154 | 16 | 16⅛ | - ⅛ |
| AirCargo Eqp | 1 | 4⅞ | 5¼ | ... |
| Air Fla Sys p | 1836 | 2 15-16 | 3 | + 1-16 |
| Alamo Sv .10b | 74 | 32 | 34 | + 3 |
| AlMutlBk 10k | 5 | 22½ | 23½ | - ½ |
| AlaskPcB .20e | 9 | 19 | 19¾ | ... |
| AlaTennRes 2 | 6 | 56 | 59 | ... |
| Alexndr Enrg | 463 | 3 | 3⅛ | + ⅛ |
| Algorex Corp | 98 | 27¼ | 27¾ | ... |
| Allco Incp .30 | 13 | 41 | 45 | ... |
| Allegh Bev .40 | 93 | 22 | 22⅜ | - ⅜ |
| Allegh LndMn | 249 | 4½ | 4¾ | ... |
| AllghWstn En | 8 | 6¼ | 6⅝ | ... |
| AlliedCapitl 1 | 18 | 26½ | 27¼ | ... |
| Alo SchererH | 15 | 10½ | 12 | + ½ |
| Alpha Micrsys | 91 | 21 | 21½ | ... |
| AltairCp 4.50t | 11 | 7¾ | 8¼ | ... |
| AM Cable TV | 231 | 6½ | 6⅝ | + ⅜ |
| Ambass Gr .28 | 73 | 8½ | 9 | - ¼ |
| Amdisco Corp | 5 | 28⅛ | 28¼ | + ¼ |
| Amerfrdl .07d | 3 | 6 | 6½ | ... |
| AmAggregat 1 | 7 | 21½ | 23½ | ... |
| AmApraisl .36 | 3 | 8¼ | 9 | ... |
| AmBcpPa 1.10 | 287 | 17⅝ | 17⅞ | + ⅛ |
| AmCityBk LA | 267 | 1 | 1 1-16 | ... |
| AmFed SL .60 | 163 | 24½ | 24¾ | + ¼ |
| Am Filtrn 1.10 | 32 | 18¾ | 19½ | ... |
| Am Fncl pf E | 3 | 8½ | 9⅛ | - ¼ |
| AmerFirst 5k | 12 | 8 | 8½ | ... |
| AmFletch 1.40 | 58 | 31 | 31¼ | - ¼ |
| Amer Furn .20 | 104 | 10⅝ | 10⅞ | - ¼ |
| AGuarnF .05e | 78 | 4⅞ | 5 | + ¼ |
| A Indem 1.12g | 5 | 20½ | 20⅞ | - ¼ |
| AmltlG pf5.85 | 10 | 133¼ | 137 | + 3¼ |
| AmInvsLf .20g | 1 | 7⅛ | 7⅝ | ... |
| AmLeisure Cp | 232 | 3⅛ | 3¼ | ... |
| AmLeisure A | 520 | 1 | 1 1-16 | ... |
| AmLeisure ut | 50 | 3 3-16 | 3⅜ | + 1-16 |
| Am Magnetics | 27 | 16 | 16½ | ... |
| AmerMgt Sys | 114 | 22¾ | 23 | + ¼ |
| Am Medi Dent | 466 | 6¼ | 6⅜ | ... |
| Am MedSv .19 | 26 | 9 | 9¾ | + ¼ |
| Am Monitor | 401 | 17 | 17½ | - ¼ |
| Am Nucleoncs | 125 | 2¾ | 3 | ... |
| Am Quasr Pet | 117 | 6⅝ | 6¾ | + ⅛ |
| ARecreatn .16 | 3 | 11 | 11¾ | ... |
| Am Secur 1.40 | 15 | 27½ | 28 | - ¼ |
| Am Software | 269 | 27½ | 27¾ | + ¼ |
| AmStLfIns .88 | 7 | 31 | 32½ | + ½ |
| AmWest Airl | 157 | 7¼ | 7½ | ... |
| AmWestrn 15k | 2 | 6¼ | 7¼ | ... |
| Ameritrst 2.88 | 358 | 44½ | 45 | - ¼ |
| Ampl A pf.40a | 3 | 17 | 18½ | - ½ |
| AnaditeInc .10 | 3 | 10⅜ | 10¾ | ... |
| Analogic Corp | 105 | 62¼ | 62¾ | + ¼ |
| AnalystIntl .30 | 134 | 13¾ | 14¼ | - ½ |
| Anaren Micrw | 242 | 11¼ | 11⅜ | + ¼ |
| Andersen 2000 | 471 | 9¾ | 10¼ | + 1¼ |
| Andrsn Ind .44 | 8 | 5⅞ | 6⅛ | ... |
| AndersenG 10i | 15 | 26¼ | 27 | ... |
| Aneco Reinsur | 7 | 3¾ | 4 | - ⅛ |
| Angeles .15f | 23 | 23½ | 24¼ | ... |
| ApogeeEnt .12 | 129 | 14½ | 14⅞ | ... |
| Arabian Shld | z54 | 10 | 12 | ... |
| Arden Group | 23 | 6¾ | 7⅛ | - ⅛ |
| ArgoSyst Inc | 106 | 24½ | 25¼ | - ½ |
| Ariz Bcw .80g | 103 | 17⅛ | 17¼ | ... |
| ArnoldInds .48 | z75 | 26 | 27½ | ... |
| ArtsWay Mfg | 20 | 6⅜ | 6⅝ | ... |
| AscBc-Cp .72g | 3 | 14½ | 16 | + ½ |
| Assoc Host .18 | 106 | 24¾ | 25¼ | ... |
| Astronics .10 | 20 | 11¾ | 12¼ | ... |
| Astrosystm ut | 2 | 31 | 33 | + 2 |
| Astrosystm wt | 100 | 6⅝ | 6⅞ | + ⅜ |
| Atico Fncl Cp | 1 | 4⅝ | 5⅛ | ... |
| Atlan-Tol Ind | 24 | 18¼ | 18¾ | + 2¾ |
| AtlGasLight 2 | 191 | 18 | 18¾ | - ¼ |
| Atl Amer .40g | 13 | 18½ | 18¾ | - ⅛ |
| AtlantBcp 1.32 | 58 | 41 | 41½ | - ½ |
| AtlSoest Airl | 79 | 15 | 15¼ | - ⅛ |
| Atwood Ocncs | 212 | 23½ | 24½ | ... |
| Autoclve .08b | 5 | 13¾ | 14½ | ... |
| Automatix Inc | 89 | 23 | 23¼ | ... |
| AutoTrol Tech | 213 | 18¼ | 18½ | - ⅛ |
| Auxton Cmptr | 85 | 23¾ | 24½ | - ¼ |
| Avatar Holdg | 77 | 15½ | 16 | - ½ |
| Aviation Grp | 83 | 26 | 26¼ | ... |
| A V M Corpn | 2 | 7 | 8¾ | + ½ |
| Aztec Mfg .20 | 19 | 9 | 9½ | - ¼ |
| - - B B - - | | | | |
| Bacrdl A 2.04a | 1 | 56 | 59 | ... |
| Baird Corp 3k | 97 | 11¼ | 11½ | ... |
| BakerFen .68a | 18 | 31½ | 33 | - ½ |
| Balco Energy | 46 | 4½ | 4⅞ | ... |
| BallysPark Pl | 22 | 14¼ | 15 | - 1½ |
| BancPop 1.80a | 7 | 28¼ | 28¾ | ... |
| BcHawaii 1.18 | 61 | 24⅛ | 24¼ | ... |
| BancOhioCp 1 | 118 | 19¾ | 20¼ | ... |
| BncpPenn 1.40 | 12 | 25 | 25¼ | + ¼ |
| BancOkla .80 | 14 | 19 | 19¼ | + ¼ |
| BancTec Inc | 48 | 16¼ | 16½ | ... |
| BncTex pf1.46 | 4 | 18 | 18¾ | ... |
| BangorHy 1.56 | 98 | 14⅞ | 15⅛ | + ⅜ |
| BankDela 2.72 | x9 | 45 | 46 | + ¾ |
| BankEast Cp | 12 | 27½ | 29 | ... |
| Bank Leumi | 56 | 1 3-16 | 1⅜ | ... |
| BkNwEng 2.60 | 94 | 62½ | 63 | - 1½ |
| Bankers Note | 95 | 9⅛ | 9⅜ | ... |
| Bankrs Tr 1.60 | 2 | 32¼ | 33 | + ¼ |
| BankIowa 1.52 | 9 | 43½ | 45½ | + ¾ |
| Bk South 1.08 | 82 | 35¼ | 36 | + 3¼ |
| BnkSecur .25d | 43 | 8¾ | 9¼ | ... |
| BantaGeor .48 | 269 | 21 | 21¼ | - ¾ |
| Barber Green | 63 | 16½ | 17 | - ¼ |
| Barden Corp 1 | 4 | 32 | 36 | ... |
| Barris Indust | 141 | 6⅝ | 6¾ | + ⅛ |
| Barton Valve | 33 | 6¾ | 7 | ... |
| BaseTnA .15g | 148 | 14 | 14½ | ... |
| BasicAm Md | 1981 | 15¾ | 16 | ... |
| Basic EarthSc | 641 | 4¾ | 4⅞ | + 1-16 |
| Basic Resour | 12655 | 1 | 1 1-32 | ... |
| BassFurn .80a | 292 | 52 | 52¼ | ... |
| BassWlkr .72b | 22 | 40½ | 41½ | + ½ |
| Baylss Mkt .60 | 3 | 17¼ | 18 | ... |
| Bayly Corp | 381 | 15⅜ | 15⅝ | - ⅜ |
| BBDOIntl 1.80 | 29 | 40¼ | 41 | + 1 |
| BearCreek .36 | 15 | 23¾ | 24½ | - ¼ |
| Beck Arnley | 78 | 14¼ | 14¾ | + 1¼ |
| Bedford Cmpt | 5 | 11 | 11¼ | ... |
| Belknap .80 | 24 | 16½ | 17 | ... |
| Bell&W Co 5i | 20 | 12¾ | 13¼ | + ¼ |
| Bell Natl Corp | 177 | 35 | 36½ | - ¼ |
| BelmoralMn p | 20 | 7¾ | 8¼ | ... |
| Belo Corp .72 | 15 | 44¼ | 44½ | - ¼ |
| Benihana Ntl | 146 | 5⅛ | 5¼ | + ⅛ |
| Benihna uts | 54 | 13 | 13½ | ... |
| BerkleyW .32g | 106 | 14¾ | 15 | ... |
| BerklineCp .50 | 19 | 12¾ | 13 | ... |
| Berkshir Hath | z54 | 980 | 995 | ... |
| Beverly Hills | 285 | 24½ | 25¼ | + 1 |
| Bibb Co .15b | 5 | 17½ | 18¼ | ... |
| Big B Inc | 101 | 19½ | 19¾ | - ⅛ |
| Big Bite .01d | 9 | 8¼ | 8½ | ... |
| Billings Corp | 91 | 4¼ | 4¾ | - ¼ |
| BingoKing Co | 33 | 5¼ | 5½ | ... |
| BioLogicls Inc | 106 | 4¾ | 4⅞ | ... |
| Biomed Scien | 401 | 3 11-16 | 3¾ | ... |
| Biochem Int | 34 | 13¼ | 13⅝ | ... |
| Biogen NV | 37 | 17½ | 18 | ... |
| Bio Response | 107 | 9⅞ | 10⅛ | ... |
| Biosrch MedP | 173 | 13 | 13½ | ... |
| Biotech Captl | 316 | 6⅞ | 7 | - ⅛ |
| Bird & Son | 71 | 17 | 17¼ | - ⅜ |
| Birtcher Corp | 45 | 8⅛ | 8⅜ | ... |
| Bishop Gr 10k | 45 | 13⅛ | 13⅜ | + ⅛ |
| BIW CblS .10a | 36 | 17½ | 17¾ | + ¼ |
| Block Drug 1g | 1 | 24 | 25½ | ... |
| BlChipSt .12b | 3 | 77 | 78½ | ... |
| BluefldSup .60 | 10 | 13 | 13¼ | ... |
| BlueWater OG | 12 | 6⅜ | 6⅝ | - ¼ |
| Btmn Bc 1.60g | 4 | 33 | 33½ | ... |
| Bohemia .40g | 74 | 26¾ | 27¼ | + ¼ |
| Bolt Tech .16b | 285 | 17½ | 17¾ | - ½ |
| Bomaine Corp | 2 | 4 13-16 | 5 1-16 | ... |
| Bonanza Intl | 37 | 4⅜ | 4⅝ | ... |
| Bonray Drillg | 84 | 3¼ | 4 | + ¼ |
| BoontonEl 10i | 190 | 12¼ | 12½ | ... |
| BootheFncl 1 | 10 | 44 | 46 | ... |
| Boston Digital | 56 | 15½ | 16 | ... |
| BPI Systms | 573 | 22¾ | 23 | ... |
| BR Commun | 21 | 36¾ | 37¼ | ... |
| Bracken Expl | 18 | 2⅝ | 3¼ | - ⅛ |
| Brae Corportn | 249 | 27⅝ | 27¾ | + 4⅜ |
| BranchCp 1.12 | 1 | 22¼ | 22½ | ... |
| Brand Insulat | 3 | 7½ | 8½ | ... |
| Brenco Inc .24 | 102 | 12¾ | 12⅞ | + ⅛ |
| Brent Petrol | 741 | 1 1-32 | 1 1-16 | ... |
| Brentn Bk .94 | 20 | 19½ | 20½ | ... |
| Bristol Corp | 87 | 17 | 17¼ | + ½ |
| BroadvFn .01d | 82 | 5⅛ | 5⅜ | - ⅜ |
| BrookFash .32 | 183 | 37⅛ | 37⅜ | + ¼ |
| Brooks Resrc | 81 | 4¾ | 5½ | ... |
| BuckeyeF .01d | 2 | 8½ | 9 | ... |
| Buldrs InvGr | 174 | 7 | 7¼ | + ⅛ |
| Burnhm Serv | 22 | 27½ | 28 | - ¼ |
| BurnupSim .20 | 195 | 7⅞ | 8⅛ | - ⅛ |
| BurrBrown Cp | 176 | 25 | 25¼ | ... |
| Burton Hawks | 60 | 2⅜ | 2 7-16 | ... |
| Business Exch | 34 | 3⅞ | 4⅛ | ... |
| B M A 1.80 | 55 | 36¾ | 37¼ | + ¼ |
| ButlerMfg 1.32 | 34 | 29¾ | 30¼ | ... |
| - - C C - - | | | | |
| Cable TV Ind | 47 | 6 | 6½ | ... |
| C A C I | 243 | 17 | 18 | ... |
| CalFsBk 1.08g | 47 | 16¾ | 17 | + ⅛ |
| CalifFed SvLn | 1536 | 25⅞ | 26 | + ⅜ |
| CalWtrSv 4.50 | 2 | 47½ | 49 | ... |
| Callon Petrol | 148 | 10⅝ | 10⅞ | + ⅛ |
| Calny Inc .20 | 21 | 15 | 15½ | - ¼ |
| CalpropCp 10i | 104 | 10¾ | 11½ | ... |
| Cam Or Incp | 12 | 11½ | 12¼ | ... |
| CambrdgR 10l | 17 | 4¾ | 5 | ... |
| Candaigua Wn | 22 | 22¾ | 23½ | - ¼ |
| Canrad Hanov | 6 | 4½ | 4¾ | ... |
| CapitlBc 1.04a | 6 | 24½ | 26 | + ¼ |
| CapitalSo Wst | 6 | 15½ | 16½ | ... |
| CapitolAir Inc | 143 | 2 | 2¼ | ... |
| Care Corportn | 2 | 21 | 22½ | ... |
| Care Enterpr | 329 | 19¾ | 20 | ... |
| Carhart Photo | 2 | 9 | 9¾ | - ¼ |
| Carlsberg Cp | 10 | 8½ | 9½ | ... |
| Cascade St .20 | 58 | 10½ | 11 | - ¼ |
| Castle Entrt | 321 | 3½ | 3⅝ | + ⅛ |
| Cavangh Com | 200 | 2 3-16 | 2 5-16 | ... |
| Cavco Industr | 48 | 10¼ | 11 | - ½ |
| CB&TBcsh .92 | 17 | 27 | 28½ | - ¾ |
| CBT Corp 1.64 | 67 | 35 | 35¼ | + ¼ |
| Cedar Pt 1.64g | 36 | 39 | 39⅛ | ... |
| CelinaFncl A | 3 | 7¾ | 8½ | ... |
| Cencor Inc .40 | 187 | 45 | 46 | - 1 |
| CenterrBc 1.80 | 261 | 23¾ | 24 | ... |
| Centocor | 33 | 17¾ | 18¼ | ... |
| CentrlBcp 1.95 | 60 | 27½ | 28 | + ¼ |
| CnBkgSys .40g | 18 | 19¾ | 20¼ | - ¼ |
| CenBcsSo 1.20 | 16 | 18⅞ | 19⅛ | ... |
| CenFidBk 1.36 | 11 | 25¼ | 25⅜ | - ⅛ |
| CenJerBT 1.10 | z1 | 16½ | 17½ | ... |
| CentrlPac .64 | 110 | 11¼ | 11¾ | + ½ |
| CPennNt 1.40a | 76 | 27½ | 28 | - ¼ |
| CentrlResv Lf | 4 | 4 | 4¼ | ... |
| Centran Cp .40 | 48 | 20¼ | 20½ | ... |
| Century Paprs | 5 | 8¼ | 8¾ | ... |
| Cenvill Devl | 65 | 20 | 20½ | + ½ |
| Cerberonics A | 44 | 22¼ | 23¼ | - 1 |
| CFS Cont .52 | 663 | 29¾ | 29⅞ | + ½ |
| Champ Pt .05b | 73 | 8⅛ | 8⅜ | + ½ |
| Chapparl Res | 786 | 2¾ | 2⅞ | + 5-16 |
| Charan Indust | 157 | 3⅜ | 3½ | + ⅛ |
| CharlesRiv .48 | 2 | 46 | 47 | ... |
| Chathm Mf .60 | 27 | 15½ | 15¾ | ... |
| Chattem .48 | 18 | 22¼ | 22¾ | ... |
| Checkpnt Syst | 98 | 24⅞ | 25⅛ | - ½ |
| ChezmDv .10f | 75 | 9¾ | 10¼ | - ¼ |
| Chefs Intl Inc | 919 | 1⅝ | 1 13-16 | + ⅛ |
| Chem Leamn | 10 | 16½ | 18½ | ... |
| Chemlawn .40 | 93 | 48½ | 49 | - ½ |
| Chemtrnc Inc | 4 | 15¾ | 16¼ | ... |
| Cherry El .06b | 26 | 18½ | 19 | + ¼ |
| Childrn World | 102 | 8¼ | 8⅜ | ... |
| Chittenden 1g | 23 | 21¾ | 22½ | + ¼ |
| Chomerics Inc | 30 | 17½ | 17¾ | ... |
| ChurchDwt .72 | 9 | 19½ | 20¼ | ... |
| ChyronCp .10b | 260 | 26½ | 26¾ | + ¾ |
| CinciFincl 2 | 63 | 61½ | 61¾ | + ¼ |
| CirclIncm 1.44 | 6 | 13⅞ | 14⅛ | ... |
| Citel Incorp | 372 | 3⅞ | 4 | ... |
| CitizenFid 1.24 | 57 | 27⅛ | 27¼ | + ¼ |
| CitizenGr .12b | 5 | 9½ | 10 | + ¼ |
| CitizenSv Fcl | 18 | 23 | 25 | - 2 |
| CitiznSthn 1.80 | 50 | 38 | 38½ | ... |
| CitzUtil A 8i | 90 | 33½ | 34¼ | ... |
| Citz UtilB 1.64 | 27 | 24¼ | 25 | ... |
| City FedSL pf | 133 | 29¼ | 31¼ | + ½ |
| CityNtlCp .88g | 24 | 30¾ | 31¼ | ... |
| CitytrBcp 1.40 | 5 | 42½ | 44 | ... |
| Clark Mfg .76 | 34 | 23¾ | 24¼ | ... |
| Classifd Fncl | 2 | 8 | 8½ | ... |
| CleveTrRl 1.20 | 1 | 14¼ | 14⅜ | ... |
| Clinical Data | 32 | 5⅞ | 6¼ | ... |
| Clow Corp | 65 | 11¾ | 12⅛ | ... |
| CMT Invst Co | 40 | 4¾ | 5⅛ | ... |

**EXPLANATORY NOTES**

z-Sales in full.

a-Annual rate, also extra or extras. b-Paid so far in 1983, no regular rate. c-Payment of accumulated dividends. d-Paid in 1982. e-Cash plus stock paid in 1982. f-Cash plus stock paid in 1983. g-Annual rate plus stock dividend. h-Paid in 1983, latest dividend omitted. i-Percent in stock paid in 1982. j-Percent in stock paid in 1983, latest dividend omitted. k-Percent in stock paid in 1983. n-Asked price not applicable. p-Granted temporary exception from Nasdaq qualifications. q-In bankruptcy proceedings. t-Liquidating dividend. ut-Units. wt-Warrants. x-Ex-dividend, ex-rights or ex-distribution. (z) No representative quote.

The Wall Street Journal, *May 23, 1983.*

| | | | | |
|---|---|---|---|---|
| AcclrtnCp .05d | 62 | 8 | 8¼ | ... |
| AccurayCp .14 | 79 | 19⅛ | 19¼ | ... |
| AcetoChem 3k | 2 | 22 | 22½ | ... |
| ACMAT Corp | 18 | 11 | 11½ | ... |
| Acme Genl .20 | 2 | 16¾ | 17¼ | ... |
| Adage Incorp | 178 | 50¼ | 50½ – 3 |  |
| AddWesley .50 | 28 | 24½ | 25 – ¾ |  |
| Advance Ross | 130 | 4⅞ | 5 | ... |
| AdvSemi Mat | 69 | 24 | 24½ | ... |
| Advn Syst .15f | 76 | 27¾ | 28½ | ... |
| AEC Inc .40 | 5 | 10¾ | 11½+ ¼ |  |
| AEICOR Inc | 1093 | 2 | 2⅛ | ... |
| Aero Services | 133 | 3½ | 3⅝ | ... |

Addison-Wesley ───────────────────────►

| Stock & Div. | Sales 100s | Bid | Asked | Net Chg. |
|---|---|---|---|---|
| AddWesley .50 | 28 | 24½ | 25 | —¾ |

You can see that the company paid a 50-cent dividend and that 2,800 shares traded on May 20.

The bid price (24½) refers to the highest price dealers offered to pay for the stock, while the asked price (25) refers to the lowest price other dealers were willing to take for the stock. These quotes were as of 4 P.M., Eastern time. Transactions occur throughout the trading day as dealers move off their bid or asked positions. The net change ( – ¾) refers to movement in the bid price from the previous trading day.

With this information, you can track the performance of any share of stock traded on the New York or American exchanges or the OTC market.

Returning to the Dow Jones Industrial Average, you know that the price of a share of stock reflects the ability of the corporation to earn profits. This relationship is expressed as the "Price-Earnings" (P-E, or price divided by per share earnings) ratio between the price of the stock and the profits per share of stock earned by the corporation (profits divided by number of shares outstanding). The price-earnings ratio answers this question: "What is the price an investor must pay to capture the earnings represented by one share of stock?" For instance, a P-E ratio of 10 might mean that a company earned a dollar per share and that a share sold for $10.

Keep in mind that the investor seeks the highest rate of return consistent with safety. The rate of return is annual profit expressed as a percentage of invested capital. If you earn $100 a year on an investment of $1,000, the rate of return is 10 percent. A P-E ratio of 10 (10/1) represents a 10 percent rate of return because earnings are one tenth (10 percent) of the price per share. Similarly, a P-E ratio of five (5/1) is the equivalent of a 20 percent rate of return because earnings per share are one fifth (20 percent) of invested capital. A

P-E ratio of twenty (20/1) represents a 5 percent rate of return. And so on.

Chart 3 shows you that the P-E ratio fell from the end of World War II until the beginning of the Korean War, because earnings grew while share prices languished. Following the uncertainties of the 1930s and World War II, investors were still unsure of themselves.

Then the great bull market (a bull attacks by thrusting upward, hence this term for a rising market) of the 1950s began and the P-E ratio rose. Investors were at last convinced of a "return to normalcy" and were willing to stake their future in shares of stock.

**Chart 3**
**Dow-Jones Industrial Average** (price), **Earnings per Share, and Price-Earnings Ratio**

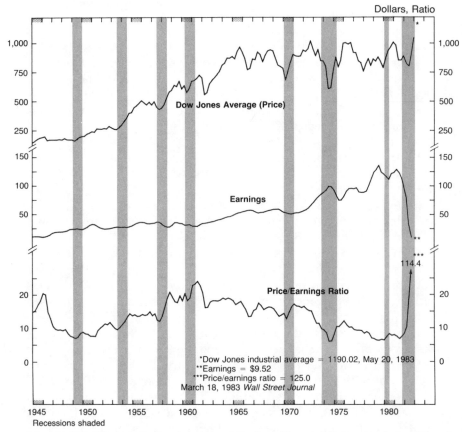

Source: Phyllis S. Pierce, ed., *The Dow Jones Investors Handbook* (Homewood, Ill.: Dow Jones-Irwin, 1983), and *Barron's*.

The market was clearly "undervalued" (a P-E ratio of seven was roughly a 15 percent rate of return), so it is not surprising that stock prices climbed rapidly. Stocks were a good buy because their price was very low compared to their earnings per share and their potential for even higher earnings. As investors rushed into the market, stock prices soared. Enthusiasm was so great and share prices advanced so rapidly that the P-E ratio rose despite stronger earnings per share.

The P-E ratio had climbed to 20 (a 5 percent rate of return) by the early 60s, so that the market was no longer "undervalued." The ratio plateaued or fell slightly to the end of the decade because share prices were no longer increasing faster than corporate earnings. The great bull market had ended.

During the next decade, investors became frightened of the impact of inflation and severe cyclical fluctuation on corporate earnings, since earnings fell sharply with each recession. At the first hint of declining profits brought on by the tail end of the cycle, investors unloaded their shares and stock prices plunged. As a result, the Dow remained in a range, fluctuating between the high 500s and 1,000 for a decade. Investors had been so badly burned by the market's decline in 1969 and 1974 that they refused to be swayed by the strong recovery of profits after each recession. Yet profits rose over the decade, and thus the P-E ratio fell, so that by the early 1980s it was almost as low as it had been at the outset of the Korean War. The market had not kept pace with profits, and stocks were undervalued once again.

Did this mean we were on the verge of another bull market, such as that of the 1950s? Was the situation similar to that of the late 1940s, with investors hesitant after years of bad news, yet willing to take the plunge when it became clear that the fundamentals had changed? One indication was that stock prices fell little in the recessions of 1980 and 1981–82 when compared with those of 1970 and 1974. It was as if investors were positioning themselves for the bull market that was just around the corner.

There were two very auspicious signs. First, the breaking of the boom-and-bust inflationary spiral with the back to back recessions of 1980 and 1981 was a key signal. Investors knew that henceforth corporations could produce growing and stable earnings. Second, the low P-E ratio meant that stocks were undervalued. Growing earnings would generate rising share prices. When sufficient numbers of investors realized that the earnings improvement was permanent, the P-E ratio would rise to higher levels as buying pressure drove stock prices up. A new bull market would be under way.

Investors anticipated this turn of events and sent stock prices soaring in the summer of 1982, when it became clear that the Fed had loosened its monetary vise. The decline in interest rates mattered to investors because the rate of interest is an alternative return to earnings per share (P-E ratio). As interest rates fall, investors move out of interest-earning instruments and into stocks.

In early 1983 corporate profits remained low because of the recession, although the Dow had gained 50 percent since the summer of 1982. This pushed the P-E ratio to a bizarre level. Investors had bid stock prices up in anticipation of greater earnings and the coming bull market. The P-E ratio will fall to a normal level as earnings improve.

Are there any flies in the ointment? Surely, and they can be placed in two groups. First, there's Murphy's Law (what can go wrong will go wrong). Unforeseen events could rekindle inflation, exacerbate the cycle, depress profits, and destroy investor confidence. Second, in order to ensure a smooth and orderly expansion, the Fed must exercise monetary restraint. Excessive ease would permit the expansion to roar ahead, rekindling inflation and instigating a renewed round of the boom-and-bust cycle. But this posture by the Fed will keep interest rates higher than they would be otherwise. And higher interest rates could depress the market by keeping the P-E ratio down. Stock prices would be prevented from climbing by the attractive alternative of high interest rates. If high interest rates are not a deterrent to the market, the Dow could easily double the levels of the early 1980s.

# CHAPTER THIRTEEN

## U.S. International Transactions

Foreign exchange rates, IMF, balance of trade, balance of payments—and the other terms used to discuss America's international economic relations—can be defined and described in the context of current events. But to understand them thoroughly, you must think back to World War II. Most of our modern international economic institutions were formed at the end of the war and immediately after, when the American dollar assumed the central role which it still occupies today. Take the time to review developments since then before plunging into the data and terminology in which current international transactions are discussed.

Well before World War II came to a close, the Allies were so certain of victory that the United States hosted a conference in the resort town of Bretton Woods, New Hampshire, in the summer of 1944 to plan international monetary affairs for the postwar years.

The United States knew that the war was taking a drastic toll on the rest of the world's economies, while the U.S. economy was growing stronger. Both victor and vanquished would need food, fuel, raw materials, and equipment, but only the United States could furnish these requirements. How were other nations to pay for these imports? They had very little that Americans wanted. If they sold their money for dollars in order to buy goods from us, the strong selling pressure on their currencies and their strong demand for dollars would drive their currencies down in value and the dollar up. Soon the dollar would be so expensive, in terms of foreign currency, that the rest of the world could not afford to buy the American goods necessary to rebuild.

It would have been very easy to say that this was everyone else's problem, not ours, but America's statesmen knew that it was our problem as well. This lesson had been learned after World War I, when similar problems had faced the world economy. Following that war, the United States had washed its hands of international responsibilities; consequently, the world economy had suffered through a dollar shortage. Many nations had been forced into currency devaluations, and the United States had ended up with most of the world's supply of gold, as other nations had used gold in desperation to settle their accounts with the United States. Moreover, each nation had sought shelter in shortsighted protectionist devices, shattering the world economy. Economic nationalism had spilled into the diplomatic arena and had been partly responsible for World War II.

Determined to avoid these mistakes the second time around, the United States convened the Bretton Woods Conference to deal with such problems before they arose. The conference's principal task was to prevent runaway depreciation of other currencies after the war. The International Monetary Fund (IMF) was established to accomplish this. The fund was a pool of currencies to which all nations (but mostly the United States) contributed and from which any nation could borrow in order to shore up the value of its own currency. If a nation's currency was under selling pressure, and weak and falling in value compared to other currencies, buying pressure designed to drive its price upward could be implemented with strong currencies borrowed from the IMF. For instance, Britain could borrow dollars from the IMF to buy pounds, thus supporting the price of the pound.

The dollar was pegged to gold at $35 an ounce, and all other currencies were pegged to the dollar, so that a dollar was worth a fixed number of francs, pounds, and so forth. At the time, the United States had most of the world's gold and other nations had hardly any, so the entire system was tied to gold through the U.S. dollar. This system of fixed exchange rates was constructed to provide stability in international economic relationships. Traders and investors knew exactly what a contract for future delivery of goods or future return on investment was worth in terms of the foreign exchange in which the contract was written. There was no need to speculate on shifting exchange rates, which could wipe out profit margins or generate large losses.

To draw an analogy, consider a shipment of oranges from California to New York and investments made by Californians on the New York Stock Exchange. Californians need be concerned about the price of oranges in New York and the price of a share of stock on the exchange, but they need not be concerned about fluctuations in the value of New York currency versus California currency, since both states use dollars.

Now think how much more difficult selling and investing in New York would be for Californians if the exchange rate between their currencies fluctuated. The diplomats wished to avoid precisely that problem after World War II, and that's why the Bretton Woods Conference established the IMF and a system of fixed exchange rates.

Unfortunately, after the war the U.S. balance-of-trade surplus (the amount by which the revenue of all exports exceeds the cost of all imports) created a greater dollar shortage than the conference had anticipated. Other nations were continually selling their currencies in order to buy American dollars with which to buy American goods. Selling pressure forced down the price of other currencies despite the IMF, which was not large enough to bail them out, and many of these currencies faced runaway depreciation against the dollar.

The United States responded to this crisis with the Marshall Plan. George C. Marshall, a career soldier, had been chairman of the Joint Chiefs of Staff during the war. At the war's end, President Truman appointed him secretary of state. Marshall understood that Europe's recovery was hobbled by a shortage of food, fuel, raw materials, and machinery and equipment and that the United States was the only nation which could supply Europe's needs in sufficient quantities. He further understood that the dollar shortage prevented Europe from importing what it needed from the United States. He proposed, and President Truman and Congress approved, a plan whereby the European nations drew up a list of their needs and the United States provided them with the dollars they required to satisfy those needs. In that way, the European nations' balances of payments were not strained and their currencies were freed from the pressure of devaluation. American exports, of course, benefited as our dollars bounced right back to us for purchases of American goods.

By the time of the Korean War, everyone was talking about the "economic miracle of Europe." The Marshall Plan had been extended to victor and vanquished, in what is probably history's greatest example of benevolence as enlightened self-interest. The United States had learned from its mistakes following World War I. Isolationism was myopic; the United States had to play an active role in world affairs. And our generosity would be repaid many times over as foreign markets for our goods recovered rapidly.

The Marshall Plan became a cornerstone of American foreign policy. Yet the United States also provided the rest of the world with desperately needed dollars in a number of other ways, all of which accomplished this purpose without being expressly designed to do so. The United States began to maintain a substantial military presence overseas, and our foreign bases provided their host countries with dollars when native civilians employed at the bases and American personnel spent their paychecks. In addition, American business firms resumed overseas investing, especially in Europe, providing dollars to countries where subsidiaries were purchased and facilities built. Finally, Americans started to travel abroad, seeding Europe with funds. All of these activities meant that dollars were sold for foreign exchange (foreign currency) and offset the constant sale by other nations of their currency in order to buy American goods.

Furthermore, whenever foreign banks, businesses, or individuals received more dollars than were immediately required, they were delighted to deposit those dollars in either American or foreign banks and to hold them for a rainy day. Since dollars were in vigorous demand because of the continuing need to buy American exports, those dollars could always be sold in the future, and meanwhile they were a handy private reserve should an occasion arise to spend them later.

By the late 1950s and early 1960s, however, some foreign banks, businesses, and individuals found that they had more dollars than they could use. They did not wish to buy American goods, and they had found making other investments more attractive than holding dollars, so they decided to sell them.

The United States did not have to rely on the IMF to support the dollar and maintain a fixed exchange rate between the dollar and other currencies. Rather, the U.S. Treasury stood ready to redeem dollars with gold whenever selling pressure on the dollar became heavy. That is, the United States propped up the price of the dollar in terms of other currencies by buying the dollar for gold. Since a foreign holder of dollars could buy gold at $35 per ounce and sell that gold for foreign exchange anywhere in the world, there was no need to sell dollars below the fixed rate of exchange. Whenever the dollar fell a little, foreigners would buy gold with their dollars and cash that gold in for other currencies at full value, which kept the dollar up. And the U.S. price of $35 per ounce of gold set the world price for gold, simply because the United States had most of the world's supply. As a result, gold started to leave the United States in a stream as dollars were redeemed for it. American holdings of gold were cut almost in half by the time increasing alarm was voiced in the early 1960s.

An alternative solution had to be found, or else the U.S. supply of gold would disappear. The foreign central banks stepped in and agreed to support the price of the dollar as part of their obligation to maintain fixed exchange rates under the Bretton Woods agreement. They had potentially limitless supplies of their own currency. If a bank, business, or individual in another nation wanted to sell dollars, and this selling pressure tended to force the price of the dollar down in terms of that nation's currency, the foreign central bank would buy the dollars for its currency and thus support the price of the dollar. This could not be accomplished by the U.S. Treasury or the Federal Reserve System because neither had limitless supplies of foreign currency. As long as the foreign central banks were willing to buy and accumulate dollars, private citizens, banks, and businesses in other countries were satisfied. In this way, the system of fixed exchange rates survived.

However, by the late 1960s and early 70s the situation had become ominous. The United States no longer had a favorable balance of trade. Other nations were selling more to and buying less from the United States. America's favorable balance of trade had been the single big plus in its balance of payments, offsetting the outflows of dollars mentioned earlier: foreign aid (the Marshall Plan), American tourism, foreign investment, and the American military presence overseas. Now the dollar holdings of foreign central banks began to swell ever more rapidly as their citizens liquidated dollar holdings. These central banks realized that they were acquiring an asset which ultimately would be of little value to them. Having been put in a position of continually buying dollars they would never be able to sell, they insisted that the United States do something to remedy the situation.

The French suggested that the dollar be officially devalued as a first step, because it had had a very high value in terms of other currencies ever since World War II. They reasoned that if the dollar were worth less in terms of other currencies, American exports would be cheaper for the rest of the world, imports would be more expensive in the United States, and thus the U.S. balance of trade would shift from negative to positive as the United States exported more and improted less. In addition, if foreign currencies were more expensive, Americans would be less likely to travel and invest overseas. This would partially stem the dollar hemorrhage. Others suggested that the foreign central banks stop supporting (buying) the dollar and that the dollar be allowed to float downward to a more reasonable level as foreigners sold off their holdings.

For many years, the United States resisted both devaluation and flotation, until, in a series of developments between 1971 and 1973, we ceased redeeming the dollar for gold and permitted it to float. It promptly fell, relative to other currencies, because foreign central banks no longer felt obliged to purchase it in order to support its price.

At the same time, the price of gold increased because the United

States would no longer redeem dollars with gold. The willingness of the United States to sell gold virtually without limit at $35 per ounce had kept its value from rising, but now the price of gold could increase according to the forces of private supply and demand. It fluctuated with all other commodity prices, rising rapidly during the general inflation at the end of the 1970s and then falling with commodity prices from 1980 through 1982.

The dollar fell until the summer of 1973, and then it fluctuated in value until the end of the decade. Foreign central banks no longer felt obliged to buy the dollar in order to support its price, though they occasionally did so to keep it from plummeting too far or too rapidly. They took this action in their own self-interest at the suggestion of exporters who knew that a low value for the dollar and a high value for their own currencies made it difficult to export to the United States.

Now the dollar has broken out of the range in which it fluctuated during the 1970s, and its value is greater than it has been for years. A discussion of the reasons for this should be put in the context of an introduction to the balance of payments, the balance of trade, and foreign exchange rates, all of which are published regularly in *The Wall Street Journal*.

Few statistical series generate as much confusion as those which portray America's international transactions. You will see that they are really not difficult to understand or follow on a regular basis.

## BALANCE OF PAYMENTS AND BALANCE OF TRADE

In order to understand the balance-of-payments accounts, think of yourself as representing the United States in all dealings with the rest of the world. If you wish to do business with the rest of the world, you must buy its currencies (called foreign exchange). Likewise, in order to do business in the United States, the rest of the world must buy dollars.

Now set up an accounting statement. The left side will include all the uses you had for all the foreign exchange you purchased. The right side of the account will include all the uses for the dollars that the rest of the world purchased. The two sides must balance, because for every dollar's worth of foreign exchange that you

**U.S. Balance of Payments**

| Money going out (−) | Money coming in (+) |
|---|---|
| Uses by United States for all foreign exchange purchased with U.S. dollars | Uses by rest of world for all U.S. dollars purchased with foreign exchange |

buy with a dollar, the rest of the world must use a dollar's worth of foreign exchange to buy that dollar. You have just constructed a balance-of-payments statement.

Once the accounting statement has been set up, you may add other details. Each side of the statement will have a current account and a capital account. The current account will be subdivided into merchandise trade, services, and foreign aid. The capital account will be subdivided into private investment and central bank transactions.

### U.S. Balance of Payments

| U.S. purchase of foreign money (debit) (−) | Foreign purchase of U.S. money (credit) (+) |
|---|---|
| Current account<br>  Goods and services<br>    Merchandise trade<br>    Services<br>  Foreign aid<br>Capital account<br>  Private investment<br>  Central bank transactions | Current account<br>  Goods and services<br>    Merchandise trade<br>    Services<br>  Foreign aid<br>Capital account<br>  Private investment<br>  Central bank transactions |

To summarize: the left side of this account (debit) shows what you, representing the United States, are doing with the foreign exchange you purchased with American dollars. The right side of the account (credit) shows what the rest of the world is doing with the dollars it purchased with its money. Remember, the two sides must be equal; a transaction can take place only if equivalencies are exchanged.

Keep in mind that nothing has yet been said about the price you must pay to buy foreign exchange or the price the rest of the world must pay to buy dollars. The rate of exchange between dollars and foreign currency will fluctuate with the forces of supply and demand. That is, if your demand for foreign money is relatively stronger than the demand of the rest of the world for dollars, your selling pressure on the dollar in order to buy foreign currency is going to force the dollar down in relative value. You will have to give up more dollars in order to get a unit of foreign exchange, or, to put it the other way around, you will get less foreign exchange for your dollars. If, on the other hand, the demand of the rest of the world for your dollars exceeds your demand for its currency, the reverse will be true and the dollar will increase in value compared to foreign currencies as the rest of the world must use more and more of its currency to buy a dollar.

Return to the balance-of-payments account. What will you do with the foreign exchange you purchased, and what will the rest of the world do with its dollars? Each category in the balance of payments will be examined in turn.

## Balance on Current Account

### Balance on Goods and Services

*Balance on Merchandise Trade.*    You can use the foreign exchange you have purchased to buy foreign goods, and the rest of the world can use dollars to buy American goods. Thus, if you import goods into the United States, you have incurred a debit ( – ) because you have sold dollars to buy foreign currency in order to make the transaction; in other words, money has left the United States. On the other hand, if the rest of the world buys American goods, you have earned a credit ( + ). It is customary to talk about the balance on merchandise trade by netting imports against exports to determine whether we have an export ( + ) surplus or an import ( – ) deficit.

*Services.*    If you use your dollars to buy foreign currency in order to travel in a foreign country, or use a foreign air carrier, or pay interest on a foreign debt, all this would be classified as an outflow of funds or debit ( – ). On the other hand, if the rest of the world used the dollars it bought to travel in the United States, or fly with an American air carrier, or pay interest on a debt to the United States, that flow of money to the United States would be a credit ( + ).

If the net credit ( + ) or debit ( – ) balance on this account is added to the credit ( + ) or debit ( – ) balance of the merchandise trade account, this subtotal is referred to as the **balance on goods and services.**

*Foreign Aid.*    If you use the foreign money you have purchased to make a gift to the rest of the world, that's a debit ( – ); and if the rest of the world uses the dollars it has purchased to make a gift to the United States, that's a credit ( + ).

When the foreign aid transaction is combined with the balance on goods and services, it completes the **balance on current account,** which will be a debit ( – ) balance or a credit ( + ) balance, depending on whether more funds flowed out of or into the United States.

## The Capital Accounts

As a private investor, you may wish to sell U.S. dollars and buy foreign exchange in order to make an investment in the rest of the world. This could be a direct investment in the form of plant and equipment expenditures or the purchase of a foreign company, or it could be a financial asset, either long-term or short-term. Stocks and bonds are long-term financial investments. A foreign bank account or a holding in foreign currency is a short-term investment. Any of these transactions will be a debit ( – ) in the American account because dollars have left the United States. Conversely, when a private investor in the rest of the world sells foreign exchange in order to use U.S. dollars to make a direct or financial investment in the United States, whether long-term or short-term, this is classified as a credit ( + ).

If, as a representative of the Federal Reserve System, you sell dollars in order to buy foreign currency, this too is a debit ( – ), and when foreign central banks buy dollars, it is a credit ( + ). These central bank transactions conclude the discussion of **balance-of-payments** components.

A further point must be made before you plow into the data. References are constantly being made to deficits or surpluses in the balances on trade, goods and services, and current account. Now and then you may encounter a comment about a deficit or surplus in the balance of payments despite this chapter's assertion that it always balances.

Trade, goods and services, and current account are easy. You already know that there can be a surplus ( + ) or a deficit ( – ) in these accounts. But how could anyone speak of a deficit in the balance of payments when it must always balance? Because that is the shorthand way of saying that the nation's currency is under selling pressure and that the value of the currency will fall unless some remedial action is taken.

For instance, at the time the foreign central banks were supporting the value of the dollar, their purchases of dollars were a plus ( + ) in the American balance of payments because they sopped up the excess dollars that their own economies didn't need. Had they not done so, the dollar would have fallen in value. Foreign central bank purchases of dollars were a "plus" in our balance of payments. Obviously, if you remove a plus from an accounting system in balance, what remains has a negative bottom line. Because the plus which made the account balance was a remedial action and because without it the account would have been negative, reference was made to a deficit in the balance of payments.

When the United States still made sales of gold internationally, in order to redeem the dollar, these sales were plus entries in our balance of payments. You may wonder why the loss of gold is a plus, but remember that anything sold by the United States is a plus because the rest of the world must pay us for it. Now if you remove gold sales from the balance of payments, the remaining items must net out to a negative balance. Therefore, people often referred to the size of the U.S. gold loss as its deficit in its balance of payments.

And now for one final tip before you look at the data: keep your eyes on the money. That's the best way to determine whether something is a "plus" or "minus" in the balance of payments. If we pay for it, that's a "minus," because money is going out. If they pay for it, that's a "plus."

The Wall Street Journal regularly publishes two Commerce Department reports dealing with the balance of payments and the balance of trade which will be useful to you.

1.  Balance-of-payments figures for the previous quarter appear between the 18th and the 20th day of the last month of each quarter.
2.  Monthly balance-of-trade figures are published between the 25th and the 28th of each month.

Look for the following in the typical (March 18, 1983) balance-of-payments article: balance on current account, merchandise trade balance, and trade in services. Very few of the items in the capital account are reported, so the article will not present a complete record of the balance of payments. (See page 185.)

# U.S. Trade Gap For Last Year Was $8.09 Billion

## White House Sees '83 Deficit On the Current Account Of a Record $20 Billion

By EILEEN ALT POWELL
*Staff Reporter of* THE WALL STREET JOURNAL

WASHINGTON—The U.S. registered an $8.09 billion deficit last year in its balance of payments on the current account, and the Reagan administration predicts a record deficit in 1983.

Robert Dederick, Commerce Department undersecretary for economic affairs, predicted that the deficit could total $20 billion this year.

Last year's red ink was the first since a $500 million deficit in 1979 and the largest since a record $14.8 billion deficit in 1978. In 1981, the U.S. registered a $4.47 billion surplus.

**{ Current Account Balance }** In 1982's final quarter, the U.S. registered a $6.1 billion deficit in its balance of payments on the current account. This was the largest quarterly deficit in the 22 years for which figures are available, surpassing the previous record of $6 billion in 1978's first quarter, Commerce Department analysts said.

### Blame Strong Dollar

Economists in and out of government blame much of the deterioration in the trade position on the strong dollar, which has made U.S. goods less price-competitive overseas. Meantime, recession abroad decreased demand for American products more than recession in the U.S. cut demand for imports.

Economic recovery in the U.S. this year probably will increase the demand for imports while the strong dollar continues to depress exports, producing the widening trade gap.

The current account is watched closely because it is the broadest measure of U.S. trade with the rest of the world, incorporating the exchange of merchandise and services, as well as some financial transactions.

Mr. Dederick said that "the current account may well improve somewhat this quarter as lower oil imports and higher exports lead to a temporary strengthening of the (merchandise) trade balance." He added, however, that "thereafter, the (merchandise) trade and current account deficits will widen again, and a current account deficit of over $20 billion is likely for all of 1983."

Jack Laver, chief economist at Merrill Lynch, Pierce, Fenner & Smith Inc. in New York, contends the administration's deficit forecast "is a bit on the high side but not unrealistic." He expects a red-ink total of $16 billion to $18 billion this year. "We're going to see the lagged effects of the strong dollar on exports, as well as lingering effects from recession abroad," Mr. Lavery said.

More imports and fewer exports translate to slower economic growth for the American economy and slower improvement in the nation's unemployment rate. However, the outflow of dollars eventually will work to reduce the currency's value on international markets and help stimulate U.S. exports.

But some economists worry that the dollar may remain strong through much of this year. C. Fred Bergsten, a Carter administration trade official who heads the Institute for International Economics here, says a continued strong dollar could produce a current account deficit as big as $40 billion this year "and continued deterioration well out into 1984."

The trade figures are seasonally adjusted. The latest report showed that for all of 1982, U.S. merchandise exports, excluding military goods, totaled $211.01 billion, down from $236.25 billion in 1981. Imports totaled $247.34 billion last year, down from $264.14 billion a year before. That produced a merchandise-trade gap of $36.33 billion last year, wider than the $27.89 billion of 1981.

Net service receipts declined to $36.11 billion last year from $38.97 billion a year earlier. U.S. financial transfers abroad, including Social Security benefit checks and nonmilitary grants, increased to $7.87 billion in 1982 from $6.61 billion in 1981.

### Deficit Was Wider

In the fourth quarter, the deficit was wider than the red-ink total of $5.21 billion in the third quarter and $927 million a year earlier. The nation registered surpluses in the first two quarters last year.

Much of the widening of the deficit from the third quarter reflected a decline in U.S. earnings on foreign portfolio investments because of lower interest rates, the department said. Also U.S. government grants—mainly to Israel, Turkey and Egypt—increased in the final quarter from the third period.

**{ Merchandise Trade Balance }** U.S. merchandise exports totaled $48.07 billion in 1982's fourth quarter, down from $52.33 billion in the third period. Imports fell to $60.21 billion in the final quarter from $64.83 billion in the preceding period. That left the U.S. with a fourth-quarter merchandise-trade deficit of $12.14 billion, compared with a $12.5 billion gap in the third period.

**{ Service Balance and Foreign Aid }** Net service receipts narrowed to $8.46 billion in the final period from $8.93 billion in the third quarter. U.S. government payments abroad totaled $2.43 billion, compared with $1.65 billion in the third period.

The Wall Street Journal, *March 18, 1983.*

*Current account balance . . . fourth paragraph*

---

In 1982's final quarter, the U.S. registered
a $6.1 billion deficit in its balance of pay-
ments on the current account. This was the
largest quarterly deficit in the 22 years for
which figures are available, surpassing the
previous record of $6 billion in 1978's first
quarter, Commerce Department analysts
said.

---

*Merchandise trade balance . . . second paragraph from end of
article*

---

U.S. merchandise exports totaled $48.07
billion in 1982's fourth quarter, down from
$52.33 billion in the third period. Imports fell
to $60.21 billion in the final quarter from
$64.83 billion in the preceding period. That
left the U.S with a fourth-quarter merchandise-trade deficit of $12.14 billion, compared
with a $12.5 billion gap in the third period.

---

*Service balance and foreign aid . . . last paragraph*

---

Net service receipts narrowed to $8.46 bil-
lion in the final period from $8.93 billion in
the third quarter. U.S. government payments abroad totaled $2.43 billion, compared
with $1.65 billion in the third period.

---

The *fourth, next-to-last, and last paragraphs* of the March 18,
1983, *Journal* article present the information you need. According
to the fourth paragraph, the current account deficit was $6.1 bil-
lion in the last quarter of 1982. This was generated by the merchandise trade deficit of $12.14 billion (second paragraph from the end)
and foreign aid payments of $2.43 billion (last paragraph) and oc-
curred despite net service income of $8.46 billion (last paragraph).
    Put these figures in the accounting format used earlier (as shown
on the top of page 187).
    The March 18 article devoted most of its attention to the annual

## U.S. Balance of Payments

| U.S. purchase of foreign exchange ( – ) | | Foreign purchase of dollars ( + ) | |
| --- | --- | --- | --- |
| Merchandise trade deficit | $12.14 billion | Service income | $8.46 billion |
| Foreign aid | $ 2.43 billion | | |
| Current account deficit (trade deficit and foreign aid less service income) | $ 6.11 billion | | |

| | |
| --- | --- |
| Merchandise trade (deficit) | – $12.14 billion |
| Service income (surplus) | + 8.46 billion |
| Foreign aid (deficit) | – 2.43 billion |
| Balance on current account (deficit) | – $ 6.11 billion |

Note: The current account deficit reported in the March 18, 1983, *Journal* article ($6.10 billion) differs from the calculations in this table ($6.11 billion) due to rounding errors.

data. See if you can put those annual figures into the accounting framework used for the quarterly data. The current account balance ( – $8.09 billion) is in paragraph 1, the merchandise trade balance ( – 36.33 billion) in the sixth paragraph from the end, and service income ( + $36.11 billion) and foreign aid ( – $7.87 billion) in the fifth paragraph from the end.

The quarterly and annual figures tell the same story. The outflow due to the trade deficit and foreign aid was not completely offset by our service income—hence, the current account deficit.

The third paragraph provides a transition for discussion of historical developments. The current account deficit was a record $14.8 billion in 1978 and then shifted to a surplus of $4.47 billion in 1981 before falling back into deficit in 1982. Use Chart 1 on page 188 to analyze these developments.

You can make two observations. First, until fairly recently the merchandise trade balance and the balance on current account were virtual mirror images of each other; only in recent years have the two series diverged. Second, the balance on current account remained positive until lately, after a brief dip in 1977 and 1978, even though the merchandise trade balance became sharply negative.

The gap between the current account and merchandise trade balances is composed of service income, such as the net earnings that the United States receives from foreign investments; the sale of banking, transport, and insurance services; and foreign tourism in the United States. In other words, until just recently U.S. service earnings grew so rapidly that the balance on current account remained positive ( + ) despite an acutely negative ( – ) merchandise trade balance.

**Chart 1**
**Balance of Payments** (quarterly data): **Current Account Balance, Goods and Services Balance, and Merchandise Trade Balance**

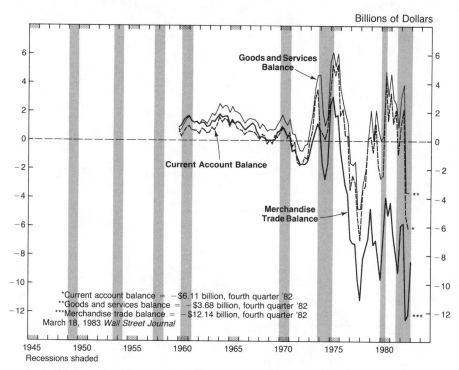

Billions of Dollars

*Current account balance = −$6.11 billion, fourth quarter '82
**Goods and services balance = −$3.68 billion, fourth quarter '82
***Merchandise trade balance = −$12.14 billion, fourth quarter '82
March 18, 1983 *Wall Street Journal*

Recessions shaded

Source: U.S. Department of Commerce, *Business Conditions Digest* and *Handbook of Cyclical Indicators,* series 622 and 667; U.S. Department of Commerce, *Business Statistics;* and *Federal Reserve Bulletin.*

How can the sharp fluctuations in the merchandise trade balance be explained, and why has the merchandise trade balance deteriorated so severely in recent years? The business cycle provides the answer to both parts of this question. Imports fell sharply in 1975 because the recession reduced demand, including demand for imports. Exports continued to grow, however, because recession had not yet gripped our trading partners, and thus 1975 was a year of trade surplus. Then, in 1976–77, recession spread internationally and exports began to lag just as our imports increased sharply with economic recovery at home. Hence, our trade balance swung into deficit and remained in deficit for a number of years as imports and exports grew at similar rates, with a steady gap between them.

Imports fell again during the 1980 recession, while exports continued to grow. As a result, the trade gap narrowed substantially. Imports hardly had a chance to recover before they fell off again during the 1981–82 recession. Consequently, the merchandise trade deficit was smaller than during the economic expansion of 1978. As the recession in the rest of the world became increasingly severe, however, our exports sank, raising the merchandise trade deficit to record levels.

To summarize, lately our merchandise trade balance has been negative, our service balance positive, and our current account balance slightly negative as the first two balances largely offset each other.

Will the current account balance remain negative? That depends on the merchandise trade balance. If economic recovery and expansion stimulate our imports, as they have in previous business cycles, expect a sizable trade and current account deficit. Remember that foreign recovery and expansion usually lag behind ours and that demand for our exports may lag accordingly, generating big trade deficits.

So it's a race between service income ( + ) and trade deficit ( – ). Chances are that the trade deficit will win as our economy expands, plunging the current account into deficit.

You can use the *Journal* to follow the Commerce Department's *monthly merchandise trade report*. The March 30, 1983, article provides data for February. Focus your attention on *imports, exports*, and the *balance* between the two. (See page 190.)

# Trade Deficit Grew Slightly For February

## Gap Was $3.58 Billion, Versus $3.57 Billion for January; '83 Estimate Is Narrowed

By LAURIE MCGINLEY
*Staff Reporter of* THE WALL STREET JOURNAL

Merchandise Trade Balance {

WASHINGTON—The nation's merchandise trade deficit in February widened slightly from January to a seasonally adjusted $3.58 billion, the Commerce Department said.

The January deficit was an adjusted $3.57 billion. The $7.15 billion deficit for the first two months of 1983 exceeded the $6.8 billion gap of a year earlier.

While still expecting a record deficit for the full year, the department narrowed its forecast for 1983 to between $50 billion and $60 billion from the $60 billion to $70 billion predicted earlier.

David Lund, a Commerce Department trade analyst, said the new projections for 1983 reflect the steep decline in oil prices and an expected rise in U.S. exports to developing nations that aren't members of the Organization of Petroleum Exporting Countries.

Even the more optimistic forecast would be sharply wider than the record $42.69 billion gap last year.

### Exports Drop 6.1%

Exports {

The department's report showed that U.S. exports in February fell 6.1% to an adjusted $16.33 billion, after rising 6.4% in January to an adjusted $17.39 billion. The February drop reflects declines in exports of machinery, chemicals, textiles, petroleum products and agricultural commodities, the department said.

Imports }

Imports last month decreased 5% to an adjusted $19.91 billion, after increasing 4.8% in January to an adjusted $20.96 billion, the department said. The report showed that a sharp drop in oil imports was partly offset by a 3% rise in non-oil imports. An increase in auto imports accounted for most of the rise in non-oil imports, the department said.

The value of imports of petroleum and related products in February fell 32.7% to an adjusted $3.19 billion from an adjusted $4.74 billion in January. It was the lowest since an adjusted $3.03 billion in October 1976, Mr. Lund said.

By volume, oil imports in February fell 29.5% to 104.7 million barrels from 148.6 million barrels in the preceding month. The average price of a barrel of imported oil fell to $30.49 in February from $31.92 in January. The February price was the lowest since $29.91 in February 1980, Mr. Lund said.

### Daily Oil Imports

Mr. Lund also noted that the U.S. imported 3.7 million barrels of oil a day in February, the lowest since "the 1960s." He said the department's records of this category don't go back far enough to provide a precise date.

The sharp decline in oil imports last month helped produce a trade surplus of an adjusted $151 million with OPEC. It was the first surplus with OPEC since an adjusted $208 million surplus last May, and only the second in a decade, Mr. Lund said. The U.S. had a deficit of an adjusted $872 million with OPEC in January.

The deficit with Japan widened sharply last month to $2.22 billion from an adjusted $1.33 billion in January. The surplus with Western Europe widened to an adjusted $417 million last month from an adjusted $292 million in the previous month.

*Merchandise trade balance . . . first paragraph*

---

WASHINGTON—The nation's merchandise trade deficit in February widened slightly from January to a seasonally adjusted $3.58 billion, the Commerce Department said.

---

*Exports . . . sixth paragraph*

---

The department's report showed that U.S. exports in February fell 6.1% to an adjusted $16.33 billion, after rising 6.4% in January to an adjusted $17.39 billion. The February drop reflects declines in exports of machinery, chemicals, textiles, petroleum products and agricultural commodities, the department said.

---

*Imports . . . seventh paragraph*

---

Imports last month decreased 5% to an adjusted $19.91 billion, after increasing 4.8% in January to an adjusted $20.96 billion, the department said. The report showed that a sharp drop in oil imports was partly offset by a 3% rise in non-oil imports. An increase in auto imports accounted for most of the rise in non-oil imports, the department said.

---

According to the *first, sixth, and seventh paragraphs*, the United States ran a $3.58 billion trade deficit in February as exports fell more than imports

The article tells you that the Commerce Department expects the merchandise trade deficit to be larger in 1983 than it was in 1982. That's consistent with an earlier recovery here than abroad.

Notice, however, that not only have crude oil prices dropped, but we are now importing less crude oil than at any time since OPEC began raising oil prices a decade ago. The reduced bill for oil is due to the recent recession and to conservation. This will help keep the value of imports down.

What bearing did these developments have on the strength of the dollar? To determine this, you must consider foreign exchange rates.

## FOREIGN EXCHANGE RATES

Recall the brief outline of the dollar's postwar history.

You can see from Chart 2 on page 193 that the value of foreign currencies in terms of dollars has declined dramatically (that is, the dollar has risen in value) in the past two years. The French franc has fallen from $0.25 to less than $0.15; the British pound, from $2.50 almost to $1.50; the Swiss franc, from over $0.60 to less than $0.50; and the German mark from $0.55 almost to $0.40. The balance-of-payments discussion will aid your understanding of the dollar's rise. The reasons appear below.

First, high interest rates have strengthened the dollar. When interest rates in the United States are higher than interest rates elsewhere, foreign exchange is sold for dollars and the capital accounts will show a net flow of private investment into the United States. The recent tight money policy of the Fed pushed interest rates in the United States higher than those in Europe and Japan, prompting heavy dollar purchases by foreign investors who wished to enjoy the high interest rates available here.

Second, the U.S. balance on current account improved dramatically until late 1982 because of rapidly growing service income and despite a sharply negative balance of trade. This positive element in the American balance of payments not only generated a flow of dollars into the United States but also encouraged private businesses and individuals in the rest of the world to invest in dollars because they believed that the dollar would remain strong in the future. And the dollar has indeed remained strong despite the recent deterioration in the current account balance.

Third, through the actions of the Fed, the United States had come to grips with inflation, driving the rate of price increase from double-digit figures to a negligible level in just a few years. Moreover, the Fed made it clear that it would not permit a resurgence of inflation. The Fed's actions gave investors throughout the world confidence in the dollar's strength because the price stability of American products would maintain America's competitiveness in world markets. This assistance to America's trading position encouraged investors to keep their dollars here, thus boosting the dollar's price.

Fourth, the decline in America's oil imports, and the weakening

## Chart 2
## Foreign Exchange Rates

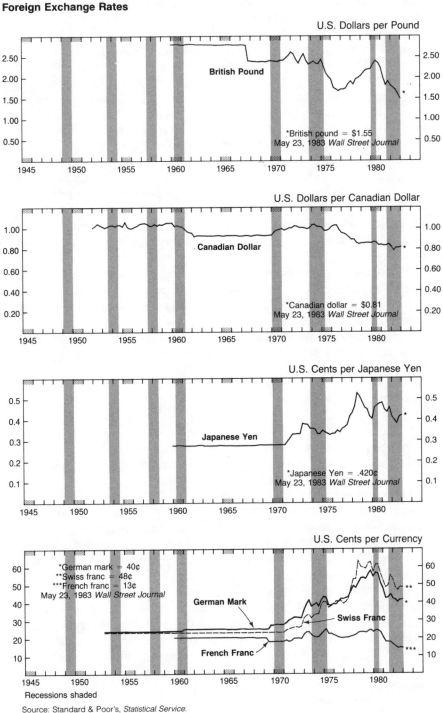

U.S. Dollars per Pound

British Pound

*British pound = $1.55
May 23, 1983 *Wall Street Journal*

U.S. Dollars per Canadian Dollar

Canadian Dollar

*Canadian dollar = $0.81
May 23, 1983 *Wall Street Journal*

U.S. Cents per Japanese Yen

Japanese Yen

*Japanese Yen = .420¢
May 23, 1983 *Wall Street Journal*

U.S. Cents per Currency

*German mark = 40¢
**Swiss franc = 48¢
***French franc = 13¢
May 23, 1983 *Wall Street Journal*

German Mark

Swiss Franc

French Franc

Recessions shaded

Source: Standard & Poor's, *Statistical Service*.

of OPEC's price grip, meant a reduced value for American imports. This helped the U.S. trade and payments balance and encouraged investors to keep their dollars here.

You can use the daily report on foreign exchange published in *The Wall Street Journal* (check the front-page index) to keep abreast of the dollar's value. For instance (see excerpt on page 196), on Friday, May 20, 1983, the British pound was worth approximately $1.55, the French franc approximately $0.13, the Japanese yen almost half a cent, the Swiss franc approximately $0.48, and the German mark approximately $0.40. Most foreign exchange trading is conducted by banks on behalf of their customers. Banks will also provide future delivery of foreign exchange for customers who wish a guaranteed price in order to plan their operations and limit risk due to exchange rate fluctuation. The price for future delivery is known as the *"forward rate,"* and you can see forward quotes for the major currencies immediately beneath the current rate. Future contracts for foreign currencies are also available on a number of exchanges.

The value of the dollar compared to a *composite of 15 other currencies* is published each Monday by the *Journal.* This information accompanies the previous Friday's foreign exchange quotations. (See excerpt on page 196.)

You can see that on May 20, 1983, the dollar was worth more than at any time since May 29, 1970. This is a remarkable comeback.

*   *   *

In conclusion, four factors have recently boosted the dollar's value: higher interest rates here than abroad, a surplus in the current account balance, the reduction in our rate of inflation due to the recession, and low oil imports.

U.S. interest rates have already fallen sharply, and the big differential which existed in 1981 has largely disappeared, and could vanish entirely in the long run. The current account surplus was temporary too, and it will turn negative as our economy recovers and expands, leading to a deterioration of the merchandise trade balance.

Under these circumstances, the dollar should fall. Yet psychological factors remain. The flight from the dollar, which brought its value down, was in part caused by the belief of the rest of the world that American inflation was out of control. Higher U.S. prices would make American exports less competitive and encourage imports, weakening the dollar. International investors now perceive that the United States is serious in its assault on inflation and that this will benefit America's trading position in the long run.

# Foreign Exchange

Friday, May 20, 1983

The New York foreign exchange selling rates below apply to trading among banks in amounts of $1 million and more, as quoted at 3 p.m. Eastern time by Bankers Trust Co. Retail transactions provide fewer units of foreign currency per dollar.

| Country | U.S. $ equiv. Fri | U.S. $ equiv. Thurs | Currency per U.S. $ Fri | Currency per U.S. $ Thurs |
|---|---|---|---|---|
| Argentina (Peso) .. | .000013 | .000013 | 75.000 | 75000 |
| Australia (Dollar) ...... | .8828 | .8820 | 1.1328 | 1.1338 |
| Austria (Schilling) ...... | .0574 | .0575 | 17.4275 | 17.3920 |
| Belgium (Franc) | | | | |
| Commercial rate ..... | .0202 | .0202 | 49.40 | 49.49 |
| Financial rate ......... | .0202 | .0202 | 49.45 | 49.53 |
| Brazil (Cruzeiro) ....... | .00216 | .00216 | 463.15 | 463.15 |
| **British Pound** → Britain (Pound) ...1.5575 | 1.5545 | | .6421 | .6433 |
| 30-Day Forward ....1.5559 | 1.5529 | | .6427 | .6440 |
| 90-Day Forward ....1.5535 | 1.5504 | | .6437 | .6450 |
| 180-Day Forward ...1.5500 | 1.5470 | | .6452 | .6464 |
| Canada (Dollar) ........ | .8178 | .8112 | 1.2228 | 1.2327 |
| 30-Day Forward ..... | .8176 | .8111 | 1.2231 | 1.2329 |
| 90-Day Forward ..... | .8174 | .8108 | 1.2234 | 1.2333 |
| 180-Day Forward ..... | .8170 | .8104 | 1.2240 | 1.2339 |
| Chile (Official-Rate) ... | .0136 | .0136 | 73.76 | 73.76 |
| China (Yuan) ............ | .5043 | .5043 | 1.9829 | 1.9829 |
| Colombia (Peso) ........ | .0132 | .0132 | 75.95 | 75.95 |
| Denmark (Krone) ...... | .1133 | .1134 | 8.8290 | 8.8150 |
| Ecuador (Sucre) ........ | .0229 | .0229 | 43.67 | 43.67 |
| Finland (Markka) ...... | .1835 | .1835 | 5.4500 | 5.4490 |
| **French Franc** → France (Franc) .......... | .1345 | .1345 | 7.4375 | 7.4375 |
| 30-Day Forward ..... | .1340 | .1341 | 7.4600 | 7.4595 |
| 90-Day Forward ..... | .1330 | .1330 | 7.5175 | 7.5200 |
| 180-Day Forward ..... | .1304 | .1303 | 7.6675 | 7.6775 |
| Greece (Drachma) ..... | .0119 | .0120 | 84.00 | 83.00 |
| Hong Kong (Dollar) ... | .1455 | .1421 | 6.8750 | 7.0380 |
| India (Rupee) ............ | .1001 | .1000 | 9.9900 | 10.00 |
| Indonesia (Rupiah) .... | .0010 | .0010 | 968.50 | 968.50 |
| Ireland (Punt) ........1.2790 | 1.2755 | | .7819 | .7840 |
| Israel (Shekel) ......... | .0232 | .0232 | 43.15 | 43.15 |
| Italy (Lira) .............. | .000680 | .000679 | 1470.00 | 1472.00 |
| **Japanese Yen** → Japan (Yen) ............... | .004268 | .004271 | 234.30 | 234.15 |
| 30-Day Forward ..... | .004279 | .004281 | 233.70 | 233.57 |
| 90-Day Forward ..... | .004299 | .004301 | 232.62 | 232.50 |
| 180-Day Forward ..... | .004331 | .004334 | 230.90 | 230.75 |
| Lebanon (Pound) ...... | .2401 | .2401 | 4.1650 | 4.1650 |
| Malaysia (Ringgit) .... | .4354 | .4346 | 2.2970 | 2.3010 |
| Mexico (Peso) ........... | .0068 | .0068 | 148.00 | 148.00 |
| Netherlands (Guilder) . | .3596 | .3597 | 2.7810 | 2.78 |
| New Zealand (Dollar) . | .6630 | .6630 | 1.5083 | 1.5083 |
| Norway (Krone) ........ | .1402 | .1403 | 7.1350 | 7.1260 |
| Pakistan (Rupee) ....... | .0826 | .0826 | 12.10 | 12.10 |
| Peru (Sol) ................. | .000724 | .000724 | 1381.92 | 1381.92 |
| Philippines (Peso) ...... | .0997 | .0997 | 10.0265 | 10.0265 |
| Portugal (Escudo) ...... | .0101 | .0101 | 99.20 | 99.25 |
| Saudi Arabia (Riyal) . | .2899 | .2898 | 3.4500 | 3.4501 |
| Singapore (Dollar) ..... | .4787 | .4760 | 2.0890 | 2.1010 |
| South Africa (Rand) .. | .9250 | .9234 | 1.0811 | 1.0830 |
| South Korea (Won) .... | .0013 | .0013 | 767.00 | 767.00 |
| Spain (Peseta) ........... | .0072 | .0072 | 138.35 | 138.00 |
| Sweden (Krona) ......... | .1334 | .1334 | 7.4945 | 7.4980 |
| **Swiss Franc** → Switzerland (Franc) ..... | .4815 | .4834 | 2.0770 | 2.0685 |
| 30-Day Forward ..... | .4834 | .4853 | 2.0685 | 2.0604 |
| 90-Day Forward ..... | .4871 | .4891 | 2.0531 | 2.0446 |
| 180-Day Forward ..... | .4926 | .4946 | 2.0300 | 2.0220 |
| Taiwan (Dollar) ........ | .0250 | .0250 | 39.98 | 39.98 |
| Thailand (Baht) ......... | .0435 | .0435 | 23.00 | 23.00 |
| Uruguay (New Peso) | | | | |
| Financial ................ | .0302 | .0302 | 33.1250 | 33.125 |
| Venezuela (Bolivar) .. | .2329 | .2329 | 4.2938 | 4.2938 |
| **German Mark** → W. Germany (Mark) .. | .4035 | .4037 | 2.4785 | 2.4770 |
| 30-Day Forward ..... | .4050 | .4052 | 2.4691 | 2.4681 |
| 90-Day Forward ..... | .4077 | .4080 | 2.4525 | 2.4510 |
| 180-Day Forward ..... | .4118 | .4121 | 2.4285 | 2.4265 |

| SDR | 1.08118 | 1.0813 | .924919 | .92481 |

Special Drawing Rights are based on exchange rates for the U.S., West German, British, French and Japanese currencies. Source: International Monetary Fund.

z-Not quoted.

## Trade-Weighted Dollar

NEW YORK - Morgan Guaranty Trust Co. reported the dollar's percentage change in market value, weighted for volume of trade with the U.S., against 15 other currencies, as of noon Eastern time, from the following dates:

| | a-May 29,'70 | b-Dec. 18,'71 | c-Feb. 15,'73 |
|---|---|---|---|
| May 20, 1983 ........ | + 1.1% | + 12.0% | + 18.7% |
| Week ago .............. | + 0.3% | + 11.2% | + 17.8% |
| Year ago .............. | 4.2% | + 6.2% | + 12.5% |

a-Parities prior to Canadian dollar float. b-Smithsonian Agreement central rates. c-Market rates following dollar devaluation.

The Wall Street Journal, *May 23, 1983.*

| | | | |
|---|---|---|---|
| **Britain (Pound)** ........1.5575 | 1.5545 | .6421 | .6433 |
| 30-Day Forward .....1.5559 | 1.5529 | .6427 | .6440 |
| 90-Day Forward .....1.5535 | 1.5504 | .6437 | .6450 |
| 180-Day Forward .....1.5500 | 1.5470 | .6452 | .6464 |
| **France (Franc)** ......... .1345 | .1345 | 7.4375 | 7.4375 |
| 30-Day Forward ..... .1340 | .1341 | 7.4600 | 7.4595 |
| 90-Day Forward ..... .1330 | .1330 | 7.5175 | 7.5200 |
| 180-Day Forward ..... .1304 | .1303 | 7.6675 | 7.6775 |
| **Japan (Yen)** ............... .004268 | .004271 | 234.30 | 234.15 |
| 30-Day Forward ..... .004279 | .004281 | 233.70 | 233.57 |
| 90-Day Forward ..... .004299 | .004301 | 232.62 | 232.50 |
| 180-Day Forward ..... .004331 | .004334 | 230.90 | 230.75 |
| **Switzerland (Franc)** ... .4815 | .4834 | 2.0770 | 2.0685 |
| 30-Day Forward ..... .4834 | .4853 | 2.0685 | 2.0604 |
| 90-Day Forward ..... .4871 | .4891 | 2.0531 | 2.0446 |
| 180-Day Forward ..... .4926 | .4946 | 2.0300 | 2.0220 |
| **W. Germany (Mark)** .. .4035 | .4037 | 2.4785 | 2.4770 |
| 30-Day Forward ..... .4050 | .4052 | 2.4691 | 2.4681 |
| 90-Day Forward ..... .4077 | .4080 | 2.4525 | 2.4510 |
| 180-Day Forward ..... .4118 | .4121 | 2.4285 | 2.4265 |

## Trade-Weighted Dollar

On May 20, 1983, the U.S. dollar was worth 1.1 percent more than on May 29, 1970.

NEW YORK – Morgan Guaranty Trust Co. reported the dollar's percentage change in market value, weighted for volume of trade with the U.S., against 15 other currencies, as of noon Eastern time, from the following dates:

| | a-May 29,'70 | b-Dec. 18,'71 | c-Feb. 15,'73 |
|---|---|---|---|
| May 20, 1983 ......... | + 1.1% | + 12.0% | + 18.7% |
| Week ago ............. | + 0.3% | + 11.2% | + 17.8% |
| Year ago ............. | 4.2% | + 6.2% | + 12.5% |

a-Parities prior to Canadian dollar float. b-Smithsonian Agreement central rates. c-Market rates following dollar devaluation.

Then, too, many foreign investors believe that the United States is the last bastion of capitalism, and thus offers a safe haven for their funds. They view with favor President Reagan's conservative administration, and have no fear that their funds or investments will be confiscated or expropriated.

Finally, the rest of the world sees many investment opportunities in this country. Business profits should be strong in the near future, and there is a good chance of a continued bull market on the stock exchange.

All of these factors encourage foreign investors and financial institutions to invest in America and keep their funds in dollars, rather than some other currency. This has pushed the dollar to its highest values in a decade.

# CHAPTER FOURTEEN

## Leading Economic Indicators

Now that you have examined the business cycle in detail, and learned to use *The Wall Street Journal's* statistical series, you may be looking for a device to make analysis somewhat easier. Perhaps, while wading through the stream of data, you felt the need for a single indicator which could predict changes in the business cycle. You wanted something akin to the meteorologist's barometer, to inform you of rain or shine without a detailed examination of cloud formations.

Unfortunately, economists have never agreed on a single economic indicator to predict the future. Some indicators are better than others, but none is consistently accurate; all give a false signal on occasion. To deal with this, economists have devised a composite or combination of statistical series drawn from a broad spectrum of economic activity, each of which tends to move up or down ahead of the general trend of the business cycle. These series are referred to as leading indicators because of their predictive quality, and a dozen have been combined into the *composite index of 12 leading indicators*.

The components of the index of twelve leading indicators are:

1. Average workweek, production workers, manufacturing.
2. Average weekly initial claims, state unemployment insurance.
3. New orders for consumer goods and materials, 1972 dollars.
4. Vendor performance, percent of companies receiving slower deliveries.
5. Net business formation.

6.  Contracts and orders for plant and equipment in 1972 dollars.
7.  New building permits, private housing units.
8.  Net change in inventories on hand and on order, 1972 dollars.
9.  Change in sensitive materials prices.
10. Change in credit outstanding—business and consumer borrowing.
11. Stock prices, 500 common stocks.
12. Money supply—M2—in 1972 dollars.

There are three general criteria for inclusion in the index.

First, each series must accurately lead and reflect the business cycle.

Second, the various series should provide comprehensive coverage of the economy by representing a wide and diverse range of economic activity.

Third, each series must be available monthly, with only a brief lag until publication, and must be free from large subsequent revisions.

The 12 leading indicators meet these criteria, and weaving these series into a composite provides a statistic which is more reliable and less erratic than any of the individual components.

Finally, some of the indicators measure activity in physical units, others in current dollars, and still others in constant dollars, and some use an index form. This variety of measurements is reduced to an index with 1967 assigned a base value of 100 percent. All other months and years are expressed as a percentage of the base year.

March's index, published in the May 2, 1983, issue of *The Wall Street Journal*, is representative. The series usually appears around the first of the month.

# Leading Index's March Increase of 1.5% Suggests a Steady Advance in Recovery

By EILEEN ALT POWELL
*Staff Reporter of* THE WALL STREET JOURNAL

WASHINGTON—The seventh consecutive monthly increase in the government's major forecasting barometer in March suggests that the recovery will continue to perk along.

But private economists say they are concerned that weaknesses in consumer spending and factory orders will hold back the economy's improvement from the 1981-1982 recession.

Index of Leading Indicators { The Commerce Department said that the composite index of leading indicators, which is designed to forecast economic trends, rose 1.5% in March after increasing 1.4% in February and 3.2% in January.

Separately, the department said that sales of new, single-family houses declined 1.7% in March to a seasonally adjusted annual rate of 577,000 units. Home sales decreased a revised 3.8% in February to an adjusted 587,000 annual rate after rising 15.3% in January to an adjusted 610,000 annual pace. The February decline had been estimated as 5.9%.

### Merchandise Trade Deficit

The department also said that the nation's merchandise-trade deficit widened in March to an adjusted $3.63 billion from $3.58 billion the month before.

In conjunction with the trade report, Commerce Secretary Malcolm Baldrige predicted that the deficit will total about $58 billion for all of 1983. That is less than the $60 billion to $70 billion projection he made several months ago, but his forecast still represents a widening from 1982's record red ink of $42.69 billion.

Economic experts in and out of government said the leading indicators report constitutes good news for the economy in the next several months.

Mr. Baldrige said in a statement that the March rise in the leading indicators "foreshadows further advances in key economic series, such as employment, production, income and business sales."

David Cross, an economist at Chase Econometrics Associates in Bala Cynwyd, Pa., agreed that the March increase "is encouraging." But he noted that the latest report shows continuing weakness in new factory orders for consumer goods and in consumers' willingness to increase their debt.

"Without some kind of pickup in consumer demand over the next couple of months, I don't see how the recovery can be sustained," Mr. Cross said. Consumer spending, he added, could get a boost in the current quarter and subsequent periods if interest rates fall further. Spending also should be helped by larger-than-usual fed-

eral income tax refunds and the scheduled July 1 tax-rate cut.

Gordon Richards, director of economic analysis for the National Association of Manufacturers, a Washington trade group, said that "the most welcome development" in the latest report is evidence that raw-materials prices are rising as industrial demand increases. But he cautioned that orders for manufactured goods continue to be weak. "A rise in new orders is critical for recovery in manufacturing, since these industries have borne the brunt of the recession," Mr. Richards concluded.

The report showed that seven of the 11 available index parts contributed favorably to the March increase: the average work-week, companies receiving slower deliveries from vendors, net business formations, orders for plant and equipment, materials prices, stock prices and the money supply.

Four contributed unfavorably: average weekly initial claims for state unemployment insurance, manufacturers' new orders for consumer goods, building permits and change in credit outstanding.

The 12th component, the change in inventories, is reported after a one-month lag.

The March increase pushed the index to 149.8% of its 1967 average, compared with 147.6% in February. (See chart on page one.)

The index has risen 6.2% since December, the month most economists say the recession ended. This is somewhat stronger than the average 4.8 percentage-point gain in the first quarter of the seven previous post-World War II recoveries, department figures indicate.

Still, the performance of a companion gauge, the composite index of coincident indicators, hasn't been as strong this year as in previous recoveries. This index, which tends to move up or down simultaneously with economic activity, rose 1.4% in the 1983 first quarter, compared with an average 2.4 percentage-point gain in the first quarter of previous post-war recoveries.

Robert Ortner, the department's chief economist, said that the difference in the performances of the leading and coincident indexes "suggests that the relatively high level of interest rates may be interfering with the usual relationship between the leading indicators and the economy's performance."

The index of coincident indicators posted a 0.7% gain in March to 134% of its 1967 average after falling 0.5% in February.

The index of lagging indicators, which tends to trail economic trends, decreased 1% in March to 114.2% of its 1967 average after rising 0.2% in February.

Index of Leading Indicators }

The Wall Street Journal, *May 2, 1983.*

## Leading Indicators

Index: 1967=100

COMPOSITE of key indicators of future economic activity rose in March to 149.8% of the 1967 average from a revised 147.6% in February, the Commerce Department reports. (See story on page 3.)

The Wall Street Journal, *May 2, 1983.*

*Leading indicators . . . paragraphs three and fifteen*

The Commerce Department said that the composite index of leading indicators, which is designed to forecast economic trends, rose 1.5% in March after increasing 1.4% in February and 3.2% in January.

The March increase pushed the index to 149.8% of its 1967 average, compared with 147.6% in February. (See chart on page one.)

The index began to recover in April 1982, according to the chart accompanying the *Journal* article, and March's figure of 149.8, as reported in the 15th paragraph and the caption under the chart, was an all-time high.

Recovery in April 82 seems hard to believe if you recall the persistent bad news during 1982, especially the rising unemployment which went to double digits by year's end. Yet Chart 1 confirms that the index has historically turned prior to the cycle, and the

1982 recovery is no exception. That's why the index is so important and so useful.

Remember, however, that this series is only a composite of unrelated series, woven together because they provide an omen of future events. You need all the statistical reports appearing in the
*Journal* in order to build an understanding of the timing, direction,
and strength of the business cycle. After all, a meteorologist needs
more than a barometer, and most Americans who make decisions in
the business community, or wish to be fully informed of current
economic events, need far more than a crude, general directional
signal to guide their long-range planning.

**Chart 1**
**Composite Index of 12 Leading Indicators**

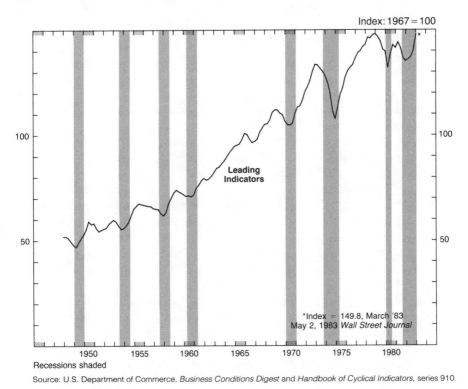

Recessions shaded

Source: U.S. Department of Commerce, *Business Conditions Digest* and *Handbook of Cyclical Indicators*, series 910.

# CHAPTER FIFTEEN

## Federal Fiscal Policy

Fiscal policy refers to the federal government's taxing and spending programs and their impact on the economy.

In order to sort out the continuing debate surrounding this topic, you must go back to the 19th and early 20th century. Economics was governed by an axiom known as "Say's Law": "supply creates its own demand." This meant that economic recession and depression and their accompanying unemployment were temporary and self-correcting phenomena. After all, capitalists produce goods for market, and workers offer their labor for hire *so that they in turn can demand goods in the marketplace.* If the goods cannot be sold or the labor is not hired, then a lower price or wage will be asked, until price and wage cutting permit all of the goods or labor to be sold. No goods will remain chronically unsold and no labor will remain chronically unemployed as long as prices and wages remain flexible.

Using this line of reasoning, economists argued that recession and its concomitant unemployment were transitory phenomena which should generate neither a great deal of concern nor any corrective policy prescription by the government. Thus, society and government ought to let well enough alone (that is, follow the policy of *laissez-faire*) and let market forces prevail. The operation of the market would eventually restore full employment.

With Say's Law as their guide, small wonder that economists could not understand the Great Depression which began in 1929 and hit bottom in 1933. Nor could they understand why the economy's performance remained anemic for so long after 1933. After all, they reasoned, the economy should naturally return to conditions of full production and full employment as business cut prices in order to sell its products and workers cut their wages in order to find employment. If the economy continued in a slump, that was the fault, not of the economists and their theories, but of employers and employees who refused to cut prices and wages.

The economists' logic did not help the businesses that were failing or the workers who were out of a job. Prices and wages had fallen, yet conditions remained dismal; something was dreadfully wrong, and somebody had to do something about it. President Roosevelt was elected and his solution was massive public works programs. These were funded by deficits, despite the economists' insistence that the federal government's efforts would merely deny resources to the private sector, and thus provide no net benefit. FDR was a practical man with a practical solution: if people were out of work, then the government would be the employer of last resort and put them to work building roads, parks, bridges, dams, and so forth.

In 1936 an Englishman named John Maynard Keynes (rhymes with *brains*) gave intellectual credentials to FDR's practical policies by proposing that the problem was the economists' theories, not the economy. Keynes tackled Say's Law (and his fellow economists) at the knees by declaring that demand could be chronically insufficient and the economy could be chronically plagued with substantial excess capacity and unemployment. Keynes scolded his fellow economists for arguing that their theories were right but that the practical world of business and work was not living up to theoretical expectations. Science—even "the dismal science" of economics—dictates that a theory that does not conform to the facts must be discarded.

Keynes declared that it was ridiculous to expect price and wage cuts to solve the economy's problem. A totally new approach had to be devised. He believed the only solution was to boost demand by the use of some exogenous (outside) force. Workers could not be expected to buy more under conditions of actual and threatened unemployment nor business to spend more on plant and equipment when excess capacity and weak profits were the rule. But if consumers and business would not spend, how could the economy pull out of its slump? Keynes argued that government spending was the answer, even if the government had to borrow funds because tax revenues were inadequate. Once government began to spend on roads, dams, bridges, and other public works and people were employed on these projects, their earnings would be spent on privately produced goods and services. In a multiplier effect, the total level of demand would be lifted and full employment restored. When the pump priming operation was over and the private economy was back on its feet, the government could gradually withdraw from the economic scene. Pump priming by government intervention became known as Keynesian economics.

Keynesian (pronounced "brainsian") theory came to dominate economics, rendering Say's Law archaic. The next generation of economists pushed Keynesian theory a bit further, reasoning that a tax cut could be as effective in priming the pump as an increase in government expenditures. Reducing taxes would increase consumers' disposable income and their consumption expenditures. The new generation believed this would be as effective as an increase in government expenditures for restoring demand to a level sufficient to insure full employment.

Economists now argued that it didn't matter how it came to pass that federal expenditures exceeded tax revenue. Putting more into the expenditure stream than was removed from the income stream (in the form of taxes) would always create a net boost in total demand. If government expenditures increased while tax revenues remained the same, the increase in public expenditures would boost demand. If government expenditures remained the same while taxes were cut, the increase in private consumption expenditures would boost demand. In either case, or in both together, the increased government deficit permitted a net addition to total demand.

Now you may ask whether government borrowing from the public has the same effect as taxing the public? After all, if the public refrains from spending to buy government bonds, isn't the public's expenditure reduced in much the same way? The answer is yes, if the bonds are purchased by private citizens; however, this is generally not the case. The largest share of bonds are sold to the banking system, which purchases them by creating a demand deposit for the government. This is known as "monetizing" the debt, as mentioned in Chapter Three. As the debt is monetized, demand increases because borrowing from the banks permits an increase in government spending without a decrease in private spending.

The federal government's attempts to influence economic activity through its power to tax and spend came to be known as fiscal policy. Although this chapter discusses fiscal policy in the context of stimulating demand in order to deal with recession, it should be clear that fiscal policy could also be employed to deal with inflation. For example, increasing taxes or reducing expenditures, thus creating a surplus, removes more from the income stream than from the expenditure stream, reducing total demand and, consequently, cooling inflation.

Fiscal policy should not be confused with monetary policy as discussed in Chapters Three, Four, and Five. Monetary policy refers to the actions of the Federal Reserve system. Fiscal policy refers to the actions of the federal government. Monetary policy works through its influence on the banking system, the money supply, bank lending, and interest rates, whereas fiscal policy works through its direct impact on aggregate demand.

Also keep in mind that fiscal policy is the province solely of the federal government, not of state or local government. Only the federal government has the flexibility to run the necessary budget deficits (and surpluses). Most state and local governments are limited, either de facto or de jure, to operating with a balanced budget.

Keynesian economics may have won the hearts and minds of economists by the early 1960s, but not everyone was convinced. When President Kennedy assumed office in 1961, he proposed a tax cut to stimulate the level of economic activity. It was opposed by Republicans and conservative Democrats in Congress, who attacked it as fiscally irresponsible. They demanded a balanced budget, and argued that tax cuts would generate unacceptable deficits. President Kennedy responded that the deficits would disappear as soon as the tax cut stimulated the level of demand, output, and income, providing even greater tax revenues despite the decline in the tax rate. These arguments did not persuade Congress, and the tax cut did not pass until the spring of 1964, following President Kennedy's assassination.

The nation enjoyed full employment and a balanced budget in 1965, and fiscal policy became an accepted method of "fine tuning" the economy to achieve the objectives of full employment without inflation. Indeed, fiscal policy became so legitimate that it was employed by the next two Republican presidents. President Nixon cut taxes to deal with the 1970 recession, and President Ford cut taxes to deal with the 1974–75 recession. In each case, the Federal Reserve also pursued an easy money policy in order to stimulate demand. Conservatives joined liberals, and Republicans agreed with Democrats that tax cuts were necessary to get the economy moving.

By the late 1970s, however, severe inflation had prompted a growing group of economists to conclude that attempts to stimulate demand with easy money and easy fiscal policies, in order to guarantee full employment, had not achieved their objectives. Escalating inflation, which reduced real income, had drawn more and more people into the labor force. The new entrants to the labor force, usually the secondary or tertiary wage earners in the family, had fewer skills and thus were more difficult to employ. Unemployment and inflation grew hand in hand. Thus, this group of economists and politicians argued that "full-employment policy" (the Keynesian prescription of stimulating demand through easy monetary and easy fiscal policies) had been a failure.

Moreover, they continued, increased inflation had discouraged savings and investment. Rising prices penalized savers for their thriftiness as the value of real savings fell. This encouraged personal indebtedness rather than saving, and inasmuch as saving is the ultimate source of all funds for investment, the level of investment was bound to shrink over time. These critics charged that the lack of savings, and the resulting lack of investment, were reflected by the low levels of business investment in new machinery and technology and by declining productivity.

Finally, they attacked the progressive income tax, which propelled people into higher tax brackets despite a drop in real income. Higher marginal tax rates removed the incentive to work more and work harder. Why should businesses invest in new ideas and new products and more efficient ways of doing things if higher taxes confiscated the profits? Why should workers put in more hours on the job if higher taxes reduced the additional pay to a meaningless figure?

The views of these economists and politicians came to be called supply-side economics, which they developed in contrast to demand-side, or Keynesian, economics. The supply-siders argued that it was more important to support policies which bolstered the economy's ability to supply or produce more goods than to enhance demand. Therefore, the supply-side economists advocated drastic federal income tax reductions over a three-year period, with deficits to be avoided by a parallel reduction in federal spending. Federal expenditure programs, in their view, tended to overregulate private activity and to waste tax dollars in needless boondoggles and unnecessary transfer payments.

A massive, across-the-board tax cut would accomplish two major objectives. First, it would provide incentives for increased effort, thus boosting output. A greater supply, or output, of goods and services would dampen inflation. Second, increased disposable income would lead to increased savings, providing a pool of funds to finance investment. Once again, the supply of goods and services would be stimulated, and increased output would reduce inflation.

Supply-side economics was a complete overthrow of the Keynesian revolution, which had prevailed for almost half a century, and was widely and correctly viewed as a device to restrict and contract the federal government. As the supply-siders began to make their voices heard, their demands caused President Carter difficulty. He had pledged to balance the federal budget by the end of his first term in office. Rapid economic expansion and inflation had pushed revenues upward more rapidly than expenditures; consequently, his goal was in sight by late 1979. But a tax cut without a spending cut would have postponed that goal, and as a Democrat, President Carter could not endorse the large reductions in federal expenditures that the supply-siders demanded.

The 1980 recession created an even sharper dilemma for President

Carter. He might have advocated a tax cut (the traditional Keynesian prescription for recession), but this would have played into the hands of the supply-siders, who by now had a presidential candidate, Ronald Reagan, as their principal spokesman. In addition, the supply-side tax cut favored upper-income groups, rather than the lower-income groups traditionally favored for tax cuts by the Democrats. Thus, circumstances precluded President Carter from trying to deal with the 1980 recession by means of tax reductions.

After his inauguration in 1981, as the economy slid into the 1981–82 recession, President Reagan pushed for and obtained the supply-side tax cuts. How ironic that 20 years after President Kennedy battled conservatives and Republicans for his tax cut, President Reagan now had to battle liberals and Democrats for his. Whereas Democrats had once advocated tax cuts to stimulate the economy and the Republicans had opposed those cuts, it was now the Republicans who were advocating tax cuts over the opposition of the Democrats. Both parties had done a complete about-face.

Debate over this matter seems to be inextricably caught up with ideological positions, but it need not be. The question can be analyzed in an objective, dispassionate way. (Remember that tax cuts are a supply-side and a demand-side prescription for economic expansion, regardless of the way in which they work.) First, if the supply-siders are correct, the tax cut will provide the incentive to work harder and produce more. If the demand-siders are correct, federal expenditures will exceed tax revenues for some time to come, and they will be financed by borrowing from banks. This will have an expansionary effect on demand. Second, both the supply-siders and Keynesians agree that the tax cut will boost personal income. The supply-siders emphasize that the chief benefit will derive from an increase in savings, which will spur investment. The Keynesians look to an increase in personal consumption expenditures. In either case, there will be positive benefits. Thus, you should be able to embrace either the novel, supply-side approach or the traditional, Keynesian approach and understand President Reagan's tax cut as necessarily expansionary.

Then what is the source of all the controversy? To begin with, most supply-siders are conservatives who wish to reduce federal domestic spending, while most Keynesians are liberals who wish to increase it. Also, the Democrats now insist that the increased federal borrowing due to the tax cut will crowd out private borrowing (and hence capital expenditures). Ironically, Republicans criticized President Carter's deficits in the late 1970s on precisely the same grounds. Yet you have seen that private borrowing exploded in those years. The shift of the mantle of *fiscal* conservatism from Republicans to Democrats is one of the most important political changes since World War II.

But the fear about "crowding out" is misplaced, for it is the Federal Reserve that will largely determine whether private borrowing at reasonable rates will be possible. If it pursues a tight money policy, private borrowers will have to compete with the government for funds. If the Fed pursues an easy enough policy, there will be room for both private and public borrowing. The point is that difficulty or ease of credit conditions will be largely determined by the Fed rather than by any crowding out. Keep in mind, too, that the Fed's objective should be to restrain the expansion rather than stimulate it, so perhaps a little crowding out, if it helps prevent credit conditions from becoming too easy, would not be unhealthy. Tight money will restrict consumer borrowing more than business borrowing, allocating funds (and resources) away from consumption expenditures toward investment expenditures in new plant and equipment. And as expansion develops, private borrowing will grow while federal borrowing shrinks.

Turning now to the business cycle, the huge federal deficits were responsible for neither the 1981–82 recession nor the recent recovery and expansion. The Federal Reserve's tight money policy generated the recession; the recession choked off inflation; and the choking off of inflation, along with the release of the Fed's grip, is what produced recovery and expansion.

President Reagan can't be blamed for the recession or lauded for the recovery and expansion. Those phenomena were produced by monetary policy, not fiscal policy.

Use *The Wall Street Journal* publication of the U.S. Treasury's *budget report* in the fourth week of the month to help you understand the federal government's current fiscal position. The headline and *first paragraph* of the April 26, 1983, *Journal* article inform you that March's budget deficit was $26.04 billion, and the *third paragraph* states that this deficit was caused by budget receipts of $43.5 billion and outlays of $69.54 billion. (See page 209.)

# U.S. Budget Gap Grew in March To $26.04 Billion

## Last Month's Figure Topped Year Ago's $18.26 Billion, February's $25.34 Billion

*By a* WALL STREET JOURNAL *Staff Reporter*

**Federal Deficit**

WASHINGTON – The Federal government's budget deficit widened in March to $26.04 billion from $18.26 billion a year earlier, the Treasury said.

Last month's deficit also was wider than the $25.34 billion posted for February.

**Federal Receipts and Expenditures**

Receipts totaled $43.5 billion in March, compared with $45.29 billion a year earlier and $38.82 billion in February. Outlays rose to $69.54 billion in March from $63.55 billion a year earlier and $64.15 billion in February.

For the first six months of the current fiscal year, which began Oct. 1, the deficit totaled $129.22 billion, compared with $71.91 billion in the first half of fiscal 1982.

The Reagan administration predicts that the deficit for all of fiscal 1983 will total a record $210.2 billion, almost double the previous record deficit last year of $110.66 billion. The administration has blamed much of the widening deficit on delayed effects of the 1981-82 recession, which has reduced revenue and increased outlays for unemployment benefits and other federal programs.

The report showed that receipts for the first six months of the current fiscal year totaled $276.87 billion, down from $289.59 billion in the first half of fiscal 1982. Almost all the decline was in corporate income tax collections, which totaled $12.29 billion in the first half of the current fiscal year compared with $22.91 billion a year earlier.

The lower corporate tax receipts reflect recession-reduced profits as well as 1981 and 1982 tax-law changes that reduced corporate tax liability.

Outlays totaled $406.09 billion in the first six months of the current fiscal year, compared with $361.5 billion a year earlier.

The Treasury also said that off-budget programs showed a deficit of $1.26 billion in March compared with deficits of $518 million a year earlier and $5 million in February. These programs, which are excluded by law from the budget, include many of the government's credit programs such as Federal Financing Bank operations.

A Treasury spokesman said the widening of the off-budget deficit reflected a pickup in Federal Financing Bank activity in March after a lull in February.

The Wall Street Journal, *April 26, 1983.*

*Federal deficit . . . first and third paragraphs*

WASHINGTON – The Federal government's budget deficit widened in March to $26.04 billion from $18.26 billion a year earlier, the Treasury said.

Receipts totaled $43.5 billion in March, compared with $45.29 billion a year earlier and $38.82 billion in February. Outlays rose to $69.54 billion in March from $63.55 billion a year earlier and $64.15 billion in February.

This data is neither seasonally adjusted, expressed at an annual rate, nor is it consistent with federal government activity as reported in the GNP accounts. Nonetheless, it will give you a feel for the relative size of expenditures, receipts, and borrowing.

You can see from Chart 1 that the federal deficit has grown enormously with each recession—for two chief reasons. First, recession reduced receipts because of higher unemployment (the unemployed pay no income tax) and lower revenues from the profits tax. Second, tax cuts accompanied the recessions of 1970, 1974–75, and 1981–82. In addition, note that federal expenditures have continued to grow during each recession despite revenue's setback. This generated the budget gap. Since the deficit grew with each successive recession, closing this deficit gap became more difficult and took longer every time.

In order to close the gap, receipts must grow more rapidly than expenditures. It took four years after the 1970 recession and five years after the 1974–75 recession. How long will it take this time? That's hard to say, but if the gap is not substantially narrowed before the next recession, many will wonder whether it can ever be eliminated.

But why worry about the deficit if its impact on the business cycle and on crowding out generates such a divergence of views? There are two good reasons for concern. First, as the federal government's debt mounts, interest payments become an increasing share of federal expenditures. There are historical examples of nations borrowing to the point that debt service composed the majority of their budget, crowding out other expenditures and compel-

**Chart 1**
**Federal Government Expenditures and Receipts**

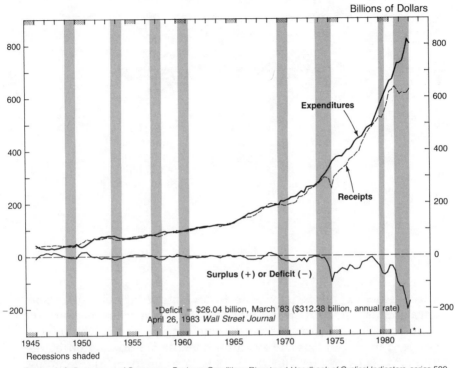

Billions of Dollars

*Deficit = $26.04 billion, March '83 ($312.38 billion, annual rate)
April 26, 1983 *Wall Street Journal*

Recessions shaded

Source: U.S. Department of Commerce, *Business Conditions Digest* and *Handbook of Cyclical Indicators*, series 500, 501, and 502.

ling increased borrowing to meet the interest payments on old debt. Second, the day could come when the creditworthiness of the federal government became suspect as the financial markets saw little chance of the federal government meeting its debts.

# CHAPTER SIXTEEN

## Summary and Prospect

The business cycle is inevitable in an unfettered capitalist economy, and its fluctuations and vicissitudes are the price that must be paid for economic progress. It's a cruel system because the price is not paid by all, just as the system's benefits are not shared by all. The price is mostly paid by workers who suffer cyclical unemployment. Their misfortune is due to the commodity they produce for market; it is not due to any fault of their own.

But, you ask, hasn't the cycle been extremely severe in recent years? Is there no era in our recent experience when the cycle was kinder to us, with less severe bouts of inflation and recession? Is that much trauma necessary?

The first half of the 1960s provides hope. Ironically, this half-decade followed the Eisenhower years, which were severely criticized by President Kennedy and his advisers for sluggish economic performance and too many recessions. Both the fiscal policy of President Eisenhower's administration and the monetary policy of the Federal Reserve at the time were excoriated for excessive concern with inflation and complacency about economic growth and unemployment. The critics charged that in the attempt to restrain demand in order to combat "creeping inflation," the economy's growth rate had fallen and recovery from frequent recessions had been weak.

All the arguments over creeping inflation seem laughable in the light of the experience of the 1970s; but inflation really did creep along at only about 2 percent a year in the early 60s. What's more, the Fed switched to a policy of relative ease in the early 60s. The low level of inflation and the Fed's easy money policy were the most important ingredients in the healthy economic expansion of the early 1960s.

Modest increases in the CPI permitted strong growth in consumer real income. As a result, consumer sentiment improved steadily. This, together with the ready availability of loans, prompted consumers to resort to record levels of mortgage borrowing and consumer credit. Home construction and automobile production set new highs. Business responded by investing heavily in new plant and equipment, so that general boom conditions prevailed by the middle of the decade.

The tax cut proposed by President Kennedy has received most of the credit for this prosperity. Inconveniently, however, it was not enacted until 1964, after his death, and it is difficult to understand how an expansion begun in 1962 can be attributed to a tax cut enacted two years later.

The relaxed and easy progress of the expansion was its most important feature. There was no overheating. Housing starts, auto sales, consumer credit, and retail sales gradually broke through to new ground. By 1965 there had been three solid years of expansion. This was reflected in a strong improvement in labor productivity and a solid advance in real compensation.

Will the next few years be like the early 60s? Will the economy expand slowly and gradually, bringing prosperity without severe fluctuation?

There are certain features today which are similar to those of the early 60s. The rate of inflation has been reduced, although violently this time, rather than gradually, as was the case 25 years ago. There is substantial slack in the economy, both in terms of low capacity utilization and high unemployment. Productivity has risen, and unit labor costs are down. All of this bodes well for continued expansion.

But there is an important difference between today and the early 60s. The Fed followed a very expansionary policy in the first half of the 60s, providing the banking system with ample free reserves. Interest rates today are far higher, and the Fed is pursuing a deliberate policy of restraint. What difference will this make?

Ironically, today's tighter conditions may help sustain the expansion. Why? Because overheating is the greater threat now. Twenty years ago, the consumer had to be cajoled into hocking the future. Not so today, when people are far more willing to borrow and spend. An easy money policy enabled the boom of the early 60s. Monetary restraint will permit the expansion of the early 80s to continue because today the chief concern is preventing a rapid increase in demand from driving production up too quickly, bringing about a decline in productivity and rapid cost and price increases. Only continued restraint by the Fed can prevent that.

But what about the fiscal policy of the federal government? As you saw in Chapter Fifteen, federal fiscal policy is injecting considerable stimulus into current economic conditions. Whether you sympathize with the demand-side or supply-side approach, the federal government, through its tax cuts and record deficits, is stimulating, and will continue to stimulate, economic activity.

But will this expansionary fiscal policy overheat the economy? Probably not. As long as the Fed exercises sufficient restraint, demand can't grow too quickly. And that is the most important policy objective.

Inflation and the volatile business cycle have generated the excessive levels of unemployment which plague society today. Rapid economic expansion will absorb labor quickly, only to generate additional layoffs in the future. Since the cycle can't be prevented, reducing its volatile nature is the only hope. Gradual expansion is the best way to secure maximum employment security for all.

# Appendixes

# APPENDIX A

## Alphabetical Listing of Statistical Series Published in *The Wall Street Journal*

| Chapter Number | Series Description | *The Wall Street Journal* Publication Schedule |
| --- | --- | --- |
| 7 | Auto sales | Monthly |
| 13 | Balance of payments | Quarterly |
| 13 | Balance of trade | Monthly |
| 5 | Bond market | Daily |
| 11 | Building awards | Monthly |
| 6 | Capacity utilization | Monthly |
| 6 | Commodity prices | Daily |
| 7 | Consumer credit | Monthly |
| 7 | Consumer Price Index | Monthly |
| 12 | Corporate profits (*Wall Street Journal* survey) | Quarterly |
| 12 | Corporate profits (Commerce Department) | Quarterly |
| 12 | Dow Jones Industrial Average | Daily |
| 11 | Durable goods orders | Monthly |
| 12 | Earnings reports | Daily |
| 7 | Employment | Monthly |
| 15 | Federal budget | Monthly |
| 3, 4, 5 | Federal Reserve data | Weekly |
| 13 | Foreign exchange rates | Daily |
| 6 | GNP | Quarterly |
| 7 | Housing starts | Monthly |
| 6 | Industrial production | Monthly |
| 10 | Inventories | Monthly |
| 14 | Leading indicators | Monthly |
| 11 | Machine tool orders | Monthly |
| 11 | Manufacturers' orders | Monthly |
| 5 | Money rates | Daily |
| 5 | Mortgage rates | Monthly |

| Chapter Number | Series Description | The Wall Street Journal Publication Schedule |
|---|---|---|
| 7 | Personal income | Monthly |
| 6 | Producer Price Index | Monthly |
| 6 | Productivity | Quarterly |
| 7 | Retail sales | Monthly |
| 12 | Stock market | Daily |
| 5 | Treasury bill auction | Weekly |
| 5 | Treasury bill rates | Daily |

# APPENDIX B

## Statistical Series Published in *The Wall Street Journal* in Chapter Order

| Chapter Number | Series Description | *The Wall Street Journal* Publication Schedule |
|---|---|---|
| 3, 4, 5 | Federal Reserve data | Weekly |
| 5 | Money rates | Daily |
| 5 | Treasury bill rates | Daily |
| 5 | Treasury bill auction | Weekly |
| 5 | Bond market | Daily |
| 5 | Mortgage rates | Monthly |
| 6 | GNP | Quarterly |
| 6 | Industrial production | Monthly |
| 6 | Capacity utilization | Monthly |
| 6 | Productivity | Quarterly |
| 6 | Producer Price Index | Monthly |
| 6 | Commodity prices | Daily |
| 7 | Consumer Price Index | Monthly |
| 7 | Personal income | Monthly |
| 7 | Employment | Monthly |
| 7 | Auto sales | Monthly |
| 7 | Consumer credit | Monthly |
| 7 | Retail sales | Monthly |
| 7 | Housing starts | Monthly |
| 10 | Inventories | Monthly |
| 11 | Durable goods orders | Monthly |
| 11 | Manufacturers' orders | Monthly |
| 11 | Machine tool orders | Monthly |
| 11 | Building awards | Monthly |
| 12 | Corporate profits (*Wall Street Journal* survey) | Quarterly |
| 12 | Corporate profits (Commerce Department) | Quarterly |
| 12 | Earnings reports | Daily |

| Chapter Number | Series Description | The Wall Street Journal Publication Schedule |
|---|---|---|
| 12 | Dow Jones Industrial Average | Daily |
| 12 | Stock market | Daily |
| 13 | Balance of payments | Quarterly |
| 13 | Balance of trade | Monthly |
| 13 | Foreign exchange rates | Daily |
| 14 | Leading indicators | Monthly |
| 15 | Federal budget | Monthly |

# APPENDIX C

## Listing of Statistical Series according to *The Wall Street Journal* Publication Schedule

| Quarterly | | |
|---|---|---|
| Day of Month Usually Published in *The Wall Street Journal* | Series Description | Chapter in Which Series Introduced |
| 1st | Corporate profits (*Wall Street Journal* survey) | 12 |
| 18th to 20th | Balance of payments | 13 |
| 20th | GNP | 6 |
| | Corporate profits (Commerce Department) | 12 |
| Last day of month | Productivity | 6 |

| Monthly | | |
|---|---|---|
| Day of Month Usually Published in *The Wall Street Journal* | Series Description | Chapter in Which Series Introduced |
| 1st | Building awards | 11 |
| 1st | Leading indicators | 14 |
| 1st week | Manufacturers' orders | 11 |
| 1st week | Mortgage rates | 5 |
| 5th | Auto sales | 7 |

## Monthly *(continued)*

| Day of Month<br>Usually Published in<br>*The Wall Street Journal* | Series<br>Description | Chapter in Which<br>Series Introduced |
|---|---|---|
| Monday of 2d week | Employment | 7 |
| 2d week | Consumer credit | 7 |
| Middle of 2d week | Retail sales | 7 |
| Midmonth | Inventories | 10 |
| Midmonth | Industrial production | 6 |
| 3d Monday | Producer Price Index | 6 |
| 3d week | Capacity utilization | 6 |
| 17th to 20th | Housing starts | 7 |
| 3d week | Personal income | 7 |
| Thursday or Friday of<br>next to last week | Durable goods orders | 11 |
| 25th to 28th | Balance of trade | 13 |
| Last Monday | Machine tool orders | 11 |
| 4th week | Consumer Price Index | 7 |
| 4th week | Federal budget | 15 |

## Weekly

| Day of Week<br>Usually Published in<br>*The Wall Street Journal* | Series<br>Description | Chapter in Which<br>Series Introduced |
|---|---|---|
| Monday | Federal Reserve data | 3 |
| Tuesday | Treasury bill auction | 5 |

## Daily

| Series<br>Description | | Chapter in Which<br>Series Introduced |
|---|---|---|
| Money rates | | 5 |
| Treasury bill rates | | 5 |
| Bond market | | 5 |
| Commodity prices | | 6 |
| Earnings reports | | 12 |
| Dow Jones Industrial Average | | 12 |
| Stock market | | 12 |
| Foreign exchange rates | | 13 |

# Index